W9-DHJ-418

PROPHETIC OBEDIENCE

PROPHETIC OBEDIENCE

Ecclesiology for a Dialogical Church

BRADFORD E. HINZE

ORBIS BOOKS
www.orbisbooks.com

TOGETHER IN GOD'S MISSION OF MERCY

Founded in 1970, Orbis Books endeavors to publish works that enlighten the mind, nourish the spirit, and challenge the conscience. The publishing arm of the Maryknoll Fathers and Brothers, Orbis seeks to explore the global dimensions of the Christian faith and mission, to invite dialogue with diverse cultures and religious traditions, and to serve the cause of reconciliation and peace. The books published reflect the views of their authors and do not represent the official position of the Maryknoll Society. To learn more about Maryknoll and Orbis Books, please visit our website at www.maryknollsociety.org.

Copyright © 2016 by Bradford E. Hinze

Published by Orbis Books, Maryknoll, New York 10545-0302.
Manufactured in the United States of America.

All rights reserved. No part of this publication may be reproduced or transmitted in any form or by any means, electronic or mechanical, including photocopying, recording or any information storage or retrieval system, without prior permission in writing from the publisher.

Queries regarding rights and permissions should be addressed to: Orbis Books, P.O. Box 302, Maryknoll, New York 10545-0302.

Library of Congress Cataloging-in-Publication Data

Names: Hinze, Bradford E., 1954–
Title: Prophetic obedience : ecclesiology for a dialogical church / Bradford E. Hinze.
Description: Maryknkoll : Orbis Books, 2016.
Identifiers: LCCN 2015032668 | ISBN 9781626981676 (pbk.)
Subjects: LCSH: Church. | Catholic Church—Doctrines.
Classification: LCC BX1746 .H555 2016 | DDC 262/.02—dc23 LC record available at http://lccn.loc.gov/2015032668

I dedicate this book to Christine,

spouse, friend, and life partner

Contents

Acknowledgments

I wish to express my gratitude to the following people who have offered invaluable help and support in the preparation of this book.

To Jim Keane and the editorial team at Orbis Books, and Carlton Chase. To those involved in the Archdiocese of New York and community organizing in the Bronx. *Archdiocese of New York*: Thomas Shelley, Ruth Doyle, Margaret Steinfels, Tyrone Davis, Maria Guarracino, Thomas Lynch, Joseph Girone, Nelson Belizario, and the members of the faith in action committee and the parish pastoral council of Our Lady of Angels. *Senate of Priests/Presbyteral Council*: John Duffell and Raymond Rafferty. *Sisters of Charity*: Regina Bechtle and Dominica Rocchio. *Parish Pastoral Councils*: Robert Aufieri. *South Bronx People for Change*: Neil Connolly, Dean Brackley, Kathy Osberger, and Angel Garcia. *South Bronx Pastoral Center*: Robert Stern and Nora Cunningham. *Northwest Bronx Community and Clergy Coalition*: Paul Brant, Roger Hayes, Jim Mitchell, Anna Marie Reinthaler, Joseph Muriana, Margaret Groarke, Mary Dailey, Yorman Nunez, Allison Manuel, Addie Banks, and Edwin Pierce, and many others involved in the work of the Coalition with whom I have worked and from whom I've learned so much. *Diocese of Brooklyn Parish Pastoral Planning*: Robert Choiniere.

To colleagues and communities that have inspired and challenged me. *Fordham University*: colleagues and friends in the theology department and across the university, including Sandra Lobo-Jost from the Dorothy Day Center for Service and Justice. *New York Theology Work Group*, for their friendship and close reading of several chapters: Teresa Delgado, Roger Haight, Jeannine Hill Fletcher, Paul Lakeland, Elaina Procario Foley, Michele Saracino, and John Thiel. *Communicative Theology Research Group*: Bernd Jochen Hilberath, Matthias Scharer, Mary Ann Hinsdale, Martina Kraml, and many others. *Critical Theory Reading Group*: Robert Davis, George Demacopoulos, Ben Dunning, Samir Haddad, Brenna Moore, Aristotle Papanikolaou. *Christian Life Communities*: members of the Peter Faber CLC in New York.

Finally, I wish to thank friends and family who have been a support during this project. George Didier, Michael Lee, Natalia Imperatori-Lee, Maureen O'Connell, Brenna Moore, John Seitz, Elizabeth Johnson, Judith Kubicki, Tom Beaudoin, and Jane Finnerty; and Ormond Rush and Stephan Bevans for comments. I thank family members for their encouragement, Sandy and John Newman, Karen Hinze, Linda and Gordy Grubb, Fran Baudhuin, Donna and Brian McLaughlin, Jane Firer, Peggy and Johnny Bishop, Paul and Linda Firer and all their children.

As always, at the end of the day, I am filled with gratitude for those closest to me: my sons, Paul and Karl, and Christine.

INTRODUCTION

How can Pope Francis's vision of the church be implemented in the local church in the Archdiocese of New York? Or in other dioceses across the United States and perhaps also in other geographical locations in the Global South? This book did not start out to address that question. In fact, it was written largely before Pope Francis was elected. Yet, in a surprising twist of fate (or perhaps providence) what follows does offer an outline and a theological justification for realizing, in parishes and dioceses, some of Pope Francis's most frequently expressed ecclesial convictions—convictions I also share. To claim that this book offers a step-by-step strategic plan would be a misleading stretch. But it does offer vital resources for faith communities discerning how, in their distinctive situations, they might embody a dynamic vision of the church as the people of God, by practicing what Francis calls missionary discipleship and what I speak of here as prophetic obedience in mission.

This book is being completed at the end of the fiftieth anniversary of the Second Vatican Council (1962–65). It commemorates a central theological motif that surfaced in many conciliar documents: the prophetic character of the people of God. Drawing on the achievements of the council, I advance a multifaceted theological and practical argument about the prophetic character of Christian discipleship and of the church's mission. I do so by exploring specific claims and implications of the council's teaching pertaining to the Holy Spirit's anointing and the baptismal participation of all the faithful in the prophetic office of Jesus Christ. This prophetic mission is a still underappreciated feature of Jesus of Nazareth's messianic identity and mission. In fact, the notions of the people of God and the prophetic character of all the faithful became contentious convictions during the pontificates of John Paul II and Benedict XVI. The beleaguered condition of the people of God, who are destined to be prophetic, provides the context and the main impetus for this project.

The constructive argument I advance here responds to the complex historical findings about practices of dialogical discernment and decision making that arose in the church in the wake of the council. These were discussed in my previous book, *Practices of Dialogue in the Roman Catholic Church: Aims and Obstacles, Lessons and Laments*,[1] and are augmented by further historical investigations reported on here. That book examined how the unprecedented attention given to the category of dialogue in the council documents motivated the implementation of a variety of dialogical practices associated with the revival, reform, and expansion of traditional synodal and conciliar practices. In the decades following the council, these practices became operative at every level of the church's existence, first from the parish and diocese, and then more widely in national and regional episcopal conferences, and then at the level of the universal church in the synod of bishops, as well as with the reform of chapters by religious congregations, in ecumenical and interfaith forums, and in numerous other innovative ecclesial forums.

Practices of Dialogue employed a historical approach informed by a phenomenological and hermeneutical method of describing participatory church practices in terms of official articulations of their aims and objectives. In an effort to acknowledge the limitations of such a phenomenological and hermeneutic approach, I identified struggles, failures, and laments of those involved in these efforts as recounted in various forms of testimony. In other words, instead of simply describing intended aims and objectives in relation to practices that emerged based on these intentions, I also sought to name *the interruptions*, to use Johann Baptist Metz's category; the negative contrast experiences, as Edward Schillebeeckx would describe them; and the unspoken, the repressed, and expressions of grief as theorized by scholars like Pierre Bourdieu and Judith Butler.[2]

To avoid approaching these social phenomena in an idealistic manner inclined to discover and impose coherence and order, I have sought to identify and dwell on the concrete realities that did not fit in well with the intended aims of various collective efforts. These were chronicled largely based on testimonies born of frustration, rather than through the more rigorously applied quantitative or qualitative social scientific and specifically ethnographic modes of analysis that have become more commonly used over the last fifteen years. While the efforts of these two books do not take the place of these modes of analysis, the approach taken here aims to be compatible with such studies, and seeks to provide an invitation to wrestle with their theological and specifically ecclesiological implications.[3]

In *Practices of Dialogue*, the biblical and theological category of lamentation surfaced as the most promising literary and heuristic vehicle for pursuing a more finely grained and textured evaluative approach to how the categories of the council were being implemented across the spectrum—from effectively to poorly, or not at all. In the present book, the category of lamentations provides an entrance point and inspiration for my principal aim: to advance prophetic discipleship as a central dimension of the baptismal calling of the people of God, an aim I pursue by reflecting creatively on the themes of lamentation and obedience in a Christian understanding of the triune God and the church.

This book begins by exploring how Vatican II's vision of the church as the people of God was received in the aftermath of the council. The first chapter portrays the reception of this vision of the church as a new dawn for a prophetic people of God as articulated in official teachings by the universal church, but also more concretely in the Archdiocese of New York, which is among the largest and most influential in the United States. The second chapter explores how Vatican II's inspiring vision of the church as a people of God seeking to fulfill its prophetic mandate became increasingly eclipsed, though not extinguished, during the pontificates of John Paul II and Benedict XVI. This eclipse is tracked both in the ascendance of a communion ecclesiology, which became delineated and transposed into policy by these popes and the Roman Curia, and in the history of practices of the Archdiocese of New York.

My constructive theological argument begins in Chapter 3, which explores the phenomenon of ecclesial impasse, using the public exchange between Cardinals Joseph Ratzinger and Walter Kasper to illustrate a much wider range of conflicts that arose in the Catholic Church during the pontificate of John Paul II. In responding to ecclesial impasse, I advance an argument for greater attention to lamentations in ecclesiology and in pastoral practice, lifting up the importance of laments in biblical literature, theology, and spirituality.

In Chapter 4, I consider the nature of obedience or responsive listening in the church, by asking where people hear God's voice within a dialogical understanding of the church. Before Vatican II, ecclesiologists gave a great deal of attention to the topic of the magisterium or the teaching office of the bishops as constituting *the teaching church*, while *the learning church*, or the obeying church, was understood as the compliant membership, beginning with the laity but including priests and members of religious congregations. A hierarchical and paternalistic vision of obedience permeated the pre–Vatican II church. This understanding of obedience often gave special attention to Jesus's obedience to the Father as the paradigmatic model of obedience to a patriarchal and paternal figure. Countering this, I offer a broader analysis of obedience by reflecting on the obedience of the triune God, giving greater attention to the obedience of the Father and the obedience of Jesus to the voice of the Spirit, and also to the obedience of the Father and the Spirit to the voice of Jesus, the son of God. This Trinitarian reflection provides new resources for an understanding of obedience in a dialogical church.

Chapter 5, a pivotal chapter in the book, offers a constructive theological argument concerning the meaning of prophetic discipleship for the people of God. Here I make my central theological argument, proposing that we explicitly recast the traditional framework for thinking about prophecy. Instead of describing and theorizing prophecy solely in terms of a word or message received and witness given, I argue for an alternative framework that gives equal attention to heeding the voice of the Spirit in the laments and aspirations of precarious peoples and in the wails of a damaged created world. This more comprehensive approach provides the basis for delineating and consolidating five dimensions of prophetic discipleship that illuminate what dialogic prophetic obedience in the church and the world requires:

- personal and communal practices of discernment;
- a mature prophetic approach to dialogue and responsibility that rejects blind obedience;
- attentiveness to the signs of the times based on honesty in facing reality;
- an abiding commitment to seek out and serve the *sensus fidelium*; and
- a missionary model of discipleship that can be described in terms of prophetic dialogue.

These five marks of the prophetic office surface in the documents of Vatican II, and here I seek to promote a deeper and more integrated reflection on their import for personal and ecclesial identity and mission.

Chapter 6 analyzes two concrete illustrations of the church's involvement in collective discernment and decision making. The first is associated with the promotion of grassroots democracy, and the second concerns locally based modes of synodality (or conciliarity). Both illuminate ways of embodying prophetic obedience in a contemporary dialogical church. I first scrutinize the church's involvement in community organizing in the Bronx, a topic introduced in Chapters 1 and 2. Second I explore the development of parish pastoral councils and planning practices in the Diocese of Brooklyn, which provides a counterpoint to the lack of a coordinated plan in the neighboring Archdiocese of New York over the last decades. In so doing, the chapter explores the connection between motifs in systematic theology and practical theology. More specifically, it offers a preliminary exploration of ways that the five distinctive dimensions of prophetic discipleship and obedience developed in the previous chapter can be useful in assessing concrete pastoral practices.

The final chapter offers a culmination of my argument by proposing that commitment to prophetic discipleship invites persons and communities into a lifelong process of personal and collective individuation, a technical term that describes individual and group identity formation. During the pontificates of John Paul II and Benedict XVI, communion ecclesiology at times became associated with the squelching of personal and collective individuation in parishes and dioceses, as well as in the Global South. My final argument is that the approach to prophetic identity and mission that emerges from Vatican II need not be viewed as antithetical to ecclesial communion. Rather, prophetic individuation and communion must be understood as necessary and mutually crucial dimensions of the church's identity and mission.

Pope Francis and a Prophetic People of God

The research on this book began roughly seven years ago, when the impact of the teachings and policies of John Paul II and Benedict XVI was at its high point and their influence seemed most entrenched. This book consequently addresses the situation in the church informed by research conducted for my previous book during the last five years of John Paul II's pontificate and research for the current book undertaken during the last five years of Benedict XVI's pontificate.

One might reasonably ask how the constructive position advanced here relates to the teachings of Pope Francis and the reforms that he has initiated. I confess that, since the election of Pope Francis, there have been moments when I have wondered whether the claims advanced in this book were rendered obsolete by his message and policies. I have come to the conclusion that this is not the case. Pope Francis's ecclesial social imaginary and mine have a large measure of compatibility and even a certain synergy. Yet they are also distinctive and have certain areas of divergence. One of the least controversial areas of difference is that while Francis's vision of the church has led him to devote himself primarily to enacting reforms of the curia and advancing the important work of the synod of bishops and episcopal conferences, this book concentrates on the local church at the diocesan and parish levels, and on the church's involvement in advancing grassroots democracy. One could say this book invites reflection on how Pope Francis's vision and policies might contribute to the reform of the local church in dioceses, parishes, and small communities.

I will not dwell on Pope Francis's contributions in this book, but let me identify here a number of key themes from his interviews, speeches, and the 2013 apostolic exhortation, _Evangelii Gaudium_, that are comparable to the themes of this work. In important ways, my vision of the prophetic mission of the church embodied in local modalities of synodality and conciliarity, and in church involvement in the promotion of grassroots democracy by means of community organizing, converges with Pope Francis's vision of the church and the church's role in civil society.

Jorge Mario Bergoglio was elected pope on March 13, 2013, and chose the pontifical name Francis, the first of many dramatic gestures signaling the profound changes that he has initiated. Numerous theologians have described the significance of Pope Francis's emerging vision of the church, and Richard Gaillardetz's essay, "The 'Francis Moment': A New Kairos for Catholic Ecclesiology," offers a most helpful overview and analysis.[4] Rather than simply revisit issues explored by Gaillardetz, I will focus on themes that intersect with aspects of my argument.

It is beyond dispute that Pope Francis has initiated a new phase in the reception of Vatican II. This became clear six months into his pontificate when in a long, widely read published interview with Jesuit Antonio Spadaro, he signaled that the long eclipse of the people of God ecclesiology had come to an end and suggested the beginning of another new dawn for the people of God teaching of Vatican II. There Francis revealed "the image of the church I like is that of the holy, faithful people of God."[5] It is not only the phrase and the theology of the people of God that he prefers;[6] in that interview and elsewhere Francis repeatedly invokes themes from _Lumen Gentium_, frequently those found in chapter two devoted to the people of God, and the paragraphs in section twelve devoted to the prophetic office of all the faithful and the supernatural sense of the faith of all the people, which provide the framework for thinking about the pilgrim people of God walking together. This formula _walking together_ alludes to the Greek word for synod, _syn odos_, together on the road.

Pope Francis has regularly accentuated the prophetic character of vowed religious life. I am inclined to think that this recognition extends to diocesan priests, for he repeatedly challenges priests to reach out to, live, and collaborate with the poor and marginalized. At the same time, in passages I will examine in Chapter 5, Francis also affirms a central claim of this book, the prophetic character of all the faithful people of God.[7] I would also argue that the pope champions each of the five marks that I here associate with prophetic discipleship and obedience: the centrality of personal and communal discernment; dialogue with, not blind obedience to, authorities; attending to the wisdom provided by the *sensus fidei* and *sensus fidelium*; facing reality and heeding the signs of the times; and a missionary discipleship that can be characterized in terms of prophetic dialogue.

More than any other postconciliar pope, Francis has accentuated the importance of promoting participatory structures of decision making in the church at the universal level in the synod of bishops, at the regional or national levels through episcopal conferences, and in the local churches through conciliar structures.[8] In an unprecedented move, his apostolic exhortation *Evangelii Gaudium* and his encyclical *Laudato Si'* have invoked and cited the magisterial teaching of national bishops' conferences and federations of national bishops' conferences as resources for the global church, rather than relying only on the papal teachings of his predecessors. This emphasis reflects his own pastoral experience as a Jesuit provincial, in diocesan pastoral life in Argentina, and as a leader in the Latin American Bishops Conference. In a brief address to the Leadership of the Episcopal Conferences of Latin America in July 2013, the pope underscored the importance of certain basic themes from the Fifth Conference of the Episcopal Conference of Latin America (*Consejo Episcopal Latinoamericano*, CELAM) held in Aparecida in 2007. He reminds his coleaders, but also the wider church that is listening in, about their shared pastoral priorities through a series of questions.

In practice, do we make the lay faithful sharers in the [church's] Mission? Do we offer them the word of God and the sacraments with a clear awareness and conviction that the Holy Spirit makes himself manifest in them? Is pastoral discernment a habitual criterion, through the use of Diocesan Councils? Do such Councils and Parish Councils, whether pastoral or financial, provide real opportunities for lay people to participate in pastoral consultation, organization and planning? The good functioning of these Councils is critical. I believe that on this score, we are far behind.[9]

Francis expands on his vision of the church when he answers Antonio Spadaro's question about how he understands Ignatius of Loyola's admonition "to think with the church" (*sentire cum ecclesia*). He begins by attesting once again to his preference for thinking of the church as the people of God, a pilgrim people "on a journey through history, with joys and sorrows."

Thinking with the church, therefore, is my way of being a part of this people. And all of the faithful, considered as a whole, are infallible in matters of belief, and the people display this *infallibilitas in credendo*, this infallibility in believing, through a supernatural sense of the faith of all the people walking together. This is what I understand today as the 'thinking with the church' of which St. Ignatius speaks.[10]

This is not populism, he insists, but "the experience of 'holy mother the hierarchical church,' as St. Ignatius called it, the church as the people of God, pastors and people together. The church is the totality of God's people."[11] In his exchange with Spadaro about what it means to think with the church, Pope Francis also explicitly elaborates on the conciliar theme of the dialogical character of the church: "When the dialogue among the people and the bishops and the pope goes down this road and is genuine, then it is assisted by the Holy Spirit."[12]

The dialogical character of the church is further developed in *Evangelii Gaudium*. There Francis encourages a rededication to pastoral dialogue, which the bishop fosters "out of a desire to listen to everyone and not simply to those who would tell him what he would like to hear."[13] In this regard he explicitly references the pastoral processes introduced or reformed after Vatican II and delineated in the Code of Canon Law, not only with bishops in mind, but also with parish priests: diocesan synods (canons 460–68), finance councils (492–502), diocesan pastoral councils (511–14), and parish pastoral councils (536–37).[14] Building on this, he accentuates the importance of reviving the parish by recognizing its flexibility, noting that "it can assume quite different contours depending on the openness and missionary creativity of the pastor and the community. . . . The parish is the presence of the Church in a given territory, an environment for hearing God's word, for growth in the Christian life, for dialogue, proclamation, charitable outreach, worship and celebration."[15] Diverse forms of pastoral dialogue inspire and orient creative strategic missionary discipleship.

The pope's advocacy of a dialogical church extends not only to diocesan synods and councils and parish pastoral councils, but also to the work of episcopal conferences, based on his personal participation in CELAM, which has championed a participatory and engaged method of collaboration with all the sectors of the people of God in its general conferences.[16] His support of CELAM's practice is likewise reflected in his call for consultation with all sectors of the church in preparation for the Extraordinary Synod of Bishops held in 2014 and the Ordinary Synod of Bishops conducted in 2015.[17]

Though it is beyond the scope of this work, it should be noted that Francis has, in keeping with Vatican II, also reaffirmed the importance of ecumenical dialogue, interfaith dialogue, and those contexts where "believers and non-believers are able to engage in dialogue about fundamental issues of ethics, art and science, and about the search for transcendence. This too is a path of peace in our troubled world."[18]

A signature motif of Pope Francis's ecclesial vision is his call for the church to promote missionary discipleship—"I dream of a 'missionary option,' that is, a missionary impulse capable of transforming everything, so that the Church's customs, ways of doing things, times and schedules, language and structures can be suitably channeled for the evangelization of today's world rather than for her self-preservation."[19] This is intertwined with his summons for the church to engage in a mission of mercy by being like a field hospital, reaching out to those who are wounded, the marginalized, those in need, and especially the poor. He develops this particular theme by reflecting on the implications of the section of *Lumen Gentium* devoted to the prophetic office of all believers.

> In all the baptized, from first to last, the sanctifying power of the Spirit is at work, impelling us to evangelization. . . . The Spirit guides it in truth and leads it to salvation. As part of his mysterious love for humanity, God furnishes the totality of the faithful with an instinct of faith—*sensus fidei*—which helps them to discern what is truly of God. . . . In virtue of their baptism, all the members of the People of God have become missionary disciples (cf. Mt 28:19).[20]

Here we find Pope Francis's call for missionary discipleship advanced precisely in terms of central motifs from *Lumen Gentium* in which the prophetic office is addressed. His message is entirely consistent with the basic features of the prophetic approach to discipleship and ecclesial mission I develop in this book, as is the particular attention he pays to the church's outreach to the poor and marginalized in the work of discerning and developing contextual missionary pastoral plans.

One final theme emerges in Pope Francis's ecclesial vision that is also a recurring motif in this book. The pope is refreshingly honest and insightful about the reality and role of conflict when advancing open dialogue in the church, such as in synodal and conciliar modes of discernment. I will address the agonistic character of synodality and democracy, a feature that corresponds with the prophetic character of discernment and obedience in the church. For Francis, "conflict cannot be ignored or concealed. It has to be faced. [One must] face conflict head on, to resolve it and to make a link to the chain of a new process."[21] At the beginning of the third extraordinary general assembly of the synod of bishops, Pope Francis exhorted the participants: in order to "bring the voice of the particular churches" to bear on the deliberations "one general and basic condition is this: speak honestly. Let no one say: 'I cannot say this, they think this or this of me. . . .' It is necessary to say with *parrhesia* all that one feels. . . . [I]t is necessary to say all that, in the Lord, one feels the need to say: without polite deference, without hesitation. And, at the same time, one must listen with humility and welcome, with an open heart, what your brothers say. Synodality is exercised with these two approaches . . . speaking with *parrhesia* and listening with humility."[22] This kind of honesty, tolerance for conflict, and humility are essential for genuine dialogue in the church. Such dialogue, in turn, provides the basis for genuine contestation, conversion, and differentiated consensus in the church, which has analogies in civil society as well.

Why Prophetic Obedience?

Prophetic obedience in a dialogical church captures the main argument being advanced in this book. The overarching theological theme pertains to the mystical and sociopolitical dimensions associated with the prophetic office. To be prophetic requires above all cultivating certain practices of personal and collective discernment and decision making, and allowing these to inform one's sense of self, one's involvement in various forms of communal life, and one's engagement with the social and environmental world, as well as the way core convictions, religious or not, influence and are weighed in everyday judgments and decisions of life. Prophetic existence demands developing a spiritual center of gravity based on a discerning way of life; this provides necessary ballast as one takes risks and acts courageously in the exercise of judgment and freedom, moving into unknown territory in order to develop one's identity and mission in the world as an individual and in community. Proceeding in this way is the mark of spiritual maturity in the life-long journey of Christian faith. Prophetic obedience is a crucial category, in my judgment, because it captures a summons to all the faithful to cultivate and exercise personal conscience, based on discernment of the apostolic faith of the church and attentiveness and responsiveness to the signs of the times.

This project develops a dialogical ecclesiology, in service to a vision of the church in which all the faithful are welcomed into the ongoing conversation that characterizes ecclesial existence, in prayer and worship, evangelization, works of mercy and work for justice, and community-building among members. In a special way, the church's dialogical character is realized through the ongoing cultivation, at all levels of the church, of participatory modes of discernment and decision making about mission. This remains the unfulfilled promise of the Second Vatican Council. I give special attention to how this takes place in the local church in the diocese and parish, and through the involvement of members of the parish in the promotion of democracy in civil society by means of grassroots community organizing with people, communities, and organizations representing and including people of other faiths and worldviews.

The church's commitment to collective modes of dialogical discernment and decision making in various expressions of synodality and democracy is only fully advanced for Christians when the prophetic character of the people of God is explicitly enacted. The Second Vatican Council's teaching about the prophetic character of all believers heralded a new call for all the faithful to work together as active agents in the church, as adult collaborators with the ordained, to discern the church's missionary mandate in local and global contexts. The council's recognition of the prophetic anointing of all the faithful should have meant the end of a paternalistic clericalism that sustains an infantile approach to the laity, including women religious, in mission and ministry. It did not. It should have meant increasing consultation and shared deliberation at all levels about the church's mission and ministry in the church and in the world. Yet sadly it did not. Affirmation of the prophetic mandate given to all the faithful should have sparked the widespread implementation of practices of mutual accountability and transparency in the church. This too has rarely occurred.

Inroads were made and experiments advanced during the first two decades after the council in all these areas, but they were too frequently restricted and undermined during the subsequent two decades. The anemic reception of the council in these matters is tantamount, in my judgment and that of many others, to structural corruption and disease in the church.

The prophetic remedy for this state of affairs is not simply for bishops, priests, and others in positions of leadership to learn how to be better listeners to the faithful or to practice wider consultation so that these voices inform their own thinking. To create the conditions for a genuinely prophetic church, a listening church is not sufficient. A prophetic remedy further requires that bishops, priests, and lay leaders enter into genuine dialogical discernment and decision making with the faithful in a robust expression of synodality, wherein the lay faithful and women religious have a far greater role in deliberative processes. The prophetic remedy ultimately demands greater mutual accountability of officeholders, community leaders, and the faithful, as the prophetic tradition emphatically insists. The missionary mandate of mercy, which has come to define the papacy of Francis, is only possible with the prophetic realization of listening, dialogical discernment and decision making, and mutual accountability.

Advancing such a prophetic vision of the church need not mean undermining the teaching office of the bishops, which represents their particular participation in the prophetic office of all the faithful. But the bishops' exercise of this office requires profound attentiveness and receptivity to the wisdom of the sense of all the faithful, along with honesty in facing, with the faithful, the signs of the times. When bishops lack these qualities, they risk jeopardizing the living faith of the church and the ongoing development of doctrine. This was John Henry Newman's momentous realization in his investigation of the history of early Christianity: the sense of faith of all the faithful is not only a source of wisdom, but also a reflection of the authentic norm of faith, of the saving gospel, and as such attentiveness to the sense of the faithful fosters a deepening awareness of how to effectively communicate the faith and the implications of this faith.[23]

The scriptures, creeds, liturgies, and conciliar formulations of official teachings provide normative expressions of the apostolic faith of the church and the basis for the obedience of faith and the various levels of response to the hierarchy of truths. Yet through the Spirit's anointing in baptism, all the faithful receive the gift of the instinct of faith and thus also share in handing on the apostolicity of the church. All the baptized are bearers and guardians of this faith, and they participate in the prophetic office. The bishops' exercise of this teaching office thus depends on their reception and embodiment of the apostolic tradition but likewise on the extent to which they have been receptive to the wisdom of all the faithful who have recognized and received the apostolic faith of the church, and who by their own prophetic anointing and mandate participate as witnesses and guardians of the faith.[24]

As I have indicated, the deeper argument I am making concerns our most basic understanding of prophecy. Usually, and based on sound judgment, the precise character of prophecy has been identified as a word or message received by prophetic individuals and communities that leads to a corresponding proclamation or witness. Frequently overlooked, however, is that prophecy is also the result of heeding, receiving, and responding to the voice of the Spirit in the aspirations and laments of vulnerable people and the wailing of a damaged world. This dimension of prophecy is also in evidence wherever prophets appear in the Hebrew and Christian scriptures, from the prototypical prophet Moses, to the messianic Jesus of the Christian scriptures, and beyond. Affirming a more comprehensive approach to prophecy and the prophetic office, by drawing on both frameworks, has immense implications for our understanding of Christian discipleship and the mission of the church. This broader understanding provides the basis for ecclesial reform and renewal based on mutual accountability and active participation of all the faithful in the life of the church, but it also nourishes the integration of mysticism and spirituality with works of mercy and work for justice, including in the social and political arenas.

A Contextual, Practical, and Politically Engaged Theology

This book shares certain orienting concerns with Johann Baptist Metz's groundbreaking work, *Faith in History and Society: Toward a Practical Fundamental Theology*.[25] I have composed here in a different key and register, and with a far simpler line of argument, in order to persent to a wider audience an approach to the church in history and society that develops certain basic categories—lamentations, prophetic obedience, and individuation-as-communion—as resources for advancing a practical fundamental and systematic ecclesiology. It appeals for a contextual and historically alert ecclesial social imaginary, one that is pastorally engaged in the cares and struggles of the people of God in everyday life in society.

Such an approach to context, history, and pastoral engagement aims to bridge the all-too-frequent gap between systematic theology and practical theology. My own attempts to bridge this gap have been motivated above all by my research into the fraught history of dialogical practices in the post–Vatican II church. Current efforts in contemporary theology to discuss the relationships between history, doctrine, and practice have been immensely enriched and made far more complex by recent debates about historiographical methods, the use of the social sciences in theology, and about how theologies of history provide tropes and plots that ineluctably inform ecclesial historiography, systematic theology, and pastoral strategies.

In addition to being influenced by Catholic, Protestant, and Orthodox theologians, my efforts have been particularly inspired and challenged by the theological scholarship of African American women and men who are the descendants of slaves, first or second generation immigrants in North America from the Caribbean and Latin America, and more widely those from the Global South who seek to bridge this gap between systematic theology and practical theology. This work has likewise been immensely influenced by my involvement in two groups. For roughly fifteen years I have participated in the Communicative Theology Research Group sponsored by the Catholic systematic and practical theology divisions of

Tübingen University and Innsbruck University. This group enterprise was initiated by collaborative effort of Bernd Jochen Hilberath and Matthias Scharer, and has many faculty and graduate student members engaged in systematic and practical theology while also being involved in various forms of pastoral ministry; it also includes as a collaborator Mary Ann Hinsdale, I.H.M., of Boston College, whose career has been distinguished by her own attempt to develop a contextually attuned and practically-engaged ecclesiology.[26]

Second, my research into the history of ecclesial practices of dialogue in the Bronx led me to become involved in community organizing through the work of the Northwest Bronx Community and Clergy Coalition. This involvement led to work with Fordham University students involved in service learning with the coalition and to my participation in the Faith in Action Committee of Our Lady of Angels Parish, one of the founding institutions in the forty-year history of the coalition. My personal commitment to the work of the coalition with my fellow parishioners, and my interpretation and assessment of what is transpiring in the Bronx, has been informed by various sociological works on community organizing, such as that of Richard L. Wood, and reflection on community organizing in relation to theology as found in the writings of people like Luke Bretherton and Mary McClintock Fulkerson.[27]

These particular illustrations of efforts to bridge systematic and practical theology are a part of seismic shifts going on in the discipline of practical theology.[28] New avenues being explored in this field reflect the impact of interdisciplinary work on praxis and practices in liberation and inculturation theologies, in the social sciences and philosophy, and in relation with developments in ethnography.

In years to come these shifting disciplinary undercurrents will inevitably leave their mark and hopefully transform not only how theologians develop ecclesiologies, but, more importantly, how the people of God advance the mission of the church in ways responsive to what is happening in local contexts, and with the collaborative involvement of varied local practices of synodality and grassroots democracy. Empowering these possibilities will be the gift and challenge of prophetic obedience.

Chapter 1

A New Dawn for a
Prophetic People of God

The Second Vatican Council captivated many by its use of classic biblical and theological motifs to advance a vision of the church as a pilgrim people of God. This retrieval came to inspire church renewal and reform, and ushered in what can rightly be described as a new dawn for Catholics. One particularly striking feature of this vision of the church was the attention given to the prophetic identity and mission of this people of God. This chapter will review these achievements and consider this question: what difference did this people of God ecclesiology make in the first stage of the reception of the council in local churches around the world, but also specifically in the Archdiocese of New York?

At the beginning of the Second Vatican Council, Pope John XXIII prayed that the gathered bishops from around the world, accompanied by their theological advisors, would experience a new Pentecost—a new outpouring of the Spirit that would bring about a new dawn of vitality in the church.[1] The bishops attending the council, with the exception of a vocal minority, came to believe that such a fresh beginning was in fact occurring in their midst. This was attributed in no small part to the recovery at the council of a vision of the church as people of God.

This configuration of the church as the people of God has provided what Charles Taylor calls a social imaginary, that is, a way people imaginatively conceive how different individuals and groups are interconnected and interact. It contributes to people's deepest understandings and expectations about social existence. Social imaginaries are not based on theories as such, although theories can help people to understand and explain such imaginaries. Rather, social imaginaries arise from images and narratives that provide a shared understanding that makes possible and motivates shared practices and legitimates common social action.[2]

The People of God in the Ecclesiology of *Lumen Gentium*

The story of how the people of God motif came to prominence in *Lumen Gentium* (cited as LG) has been told often, but a selective outline of this history bears repeating here. There was much consternation among bishops and theologians preparing for the council about the original schema of the decree on the church, which was recognized as the council's main agenda.

1

Sebastian Tromp, S.J. prepared the preliminary draft of the schema—the same theologian who had been the main author of the encyclical *Mystici Corporis Christi,* issued by Pius XII in 1943. The original council schema recapitulated main elements found in that earlier encyclical.

Mystici Corporis had been widely appreciated for giving greater attention to biblical and patristic treatments of the theology of the body of Christ as a spiritually and pastorally inspiring notion for the church and to the charisms of the Holy Spirit at work in the church. Yet this was achieved without denying the main tenets of the *societas perfecta* ecclesiology that predominated in the counter-Reformation mind-set, particularly in neoscholastic theology.[3] The Catholic Church is perfect on this view not in any moral sense, but because it has the parts necessary to complete its divinely established purpose of mediating salvation. This ecclesiology affirms the visible character of the church in its institutions, ordained offices, dogma, codes, and sacraments, in contrast to the Protestant emphasis on the invisible character of the true church of the justified. Pope Pius XII's vision of the *body of Christ* view of the Catholic Church incorporated the perfect society ecclesiology and thus maintained a staunch defense of the inequality among members in the church, a juridical approach to the institution of the church, a paternalist model of hierarchy and clericalism, and a triumphalist identification of the mystical body of Christ with the Roman Catholic Church. The original schema "*De Ecclesia*" seemed to portend more of the same.

Deeply dissatisfied with Tromp's schema, many national and regional groups of bishops and theologians prepared alternatives. At one point there were fifteen versions. Nine received considerable attention from the council's doctrinal subcommission. The alternative schemas were then fashioned into one, without unduly discrediting the original draft, in the hope of gaining the support of a majority of the bishops.[4] In this process, certain aspirations of disparate groups converged. In contrast to a juridical, propositional, and syllogistic style of reasoning, these groups sought to reclaim biblical and patristic sources and fashion a rhetorical style that would contribute to a more compelling vision of the church and the church's place in the world for a modern audience. By developing a more pastoral, persuasive style, the aim was to attract, sustain, and motivate the faithful, while respecting and engaging other Christians, people of other religions, and a wider nonreligious public.[5]

From the original schema of eleven chapters crafted with logical and juridical precision, the second version emerged with four chapters and a pastoral quality.[6] The revised first chapter spoke volumes by its very title, "The Mystery of the Church," and introduced a style that was distant from neoscholastic logic. It depicted the origins, identity, and mission of the church in relation to the Trinity. The second chapter concentrated on the hierarchical constitution of the church and the episcopacy. The topic of the episcopacy was conceived by some as the main agenda of the council, which was needed to complete the work of Vatican I that had concentrated on the papacy in relative isolation. The third chapter in this new draft was devoted to the people of God and the laity in particular, and incorporated material from the original schema. And the fourth addressed the holiness of the church, in contrast to the original draft's treatment of the states of evangelical perfection.

During the second session of the council, following months of discussion in various quarters, a momentous development took place. On October 9, 1963, a proposal was introduced by Belgian Cardinal Léon-Josef Suenens and agreed on by a majority of the bishops: the current draft of chapter three, on the people of God and the laity, often viewed as dealing with overlapping topics, would be divided into two. The topic of the people of God would now treat all the baptized faithful, equal in dignity and freedom, who are all destined for holiness, rather than stand as prelude or proxy for the category of laity. This topic would be addressed in its own chapter, before the treatment of specific offices and roles in the church—the hierarchy, the laity, and the religious.[7] This change introduced the possibility that the people of God motif would provide a framework for understanding the relationships of all groups in the church.[8]

The category of communion provided the other prominent framework at the council. Introduced in chapter one of this revised draft document, it drew its inspiration from the body of Christ ecclesiology that was in vogue before the council. It provided a sacramental and Eucharistic introduction to the church's identity and mission, which would eventually be integrated with a Trinitarian theology and anthropology.

In the end, the second chapter on the people of God received wide approval from the bishops, due in no small measure to its scriptural and classical theological resonance and its appealing logic. After the first chapter treated a diversity of images for the church found in the scriptures and treasured in early Christianity, it made abundant sense to focus on the people of God, a notion that was being recovered in recent biblical studies. The Christian community is a people with roots in the call of the Israelites—a community chosen and sent on pilgrimage in history.[9] This people that is called forth brings together Jews and Gentiles in a new covenant as taught in the letters of St. Paul, but it also extends to many clans and tribes, ethnic and racial groups, and nations who are united by covenant into one messianic people characterized by a catholicity of outreach. The people of God are commissioned to welcome those considered outsiders and strangers, reaching to all peoples created by God.

Karl Rahner thought this offer of salvation warranted extending the category of people of God to include all of humanity, but Yves Congar believed that "scriptural usage as well as liturgical and patristic tradition do not justify this way of speaking."[10] The council fathers chose neither to adopt nor reject the more expansive sense. In the words of the document, "this messianic people, although it does not, in fact, include everybody, and at times may seem to be a little flock, is, however, a most certain seed of unity, hope and salvation for the whole world" (LG, no. 9).

The people of God motif brought into focus a human community responding to a divine initiative, a people transformed into a collective historical subject in bodily form, and transfigured into a sacrament of God. The notion thereby captured the dynamic character of God's people as historical and eschatological: a pilgrim people searching; sinful; in constant need of renewal, conversion, and reform; and a messianic people on mission. The council never set the people of God motif in tension or opposition with the motif of the body of Christ or, by extension, with Eucharistic and communion motifs. Most revolutionary for Catholic theology at the time was the way the people of God reflected a renewed appreciation of the theological affirmation that through baptism all the faithful are equal, gifted with and by the Spirit of God, and incorporated into the church, regardless of any subsequent office and state in life. Every individual is called to holiness, to become a full and active participant in the life of the church, to develop spiritual practices, and to play a part in the mission of the church.

Most important for this study, chapter two of *Lumen Gentium,* devoted to the messianic people of God, reclaimed and rejuvenated the conviction that all the baptized, all the faithful regardless of office, share in the threefold office or mission of the messiah Jesus Christ as priest, prophet, and king, in the work of worship, witnessing to the truth, and contributing to the exercise of governance (LG nos. 10–12). As it was restated in the Decree on the Laity (*Apostolicam Actuositatem* [cited as AA]), "In the church there is diversity of ministry but unity of mission. To the apostles and their successors, Christ has entrusted the office of teaching, sanctifying, and governing in his name and by his power. Laypeople too, sharing in the priestly, prophetical, and kingly office of Christ, play their part in the mission of the whole people of God in the church and in the world" (AA, no. 2). All the faithful, not just the hierarchy or clergy, contribute to the building up of the church and advance God's kingdom by living out their baptismal inheritance.

The identification of the prophetic mission of Jesus Christ with the sense of the faith of believers merits particular attention.

> The holy people of God shares also in Christ's prophetic office: it spreads abroad a living witness to him, especially by a life of faith and love and by offering to God a sacrifice of praise, the fruit of lips confessing his name (see Heb 13:15). The whole body of the faithful who have received an anointing which comes from the holy one (see 1 Jn 2:20 and 27) cannot be mistaken in belief. It shows this characteristic faith, when "from the bishops to the last of the faithful," it manifests a universal consensus in matters of faith and morals. By this sense of the faith, aroused and sustained by the Spirit of truth, the people of God, guided by the sacred magisterium which it faithfully obeys, receives not the word of human beings, but truly the word of God (see 1 Th 2:13) . . . The people unfailingly adheres to this faith, penetrates it more deeply through right judgment, and applies it more faithful in daily life. (LG, no. 12)

This passage identifies the people of God as a prophetic people called to witness to the truth of faith. Moreover, it connects this prophetic identity and mission with a sense of the faith of individuals and, by implication, the sense of the faithful as a collective whole, which is the basis of "a universal consensus in matters of faith and morals."

In the context of affirming the sense of the faith given to each individual, one particular phrase asserts that this prophetic sense of faith of the people of God is "guided by the sacred magisterium which it faithfully obeys." Does this passage introduce a tension between obedience to the faith of the church and obedience to the magisterium? Is the sense of the faith of all the faithful simply identified with what the magisterium teaches? Is it possible that there are instances when the magisterium has not accurately or fully perceived and articulated the sense of the faith of the faithful? Could obedience to authority ever be in conflict with obedience to the sense of the faithful? Is the magisterium also bound in obedience to the *sensus fidelium*? Such questions point to the crux of the problematic nature of prophetic obedience and its relation to obedience to authority that we will seek to address in the following chapters.

The retrieval of the baptismal inheritance of all who comprise the people of God in chapter two of *Lumen Gentium* was combined with the teachings about the dignity of the office of bishops flowing from their episcopal consecration and the authority of the college of bishops in chapter three. Together these teachings provided the theological underpinnings for a dialogical understanding of the church, both internally among the church's members and externally with groups ranging from other Christians (ecumenical dialogue), other religions (interreligious dialogue), and people with different worldviews. Together they provided a theological framework for advancing the reform of specific structural changes in the practices of the church.[11]

The doctrines of the people of God and of episcopal collegiality provide the theological justification for dialogical practices and participatory structures in the church. Just as the dignity and authority of the college of bishops was being firmly established as a complementary corrective to the one-sided doctrine of papal primacy established at Vatican I, so the dignity and authority of all the faithful people of God were recognized, as was their role as genuine agents in the church's mission rather than as passive recipients.

What could hinder these dynamic movements? What might provide an alternative framework for envisioning the nature and mission of the church? For some, it would be the motif of communion, a theme that, like the people of God, was developed in *Lumen Gentium* by drawing on biblical and classic theological motifs. Vertical communion with God and horizontal communion among church members find their source in Eucharistic and body of Christ themes. The church as communion finds its ultimate justification in the deepest doctrinal convictions about the unity of the triune persons in the Trinity.

In principle, there need not be a contrast or conflict between viewing the church as communion and as people of God, and this is how the participants at the council viewed the matter. The bishops saw them as different theological motifs opening up interrelated semantic fields, serving complementary rhetorical purposes, each offering multilayered narratives, and lending credence to a combination of theological claims about the nature and mission of the church.

The church as communion and as people of God provided deeper frameworks that contributed to the treatment of the subject of chapter three of *Lumen Gentium*, the hierarchy, as well as the subsequent chapters on the laity, the universal call to holiness, religious life, the pilgrim church, and Mary. Many still remained convinced that the treatment of the episcopal hierarchy was the main agenda of the council, to redress the unfinished business of Vatican I on papal primacy and infallibility. And the council did so, especially in chapter three of *Lumen Gentium*, by affirming the integrity of bishops' sacramental ministry and their authority in their own particular churches, their dioceses, as well as the collegial exercise of their ministry with each other and the pope, the bishop of Rome, for the good of the universal church. A vocal minority of bishops pressured Pope Paul VI to mitigate against this teaching on episcopacy and collegiality in the interest of underscoring the hierarchical authority of the pope in relation to the college of bishops by having a prefatory note of explanation (*nota explicativa praevia*) added without the vote of the council to the beginning of chapter three.[12] Nevertheless, in the aftermath of the council, the treatment of the church as people of God in *Lumen Gentium* and the other documents generated considerable momentum around the world.

What Difference Has the People of God Ecclesiology Made?

If one were searching for indications that the council's teaching on episcopal collegiality has been fruitful, the most important avenues to explore would be how synods of bishops and episcopal conferences developed in the decades following the council.[13] Evidence of the teaching on the people of God's contributions to the exercise of episcopal collegiality would require examining how synods of bishops and episcopal conferences engage representatives of the people of God in their deliberative procedures. The most significant proof of the implementation of the people of God motif is provided by the establishment of diocesan and parish councils and diocesan synods, as the laity and women religious made great strides to collaborate as partners with the local bishop and parish priests in ministry and missionary activities in everyday practices of faith and mission of inculturation and social outreach.

Two additional conciliar mandates intersect and are interwoven with the influence of the people of God ecclesiology, and the mandates also came to influence the local church and the church universal. Presbyteral councils, which were initially called priest senates, were established as a means for the bishops to collaborate with the collective body of priests (the presbyterum) of the diocese. Congregations of religious women and men were also called on to enter into a prolonged process of communal reflection and deliberation in the interest of revitalizing and renewing their orders. These various efforts at collaboration and co-responsibility are associated with a synodal way of being church in dialogical practices of collective discernment and decision making.

Local Synods, Councils, and Forums

One of the most profound changes that resulted from the teaching on the people of God was that new avenues opened for laypeople to participate in the life of the local church through synods, councils, and other collegial forums. As the Decree on Bishops states, "This sacred Ecumenical Synod expresses its earnest hope that these admirable institutions—synods and councils—may flourish with renewed vigor so that the growth of religion and the maintenance of discipline in the various churches may increasingly be more effectively provided for in accordance with the needs of the times" (*Christus Dominus*, no. 36). Diocesan synods were no longer to be assemblies of priests implementing legislative decisions reached by bishops in national and regional councils, but rather were to engage the faithful in reflection and discussion about pastoral priorities and planning for the life of the local church. A small number of bishops implemented the new approach to diocesan synods during the first two decades after the council, and the number increased slowly after the revised Code of Canon Law was issued in 1983. Some diocesan bishops and chancellors resisted implementing the newly restructured diocesan synods, while in other dioceses, alternative pastoral planning processes were designed and utilized as the functional equivalent of synods, without the canonical requirements of diocesan synods. The formation of diocesan pastoral councils and parish pastoral councils were explicitly recommended, but not required, in Paul VI's Apostolic Letter *Ecclesiae Sanctae* (1966). Consistent with the teaching on the people of God, laypeople were to join religious and priests in deliberating with their bishop or archbishop about the pastoral work of the local church. The main problem from the very beginning, however, was that pastoral councils and synods were never mandated, only encouraged. Moreover, those preparing for priestly ordination received little to no pastoral training in the practical skills necessary to run effective councils and synods, or how to collaborate as equals with lay leaders and parish members. Still, these new structures offered the most important concrete manifestations of the people of God in action and had ripple effects in the ministries and mission outlook in the local church.

The Many Faces of Catholic Action

The people of God ecclesiology provided valuable theological moorings for postconciliar lay involvement in the mission of the church in the world. Lay involvement had previously been associated with the term *Catholic Action*, which had been heralded by Pope Pius XI in 1931 in the encyclical *Quadragesimo Anno*, on the Reconstruction of the Social Order, as "the participation of the laity in the apostolate of the hierarchy."[14] At the time of the council, there was a debate concerning the relative adequacy of general Catholic Action and specialized forms of Catholic Action.[15] The general form, which began in Italy, espoused a paternalistic approach to the laity's participation in the hierarchy's apostolate of advancing Catholic

Christendom against liberalism and Protestantism and was sometimes tainted with anti-Jewish animus. Specialized forms of Catholic Action advanced formation of associations among social groups (e.g., workers, students, doctors, lawyers, married couples) interested in addressing social issues, often those pertaining to poverty and the promotion of grassroots democracy such as the rights of laborers.[16] One of the most influential forms of specialized Catholic Action was associated with Belgian priest Joseph Cardijn who developed an inductive approach to surfacing and analyzing pressing social issues combined with a review of life, spiritual and social–political, as a means for promoting strategic social action that would foster lay leadership in collaboration with clergy. Sometimes contrasted with devotional societies and ecclesial movements fostering personal spirituality, all these various socially and politically engaged groups made some claim on the category of Catholic Action.

Cardinal Léon-Joseph Suenens, the cardinal archbishop of Malines-Brussels, who would become one of the most influential figures at the council, voiced the opinion at the World Council of the Lay Apostolate in October 1957 that the name Catholic Action was too narrowly associated with particular social action groups who promoted activist practices. Suenens had in mind Cardijn's method of see, judge, act used by the Young Christian Workers initiated by Cardijn, groups that could be confrontational in social and political affairs. Suenens argued during the council that the term *Catholic Action* should refer to a multiplicity of forms that would include groups oriented toward spirituality and the spiritual works of mercy. In the end, the council commended Catholic Action explicitly, yet in a concession to critics defined it broadly and acknowledged associations of all sorts (AA, no. 20). The council's affirmation of a plurality of forms of grassroots associations and movements in the promotion of contextualized missions established an important principle for inculturation and social outreach.[17]

The people of God ecclesiology did more than provide a rationale for an older approach to Catholic Action. In some instances it was reformulated, freed from hierarchical paternalism and clericalism. This theology not only justified the vocation of the laity in secular society, it also motivated the participation of the laity in the saving mission of Jesus Christ as priest, prophet, and king in worship, witness, leadership, and service. This manifested itself in various forms as more and more laypeople and women religious took on active and leadership roles in parish councils, and in lay ecclesial ministries in liturgy, in religious education, and in social outreach. The people of God motif thus offered an invitation to bishops, priests, religious, and the laity to rethink and refashion their relationships with each other in a collaborative manner beyond the hierarchical and clerical paradigm of the medieval and Tridentine church embedded in neoscholastic theology.

The people of God ecclesiology established the bedrock teaching of Vatican II that all the faithful, ordained, religious, and laity are equal and are called to be active and fully participating in the life and mission of the church (*ad intra* and *ad extra*). This doctrine was juxtaposed with the teaching that the laity had a secular vocation (LG nos. 31, 35–36) to work in the world (*ad extra*) while the clergy were ordained for a mission in the religious realm at work in the church (*ad intra*). The council affirmed all these claims, holding them in balance if not tension.

The People of God in the Local Church of New York

The response in the Archdiocese of New York to Vatican II exemplifies the dynamic reception of the prophetic impulses of the Spirit at work in the people of God ecclesiology, and, as well, the forces that threaten to undermine those energies. New York was at the time of the council the largest US metropolitan See and the most cosmopolitan, with the most numerous and diverse immigrant membership. New York encompasses the greatest variety of intersecting social realities that people face every day: those living in extreme poverty share the same streets and subways with the wealthy; and ethnically and racially diverse people encounter each other daily. This creates possibilities for friction and for fusion. Everywhere in the city, one discovers openness in the population toward those who are different, based on ethnicity, race, gender, and sexual orientation, side by side with those who are prejudiced toward these same groups. One experiences the shame and glory of ecumenical and interreligious relations, and manifestations of secularity and worldliness in every cultural form and way of life. New York culture is a symbol of the free market and consumerism, of the arts found in theaters, museums, concert halls, pubs and clubs, street murals and graffiti, and every form of music.

How was the ecclesiology of the people of God received by the members of this archdiocese in the aftermath of the council? The implementation of Vatican II in the local church that is the Archdiocese of New York can be detected in shifting social formations among priests, women religious, and the laymen and women working alongside and in collaboration with them.

The Senate of Clergy

Paul VI implemented Vatican II's call for the formation of senates of priests in August 1966.[18] Cardinal Spellman initiated their development in the Archdiocese of New York on October 24, 1966; the process came to completion with May elections, and the first meeting convened on June 21, 1967. There were forty-nine priests elected, including a designated number of pastors (twelve) and associates (twenty-three), according to archdiocesan regions. All the priests of the archdiocese from six newly established vicariates were invited to elect the entire membership of the senate, according to area priests' conferences based on population. The statutes established by the first senate stated that the archbishop is encouraged to attend the meetings periodically but should definitely meet monthly with the executive committee of the senate during those months when a senate meeting takes place to discuss pertinent issues. The senate executive committee set the agenda until the New Code assigned this duty to the ordinary. At the first senate meeting, it was decided to survey the priests of the archdiocese to identify areas of concern. Six categories were identified and became the purviews of six standing committees of the senate: priestly life, pastoral renewal, personnel, education, social action, and ecumenical action.

Spellman died five months after the first senate meeting was held on December 2, 1967, and Terence Cooke, a New York priest, was appointed archbishop in March and installed in April of 1968. In the intervening period, the former members of the senate convened unofficially as the Priests' Interim Advisory Committee and prepared a Memorandum of Priorities to assist Cooke in making his transition. This rare document offers clear evidence that the theology of Vatican II was taking root in the archdiocese. The list of eight priorities began with the urgent need to implement and utilize participatory structures in the archdiocese—a priests' senate—and called for the quick implementation of a diocesan pastoral council, which could serve as a model for the establishment of parish councils. These collective bodies, it asserted, can best serve in the assessment of programs and budgets, hiring at the seminaries, and nominations for diocesan officials. The directive identified research-based pastoral planning as one of the highest priorities, and also highlighted social issues, especially racial justice, housing, and the poor.[19]

Initially Cooke attended every meeting of the priests' senate. He was so talkative, however, that some members reached the conclusion that he made it difficult to implement a broad dialogical process to work through their agenda. Eventually, the executive committee asked Cooke not to attend so regularly and instead to devote himself to discussions with the executive committee. He agreed.

During the Cooke era, the senate devoted itself to a variety of issues. Implementing the office of episcopal vicars in order to promote more local decision-making structures (*decentralization*) was a repeated theme and resurfaced again during Cardinal O'Connor's era when the 1983 Code of Canon Law was issued. The role and status of episcopal vicars was treated in great detail, including the processes involved in their nomination, voting in vicariates, and area priests' conferences. The senate selected a prioritized list of three names that would be submitted to the archbishop for his approval or rejection. Other issues received considerable attention: the tenure terms for pastors (six-year terms, with two terms maximum), recommended periodic peer evaluations of pastors and associates, and the establishment of personnel boards in the archdiocese that would identify new openings and offer assessments of eligible candidates to the archbishop.

A great deal of attention was also devoted to a range of issues pertaining to the life and ministry of priests. The topic of low morale among priests began to surface early during the Cooke years. A great number of priests were leaving ministry. Many felt overextended. Numerous difficulties surfaced associated with laicization, salaries, benefits, and mandatory retirement. It was strongly recommended that priests be chosen to be pastors based on genuine leadership skills, not years of service. The option of creating team ministry with women religious and lay leaders was recommended by a simple majority. Social issues were regularly raised during these meetings. Topics considered included the war in Vietnam, the position of conscientious objectors, protests against the war and against nuclear weapons, the Civil Rights Movement, and boycotts initiated by the United Farm Workers. Racism and the exodus from the black Catholic parishes in Harlem and elsewhere received increased discussion, and members of the senate voiced the growing need for development of Hispanic ministry. An annual assembly of priests of the archdiocese was launched in June 1969, at which the archbishop and chancery officials would meet for a few hours in the afternoon for an open discussion with the priests of the archdiocese about the reports from the standing committees, especially on pressing issues. Topics treated at senate meetings were discussed and voted on during these annual assemblies.

The new Code of Canon Law was promulgated on January 25, 1983, and went into effect on the First Sunday of Advent, November 27, 1983. The new precepts required the establishment of a presbyteral council to replace the senate. On October 13, the senate submitted its final recommendations based on its positive and negative experiences. The positive experiences reflected aspects of the people of God ecclesiology: the diversity of the presbyterum was represented by age, geography, ideology, and ministry; there was open discussion between the executive council of the senate with the archbishop during monthly meetings; the minutes, the resolutions agreed on, and the archbishop's response were distributed to the presbyterum in the Senate Progress Report; freedom of discussion in the senate permitted any topic to be raised and ideas, projects, and resolutions deliberated on. The report lamented the lack of enthusiasm for the work of the senate, the inconsistency in the archbishop's and archdiocesan offices' consultation with the senate before decisions were reached, the lack of coordination among consultative bodies (the senate, archdiocesan council of women religious, and archdiocesan pastoral council, and their respective standing committees), and the lack of contact between committees and corresponding archdiocesan offices.

Women Religious in New York: The Example of the Sisters of Charity

Women's religious communities have been the most dedicated and most astute in putting into practice Vatican II's teaching about the people of God, and this has frequently been in evidence in the Archdiocese of New York. The reforms of religious congregations in the wake of Vatican II incorporated the teaching on the people of God through their growing emphasis on the equality of members, the diversity of personal gifts, lifestyles, and missions, and above all their hard-earned cultivation of communal processes of discernment and decision making about identity and mission. If we were to measure "The Impact of Women Religious on the Church of New York," as Sister Regina Bechtle formulates the issue, we have to realize with her that

In New York City, where real estate rules and media coverage makes you
or breaks you, some judge impact in terms of stone and steel, of buildings
constructed, renovated, retrofitted. Some measure impact by best sellers
and column inches, by prime-time coverage and website hits. Others
measure impact in the flesh-and-blood realities of bodies blessed and
bandages, minds mentored, hearts healed, spirits sustained. Impact is
about relationships as much as headlines.[20]

Of all the congregations of women religious that have left their mark on the
Archdiocese of New York, a compelling choice for special consideration is the Sisters
of Charity. These women have, throughout their history, dedicated themselves to
working with the poor, especially women and children. They have opened orphanages,
hospitals, and schools. They have worked as caregivers, administrators, teachers, and
counselors. After the council, they increasingly engaged as social activists in New York
and as cosmopolitan agents of compassion and justice advocates around the world.[21]

At least a decade before Vatican II had been announced, the Sisters of Charity
had launched an ambitious program of education and deliberation about the reform
of their community government, lifestyles in local communities, and their apostolate, in response to Pope Pius XII's appeal in 1950 to congregations of religious
men and women to update their practices.[22] Under the truly prophetic leadership of
Sister Loretto Bernard Beagan, who was elected mother general in 1960, there were
frequent monthly lectures given by Catholic pioneers, some from other continents,
in the fields of psychology, sociology, immigration, and race relations, as well as in
biblical studies, liturgy, and theology, and by pastoral leaders in the archdiocese.
Cardinal Leo-Josef Suenens addressed the community on the renewal of women's
religious life in May 1963 and again in 1964. Daniel Berrigan, S.J. challenged the
sisters in 1962 to rediscover their apostolate: "go to the poor, live among them,
learn from them, love them, serve them, plan with them."[23]

In 1964, Sister Margaret Dowling, a visionary and activist in the congregation, asked Fr. Robert Fox, a social worker who subsequently became the director
of the Office of Spanish Catholic Action, to help design a program for the sisters
to work on a volunteer basis with the Puerto Rican immigrant community. Fr. Fox
addressed the sisters and encouraged them to begin in that same year to deepen
their commitment to poor immigrant communities. By so doing Fox was carrying
on the influential work of Fr. Ivan Illich and Fr. Joseph Fitzpatrick, S.J. who, during
that same period in the 1960s, pioneered ministries with immigrant communities,
especially among Puerto Ricans, and subsequently with new waves of immigrants
from other Caribbean and Latin American centers. Fox invited the sisters to visit
immigrants in their homes and to work with the young:

> Go to a city-owned housing project, Lillian Wald, filled with people of
> all races and religions, and just be with people. 'Don't give lessons. . . .
> Don't do nursing, don't try to teach anything. . . . Just be with the people.

Go to the playground there and draw with the children when they feel like drawing and swing with them when they come around and spend the whole summer like that.[24]

This program paved the way, with Dowling's collaboration, for the Summer in the City program that began in the summer of 1965 and that reached out to twenty-nine poverty areas in New York City. About 30 Sisters of Charity, joining more than 250 priests, religious brothers and sisters, representing 28 congregations, participated that first year. This program fostered the formation of closer relationships, sometimes friendships, among people, many of whom were poor, often isolated in their high-rise apartments, and ill at ease because of racial and cultural differences. The program's aim was simple: promote informal contacts by means of imaginative activities on the streets, sidewalks, and recreation areas of large housing projects. Latin American music played, people danced, professional art and drama people and recreation leaders taught arts and crafts; poetry, folk singing, the sounds of guitar and percussion filled the streets; there were banners and parades, movies, and weekly carnivals. This was an experiment in creating a local social imaginary that captivated and energized.[25]

More activist dimensions of their own social imaginary were on display when about 700 Sisters of Charity marched in a civil rights demonstration in Harlem on March 14, 1965, more than seven months before Vatican II's Decree on Religious Life was approved. The Sisters of Charity were becoming committed to developing programs to address the needs of new waves of immigrants in New York. This commitment also led them to expand beyond their mission in the Bahamas, established in the late nineteenth century, to pursue missions in Guatemala, Chile, and Peru to advance the role of women and the laity in the church and society.[26]

The mission of the Sisters of Charity has always been defined in terms of responding to those in great need. Like so many other congregations of religious women, however, their lifestyle—the practices of governance and the rigorous daily schedule of communal prayer, meals, and work—often fostered dependency, obedience to authority figures, and uniformity of lifestyle rather than independent thinking and creative initiative in their ministries. After the council, community members devoted themselves to reflect personally, in small groups, and in larger assemblies on their own personal aspirations for autonomy and interdependence, and to search for lifestyles, forms of community, and patterns of governance conducive to flourishing in this calling and commitment to be a Sister of Charity. They developed discernment practices in their own personal spiritual lives as they made important decisions about their own lifestyles, living arrangements, and ministries; and together they cultivated processes of group discernment as a method for corporate decisions.[27] This was articulated most clearly in the Chapter of Affairs that took place in 1969–70, during which the sisters reached corporate decisions on every aspect of their life in community.[28] Through this process they explored a variety of options about the government of their local community, with many ultimately choosing corporate or team government "by all members of the entire community, who would strive to reach consensus on significant issues concerning life-style and witness, through deliberation and dialogue."[29] In time, all members were to discern their choice of living arrangements, their own daily schedules, and their ministries. By the end of the 1969–70 chapter, the community had sanctioned a plurality of lifestyles, community forms, and ministerial options for individual members as they strove for a rich vision of life and mission in community, not without some tension.

This period of transition was aided by sociological studies of the views of the membership, the Sisters' Survey in 1967 and 1968 and by a ten-month Stanford Research Institute Study in 1969, which gave a clear sense of the fears and aspirations of the group and guided the development of proposals for reform that took place during the years that followed.

During the two decades that followed the council, the Sisters of Charity deepened their reflection on the implications of the chapter of 1969–70 and embarked on a period of great transition. In 1971, a new and more open and collaborative government structure, which was agreed on at this chapter, was established. The regular chapters were now called assemblies, and they began to offer a valuable model for group discernment and decision making about mission in local communities such as parishes and dioceses. In the assembly of 1971–73, the first in a series of "Assemblies of Vision," the sisters devoted themselves to four goals: (1) to become better informed on an ongoing basis of what the sisters feel are their needs and purposes, and the obstacles involved; (2) to strengthen and develop local communities to promote personal growth and service; (3) to foster better communication and participatory decision making; and (4) to develop "greater awareness of the needs and struggles of today's world, to encourage and assist their abilities to relate to these in constructive and creative ways, so that they may see themselves as part of, and in meaningful relation to, the great issues of our times."[30]

In response to the challenges entailed in renewing their communal practices, Sister Margaret Dowling made clear in a letter addressed to all community members, "The Executive Council . . . has prepared a program [for the final meeting of the assembly] which will offer to every sister multiple opportunities to share in this discernment and decision-making. It will be effective only to the degree that every sister participates." The assemblies held during the 1970s and 1980s continued this process of deliberation that culminated in the revision of their constitution, which was adopted in September 1984.[31] At their 1978 assembly, they agreed on the following mission statement: "Our mission as Sisters of Charity is to share in the ongoing mission of Jesus by responding to the signs of the times in the spirit of St. Vincent de Paul and St. Elizabeth Ann Seton, by revealing the Father's love in our lives and in our varied ministries with and for all in need, especially the poor."[32]

It is clear that the Sisters of Charity became important advocates of the people of God theology not only as a result of their own process of discernment and decision making, but also by promoting these methods in the local church at parish and archdiocesan levels. In their revised constitution, the sisters articulated for their own time the prophetic vision that guided their founders, St. Vincent de Paul and St. Elizabeth Seton:

> We are called to be witnesses to the faithfulness of God's love by our fidelity to our convent relationship with Him.
>
> We are called to share with others the life-giving bread of His Word and the material bread that sustains life.
>
> We are called to be women of healing, sensitive to the wounds of person and to the social evils of our times.
>
> We are called to use every means in our power to reconcile and bring into unity persons and groups who are alienated or divided.
>
> We are called to share with others in a ministry of liberation from multiple forms of oppression and injustice.
>
> In every area of our lives, as we strive to live the evangelical counsels, in prayer, community, and ministry, we share and prophetically call others to share the ongoing mission of Jesus: to reveal the Father's love, to promote and foster life in all its aspects.[33]

Parish Councils

Shortly after Terence Cooke was installed as archbishop in April 1968, he appointed a group of twenty-one priests, religious women, and laity to study the best methods for implementing parish councils. They first met on October 10 of that year. Parish councils were not mandated, but the archbishop wanted to promote them as a necessary part of the commitment to the vision and goals of Vatican II. As he later stated in a letter read at all masses in February 23, 1969, "I am convinced that each parish of the Archdiocese should now begin to set up its Parish Council, so that the parish apostolate may be enriched by the common thinking and working of all its members—priests, religious and laity."[34] Implementing parish councils was a part of a larger plan to initiate councils on the regional (what would later be designated vicariate) and diocesan levels. More than two-thirds of the twenty-one members of this committee, which included two religious women and two laymen, played a role in getting councils up and running in their parishes. Many expressed positive reactions among council members and parishioners, but there were also concerns raised about the need for more formation, direction, for strong laypeople, and above all the need for the pastor's collaboration. This committee was urged to consider "the best way for the Archbishop to move ahead on PC!"[35]

In response, the archbishop decided to release six pastoral letters to orient the laity on parish councils. These letters addressed a theological rationale for the councils, religious education, liturgy, and ecumenism, and two were devoted to social action. Msgr. Myles Bourke, a respected biblical scholar at New York's Dunwoodie Seminary, drafted the first letter. Bourke chose Paul's first letter to the Corinthians to make his main argument: "God has appointed in the church first apostles, second prophets, third teachers, then workers of miracles, healers, helpers, administrators" (1 Cor 12:28). Bourke gave special attention to the call of the laity to be prophets.

> There is no doubt that the majority of people of whom Saint Paul wrote were laymen. May I draw your attention particularly to the function of the prophet? The people who had it were not outstanding and unusual people like the great prophets of the Old Testament, Jeremiah, Isaiah, or Amos. They were quite "ordinary" members of the congregation of Corinth. In the fourteenth chapter of that same epistle . . . we see that their God-given work was to speak to the situation of the church, and to give guidance. Not everything that they said was accepted by the rest of the church; their words were weighed and tested. . . . But it is clear that Paul cannot imagine a Christian congregation which could go its way without the enlightenment given to it by the Holy Spirit through the prophets.
>
> I think that we may say that the principal reason for the parish council is that a vehicle may be given whereby the prophetic witness of the Christian layman may be made more readily available to the Church of today. The prophetic office is not something that went out of existence in the first century of the Church's life; the Holy Spirit still speaks to the Church through the prophets of our own times. Unfortunately, some who claim that they are speaking prophetically do so in a manner which could hardly pass the test of true prophecy which Paul gave. But this is surely no reason why a genuine prophetic witness of the layman should be stifled. And one of the most effective means whereby the bishops can hear that authentic witness is the parish council. There the "ordinary" Christian layman is able to speak and make his invaluable contribution to the life of the Christian community.[36]

Bourke appreciated the prophetic charism given to laypeople as decisive for the work of parish councils, but the cardinal or someone in his inner circle judged that this motif, for whatever reason, was counterproductive and replaced it with the no less important motif that the whole church is the temple of the Spirit of God in which all members are given gifts and talents for the good of the whole church. Counterproductive could have different meanings—from being rhetorically ineffective to raising questions about countervailing power and authority of the laity in relation to officeholders that would best not be discussed. In any event, sadly, Bourke's sound argument was not used.

By September 1969, Cardinal Cooke had opened an office for the Commission on Parish Councils, whose charge was to launch parish councils in the archdiocese, with a full-time director, Msgr. William O'Brien. In 1972, Msgr. Henry Mansell took over as director of what was now called the Office for Parish Councils, a position he would hold until 1985.[37] In 1972, Fr. Philip Murnion, with a doctoral degree in sociology, opened the Office of Pastoral Research and Planning, and collaborated with Ruth Doyle to compile data about immigration patterns and the composition of the membership of the archdiocese.[38] Increasingly this office gathered information about individual parishes for the pastoral planning of the archdiocese and parishes.[39] In 1978, Murnion left the office to become the head of the Parish Project of the National Catholic Conference of Bishops, but the office continued under the leadership of Doyle, who oversaw major studies of the Hispanic and black populations of New York.[40]

By October of 1969, an elaborate program for implementing councils was in place that included official guidelines on parish councils in English and Spanish, a leadership training manual, three brochures (*How Not to Form a Parish Council, Why the Parish Council?,* and *The Steps to a Council*), sample constitutions, and the inauguration of a regular newsletter on parish councils. Leadership training and professional training for priests was run through the Pastoral Institute. By May 1969, of the 409 parishes in existence at the time, there were 155 councils (48 percent); by November 1970, there were 231 (57 percent); by December 1971, the percentage had risen to 64 percent. While 139 parishes were without councils, 20 of which were judged to have good reasons for not having them. The other 110 pastors were considered hard-hat holdouts.

Why were some priests against parish councils? One former head of the Office for Parish Councils said that there were three basic reasons: priests did not have the skills to create and effectively maintain a council; they had negative experiences with parish councils and did not know how to improve them; and with the development of so many different apostolates and offices in parishes, sometimes run by paid officials, parish councils were sometimes overlooked or viewed as unnecessary compared to the elite professional class of lay ministers who were collaborating with the pastor and priests.

After its meeting of December 10, 1971, the Commission on Parish Councils, which at the time had four priests, one laywoman, one layman, and one woman religious, was to be replaced by a new regional commission that would have twelve regional representatives as well as a black and Puerto Rican representative, one pastor, one other priest, and two religious women; this new organization, it was hoped, would foster better coordination and communication. Many believed it was time to mandate the implementation of parish councils. Ten feedback sessions were held late in 1971 and early 1972 that identified parishes that were not making any headway on forming councils.[41]

The formation of parish councils into well-functioning deliberative bodies could not take place overnight. Those chosen to initiate parish councils in the

Archdiocese of New York understood that and developed programs of formation for pastors, religious, and laypeople to make them work. This was not sustained later on. Moreover, during the first twenty years of parish councils, people experimented with different models of decision making with different goals and agendas, and with various approaches to selecting council members. It was not always easy or effective. At times there was resistance on the part of the pastor and the parishioners. Even in the best of parish councils, there were struggles and lessons to be learned. Often there was a steep learning curve.

Over time, however, many councils grew together in identifying the animating concerns of the parish and came to greater clarity about the gifts and needs of the parish community in terms of adult faith formation, and in the areas of liturgy, religious education, ecumenism, and social outreach. Some parish councils passionately promoted and became recognized for their excellence in programs in liturgy and spiritual formation. Others devoted themselves to advancing religious education for children and adolescents but rarely for younger and older adults. Still others were motivated to engage with ecumenical issues with prominent churches in their neighborhood or the city, or with interfaith issues, particularly with Jewish neighbors and synagogue congregations. There were many parishes that enthusiastically committed themselves to social service and outreach, developing soup kitchens, food pantries, clothing drives, shelters, and procedures for helping the homeless. These various centers of energy evolved based on the needs of the community and the responsive engagement of council members, pastors, and parish priests. In many cases, there were efforts to listen to the animating concerns of the parish community.

Parish communities and pastoral councils in New York were confronted before and immediately after the council with issues raised by the arrival and increasing numbers of black and Puerto Rican families moving into parish boundaries and the white flight that ensued. Parish councils provided opportunities to foster lay pastoral ministries and to address broader social problems, and some parishes promoted hospitality toward blacks and Puerto Ricans, a few toward gay and lesbian populations; others addressed problems of racism, poverty, substance abuse, gangs, and violence. These social issues became increasingly pronounced in the Bronx.

The Archdiocesan Pastoral Council

The US Conference of Catholic Bishops (USCCB) during their 1971 fall meeting strongly recommended that diocesan pastoral councils be implemented as soon as possible. The Archdiocesan Commission of Parish Councils, in a letter to Terence Cardinal Cooke, expressed the concern of the members:

> The reality of dioceses that have rushed head-long into diocesan pastoral councils as a first stage without prior programming on the parish and regional levels have unwittingly created more problems than they have solved. These diocesan pastoral councils, having little or no parish council

energy, have foreclosed on vertical communication from the start and exposed themselves to charges of imbreeding [sic], pro-forma activity. We recommend the establishment of a diocesan pastoral council at a time when parish councils are in the majority (New York is now 65%) and when regional (vicariate or deanery) councils have begun. Then will the diocesan pastoral council represent the flowering of an awakening and involvement of a substantial segment of the People of God.[42]

By the end of the year, the Commission on Parish Councils confirmed that it was the intention of Cardinal Cooke to establish the archdiocesan pastoral council at the earliest possible date.

Fr. Henry Mansell, the director of the Commission on Parish Councils, began planning for the formation of the archdiocesan pastoral councils in earnest in 1972. By the spring of 1974, a proposal for an interim archdiocesan pastoral council was submitted for consideration to the priests' senate, but it was not approved until the October meeting.[43] The original proposal was that the twenty-four vicariate (or district) conferences would each elect one woman and one man. There would be youth representatives, one male and one female from the university apostolate and one from the Teen Age Federation, and ten at-large representatives "to provide ethnic, racial, age balance."[44] The council would also include various officials from the offices of the archdiocese, various consultative bodies in the archdiocese (priests, women religious superiors, women religious) and five representatives from the Coordinating Committee of Catholic Lay Organizations.

Several members of the priests' senate argued that the archdiocesan pastoral council should be designed to promote grassroots involvement, which might be mitigated if most members were chosen from vicariate councils and archdiocesan offices. A question was also raised about how consultative this deliberative body would actually be. Despite these concerns, the priests' senate approved the proposed council in October 1974, and the council, composed of 106 members, was formed in 1975. The council met four times a year to discuss such issues as communication in the archdiocese and evangelization. Often, the group considered documents from the pope and from the USCCB. The executive committee formulates each meeting agendas, which is approved by the archbishop. Items for the agenda can be proposed through many channels including individual committees and members of the archdiocesan pastoral council.[45]

Facing Reality in the Bronx

In the aftermath of Vatican II, the vision of the church as a prophetic people of God became reality wherever laypeople, women religious, and priests were encouraged and thriving in collaborative mission and ministry. Two centers of activity in the Bronx that emerged during the 1970s offer particularly compelling illustrations and merit special attention.

Let me begin by describing the Bronx at the time. During the 1970s and 1980s, the Bronx became known as the worst slum in America; today it is still known for having the poorest congressional district in the nation (the fifteenth district), with the highest levels of poverty and unemployment. The Bronx did not always have this reputation. In the nineteenth century, it was a rustic community of farms, little towns, and a small number of larger estates, home to roughly ninety thousand people by the end of that century. By contrast, over 1.5 million people lived in downtown Manhattan, many of them European immigrants suffering from overcrowding and poor living conditions in high-rise tenement buildings. During the second half of the nineteenth century, a growing percentage of more successful immigrants living in the Lower East Side of Manhattan moved to the Bronx. The Germans relocated in the Melrose neighborhood and were joined by the Irish "in Mott Haven, Melrose, and Highbridge, the Italians in Morrisania and Belmont, the Jews, by far the biggest contingent, in Hunt's Point, West Farms, East Tremont, and bordering the Grand Concourse, the wide boulevard sweeping the length of the borough."[46] By the 1930s there were over 1.25 million people living in the Bronx, and the population continued to grow through World War II. This was the heyday of the borough, which boasted great thoroughfares for cars, trendy Art Deco apartments along the Grand Concourse Boulevard, Yankee Stadium, the Bronx Zoo, and the New York Botanical Gardens.[47]

The northern migration of African Americans to escape the legacy of slavery in southern US states and the immigration of Puerto Ricans precipitated by the global depression of the 1930s were important factors contributing to the transformation of the borough. In 1910, the Bronx population included roughly four thousand blacks; by 1960, there were over a million.[48] In 1930 1,200 Puerto Ricans lived in the Bronx (and 45,000 lived in New York City); by 1960, there were 612,000 Puerto Ricans in New York City, including hundreds of thousands in the Bronx. By 1970, the total number of Bronx residents had grown to almost 1.5 million, including large numbers of blacks, Puerto Ricans, and Latinos from the Dominican Republic and other countries in Central and South America.[49]

Just as many African Americans and Puerto Ricans *entered* the Bronx, a significant percentage of ethnic Europeans *left*. Waves of Irish Americans left in the 1930s, followed by German Americans in the 1940s, Italian Americans in the 1950s, and Jewish Americans from Russia and Eastern Europe in the 1960s. This departure of first- and second-generation European Americans between the 1950s and the 1970s was accelerated by the construction of planned suburban communities filled with mass-produced houses and crisscrossed by new superhighways. As one historian reports, "The exodus left the borough with empty apartments and storefronts and dwindling congregations in churches and synagogues."[50]

During the 1950s and 1960s, many neighborhoods in the Bronx showed signs of decline: apartment buildings deteriorating, leaking roofs not fixed, buildings not painted, holes in walls not repaired; increasing litter on the streets. In this environment, rats and cockroaches thrived, and crime, robbery, domestic abuse, and drug use escalated. Gangs affiliated with different ethnic groups targeted young boys to join them in selling drugs and urban warfare. Between 1961 and 1971, "the number of murders increased from 18 to 102, robberies jumped from 183 to 2,632, and burglaries rose from 667 to 6,443."[51] As blacks and Puerto Ricans moved into the Bronx, real estate agents steered whites into the newer, suburban enclaves, and real estate in the borough declined in value. Landlords neglected their properties. Banks gave fewer and fewer loans to landlords for the maintenance and improvement of their distressed buildings, even though neighborhood residents kept their money in these banks and patronized their mortgage companies. And, in a devastating symbol of urban distress, an epidemic of fires swept through apartment buildings across the South Bronx, with fires breaking out by the tens, the hundreds, the thousands. One firehouse, Company 82, in a Bronx neighborhood called Park East, received over three thousand calls in 1967, twice as many as ten years earlier. Three years later, in 1970, "the firefighters of Company 82 made 6,204 runs to 4,246 fires, or 11 runs a day."[52]

Why was the Bronx burning? Many believe that the main cause was arson. The reality was more complex but no less criminal. A negligible number of the fires were accidental. But throughout the Bronx, the fires were made possible by common conditions in tenement housing: overcrowding, old buildings and outdated electrical wiring. More perniciously, bureaucrats trying to save city money closed a significant number of fire stations in the South Bronx. Fire departments could not reach many jobs soon enough to stop the fires, and buildings burned down. This resulted in more overcrowding and further deterioration of neighborhoods.[53] Landlords who wanted to collect insurance money and to get rid of properties that were rapidly declining in value also started some of the fires. In some cases, tenants were paid by landlords to start fires; others did so hoping to get on waiting lists for better housing. Desperately poor and addicted residents at times expressed their rage and nihilism by vandalizing and torching apartment buildings. Fueled by this combustible combination of the actions of landlords, banks, insurance companies, and criminals, the South Bronx fires came to symbolize the destruction of neighborhoods and a way of life.

A theologian who lived in the South Bronx during these years recalls, "A plague of abandonment—by banks, landlords, and government—eventually wrecked South Bronx neighborhoods in the late 1960s and 1970s. It destroyed over 100,000 housing units and displaced more than 250,000 persons. Never before had such destruction taken place apart from war or natural disaster. Maybe it was war."[54] In these dire conditions, human hope and a sense of human agency were going up in flames. A *New York Times* columnist declared at the time that a visit to the South Bronx was "as crucial to the understanding of American urban life as a visit to Auschwitz is to understanding Nazism."[55]

The Bronx was particularly hard hit by a further confluence of social developments in the years encompassing the Second Vatican Council. In the 1960s and 1970s, the Civil Rights Movement and the Vietnam War protests were keenly felt in New York and helped stoke the energies of a new generation of activists, including Catholics inspired by their church's social teaching. Thanks to their efforts, Vatican II's invitation to become agents in history as a pilgrim people of God took on concrete form amid the struggles of the Bronx. *Gaudium et Spes's* summons to discern the signs of the times and to develop practical courses of action to address these signs was realized. People of the Bronx, Catholic, Protestants, Jews, and the religiously unaffiliated, led by coalitions of clergy, lay and secular leaders, and organizers, accomplished something remarkable. They joined together to confront powerful forces of destruction by building bonds of solidarity, by undertaking collective action for social justice, and by creating communal geographic and cultural oases of hope.

A Prophetic Summons

Two Catholic parish-based examples from South Bronx neighborhoods merit special attention. One is associated with St. Athanasius Parish, where a pilot program of community organization and pastoral leadership formation in the 1960s developed into regional efforts that culminated in the founding of, in 1978, two influential coalitions: South Bronx People for Change and South Bronx Pastoral Center. A second illustration is the Northwest Bronx Community and Clergy Coalition, founded in 1974.

Typical renderings of these two stories cast priests and other clergy as the heroes. Diocesan priests Neil Connolly of St. Athanasius Parish, Bob Stern and Neil Graham of Our Lady of Victory, Jesuit scholastic Paul Brant teaching at Fordham and working as liaison between the university and the neighborhood, Auxiliary Bishop Patrick Ahern of Our Lady of Angels, and Rev. Dr. Basil Law of St. James Episcopal Church are just a few of the magnanimous and courageous clergy who deserve immense credit for what they were able to accomplish. These priests responded to immense suffering occurring in their neighborhoods by encouraging parishioners to become social and political agents in a volatile situation, disregarding the neoscholastic chasm between religious and secular apostolates to work not only for, but in collaboration with, their parishioners. "Collar power," as Connolly tagged it, symbolized a bonding among priests in this vicariate committed to mobilizing the people of God for mission, and to nurturing leadership and bonds of solidarity and collective agency among the laity in their Catholic parishes, with other Christians, and with people of other faiths and worldviews. But often in these stories not enough is said about the laity and women religious who became partners with these priests, and who acted as leaders in their own rights, mobilizing members of their parishes and neighborhoods.

None of these community groups explicitly espoused the power and potential of parish councils. But they do provide valuable lessons that can be extended to parish councils. Among Bronx Catholics and their neighbors during these years, there emerged bonds of intercultural solidarity and social action in concrete struggles against social injustices cemented by institutionalized racism and rank greed; these struggles, in turn, contributed to the development of lay leadership and lay ministry. The narrative of what transpired in the Bronx during these years offers a worthy example of the drama of the people of God seeking to read the signs of the times in their communities, and to respond to the grief, anguish, and aspirations of men and women in their own day and place.

South Bronx People for Change

In the South Bronx, two Catholic groups started as parish-based and later became regional. Committed to revitalizing parish and neighborhood life in the area, these groups offer compelling examples of the people of God theology in the 1970s, with laypeople, priests, and women religious collaborating in team ministry to enact a mission-oriented way of life.

Fathers Neil Connolly and Louis Gigante, ordained in 1958 and 1959, were first assigned to St. Athanasius parish in the South Bronx. After ordination, they received summer language training and pastoral experience in Puerto Rico, an immersion experience designed by New York priest Ivan Illich and Jesuit sociologist Joseph Fitzpatrick, which introduced them to poor people living in rural areas, hospitable families, close-knit communities, and a more informal style of worship. Taking what they learned from this experience and from liturgical conferences held in St. Louis that they attended annually between 1966 and 1970, these two young priests enthusiastically implemented changes in their parish. And with the Sisters of Charity teaching in the parish elementary school, they experimented with forming a faculty that would be attentive to the challenges facing family life for immigrants amid a diversity of cultures in the neighborhood.

Connolly dedicated himself to developing a community attuned to the everyday joys and sorrows of people, a community full of life, with rich liturgical expression, strong lay leadership, and, as time went on, community social action, *people development* as he called it, on a range of issues confronting those in the neighborhood—rent control, keeping heat and hot water running, confronting substance abuse, and the problems with arson and fires.

Gigante, by contrast, dedicated himself to brick and mortar development. He worked with organizations, initially thirteen of them—churches, business institutions, and civic associations—to address the destruction of apartment buildings. With these groups, Gigante established the South East Bronx Community Organization (SEBCO) that elicited funding from the Model Cities Program for urban development. This program, an element of Lyndon B. Johnson's War on Poverty, aimed to improve schools, parks, and organizations in order to pave the way for a more elaborate program of rehabilitating area apartments. Gigante's efforts with SEBCO represented a contrasting approach to the situation in the South Bronx than that pioneered by Connolly.

Connolly was especially inspired by the Summer in the City program pioneered by Sister Margaret Dowling and Fr. Robert Fox in East Harlem—El Barrio—which created a public forum for people to foster relationships through creative activities. In this spirit, in 1967, Connolly initiated a similar effort with the staff at St. Athanasius, including Gigante and Fr. Richard Adams (who joined the staff in 1965) and four Sisters of Charity. The idea was to experiment with Summer in the City activities in the parks on the Hunts Point peninsula of South Bronx, which was being threatened by escalating drug use, robbery, and violence.

This effort had a real impact. For several years parishioners and neighbors gathered for street masses, social gatherings, and sports nights. These events provided an opportunity for people to form communities, to share the joys of everyday life, but also to create bonds of solidarity among those struggling with tenement living under poor conditions, economic hardship, and neighborhood unrest. In 1968, there was a public forum for dialogue with the local residents involved in this effort, and Connolly asked the people what they wanted to do with their collective experiment. They wanted it to continue. Connolly made it clear that if residents wanted this to happen, they were going to have to make it happen. The parish priests and staff were overextended as it was. But the question was, how?

Together they decided that it would be good to have a weekly Mass in English and one in Spanish, and continue their social events and social outreach. Connolly was happy to celebrate Mass with them, but the people in the neighborhood had to be responsible for building upkeep, budgeting, and planning activities. What began on the streets eventually led to renting a storefront on the Hunts Point peninsula that could serve as a center for people from this outlying region of St. Athanasius parish to foster community and meet the needs of neighborhood members. This was the beginning of the Seneca Center.

The Seneca Center, a satellite of St. Athanasius Parish, provided a unique and effective experiment in a lay-led faith community for over one hundred people. These people took charge. The Seneca Center served two objectives, a religious mission and a social outreach mission. In practice, the religious mission became identified as St. Athanasius Chapel and the social outreach program as the Seneca Center, but the collective enterprise was known in the neighborhood as the Seneca Center. The first thing the pastoral team of priests, women religious, and those actively involved from the neighborhood decided to do was to establish a storefront chapel on Seneca Avenue. Although the center had no formal parish council, the people made decisions together. Second, they developed the Seneca Center as a distinct nonprofit group that would include a board composed of people from the neighborhood, parishioners as well as non-Catholics. The Seneca Center developed programs to address the needs of those in the neighborhood and was also distinctly identified with the evangelical mission of the chapel. The formation of the center in 1968 planted the seed for the South Bronx People for Change, an organization established in 1978 devoted specifically to promoting local social action.

There were other factors that paved the way for the development of the South Bronx People for Change, all of which reflected this emerging people of God theology being received and implemented. One was the formation of the South Bronx Catholic Clergy Association during the 1960s, under the leadership of the priests at St. Athanasius, to bring priests from the South Bronx together to talk about collective concerns about the neighborhood. In 1974, following up on the team ministry formed with women religious and laypeople during the Summer in the City program, the association decided to explore reaching out and joining forces with women religious and some lay leaders to establish the South Bronx Catholic Association. This group comprised pastoral ministers, lay and ordained, in the twenty-four parishes of the South Bronx and provided often-monthly opportunities to meet to discuss their ministries with those struggling with poverty, institutional injustice in housing and employment, and crime and prejudice that fueled local violence. Besides surfacing local signs of the times, this group cultivated a social analysis of the dynamics that were contributing to these problems and often devised strategies to address them that called for additional ad hoc meetings. At these gatherings members also prayed together, shared meals, and formed community among themselves. No other clergy conference in the archdiocese had combined forces with women religious and lay leaders to develop such local processes of communal discernment and decision making.

When the archdiocese established additional vicariates around 1976, there was a need for a vicar of the South Bronx. Neil Connolly, at the time still the pastor of St. Athanasius, was first on the list of three pastors chosen and ranked through communal deliberation by the South Bronx Catholic Association submitted to Cardinal Cooke for his own decision. Cooke approved their nominee as regional vicar in 1976 for a three-year term. Connolly had a deep conviction that the people of God theology should make all the difference in the life of pastors and parishes. As he wrote in 1978 in the newsletter *Clergy Report*, sent to all priests of the Archdiocese of New York, "once the concept that the Church is the People of God becomes operational in a Pastor and is more than just a conversation piece on priestly renewal weeks, then a pastor must sort out in his head the implications that it has for his parish. It cannot be 'business as usual.'" As Connolly explained, the pastor should be

> developing God's people and forming them into a community that speaks and acts like Christ for the local scene. . . . To be effective, a pastor must gain the confidence of the parish council and the staff and must learn, as does the rest of the staff, to be faithful to the parish goals and objectives. It is this posture that will engage the necessary trust of the inner few so that he can win entrée to the wider parish community.[56]

As vicar, Connolly made it a point to meet and get to know every individual staff person in the rectories, convents, and parishes. He was elected for a second three-year term in 1979. His driving goal was to develop the people by encouraging them to take responsibility for the church. He served as vicar for eight years.

While sinking his roots deeply into the church in the South Bronx, Connolly also benefited from national contacts. Around the time that he was elected vicar in 1976, New York priest Phil Murnion invited him to become a board member of the Catholic Committee on Urban Ministry (CCUM). Msgr. Jack Egan and Peggy Roach from Chicago had launched this national organization a decade earlier, in 1967. CCUM channeled the energy forming through the development of diocesan offices of social action and urban affairs stretching back to the late 1950s.[57] This national organization became a prime center for developing social ministry in light of the council's people of God vision of the church.

Through mutual CCUM contacts, Connolly met Kathy Osberger in spring of 1977, a Notre Dame graduate recently back from pastoral work in Chile and Peru, where she had worked with Holy Cross priests, women religious, and lay leaders with the poor and base Christian communities. Connolly recommended her for a position as staff member at the Seneca Center. There, Osberger joined others on the team in developing lay leadership; she served as staff representative to the parish for its religious mission; and she fostered the nascent work of the Seneca Center, the nonprofit subgroup. The Seneca Center offered a variety of service programs, including meal programs for seniors, family counseling, summer youth programs, an after-school program for middle school children, and a tenant organizing program. About half of the first board of the nonprofit Seneca Center was drawn from the religious program of St. Athanasius, and the rest were from the neighborhood, including Jewish and Protestant members.

In the summer of 1977, Connolly attended a Chicago training workshop sponsored by CCUM where he heard Marjorie Tuite, O.P, who spoke about the need for social analysis in local settings; Harry Fagan, a layman, who offered training in community organizing following the methods of Saul Alinsky; and Fr. Larry Gorman, a priest from the archdiocese of Chicago who had developed a pastoral theology of lay empowerment. This training session sparked Connolly's imagination.[58] At the next meeting of the South Bronx Catholic Association, he floated the idea of having Tuite, Fagan, and Gorman come to the South Bronx and offer their workshop, which the association endorsed. In October, a workshop was held at St. Athanasius for about one hundred pastoral workers—lay, women religious, brothers, and priests. At the end, the presenters offered to come back to train leaders from the various parishes in the region. There was an enthusiastic response.

They returned for about ten training sessions, and formed a local team of twenty-one trainers for bilingual audiences who would replicate these workshops in parishes in the South Bronx. With the new team of trainers prepared, pastors, staff, and lay leaders were asked to sponsor a mission kick-off weekend. These kick-off missions were designed to encourage entire parish communities to explore the connection between their faith lives and their everyday lives, and to place social concerns at the core of their parish ministry, which included the formation of a large parish social action committee of between twelve and thirty people. The goal was to promote parish involvement in civic life and social transformation in the neighborhoods. Major issues percolated over the kick-off weekends, and these were subsequently refined by the parish social action committees and became issue campaigns. This program also ignited the imagination to develop a new program devoted to the formation of people committed to promoting change.

The South Bronx People for Change effort was formally launched in 1978. That same year the Catholic Campaign for Human Development (CCHD), administered by the US Catholic Conference, the administrative arm of the National Conference of Catholic Bishops, awarded the South Bronx People for Change its largest level of award at the time, $300,000, in increments of $100,000 for three years. This CCHD grant was a part of a nationwide strategy of the bishops to help impoverished communities across the country. Catholic parish communities, priests and parishioners together, were the target audience, but other neighborhood organizations were included: participation by social service centers and other churches was welcomed. In April 1979, St. John Chrysostom Parish initiated the CCHD-funded program for the South Bronx. In the years that followed, eight to ten Catholic parishes got involved.

The lifeblood of this enterprise came predominantly from a younger generation of people, laywomen and men, often college-educated children of immigrant parents. The rich intercultural composition of this group of leaders can be detected in their names. The first executive director was Nelson Rodriguez, a Puerto Rican with training in social service; Angel Garcia came from the neighborhood and had a degree from Princeton; staff members included Mili Bonilla, Wilson Martinez, Elsie Cabrera, and Tom Amato, all from the South Bronx. Fr. John C. Flynn was an inspirational resource who was deeply committed to the vision of South Bronx People for Change and served in several parishes in the area. Dean Brackley, a New York Jesuit who had recently completed his doctoral dissertation on liberation theology at the University of Chicago, joined the staff in November 1980. Like the people associated with St. Athanasius Center and the affiliated Seneca Center, this nascent group cultivated a dynamic approach to parish-based neighborhood community action.

Community organizing was the organizational heart of South Bronx People for Change. Connolly was a disciple of Fr. Robert Fox, one of the inspirations for the Summer in the City program and founder of the Office for Spanish Catholic Action. For Fox the mandate was to enter into relationships with people in the parish and in the neighborhood, and learn about their struggles and aspirations. From Tuite, Fagan, and Gorman, the team at St. Athanasius learned about social analysis of the problems the people were facing, about community organizing to address these issues, and about constructing a local theology to address the situation on the streets. The newly trained team of priests, women religious, and lay leaders spread this program throughout the South Bronx.

Dean Brackley was reassigned in 1987 after seven years of work with South Bronx People for Change. Based on his experience in predominantly Catholic settings with people promoting social engagement on social issues, he wrote two booklets and two training manuals. The first was a pamphlet, *People Power*, which used a comic book format portraying people of different ethnic and racial groups— with New York attitude and flair—to convey the kind of social analysis of local situations taught by Marjorie Tuite.[59] What do you do when you don't have heat or hot water in your apartment? And your landlord doesn't seem to care? And your neighbors are apprehensive about joining forces to address the situation? The comic book offered six basic ideas about people's attitudes and group dynamics concerning the problems of perceived inequalities and social pyramids, the tendency for individuals to ignore each other and for groups to be in disarray, and the need for people to form a team of equals. What is ultimately needed, the comic concluded, is a social vision that will utilize power and confront, in a constructive manner, in situations of injustice.

The second short booklet, *Organize! A Manual for Leaders*, drew especially on the methods learned from Tuite and Harry Fagan to explore two key concepts: power and social action.[60] A central need was to develop communication and research skills that would enable leaders to bring people together to identify and work on pressing social issues. The goal was to strategize an effective campaign for social change, then to work on tactics, public meetings, negotiations, evaluation, monitoring agreements, and celebrations![61]

These tracts were not replicas of Saul Alinsky's *Rules for Radicals* and *Reveille for Radicals*, which served as the inspirational source for community organizers going through training in the program launched by Alinsky—Industrial Area Foundation (IAF). Rather, they were theological, and drew on biblical stories and Christian beliefs to make their point. One could say that they offered a homegrown version of liberation theology, South Bronx style, which combined the principles and practices of Alinsky's community organizing with theological inspiration from Vatican II and Latin American liberation theology.[62] Their mandate was to build communities that helped people become agents in their own history, by working for meaningful change in their social environment as a sign of their dignity and prophetic calling. Their call to social action exemplifies a genuine reception and realization of the prophetic people of God vision of *Lumen Gentium* and *Gaudium et Spes*.

South Bronx Pastoral Center

In contrast to South Bronx People for Change, whose model of empowering people for social action was influenced by Latin American liberation theology and Saul Alinsky's brand of community organizing, the South Bronx Pastoral Center, subsequently called South Bronx Center for Lay Leadership, employed an approach to religious education based on the teachings of Vatican II but also incorporated interests that became associated with inculturation and contextual theologies then emerging in Latin America, the Caribbean, Africa, and Asia. This center wished to promote a model of team ministry among priests, women religious, and laypeople, and sought to promote lay ecclesial ministry, lay leadership, and community formation. It began with a few priests from the Lower East Side Area Clergy Conference: Frs. Robert Stern, Peter Gavigan, and Neil Graham. They had experimented with such an approach in a parish on the lower East Side of Manhattan, but the parish struggled to make the transition, and so they asked to be reassigned to the beleaguered Our Lady of Victory in the South Bronx.

Robert Stern's role was pivotal. He studied Spanish and learned the indigenous culture in Puerto Rico after ordination in 1959 and returned the following summer for a Latin American Studies program. After serving three years in a parish, he went to Rome to earn a doctoral degree in canon law. This took place during Vatican II, which he witnessed firsthand. After he returned from his studies, he spent four years in the chancery office and then was selected for a new position that could draw on his background in Spanish and Hispanic culture.

Cardinal Cooke had misgivings about Fr. Robert Fox's approach as the head of the Office of Spanish Community Action, which promoted engagement on urgent social issues in the local community. Cooke, who wanted a more broad-based pastoral orientation, wanted Fox to step down. At Fox's insistence, Stern was assigned to replace him, a post Stern accepted in 1969. During Stern's four years in this position, he reoriented the focus of the office so that it more broadly reflected its new title, the Office of the Spanish-Speaking Apostolate. Its activities now included research and pastoral planning; linguistic and cultural formation; the apostolate of religious, priests, and the laity; community relations; ecumenical relations; press, radio, and television; liturgy; and catechetics. Stern promoted a team approach to the office, and together with his team generated an impressive set of programs reaching out to the predominantly Puerto Rican immigrant community but appealing to other Hispanic populations as their numbers increased. But certain people in the chancery became concerned by the increasing power of Stern's Office of the Spanish Speaking Apostolate. The decision was made to break up his office and *mainstream* the Spanish apostolate into the various offices in the chancery; in practice this meant that each office would have its Hispanic representative who would in effect be only a token member of the group. The ascendance of the Spanish apostolate was dealt a blow. Stern's program was in effect being dismantled, and he wanted out of the program. He later decided not to hand in his resignation, but eventually he was forced by chancery officials to leave the office in 1972.

In 1973, Stern became parish administrator at Our Lady of Victory parish in the South Bronx, with Graham and Gavigan as pastoral associates. Together they started a team ministry with two Sisters of Charity, Nora Cunningham, an elementary school teacher with ten years of experience, who arrived in 1974, and Muriel Long, also a teacher and administrator who arrived a year later, along with a lay administrator, Carmen Goytia.

This team of three priests, two women religious, and one laywoman prioritized the parish needs. They restored the church building; developed liturgy preparation in English and Spanish; and explored the needs of their members, some living in one of the largest housing complexes in the Bronx. They designed a ten-week program introducing the scriptures. It was so well received, they offered another. Over time they developed a three-year program that included courses on the scriptures, the church, and also courses on communication, group dynamics, and communal decision making. They developed these courses together as a team.

Eventually they added training programs for every area of lay ecclesial ministry: Eucharistic ministry, lector, music, baptism preparation, evangelization, youth leadership, and family ministry. Intercultural courses, on the Hispanic community in New York, and black American history and awareness, were also designed. Courses were developed on the Charismatic Renewal Movement and the Cursillo Movement.

This program at Our Lady of Victory was so effective that the team decided to expand its outreach and program, founding the South Bronx Pastoral Center in 1978 to promote lay leadership in regional parishes and the local church.[63] During its first three years, the course offerings and programs grew from serving 209 people from 26 parishes with 15 faculty members to serving 448 people from 39 parishes with 31 faculty members. In the sixth year, there were over 647 people participating from 40 parishes: 21 from the South Bronx vicariate and 19 from neighboring areas of the Bronx, Manhattan, New Rochelle, and Yonkers. Over fifty parishes were served during this period.

Northwest Bronx Community and Clergy Coalition

As the situation in the South Bronx deteriorated at the beginning of the 1970s, fear spread among residents of the Northwest Bronx that the same situation of fires, neglect, and crime would be replayed in their own communities. In 1970, Jesuit scholastic Paul Brant, a graduate of the Jesuit seminary in Milford, Illinois, was assigned to Fordham University to teach philosophy and to serve as Fordham University's liaison with the Northwest Bronx neighborhood. Living in an apartment in this area allowed Brant to experience firsthand some of the challenges faced by his neighbors. He recruited students from his Elements of Social Thought class to help him pick up waste on the streets. When he appealed to Catholic pastors in the area to try to stabilize the neighborhood, he got mixed responses: "Some of them didn't think the church should be involved, others were afraid it would incite racial conflict."[64] One priest was not afraid: Msgr. John Charles McCarthy of Holy Spirit Parish. Brant joined forces with McCarthy, and in 1972, they established the Morris Heights Neighborhood Improvement Association, whose aim was to address threats to neighborhood well-being through community organizing.

The spirit generated in this parish-based association emboldened Brant and McCarthy to broaden their reach, joining with priests from sixteen parishes to form the Northwest Bronx Clergy Conference (NWBCC).[65] A few of the priests recruited Auxiliary Bishop Patrick Ahern, pastor of Our Lady of Angels parish and vicar for the Bronx, to join the group. Motivated by the concerns of his fellow priests, Ahern did join, and became a passionate advocate for the people of the Bronx. An exceptional fund-raiser, Ahern was a genius at crafting razor-sharp letters to elected officials and bureaucrats denouncing their failures to address the needs of Bronx residents.[66] Priest members of the NWBCC gathered regularly for prayer and to discuss problems confronting their parishioners at meetings accompanied by, so it was reported, Irish soda bread, tea, and coffee. Attentive to the signs of the times and the grief and anguish in their midst, and eager to discern together and commit themselves to do what was necessary to help out, this clergy group captured the spirit of a people of God ecclesiology.

In June 1974, a three-day conference at Fordham University titled "Strategies for Ministry in the Urban Struggle" featured members of the Jesuit community at Fordham, notably sociologist Fr. Joseph Fitzpatrick and, from the neighborhood, Bishop Ahern for Our Lady of Angels parish. Also in attendance were Msgr. Jack Egan, a Chicago social activist priest who had moved to the University of Notre Dame, and bishops from Detroit and Denver. In his keynote address, New York Cardinal Terence Cooke endorsed the example of South Bronx parishes. These parishes, he declared, "are a promise of stability, of permanence in a storm of change, of security that at least one of the major structures of our society, the church, has not pulled out and thrown up its hands in frustration at the appalling convergences of urban crises." Cooke explicitly affirmed these parishes' engagement in the civic life of their neighborhoods: "The urban ministry of the local parish encompasses its role of service in housing, in education, in opportunities for employment, in the very critical area of personal safety for the people who dwell within its boundaries."[67] When Fr. Louis Gigante delivered a keynote speech accompanied by pictures of South Bronx neighborhoods decimated by fires, his message to audience members residing in the Northwest Bronx could not have been clearer: the situation in the Northwest Bronx is volatile, and this will become your neighborhood, too, unless you do something about it.

The NWBCC and Morris Heights Neighborhood Association became the catalysts for the formation of the Northwest Bronx Community and Clergy Coalition later that year. This larger coalition was launched in the fall of 1974 with initial funding of $15,000 from the chairman of Dollar Savings Bank and from collections taken by area churches.[68] With this money, the fledgling organization hired six full-time organizers. Comprising an interracial group of Latinos, African Americans, and whites, and composed of people of different faiths—Catholic, Protestant, and Jewish—and different nonreligious worldviews, the Northwest Bronx Community and Clergy Coalition was established by religious leaders and lay leaders from parishes and congregations, neighborhood and tenant associations to advance racial and economic justice.[69] Catholic clergy from the original sixteen parishes, along with Episcopalian Rev. Dr. Law, were key in the formation of the Northwest Bronx Community and Clergy Coalition (the Coalition) but Protestant clergy and church involvement grew quickly; by the end of the its first decade, the coalition included Presbyterians, Lutherans, and Methodists.[70]

Of utmost importance for my argument is the fact that in this undertaking, Catholic priests collaborated closely with an ever-widening circle of laypeople and women religious, and with them they became leaders and agents of social action. Among the lay leaders who played a crucial role in this enterprise were many trained in the community organizing methods of Saul Alinsky.[71] Paul Brant initially gathered a group of community organizers led by two of his friends and former Jesuit seminary classmates, Roger Hayes and Jim Mitchell. Hayes was trained in Alinsky's methods of community organizing in Chicago and knew Spanish from a year in formation with the Jesuits in Peru, and Mitchell had worked with a construction company started by Jesuit brothers in Detroit.[72] This group of organizers was joined by Fr. Jim McNally, an Augustinian priest serving at St. Nicholas of Tolentine parish, and Sister Pat Dillon, a native of the Bronx and a member of the Congregation of the Religious of Jesus and Mary, who had trained in community organizing in Rhode Island and who subsequently worked as an organizer at the coalition for twenty-five years. This first group of Coalition organizers working with largely Hispanic and African American populations in the area were young, predominantly white men, all under the age of twenty-five, some with degrees from Fordham University: Bill Fischer, Ralph Menendez, Jim Vogt, and Bill Frey, who received $6,000 a year for their work. And the number of white female organizers grew quickly over the first decade.

Coalition organizers' first goal was to establish ten neighborhood associations across the Northwest sector of the Bronx that would include members from various Catholic parishes, Protestant congregations, and tenant associations.[73] Organizers invited individuals to gather together to identify their concerns about the state of their buildings and neighborhoods. Participants in these gatherings began to form community and civic friendships, and many went on to forge partnerships to address their situations. Clergy and the community organizers worked with sixteen Catholic parishes, approximately six Protestant congregations, and they collaborated with the West Bronx Jewish Community Council,[74] as well as with people that had no religious affiliation. Together they promoted grassroots citizen leadership and mobilized members of churches, apartment buildings, and neighborhoods to address a range of issues pertaining to building and neighborhood conditions, including lack of heating and hot water, sanitation problems, crime, and the threat of fire.

Anna Marie Reinthaler is a good example of a local leader in these efforts. Her home was in Our Lady of Refuge parish in the Northwest Bronx, an increasingly Hispanic parish located not far from Fordham University.[75] Anne Marie was known in her parish as soft-spoken. But when she attended the 1974 conference at Fordham on the future of the Bronx that had been advertised at her parish, she felt compelled by what she heard to get involved.

Anne Marie subsequently attended a meeting at a nearby church for people in her neighborhood set up by organizer Bill Fischer. Participants were encouraged to reach out and invite their neighbors to come together to talk about the issues that were of concern to them. Anne Marie went home and made a list of possible topics of concern and delivered copies door-to-door along with an invitation to attend a meeting at her parish on August 15, the Feast of the Assumption. She expected twenty or thirty to attend; to her astonishment, over two hundred turned out. They set as their immediate goal to form a neighborhood block association, with an eye toward a tenant association later. Anne Marie's block association elected her to represent the group at the first board meeting of the fledgling Coalition, and she went on to become one of the coalition's most effective and committed activists.

Each of the ten neighborhood associations in the coalition developed their own board of directors with a president and committees composed of organizers and members to work on the most pressing concerns. These committees conducted research on critical issues, brought problem issues into focus, identified strategies for direct action, and targeted leaders for the group to hold accountable and challenge in public venues.[76]

The original board of directors of the coalition combined roughly fifteen clergy with ten laypeople representing the spectrum of affiliated groups: neighborhood associations and tenant associations.[77] Regularly, organizational tensions flared between the coalition board and the presidents and representatives of the individual associations over campaign priorities such as housing maintenance, vandalism, and drugs.[78] Each member group could select up to twenty-five members annually to serve on coalition standing committees. Four neighborhood associations had to be involved on an issue in order to establish a coalition-wide standing committee. The annual meeting of the coalition provided an opportunity for the membership to ratify standing committees, which were formed around issues such as housing, security, city services, young people, and health care issues. These annual meetings also provided the occasion to affirm the primary campaign agendas for the coalition for the coming year.

From its inception in 1974, the Coalition set out to organize the growing Latino and black populations of the Northwest Bronx, with a staff and board that was initially composed primarily of white men and an increasing number of mostly white women. Attention would be given to increasing the black and Hispanic composition of the board officers and staff in the decades that followed.

Anne Devenney, the third president of the coalition board, was the first layperson and first woman to serve in that position. The former president of the Altar and Rosary Society at her parish, St. Brendan's, Devenney was involved with the coalition from its inception. She went on to become longtime coalition board president and one of its most effective and beloved leaders. She collaborated with clergy, organizers, and lay leaders on the key campaigns that defined the first twenty years of the coalition.

Coalition members mobilized people to hold accountable the area's slumlords, insurance company officials, bankers, and politicians who were not addressing the real-life problems that were being faced every day by people in the Northwest Bronx. A key leader, Devenney was often described as a grandmother-like figure: a person filled with compassion toward struggling neighbors, someone with a quick and wicked wit in tense situations, and a person with nerves of steel in calling on people with power to listen up and do the right thing. She mobilized people—parishioners, neighbors, and fellow leaders—and was instrumental in facilitating the joining of forces among blacks, Latinos, and ethnic whites of Irish, German, and Italian descent.

Of the many campaigns that defined the work of the coalition over its first two decades, housing was an ongoing issue and an impetus for ever-deeper analysis and diverse action strategies. Initially the coalition's housing standing committee focused on holding tenement superintendents and landlords accountable for building problems experienced by renters. The committee identified a pattern of violations and organized renters' protests.

Over time, coalition members learned the problems went deeper than the lack of hot water, heat in winter, and building upkeep. Some landlords were not making improvements and abandoning buildings, while other decent landlords were having difficulty getting loans to perform building maintenance and improvement. It became apparent that it was no longer sufficient to confront landlords. The coalition established a new committee on city services to compile data about poor building maintenance. Their aim was to keep pushing these issues with the New York City Department of Housing Preservation and Development, which had "the mandate to preserve low-income and affordable housing and enforce a local house code."[79] They established an emergency number for Bronx residents to call with housing complaints to the city's Housing and Development Administration. But that was not enough. Community development funds were being denied to Bronx properties.[80] The problems went deeper.

A breakthrough year on the housing issue at the coalition and across the country was 1975, when the US Congress enacted the landmark Home Mortgage Disclosure Act (HMDA). This legislation requires that financial institutions publicly disclose mortgage data to determine if they are serving the neighborhoods justly.[81] Housing issues were receiving increased attention nationwide at this time; that same year a nonprofit organization, the National Housing Institute, was formed to address issues of affordable housing and community development.[82] Also in 1975, organizers from the coalition attended the annual meeting of the National People's Action assembly in Washington DC, which gave them an opportunity learn about redlining. Redlining is the widely used term describing the practices of banks and other lending institutions that deny loans to landlords of apartments in certain areas of the city map, color-coded by the perceived financial risk. Places like the Bronx may have been considered financially risky because of poverty and low incomes, but this fails to account for the fact that neighborhoods were populated, and increasingly so, by black and Latino majorities.[83]

Facing escalating arson, crime, and the combination of the government housing subsidies for welfare recipients with the uncapping of rent controls by the government landlords to increase their profits, waves of people left the Bronx out of frustration and fear. Coalition board president Anne Devenney championed the rallying cry, *Don't Move, Improve!* as she partnered with members to address these problems in a multipronged attack. This motto called on neighbors to stay in the Bronx and take a stand against racism by forging new forms of intercultural communities.

Housing issues remained the driving concern during the first two decades of the Coalition. Rent strikes and demonstrations against landlords procured short-term gains through the use of countervailing power. But a broader strategy was needed to address the lack of loans being given to improve apartments. In 1976, the coalition established a neighborhood redevelopment committee to track where the monies from the federal Community Development Block Grant program that were being allocated in New York. President Gerald Ford had enacted this block grant program in 1974. Eventually one question stumped coalition leaders. Why was so little grant money going into the Bronx? The Home Mortgage Disclosure Act of 1975 enabled communities to find out where local lending institutions were investing and to uncover redlining practices. In 1976, the Coalition established a reinvestment committee to compile information about lending practices of local banks and to encourage local investment.[84] In an inspiring fashion, the Coalition was relentless in gathering further information and in learning about how government institutions and lending agencies contributed to the problem, and the members of the Coalition worked tenaciously to bring their problems into focus and to develop new strategies for addressing them.

Clergy leaders like Bishop Ahern and Father McCarthy became active on the Neighborhood Development Committee, working with organizers and core community leaders to develop solid social analysis and to mobilize people in the churches, tenements, and neighborhoods to speak up in front of officials from banks and lending institutions, just as they had previously done before their landlords.[85] These clergy, who were comfortable around elite members of society as golf partners and dinner guests, now stepped forward to hold them accountable on the issue of housing. The gospel of economic and interracial justice suddenly became quite concrete.

With fears of apartment building deterioration and fires looming large, landlords in the Northwest Bronx needed reinvestment loans from mortgage companies to improve their buildings and to maintain their insurance. Banks, mortgage companies, and insurance agencies were not giving loans to the neighborhood people who had money in their banks; insurance companies were not renewing insurance coverage or granting new coverage to people in the Northwest Bronx. Over time, and with assiduous effort, the tables were turned, and by the mid-1980s the coalition had been able "to attract $37 million for the rehabilitation of seven thousand apartment units" and continued work to identify insurance programs to offer policies to people in the Northwest Bronx.[86]

At their tenth anniversary celebration held in 1983, the coalition celebrated its involvement and achievements on a range of projects. Tenant organizations had pushed for over forty-five thousand building violations to be corrected by organizing thirteen hundred apartment buildings. Neighborhood organizations had developed employment training programs, fire and arson prevention programs, and youth programs. And the Coalition had addressed the neighborhood reinvestment and insurance problems through collaboration with financial institutions.[87] Also in 1983, New York State awarded the coalition a $100,000 contract "with no guarantee of renewal" for a project of weatherization of apartment buildings to fight against the rising costs of fuel oil being passed on to tenants. Under the leadership of Fran Fuzelli, longtime collaborator with organizer Sister Pat Dillon, the coalition has received state funding for this weatherization program ever since.

Over time, different aspects of the problems faced by the people of the Bronx were identified, analyzed, and strategically tackled: in housing, education, policing and prisons, health care, labor, immigration, and environment. But it also became increasingly clear that these diverse problems were interrelated aspects of structures of racial and economic injustice that contributed to transgenerational poverty. This is the long legacy of slavery and colonialism as it manifests itself in the Bronx and in countless neighborhoods in the United States. In time new manifestations and dimensions of this legacy would surface in the Bronx, and the coalition would develop new proactive strategies for confronting them. In struggling with these deeper levels of injustice, the coalition undertook practices that have helped form Bronx parishioners and neighbors into a prophetic people of God committed to the promotion of grassroots democracy. In particular, the coalition set itself on a path toward a dialogical model of discernment and decision making based on basic religiously inspired values about human dignity, the common good, and the promotion of racial and economic justice. In this process, a great deal of effort was given to bringing into focus the laments of the community and the signs of the times in social and economic terms. Much of the membership of the coalition was motivated by gospel values and vision, but these were articulated in ways that could appeal to diverse faith traditions and to those with no explicit faith commitment other than to work for the common good for the poor and the marginalized.

Concluding Remarks

This chapter has introduced the emergence of the people of God ecclesiology at Vatican II and explored how this social imaginary was received, and how it motivated the implementation of structural innovations and reforms in the Archdiocese of New York at the diocesan level, the parish level, the neighborhood level, and among priests and religious congregations. Special attention was given to the prophetic character of this social imaginary as it surfaced in various contexts among the Sisters of Charity, in the development of parish councils, and among priests, women religious, and lay leaders who developed faith-based community organizing to promote civic engagement in the Bronx. The next chapter will explore the shifts that occurred in official Catholic teachings during the pontificates of John Paul II and Benedict XVI, and how the influence of these shifts can be detected in the various examples we have introduced here.

Chapter 2

THE PROPHETIC PEOPLE OF GOD ECLIPSED

In the aftermath of the Extraordinary Synod of Bishops held in 1985, which was devoted to evaluating the reception of the Second Vatican Council, an unsettling opinion surfaced and soon spread. There was a growing conviction that the new dawn in the church ushered in by the implementation of the people of God ecclesiology (as well as the doctrine of the collegiality of bishops), attributed by many to a new outpouring of the Spirit at the council, was being eclipsed. Various groups of theologians in Europe and in the United States and organized networks of active laypeople, women religious, and priests expressed the fear that the reception of the Spirit and the prospect of a new Pentecost in the church made possible by the council was being stifled, if not extinguished.[1]

Over the subsequent three decades, many associated this eclipse of the people of God ecclesiology with the emergence of what is known as the official papal and curial expression of communion ecclesiology. I contend, and I am not alone in so doing, that communion ecclesiology as such is not the source of the problem and consternation since the mid-1980s. The understanding of the church as communion, as indicated in the last chapter, offers a vision of the church's identity and mission informed by the Christological, sacramental, and Eucharistic character of the church as the body of Christ, all of which are central motifs in the documents of Vatican II. The conciliar vision of the church as communion is both beautifully simple and richly complex. However, for all that is gained by this approach, to dwell predominantly or exclusively on the church in terms of communion accesses only part of the truth of the full splendor of the church and its mission.

As this chapter will seek to demonstrate, official Roman Catholic communion ecclesiology, as it was advanced especially during the pontificates of John Paul II and Benedict XVI, offers certain important and legitimate ecclesiological claims and clarifications, and rightly points out certain risks and problems in alternative orientations, specifically those associated with a people of God ecclesiology. At the same time, the officially promulgated communion ecclesiology has imposed certain unjustified or at least highly contested restrictions over the last thirty-five years that became detrimental to the vitality of the church in various ways. It can be argued that these problems and contestations are associated with one particular version or species of communion ecclesiology associated with the official Roman Catholic or papal and curial version of communion ecclesiology.[2] It can likewise be contended that during this period in history, we are witnessing a protracted conflict between alternative communion ecclesiologies as these bear on debates about the relationship of the exercise of papal primacy and episcopal collegiality; about the relationship of the universal and local church, the center and the periphery; about the nature of lay and ordained ecclesial ministry; and about the evangelical and social mission of the church. The diverse communion ecclesiologies, which have developed as alternatives or corrections to the official papal and curial version, merit attention, have much to commend them, and, in certain ways, I am convinced, are correct. I will not, however, directly engage the challenges that surfaced over the last thirty years in terms of vying views of communion ecclesiology.

Rather, I will argue that at a more fundamental and no less important level, the ascendancy of the official communion ecclesiology eclipsed the new dawn of the people of God as it was emerging during the two decades after the council. As I advance this argument, I will give special attention to the prophetic character and mission of the people of God associated with the Spirit's anointing, and with the messianic and specifically the prophetic identity and mission of Jesus Christ. This line of inquiry brings into focus an underdeveloped counterpart to the church understood as communion. This historical development of the eclipse of the people of God ecclesiology must be understood in order to foster a new phase in the history of the reception of this great council, which is in the early stages of being initiated by Pope Francis. I am particularly convinced that reclaiming the prophetic character of the church as people of God is crucial for further cultivating the dialogical practices of the church associated with all forms of synodality, including those forms practiced in the diocesan and parochial church and, by extension, in base communities, as well as in the church's mission in the world for the poor and oppressed through the promotion of grassroots democracy. The prophetic character of the people of God is realized in and through synodality in the church, and in and through democracy in civil society.

How could such an eclipse have occurred? This is not a mystery. The vocal minority of bishops during the council, many representing the institutional commitments of the Vatican curia and an older vision of the church that has been variously described as triumphalistic, juridical, hierarchical, and paternalistic, resisted and complained relentlessly about the changes being introduced by the council majority. After the death of John XXIII, Pope Paul VI chose to exercise a more active role in the council. He was especially concerned about the minority at the council being marginalized, which he believed risked undermining unity in the church and his own effective implementation of the council's teachings after its completion. Pope Paul went to great lengths to promote a sense of communion in the church with this traditionalist group and in the end made certain concessions on pivotal issues. This is associated in dramatic ways with the inclusion of the Preliminary Explanatory Note, which I will refer to by its Latin formulation, *Nota explicativa praevia*, and Paul VI's preemptive articulation of the nature and operating procedures for the synod of bishops in his *motu proprio, Apostolicam Sollicitudo*.

These papal interventions set up the conditions for the conservative minority, through the activities of curial officials, to significantly influence the implementation of the council. Over time, this minority undermined certain teachings of the majority. With the appointment of an increasing number of bishops who adhered to aspects of this minority outlook during the pontificates of John Paul II and Benedict XVI, the minority outlook grew in power and influence around the world. In order to understand the struggles going on in the Roman Catholic Church during the beginning of the pontificate of Francis, this sequence of events must be understood. Ultimately, they must be assessed in terms of their impact on concrete practices in local churches around the world as well as in the universal church.

Two decades after Vatican II, the influence of chapter two of *Lumen Gentium* (cited as LG) was being felt in local churches around the world. Bishops, priests, religious women, and laity were collectively renegotiating their relationships and modes of collaborative behavior. These changes were certainly difficult and raised new questions and problems. Yet, a new way of being church that was synodal and conciliar, in other words, a dialogical vision of the church, was emerging, and supplanting the triumphalistic, juridical, and paternalistic brand of hierarchy and clerical behavior that shaped the way of being church that was in existence before Vatican II.

There were pockets of resistance to the people of God ecclesiology of Vatican II among some curial officials and certain bishops around the world, especially in the center of Europe, as would become clear at the time of the Extraordinary Synod of 1985. These opinions were at times associated with the views held by the minority of bishops who had urged Paul VI to add the *Nota explicative praevia* to *Lumen Gentium*. During the two decades that followed the council, significant conflict over the interpretation of the council and its aftermath emerged.

Paul VI's *motu proprio Ecclesiae Sanctae I*, issued on August 6, 1966, established the initial outline for implementing the council's work, and introduced synodal and conciliar practices in the local church, which were widely welcomed. Yet over time, critics of the experiments inspired by the people of God ecclesiology and its dialogical approach to discernment and deliberation became more vocal.

There are some who might be inclined to argue that during the pontificates of John Paul II and Benedict XVI, the inspiration and power of the Spirit of God was being extinguished. That would be going too far. I want to offer a more differentiated argument by claiming that during this period of time, the people of God ecclesiology and particularly its prophetic character were being eclipsed; the inspiration and power of the Spirit was being stifled and restrained, yet both remained operative in obscure ways without being extinguished. Let me offer evidence to support this thesis.

The New Code of Canon Law

John Paul II promulgated the new Code of Canon Law on January 25, 1983, almost eighteen years after the council ended and twenty-four years to the day from the moment in 1959 when John XXIII both called for the revision of the 1917 code and convoked Vatican II. John Paul II explained the nature of the revision in this way:

> This new Code could be understood as a great effort to translate [the] doctrine and ecclesiology [of Vatican II] into canonical language. If, however, it is impossible to translate perfectly into canonical language the conciliar image of the Church, nevertheless the Code must always be referred to this image as the primary pattern whose outline the Code ought to express insofar as it can by its very nature.[3]

The new code offered something different from a translation of the council; it offered an interpretation. In the process, the architects of the new code were providing an assessment and even an adjudication of postconciliar debates about the interpretation of the council, particularly the varying emphases offered by the people of God and communion motifs in the council documents.[4] So how were the two images of the church, people of God and communion, and their underlying theological and pastoral implications, transmuted into canon law?

On the face of it, one can easily discover that the code sought to affirm these two important approaches to the church and to recognize the basic claims and impulses of each. Thus, after the general norms are established in Part I of the new code, Part II is announced with the title "The People of God." The first canons of this section echo themes from the people of God ecclesiology:

> The Christian faithful are those who, inasmuch as they have been incorporated in Christ through baptism, have been constituted as the people of God. For this reason, made sharers in their own way in Christ's priestly, prophetic, and royal functions, they are called to exercise the mission which God has entrusted to the Church to fulfill in the world, in accord with the condition proper to each. (204, § 1)

The next two formulations, however, assert the importance of communion, and in fact provide what can only be called in the strict sense a governing framework for the new code: "This Church, constituted and organized in this world as a society, subsists in the Catholic Church governed by the successor of Peter and the bishops in communion with him" (204, § 2). "The baptized are fully in the communion of the Catholic Church on this earth who are joined with Christ in its visible structure by the bonds of the profession of faith, the sacraments, and ecclesiastical governance" (205). The two motifs, people of God and communion, have been virtually fused, becoming one amalgam. In the process, hierarchical communion became the code's dominant and controlling notion. This resulted in tendencies to place restrictions on the authority of the people of God and also to limit the participation of the laity in the ministry and mission of the church as was intended by council teachings that all the faithful share in the prophetic, priestly, and kingly mission of Christ and are bestowed with the anointing and gifts of the Spirit for the good of the church and the world. In all this, the influence of the *nota explicativa praevia*, which accentuated papal authority in relation to the college of bishops, as mentioned in the previous chapter, is clearly manifest.[5]

This eclipse is also in evidence a few canons later. Only one canon speaks of the equality of all the faithful: "there exists among all the Christian faithful a true equality regarding dignity and action by which they all cooperate in the building up of the Body of Christ according to each one's own condition and function" (208). But this is immediately followed by the claim that "The Christian faithful, even in their own manner of acting, are always obliged to maintain communion with the Church" (209, § 1). The code acknowledges that there are various rights of the Christian faithful to promote the mission of the church in the world (211–19), including the right and duty to voice their views to their pastors concerning the good of the Church (212, § 3), but these rights are restricted, if not eclipsed, by the canon that states "the Christian faithful are bound to follow with Christian obedience those things which the sacred pastors, inasmuch as they represent Christ, declare as teachers of the faith or establish as rulers of the Church" (212, § 1). An individual or a group speaking out for, witnessing to, the perceived good of the church has no weight relative to the obedience due to clerical, hierarchical authority in canon law.

In keeping with the council's teachings on the people of God and the collegiality of the bishops, the revised code introduced new or refurbished structures to foster collaboration in the church: the synods of bishops to promote collegiality among bishops with and under the pope; episcopal conferences for national and regional collegiality among bishops; and at the diocesan level, diocesan synods, diocesan presbyteral councils, diocesan pastoral councils, and parish pastoral councils. However, what the code establishes, on the one hand, it restricts and constrains, on the other, by stipulating that all of these deliberative bodies are only consultative and not genuinely decision making. Now, it has been argued that in the code "consultation . . . is not a mere sounding of opinions, but a seeking of the wisdom resident in the Church. The freedom of Church authorities to act is preserved, but those in positions of authority are continuously called on to listen to the wisdom in the Church through various forms of consultation."[6] Yet, the person canonically charged with governing, pope or bishop or priest, is by ordination and office canonically designated as authorized to make many decisions. This leaves the issue of accountability and meaningful participation of laity, religious women, and priests in question.[7] The pope, with the curia's assistance, is given the final judgment and decision in matters of the synod of bishops and episcopal conferences; bishops decide in matters pertaining to the presbyteral council, which are mandated by canon law and diocesan pastoral councils, if they do exist (in many cases, they do not); and parish pastors decide in matters pertaining to the parish councils.

For many in the church, this reassertion of top-down authority is a source of considerable frustration and reflects the failure to move forward in developing a model of leadership that employs a genuinely collective model of discernment and decision making. In fact, diocesan synods and diocesan and parish pastoral councils are not required. As a result, the authority of all the people of God based on baptism, the equality of believers, and their anointing to share in the three-fold mission of Christ, especially in terms of decision-making authority, is being restricted and denied. Joseph Komonchak discovers in the new canon law "the absence . . . of one of the most important assertions of a right and duty to be found in a conciliar text," *Apostolicam Actuositatem* (cited as AA) 3, which reads,

> From the reception of these charisms, even the most ordinary ones, there arises from each of the faithful the right and duty to exercise them in the Church and in the world for the good of men and the upbuilding of the Church, in the freedom of the Holy Spirit who "breathes where he will," and at the same time in communion with their brothers and sisters in Christ, especially with their pastors, whose role it is to pass judgment on the authenticity and orderly exercise of the gifts, not indeed in order to extinguish the Spirit but to test all things and to keep what is good.[8]

A related discovery is made by James A. Coriden: there is a virtual "canonical silence about the Spirit['s] . . . influence and activity in the Church."[9] He identifies seven canons where the Holy Spirit is mentioned, but none pertain to the people of God and how all the baptized and anointed share in the priestly, prophetic, and kingly offices of Christ.[10] He goes on to develop a set of proposed amendments to the code that would make explicit the agency of the Spirit at work among all of the faithful in the life of the church as well as in the special charisms received and special offices exercised in the church. Coriden gives close attention to the role of the Spirit in the work of synods and pastoral councils in the life of the church, and to the importance of the Spirit in processes of ecclesial discernment.[11]

In short, central impulses in the council were dampened by the new code. Providing background, Joseph A. Komonchak helpfully explains the negative currents operative during the drafting process.

> These [draft] texts [of the code] were elaborated by the *coetus* [the commission for the revision of the code] on the basis of an interpreta-tion not only of Vatican II but also of events that have taken place in the Catholic Church since the Council. That the latter should be true is, of course, legitimate and necessary; but it is also clear from the discussions that the dominant interpretation of post-conciliar events has been rather narrow and fearful. There are many protests about abuses and many warn-ings of dangers; there is less evidence of a feeling that the developments set in motion by the Council have enriched the Church's life. One senses also a feeling that it is necessary to hurry the promulgation of the Code, that the Code will supply the needed remedies for these "anti-juridical times."

This interpretation of events since the Council also affects the interpretation of the Council itself. Its texts are read, selected, and modified in the light of those events as interpreted. The Council's deliberate refusal to settle disputed points—its "ambiguity," if you prefer—at not a few points permits a "business as usual" canonical determination: the voice is the voice of Vatican II, but the hands are the hands of the Code.

For that reason it becomes important to express reservations about considering the new Code to provide "an authentic interpretation on many points of the teachings of Vatican II." It will, of course, be an authoritative statement in many, many areas, and it may be that some will even present it as *the* authentic interpretation of the Council. But surely it is the Council that must interpret the Code, and not the Code the Council.[12]

As Komonchak and Coriden suggest, the renewed vitality and updating of the church promised by the prudential wisdom being cultivated by synodal and conciliar practices at every level of the church was, in the new code, being restricted. The invitation to develop communal processes of discernment concerning the pastoral mission of the local church at the diocesan and parish levels was welcomed, often with enthusiasm, in the first two decades after the council—not without struggles, pitfalls, and frustrations, but with genuine good will and openness to growth. During the subsequent years, these efforts were consistently challenged and undermined by an increasingly centralized, clerical exercise of authority at every level of the church, although not in every parish, diocese, and episcopal conference, or at least not to the same degree.[13] The last generation or two of bishops and priests have frequently imitated the model and style of centralized clerical authority exercised by John Paul II and Benedict XVI.

Some canon lawyers and theologians involved in the process of drafting and revising the new code raised the kinds of concern articulated by Komonchak. However, in the final phase of preparing the code, John Paul II chose not to continue the broad collaborative process of deliberation and revision, and instead selected a commission of six canonists. Msgr. Edward Egan, a highly regarded canon lawyer who ultimately became Cardinal Archbishop of New York, was the only person from the United States involved in making the final revisions, which were then approved by a small commission of four bishops, which included Cardinal Joseph Ratzinger.[14]

There is sufficient evidence to conclude that, though there was a spectrum of theological and canonical positions among the framers of the new code, a small group who shared sympathies with certain impulses associated with the *nota explicativa praevia*, which was added to chapter three of *Lumen Gentium*, methodically implemented a more narrow understanding of hierarchical communion. This reasserted and reinforced a centralized vision of authority and power over and against synodal and conciliar practices. As a result the authority of the college of bishops and the people of God and the importance of the charisms of the local churches were not fully recognized and, consequently, eroded. The canonical promotion of communion in the church has undermined legitimate diversity and the genuine contributions of local, regional, and national churches for the universal church. This is no small loss. Not only has the code effectively restricted the decision-making power and authority of collegial bodies of bishops (the synod of bishops and episcopal conferences) and communal bodies of discernment in the local church, it has offered no explicit mention of the right and duty to the free exercise of charisms in an orderly manner for the good of the church (LG, no. 12; and especially AA, no. 3) and has made no mention of the *sensus fidei* of the faithful, which is witnessed to by the prophetic character of the people of God and serves as a genuine guardian of the faith of the church.

The 1985 Extraordinary Synod of Bishops

John Paul II announced the convocation of an Extraordinary Synod of Bishops on January 25, 1985, with the aim of deliberating about the reception of the council. Archbishop Jozef Tomko sent a letter in April to the 165 representatives chosen to participate in the synod asking them to consider the reception of the four conciliar constitutions on liturgy, revelation, church, the church in the modern world, and to respond to four questions:

1. How was the council made known, received, and implemented?
2. What benefits did the churches derive from the council?
3. What errors or abuses have there been, and what was done and still needs to be done to correct them?
4. What difficulties, new or old, remain in the way of an implementation of the council, and how can they be met?

Those leading the synod wanted to focus on the difficulties of reception identified as errors and abuses, so as to devise ways to address these problems.

The centerpiece of the response devised by the synod is found in the Final Report of the Synod, which reached the conclusion that "The ecclesiology of communion is the central and fundamental idea of the council's documents. . . . [and] is [. . .] the foundation for order in the church especially for correct relationship between unity and pluriformity in the church."[15] After six months of reflection before the synod and the four weeks of discussion at the Extraordinary Synod the bishops judged that postconciliar difficulties, errors, and abuses needed to be addressed. They chose to do this by reaffirming the place of mystery in the church, above all by establishing communion as the governing framework for the vision of the church for the council. The pivotal role played by the people of God motif in the council documents was thereby displaced. Only three passing references were made to the people of God in this synodal document. First, it is included on a list of images of the church used at the council: people of God, the body of Christ, the bridge of Christ, the temple of the Holy Spirit, the family of God (II.A.3). Second, an eschatological note is sounded when it speaks of "the pilgrim church on earth [as] the messianic people" (II. A.3). Third, we read, "In the unity of the faith and the sacraments and in hierarchical unity, especially with the center of unity given to us by Christ in the service of Peter, the church is that messianic people of which the Constitution *Lumen Gentium* speaks" (no. 9).

These fleeting references render the richness of conciliar teaching on the people of God mute in contrast with the communion motif. Confirming the bishops' selectivity is the fact that there are absolutely no references to other topics associated with the treatment of the people of God in *Lumen Gentium*: the equality of all the baptized in the church; the participation of all the faithful in Christ's threefold mission as priest, prophet, and king; the important category of the *sensus fidei* of all the faithful—and nothing on the role of the people of God in advancing the kingdom of God, which is not to be identified with the church. Correspondingly there is no urgent call for implementing participatory structures at every level of the church for collective deliberation about the signs of the times and the church's mission. Rather, we find this weak formulation: "diocesan synods and other ecclesial conferences can be very useful for the application of the council" (I.6). This conclusion subverts central processes that were being encouraged and put into place after the council. The formulation implies that such participatory structures can be useful, but they might not be; and they certainly are not necessary. The conclusion offered is clear and course changing: where the council offered two orienting frameworks, people of God and communion, the Final Report offers one.

Why did the Extraordinary Synod of Bishops ignore the substance of the council's teaching on the people of God and choose a communion ecclesiology as the governing framework through which to interpret Vatican II? Cardinal Godfried Danneels, the general secretary of the synod, wrote an Initial Report, which identified, in his summary comments on the written responses from bishops, three perceived problems with the reception of the people of God motif.[16]

- Promotes a democratic ideology in the church, grassroots movements, a popular church from below, a church of the poor, a sociological approach to the church.
- Focuses on the human character of the pilgrim church in history without being integrated with the supernatural gift character of the church identified with the body of Christ.
- Threatens the mysterious divine sacramental character of the church, which serves as the foundation of the church's hierarchical and clerical identity in the mediation of salvation.

Even if these three characterizations reflect possible trends or tendencies in the reception of the people of God notion with any degree of accuracy, which some seriously doubted at the time and still question, the response of the synod was deeply flawed. Instead of working through the variety of positive and questionable receptions and the complementary and contrasting insights of the council offered by the people of God and communion motifs, the virtual silence of the Final Report on the people of God set up a dichotomy between these two ecclesiological orientations that discredited the opposing position. It discredited what is being described here as the prophetic character of the people of God associated with synodal and conciliar forms of discernment and mission orientation in the church.[17] In so doing, the synod offered an overcorrection to an alleged problem that, arguably, has had damaging effects on the vitality of the church.

This Extraordinary Synod was a harbinger and influence on subsequent official teachings, policies, and actions, which in many cases have been restrictive and destructive. And in fact, the story of the synod proceedings and the underground currents that continued on after the synod are even more complex and multilayered. For our purposes, it is important to remember the responses to the original questionnaire, which the council participants had six months to prepare, often in consultation and collaboration with episcopal conferences and working groups. Many responses offered positive assessments of the various ways in which the teachings of chapter two of *Lumen Gentium* were being received, even though they were combined with struggles and difficulties in implementation, or partial receptions. These more positive assessments of the reception of the council stood in tension with Cardinal Joseph Ratzinger's influential thesis that the postconciliar period is a period of crisis and increasing deterioration.[18]

It is also significant that, throughout his career as a theologian and during his years as Pope Benedict XVI, Ratzinger consistently judged the people of God ecclesiology in light of the postresurrection theologies of the Eucharist and the body of Christ, without giving much attention to Jesus's mission and ministry as exorcist, healer, and teacher, and his conflicts with Jewish and Roman officials. This may help explain his more narrow assessment of the dynamic of the biblical approaches to the people of God and their postconciliar reception.

In 1985, the year of the Extraordinary Synod, there was widespread resistance to Ratzinger's negative assessment of the postconciliar period by representatives from episcopal conferences in the United States, Canada, the United Kingdom, and in the Southern Hemisphere. By contrast, primarily among bishops in central Europe, especially a few Germans, Cardinal Joachim Meisner (Berlin) and Joseph Höffner (Cologne), there was a profound pessimism about the reception of the council that echoed "Ratzinger's long-standing critique of the way the Church in Germany has become 'synodalised' and bureaucratized."[19] The situations surrounding the Pastoral Council of the Netherlands Church (1969–70), the Joint Synod of the Dioceses of the Federal Republic of Germany (1971–75), and the activities of the Central Committee of German Catholics (an organization of lay Catholics representing various Catholic diocesan councils and associations), are reflected in these dim assessments. One finds, moreover, statements that seem to be sparked by echoes of the influential We Are the Church Movement that developed initially in Austria and Germany. A few German cardinals spoke of "the tendency to want to make the Church ourselves rather than to receive it from God. From the [doctrinally] correct statement, 'We *are* the Church,' it is often mistakenly concluded, 'we *make* the Church.'"[20]

Although the first week of the synod was devoted to identifying the positive fruits of the council, which were widely acknowledged, the Final Report echoed little of this. At the urging of Cardinal Danneels, the participants were encouraged during the deliberations in the second week of the synod to "to concentrate on present problems and on how to meet them."[21] A far more positive approach to the people of God was readily available but not used.[22]

Many theologians from around the world criticized the Final Report, but *not* for what it commended—the importance of the mystery of the church, its sacramental and eucharistic character, and central notions of the body of Christ and communion for understanding the church. They criticized it for what it left out and thereby discredited—the people of God, the equality of all believers and their participation in the threefold mission of Christ—rather than trying to deepen our understanding of these motifs and work to integrate them. Again, Joseph Komonchak has put the matter most clearly:

> On the basis of the Final Report, one could never think that "People of God" had been the title of an entire chapter of *Lumen Gentium*, that it had been one of the overarching themes of the Council's ecclesiology, and that it had been introduced precisely as an organizing principle of the true mystery of the church in the time between the Ascension and the Parousia.[23] Somewhere between the Council and the Synod, it came to be believed that to stress the mystery of the Church required one to underplay the Church as the People of God, to the point that some observers even speak of the Synod's having "entombed" the expression "People of God." Neither the pre-synodal responses nor the synodal interventions required this development. Several of them indicated how significant and beneficial it was that Christians began to see the Church as the People of God. . . . [The] alleged misuse of the term seems to account for its *near-disappearance from the Final Report*, an astounding development for a document which warns against partial and selective readings of the Council's texts.[24]
>
> Since . . . the Final Report does not reflect with complete accuracy the variety of viewpoints expressed at the Synod, the question arises as to the source of the reading of the postconciliar developments which it does present. The answer, it appears, must be found in the contributions of the middle-European and especially the German members of the Synod. The Final Report faithfully echoes the views expressed by Cardinals Meisner, Hoeffner, and Ratzinger.[25]

Belgian priest and theologian José Comblin, who worked in Latin America for over fifty years, concludes that the Final Report's critique of a sociological approach to the church is correlated with the negative assessment of the people of God and shows ignorance of both the Bible and sociology. Comblin reached the harsh conclusion:

> The synod sought to remove any theological consideration of the church's human reality. The council's adversaries knew this could be accomplished by removing any consideration of the "people of God." The hierarchy would not be threatened because it would be regarded as part of the mystery of the church rather than a human reality in the church. The hierarchy wanted to return to the pre-conciliar theology based on the documents of the sixteenth-century Council of Trent. The synod's solution (although most participants probably did not realize this) was to suppress Vatican II's chapter on the people of God. This is a return to Tridentine ecclesiology: everything in the church is divine. . . . The synod did more than simply interpret or explain the council, it changes its content on essential points. . . . The concept of the people of God must be restored—even with all necessary explanation. Otherwise the council's ecclesiology would be largely eviscerated.[26]

German theologian Elmar Klinger, a former student of Karl Rahner with long-standing sympathies for liberation theology, offered the trenchant critique that the virtual silence of the Final Report on the people of God was in effect a *coup d'etat*.[27]

Communion, Centralization, and the Clerical Difference

Catholic protests against the negative assessments of the people of God theology that prevailed at the 1985 Extraordinary Synod did not subside in its aftermath. They did not really begin to diminish until the first year of Pope Francis's pontificate. The synod did represent the beginning of increased attention among Catholics to the vision of the church as *communio*.[28] More important for this chapter, *communio* ecclesiology in the aftermath of the synod provided the definitive theological frame of reference and justification for growing centralization and the reassertion of clerical authority in the Catholic Church. This led to increased restrictions placed on open dialogue in the church and a lack of collective mutual responsibility and accountability. These are results of the teachings and policies of John Paul II and Benedict XVI, along with the documents and disciplinary procedures taken by various curial offices.

Before exploring how this new phase in the reception of Vatican II unfolded in the Archdiocese of New York, it is helpful to recall briefly how the ascendance of the official papal and curial version of communion ecclesiology fostered a policy of centralization, enhanced clerical authority, and with them, the suppression of the prophetic character of the people of God.

The Debate about Communion Ecclesiology

The 1992 Letter of the Congregation for the Doctrine of the Faith to Catholic Bishops on "Some Aspects of the Church Understood as Communion" (1992) has been criticized for offering a justification of a policy of Roman centralization in the exercise of the papacy and the curia. This document aimed to defend "the unity of the Church at the visible and institutional level" (no. 8) that was allegedly being undermined by an ecclesiological unilateralism that asserts "that every particular Church is a subject complete in itself, and that the universal Church is the result of a *reciprocal recognition* on the part of particular Churches." Such a view was judged suspect because it "impoverishes not only the concept of the universal church, but also that of the particular Church, [and thereby] betrays an insufficient understanding of the concept of communion" (no. 8). This document defended the position that the universal Church "is a reality *ontologically and temporally prior* to every *individual* particular Church" (no. 9).[29]

German theologian Walter Kasper in 1999 expressed the suspicion in an essay published in a German collection honoring a Catholic theologian that the formula expressed by Cardinal Ratzinger in the 1992 letter justified a "reversal" of the teachings of Vatican II, by fostering at the level of practice "a theological restoration of Roman centralism . . . [that] appears actually to be in progress."[30] Cardinal Ratzinger responded to Kasper's remarks in the US Jesuit journal *America* and not in a European journal, which may reflect Ratzinger's perception that the United States is a center of the problem he wished to quell. This resulted in what can only be described as a civil exchange between the two about the theological, historical, and practical issues involved. This debate has repercussions for how episcopal collegiality and authority are exercised in the synod of bishops, episcopal conferences, and in the local church, and also bears on the ramifications of the people of God ecclesiology.

Episcopal Conferences

Since the 1970s certain curial officials have been critical of the practice of national and regional episcopal conferences generating pastoral teachings and pastoral plans and priorities, and, in particular, the collaboration of the episcopal conferences with wider circles of the people of God in these efforts.[31] This conflict surfaced during the Extraordinary Synod of 1985, culminating in a call for a study of episcopal conferences. Several curial offices prepared a draft statement issued in 1988.[32] This document, which reflected certain influential curial views, argued that episcopal conferences of bishops do not exercise any collegial authority in their pastoral teaching (*actio collegialis*), but rather foster collegial relations (*affectus collegialis*). The document's distinction between effective collegiality and affective collegiality has been judged by many to be an attempt by curial officials to undermine the pastoral authority of episcopal conferences in the interest of strengthening centralized authority. Nonetheless, it has since been assumed to be a guiding curial norm.[33] Corresponding to this teaching, the work of episcopal conferences around the world, both in their deliberative processes and their pastoral teachings, have been increasingly scrutinized and curtailed by curial officials and new policies. Bishops appointed by John Paul II and Benedict XVI were expected to adhere to this official theology of communion, and to this doctrine and policy on episcopal conferences.[34]

Diocesan Synods

The 1997 Instruction on Diocesan Synods issued jointly by the Congregations for Bishops and for the Evangelization of Peoples reaffirmed canon 465 when it stated that "all questions proposed are to be subject to the free discussion of the members in the session of the synod." The document practically contradicted this claim, however, by further stating that "the bishop has the duty to exclude from the synodal discussion theses or positions . . . discordant with the perennial doctrine of the Church or the magisterium or concerning material reserved to supreme ecclesiastical authority or to other ecclesiastical authorities."[35] The findings of synods are sent to various curial offices in Rome so that they might learn about the views of priests, religious, and laity in the diocese. With this instruction, open discussion with various sectors of the people of God about non-infallible and disciplinary norms was now officially restricted. The message is clear: bishops are strongly encouraged to deter participants at synods from raising critical questions and concerns about pressing issues facing the church, such as questions concerning homosexuality, ministry to divorced and remarried Catholics, the role of women in the church, the requirements and restrictions for priestly ordination, and any other position the bishop chooses to state as out of bounds.

Pastoral Councils

Numerous papal and curial documents have been issued since the new code was promulgated insisting that hierarchical and clerical authority not be undermined by the exercise of pastoral councils. John Paul II echoed in his postsynodal apostolic exhortation, *Christifidelis Laici*, the proposition of the 1987 Ordinary Synod of Bishops that asserted the need for diocesan pastoral councils (no. 10) but diminished its force by adding that diocesan pastoral councils could be "a recourse at opportune times" (no. 25). John Paul II repeatedly urged Catholics to avoid confusing and equating of the common priesthood and ministerial priesthood (no. 23). In 1994, he warned against any tendency to clericalize laity and laicize priests.[36]

The 1997 Instruction on Certain Questions Regarding the Collaboration of the Non-Ordained Faithful in the Sacred Ministry of Christ, issued by six curial congregations and two pontifical councils, begins with the affirmation that "the source of the call addressed to all members of the Mystical Body to participate actively in the mission and edification of the People of God, is to be found in the mystery of the Church. The People of God participate in this call through the dynamic of an organic communion in accord with their diverse ministries and charisms."[37] But the main purpose of this document is to underscore that "the exercise of the *munus docendi, sanctificandi et regendi* (the teaching, sanctifying, and governing offices) by the sacred minister constitute the essence of pastoral ministry. . . . Only in some of these functions, and to a limited degree, may the non-ordained faithful cooperate with their pastors should they be called to do so by lawful authority and in accordance with the prescribed manner" (no. 2). Moreover, pastoral councils are consultative only "and cannot in any way become deliberative structures" (Article 5, § 2). A special emphasis was placed on the norm that "it is for the Parish Priest to preside at parochial councils. They are to be considered invalid, and hence null and void, any deliberations entered into, (or decisions taken), by a parochial council which has not been presided over by the Parish Priest or which has assembled contrary to his wishes" (Article 5, § 3).[38]

The Eclipse of the People of God in New York: Has the Spirit Been Extinguished?

The ascendance of the official communion ecclesiology was accompanied by (especially among curial officials) little enthusiasm for, and even evidence of resistance toward, the theological motifs associated with the people of God ecclesiology. This disposition has been especially pronounced with regard to the prophetic dimension of this ecclesiology. Is there evidence of this in the Archdiocese of New York?

The primary measure that will be used here to assess the situation is to examine the vitality of participatory structures dedicated to discerning the apostolic mission of the local church at the archdiocesan and parish levels. To a certain extent, the ebbs and flows in the vitality of these participatory structures can be correlated with the time frame offered by who is the archbishop: Francis Spellman, 1939–67; Terence Cooke, 1968–83; John O'Connor, 1984–2000; Edward Egan, 2000–2009, Timothy Dolan, 2009–. In the first chapter we sought to identify the positive impulses of the reception of the people of God theology in the archdiocese during the episcopacies of Spellman and Cooke. In this chapter we will explore ambiguous indications during the periods of O'Connor and Egan, with the cumulative effect that the conditions of eclipse are widely experienced. Since Cardinal Archbishop Dolan is currently holding his office, I will not consider the transitions that have occurred in the policy of the archdiocese during the years he has been New York's prelate.[39]

If one focuses only on the implementation of participatory structures of councils and synods, as distinct from matters of leadership substance and style, the storyline could be constructed in a simple manner. Cardinal Spellman launched priests' senates during the last years before his death, and his staff in the chancery laid the foundation for the formation of parish councils and vicariate councils.

Cardinal Cooke authorized the development of a comprehensive plan for developing parish councils, vicariate councils, and eventually when parish and vicariate councils had reached critical mass, an archdiocesan pastoral council. However, it should be noted that a high percentage of priests (between 30 and 45 percent) resisted implementing parish councils.

Cardinal O'Connor convened the first post–Vatican II archdiocesan synod in 1985 (the last one had been called by Spellman in 1950). He subsequently gave considerable attention to developing participatory structures of consultation at every level of the archdiocese that were representative of the diverse populations of the parishes, as long as they followed closely the consultative-only policy. The years that Cardinal Egan was archbishop of New York represent the low point during the postconciliar period in terms of promoting and fostering participatory structures. While the archdiocese faced considerable financial difficulties and pressure to consolidate and close parishes, Egan closed the Office for Parish Councils, stopped the publication and distribution of the *Handbook for Parish Councils*, and closed the Office of Pastoral Research and Planning. Eventually Cardinal Egan stopped convening the archdiocesan pastoral council. These are the policy decisions of a man who served on the small group of canon lawyers that worked closely with John Paul II on the final revision of the new code, and one might argue that Egan's actions exhibit a certain pastoral posture associated with the official ecclesiology of communion.

This is an admittedly simplified narrative, but it highlights the resurgence of centralization and clericalism in the Archdiocese of New York during these years. It also gives evidence that the outpouring of the Spirit associated with the implementation of the people of God ecclesiology, and promotion of the active participation of the laity and women religious, and to a certain degree even priests, was being eclipsed. Multiple forces were operative during this period, and they must be honestly acknowledged. Attention must be given to specific, if fragmentary, evidence contributing to a more complex telling of the story about how the inspirations of the Spirit were being resisted and restrained. Nevertheless, even during this period there are signs of pneumatic energies of the people of God, sometimes as a countervailing power of resistance, in the Archdiocese of New York.

Archdiocesan Synod 1988

We will now reflect on the use of participatory structures of dialogical discernment and decision making as practiced by the presbyteral council, the archdiocesan pastoral council, and parish pastoral councils, all in relation to the work of the archdiocesan synod held in 1988. The last archdiocesan synod held in New York, in 1950, had followed the older paradigm prescribed by the 1917 Code of Canon Law. The bishop assembled only with clergy. They deliberated about issues pertaining to the local church. The result was legislative actions taken by the bishop.[40] Cooke did not hold a synod while he was archbishop. O'Connor, at his very first meeting with the presbyteral council in September 1984, six months after his installation, stated his desire to convene a diocesan synod, just as he had done after being installed as bishop of Scranton in 1983. The presbyteral council urged a pastoral rather than a legislative synod. The archbishop subsequently informed the archdiocesan pastoral council of his decision to proceed with the synod. There is no indication that the archbishop consulted with either the presbyteral council or the archdiocesan pastoral council about whether they thought such a synod would be either timely or a good idea.

At his 1984 meeting with the presbyteral council, O'Connor indicated that a presynod commission would be appointed to conduct an archdiocesan-wide survey that would involve all the members of the archdiocese. He followed closely the theology of *Lumen Gentium* by indicating that two purposes would be served by the synod: "to initiate a process whereby all the faithful would be given the opportunity to participate in the life and mission of the local church" as a collegial process pursued in the interest of communion. Its main objective would be to implement the Second Vatican Council at "the grass roots."[41] People of God and communion motifs were here emphasized and combined. O'Connor described the synod as collegial and consultative, but following Paul VI's *Ecclesiae Sanctae* and the new code, indicated that it would only be consultative, not deliberative, and that he would be the one to make any decisions concerning new policies, statues, and decrees for the archdiocese, as invested in him by the power of episcopal ordination.[42]

It was subsequently decided, after consulting with the Metropolitan Tribunal of the Archdiocese of New York, that the outcomes of the synod would be designated proposals or directives rather than decrees or local legislations. This was offered as a way to safeguard the authority of the diocesan bishop as the sole legislator of his diocese, while granting a role to the synod for pastorally applying the general law of the church.[43]

The questions that need to be asked are these: Does such a hierarchical approach to decision making leave room for a genuinely collaborative mode of discernment and deliberation about the apostolic mission of the local church? Or can the two modes of decision making, hierarchical and collaborative, be interrelated? What discernment and deliberation role do the various councils, presbyteral, archdiocesan pastoral, vicariate, and other such archdiocesan bodies, serve during the formal synod process itself?

The archdiocesan synod of New York offers a valuable case study because it was well designed and executed. There were five basic phases. First, the Office of Pastoral Research used social scientific methods to design an initial phone-interview questionnaire to be used with a proportionally selected random sample of roughly two thousand members of the archdiocese to identify the basic issues. The question raised was, What are the most important concerns of Catholics and what needs are not being met by the archdiocese? Second, the results from the initial questionnaire were made available to the general public and provided the database for the preparation of a written questionnaire sent to all Catholic parishes and institutions with a total of approximately sixty thousand surveys to rank concerns, needs, and needs not being met. Third, from April to December 1987, the results from these were compiled into a report, *Concerns of the People*. These were studied in parishes in small group meetings with prayer, scripture reading, and reflection based on a booklet, *Outlines on Vatican II Teachings*, prepared for this purpose by a synod planning group. The aim of these discussions was to consider these teachings in relation to the areas of concern with the goal of "synthesizing the teachings and concerns into statement(s) to the Synod about what the Archdiocese should do."[44] Fourth, over 3,000 statements (proposals) were received and combined into 564. Carefully selected delegates were commissioned to select seventy-five of these proposals in five areas, fifteen for each area: (1) people of the church, (2) prayer of the church, (3) family and church, (4) education and formation of the church, and (5) social concerns. These were then reduced to sixty-five by combining some proposals. Fifth, Fr. William Belford was chosen in 1987 as the synod coordinator and was commissioned to focus on parish involvement in the synod process. Sister Rosalie Kaley, a Sister of Charity who had considerable formation in communal discernment processes with her religious congregation, was appointed later that year to serve as associate coordinator. Belford and Kaley instructed the 239 synod delegates to be ready to offer a priority rank of importance to the sixty-five proposals that followed at the synod assembly on September 23–25, 1988. The findings of the synod offer an important sounding of the people of God in the archdiocese speaking out at this time.

What were the findings of the synod? The highest percentages were given to a variety of issues pertaining to the involvement of fostering lay leadership in parishes through participation in parish councils, ecclesial ministries at liturgies, in religious education, and in social action. The greatest concern, however, was expressed about the need to increase the role of women at every level of church activity and decision making. Urgent attention was also called for issues surrounding ethnic and racial diversity in the archdiocese, with its storied history of European ethnic groups, but its dramatically increasing numbers of African American, Puerto Rican, other Latin American and Caribbean, and Asian populations in New York. There were strong proposals about the need to fight against racism and prejudice in employment, housing, and education, and to promote diverse cultural expressions and intercultural relations in parishes and neighborhoods.

Two of the top concerns raised in the initial phone interviews were summarized for synodal deliberation in terms of the need to "reach [. . .] out to alienated Catholics" and "a pastoral concern for Catholics who express a difference with church teachings."[45] Any official mention of differences with church teachings was omitted in the final synod document, which simply stated "that Archdiocesan leadership encourage[s] the development of programs at the parish level which address the problem of alienation and emphasize lay participation" (People 4). There was a concerted effort on the part of the archbishop and the clergy synod leaders to avoid open discussion of controversial church teachings and practices by indicating that they are beyond the competence of this body and the ordinary. These topics were raised in the initial phone interviews, again on the written surveys, and during the synod itself, but were not actively engaged during the synod; and any echo of them is filtered out of the final directives.[46]

Was the synod implemented? There was a collaborative effort by O'Connor and the synod coordinators to foster implementation. The Synod Implementation Review Board was established in January 1989 and composed of ten members: two priests, two women religious, two laywomen and two laymen, as well as Bishop Patrick Sheridan, the vicar general, and Msgr. William Belford, the director of the Office for Parish Councils. They met periodically until 1993, and during these years, they recommended that certain proposals be put into action in parishes in each of the five thematic areas: people, prayer, family, education, and social mission. For instance, in 1992, the board recommended implementing African American and Hispanic styles of worship, music, and preaching; fostering closer relations with other Christian churches and the congregations of other religions; promoting interracial and intercultural understanding and collaboration; and establishing practices of hospitality and fellowship. In addition, during the first four months of 1989, Cardinal O'Connor visited all of the counties in the archdiocese to discuss with priests, religious, and the laity his hopes and expectations for implementing the synod. A convocation commemorating the fifth anniversary of the synod was scheduled for March 13, 1993, which would provide an opportunity for the cardinal to assess the implementation. The event was canceled due to a terrible snowstorm.

Did the synod have any effect on the life of the archdiocese? Some say no, for instance, in the area of preaching, where there is no indication that any process of archdiocesan-wide workshops for the clergy to improve their homilies was introduced; nor was there any call for clergy to develop feedback procedures from parishioners that would promote some degree of accountability. The topic of the concerns of women was repeated so often and pointedly at the synod that O'Connor established an Office for Women's Concerns, which was led by Maria Guarracino. To what extent women have come to play important roles in the life of the archdiocese and parishes merits further attention. Overall, Cardinal O'Connor did continue to support the work of the presbyteral and the archdiocesan pastoral councils, and he gave fresh attention to the need to promote the ongoing development of parish pastoral councils.

Presbyteral Council

Cardinal Terence Cooke died on October 6, 1983. On October 13, the senate of the clergy issued a document, "Recommendations of the Senate of Clergy Concerning the Formation of the Presbyteral Council." This document, in preparation before Cooke died, was offered in part as a response to the constitution of the presbyteral council as specified in the new Code of Canon Law issued on January 25 of that year. John O'Connor was appointed Archbishop of New York on January 26, 1984.

This document offered observations on the positive and negative experiences of the senate. There were five assets identified. The clergy elected the entire membership of the senate, which represented the diversity of age, geography, ideology, and forms of ministry among the priests in the archdiocese. The body met monthly with the archbishop and offered access to the vicar general. Senate resolutions that were adopted by the cardinal were published in the monthly *Progress Report* that was mailed to all the clergy. There was freedom to raise topics of discussion. The senate developed its own standing and ad hoc committees.

Four negative experiences were treated. First, there was a significant lack of participation in voting on senate elections (40 percent) and in responses to requests for input.[47] Second, consultation did not regularly occur in archdiocesan decision-making processes on important matters. Third, the senate of the clergy had no regular meetings with either the archdiocesan council of women religious or with the archdiocesan pastoral council and their respective standing committees. Fourth, little contact took place between the senate of the clergy and archdiocesan offices.

John O'Connor was installed as the eleventh Bishop and eighth Archbishop of New York on March 19, 1984, four months after the new code was issued and the death of Cooke. Eight days after O'Connor's installation, on March 27, he met with the standing senate of priests and offered his own views on the impending implementation of the new code in the formation of the presbyteral council. In the process, he touched on issues raised in the recommendations offered by the senate of the clergy in their October 13 document. The new archbishop spoke about his experience of priests' senates during his short time, seven months, in Scranton, Pennsylvania. He observed "increasing maturity" in priests' senates, but believed that some "malfunctioned" and some were "adversarial," presumably toward the bishop. He was upbeat about his experience with the senate in Scranton. He stated his intention to be at every meeting, as *ex officio* president, while the elected chairman would run the meeting. It was most important in his judgment that the membership be representative of the variety of priests in the archdiocese.

The new code required dramatic changes in this deliberative body, which reflected the increased power being accorded to the archbishop in relation to the council and an increased attention to the authority of the priests relative to that of deacons. Deacons would no longer be eligible to participate. Only half the priest membership would be elected by the presbyterate of the archdiocese, while a full half would appointed by the ordinary, a momentous change from the senate of priests when all of the members were elected entirely by the clergy. O'Connor indicated no desire to "stack the membership" in his own interests and emphasized that he did not perceive, nor did he wish to promote, an adversarial relationship between the senate and the bishop in New York. He expressed agreement with the recommendation that "ethnic diversity be assured" on the council. Concerning the senate's "proposed agenda items," he said without discussing any details that "he found himself able to say 'yes' to each with one or two exceptions. In these cases he had some questions," without identifying what those issues or questions were. He concluded his remarks by stating "his desire that the discussion in the Presbyteral Council be honest and open. He stated that there would be no problem because of discussion. He stated that it is the bishop who must always make the decision. He would ask for the full support of the Presbyteral Council in his decisions."[48] The code's approach to the presbyteral council emphasized the authority of the bishop, and those participating in the presbyteral council perceived this shift during the O'Connor years as a major change. Nevertheless, of all the conciliar forums in the archdiocese, O'Connor made it clear that the presbyteral council was the most important one for him. That all of these forums were consultative only and not decision making was emphasized in the new code and was made abundantly clear both in the cardinal's style of leadership and in practice. The priests could easily have inferred that their role in this council had only minimal impact and that the archbishop would do what he wanted to do regardless of the opinions expressed by the council.

One particularly significant item surfaced at the meeting of the presbyteral council on December 4, 1984. O'Connor reported on five listening sessions he conducted with women religious throughout the archdiocese. Sisters were asked to submit cards expressing their concerns, and 809 were received, which were broken down into eight or nine categories. The concern most often raised (259) was about the poor quality of the relationship with priests at the parish level or in schools or hospitals. A significant number of women religious in the archdiocese believed that, in many instances, they were not consulted and they were not being treated professionally. While this issue was added as an agenda item that should receive subsequent attention, it was also telling that the presbyteral council expressed unanimous interest in having similar *listening sessions* with the priests of the archdiocese, something the archbishop readily agreed to, but no further indication about the substance of these meetings appears in subsequent minutes or whether they occurred. Four years later in January 1988, the cardinal reported that the women religious of the archdiocese had presented for his approval a conflict resolution process to negotiate problems between priests and sisters. The cardinal felt some kind of process would be helpful. Members of the presbyteral council at their next meeting discussed the idea of such a process but responded that there already were due process procedures in place and that the issue was not a need for new structures, but rather for improving poor communication. It was decided that representatives of the presbyteral council should set up a meeting with leaders of congregations of women religious in the archdiocese and proposed a workshop for priests, women religious, and laity on cooperation and communication in pastoral ministry in order to develop some guidelines.

John Cardinal O'Connor died on May 3, 2000; Edward Egan was named the new ordinary of New York on May 11, 2000. As mentioned, Egan had served in the small inner circle of six consultants for Pope John Paul II in the final revisions of the Code of Canon Law; he subsequently served as vicar of education in the Archdiocese of New York from 1985 to 1988; and then he served as Archbishop of Bridgeport, Connecticut, from 1988 to 2000.

On May 18, the presbyteral council, with thirty-eight voting members, prepared a list of four priority recommendations for Egan. The list of recommendations (like the Memorandum of Priorities prepared by the senate of the clergy for Terence Cooke in March of 1968) offers rare insight into the assessment of the priests' council about the pressing concerns in the archdiocese as well as the functioning of the council. Pastoral planning was ranked first, and the issue was framed in terms of the twofold dynamic of the diminishing number of priests and demographic changes relative to the effectiveness of the evangelical mission of the archdiocese. Decisions about parish closings, mergers, and the formation of parish clusters, it was stated, needed to be made on the basis of objective criteria and through broad consultation. Special attention should be given to evangelizing youth, the poor, and the Hispanic and African American communities. The second and fourth priorities concerned the overall pastoral care of all priests and their compensation and benefits. The third priority area pertained to the perceived lack of communication and lack of support for priests, and their desire to be listened to and heard when decisions were being made about archdiocesan governance structures. In response to this neuralgic communication problem, one pertaining to effective consultation as it bears on participatory structures in decision making, the document made two recommendations: on the one hand, that the principle of subsidiarity be honored and put into practice as appropriate with those influenced by particular decisions; and, on the other hand, that practices of accountability and transparency be implemented in the areas of finance and governance policies.[49]

During his tenure, Cardinal Egan reportedly did not have a good working relationship with the body of priests of the archdiocese, and this was reflected in his work with the presbyteral council. The senate of priests and then the presbyteral council during the Cooke, O'Connor, and Egan years met approximately ten times a year, usually once a month, but the Egan decade represents the low point of collaboration between the presbyteral council and the archbishop. Egan's tenure offers one particularly clear interpretation of John Paul II's understanding of participatory structures for priests, religious, and laity in the church.

Near the end of his first year, Cardinal Archbishop Egan, citing budgetary constraints, closed eleven offices in the archdiocese including: the Office of Pastoral Research and Planning, the Office of Community Relations, the Italian Apostolate, the Chinese Apostolate, the Office for Women's Concerns, the Liturgical Commission, and the Liturgical Music Commission. There were twenty-three people who lost their jobs, six nuns and seventeen laypeople. Priests working in many offices were reassigned.[50] The offices that were closed had certainly served the archdiocesan population but, in particular, the priests and the parishes. Moreover, they represented the leading edge of post–Vatican II concern for renewed parish life, liturgy, liturgical music in particular, and attentiveness to the burgeoning concerns of women and cultural diversity in the archdiocese that were accentuated at the Archdiocesan Synod of 1988.

In October 2006, an anonymous letter was sent to the priests of the Archdiocese of New York calling for a no confidence vote at each vicariate meeting on Cardinal Egan's episcopal leadership in the archdiocese as he approached his seventy-fifth birthday, when he would become eligible to retire. The letter found its way onto a popular national Catholic blog and was covered in a *New York Times* article.[51] The controversy and news frenzy surrounding this public posting have no direct bearing on assessing the presbyteral council, but the letter and public comments by priests made in its aftermath reflected widespread concern among the clergy about the pastoral effectiveness of the leadership style of Cardinal Egan accompanied by frustration, estrangement, and hostility during this period in the archdiocese. The presbyteral council was convened for an unscheduled meeting to discuss the controversy with the archbishop. Without addressing the substance of the concerns raised in the letter, a carefully worded statement by the council was crafted expressing solidarity with Cardinal Egan and dismay at the tone of the no confidence letter. When speaking about this period in the history of the presbyteral council, one respected priest of the archdiocese was reminded of the saying, apathy is frozen violence. Whether issuing in angry outcry or apathy, this period and this episode symbolized virtually a total eclipse of the people of God ecclesiology by one influential rendering of communion ecclesiology.

Women Religious: The Sisters of Charity

Individual Sisters of Charity were on occasion invited to take leadership roles in key archdiocesan positions charged with cultivating practices of participatory governance. Sister Rosalie Kaley, for example, was chosen as associate coordinator on the archdiocesan synod and in the Office for Parish Councils. Other sisters were leaders in team ministry in parish settings such as Sisters Nora Cunningham and Muriel Long at the South Bronx Pastoral Center. The postconciliar formation and transformation of the Sisters of Charity in processes of group deliberation and decision making offer a valuable illustration of why this was so. As we have noted in the previous chapter, in keeping with the Chapter of Affairs in 1969–70, the Sisters of Charity in their periodic assemblies continued the process of clarifying their lifestyle and mission, and accordingly devoted themselves to revising their constitution and directory enacted in 1984. In the years that followed they continued to develop a mission-oriented process of discernment and decision making.

The convocation of 1986 concentrated on the gospel call to discipleship and mission. The Sisters of Charity have always been committed to serving the poor and the needy in hospitals, orphanages, and schools. Since the 1960s, however, they have increasingly attended to immigration issues and with local populations suffering from hunger, homelessness, and racism. Moreover, in keeping with developments in Catholic social teaching and theological developments, they addressed the social structural problems contributing to social injustice. This is illustrated, for instance, in their 1987 general assembly in which they rededicated themselves to continue to promote a process of communal conversation and renewal in the interest of promoting corporate responsibility by promoting structural change. During their 1991 assembly, they considered the painful signs of the times in Northern Ireland, apartheid in South Africa, third-world debt, and environmental degradation. In their 1995 assembly, they articulated a moving Vision 2000 statement that would orient them for the next four years:

> Impelled by the love of Christ and a yearning to live our Eucharistic Heritage more passionately in this new time of Charity, we, Sisters of Charity of New York, joyfully bonded in mission celebrate our corporate vision. As ecclesial women in collaboration with our Associates and with all who seek to renew the face of the earth, we focus our energies to embody this vision:
>
> > to be visible, effective risk takers standing with and for the poor
> >
> > to respond to the needs of women and value women's experience as sisters, weaving our gifts into the fabric of contemporary society
> >
> > to reverence creation in a spirit of interconnectedness with all that is, living responsibly
>
> We claim the power of our charism, clothing ourselves in humility, simplicity and charity so that the power of God may do through us more than we can ask or imagine.

During the assemblies in 1999 and 2003 this vision was embraced and elaborated on but always with a keen eye on mission. They dedicated themselves in 2003 to be a community engaged in "ongoing learning, . . . respectful dialogue about difficult decisions," and "to personally promote simplicity of life and responsible interdependence with the local community, the Congregation, and the world; to live lives that challenge consumerism, individualism and a sense of entitlement."[52]

Sister Regina Bechtle, who played a pivotal role on many committees and in the leadership of the Sisters of Charity in the years following the council, summarized what was required:

> Many writers identify the emerging paradigm of religious life as prophecy and contemplation. . . . Standing within our culture but not mesmerized by it, religious must engage it reflectively, discerning and addressing the fears and hungers of the Spirit that lie beneath the surface. We know that we, too, are shaped by our culture, called to our own conversion even as we seek to transform the world. Where is God in all of this? Only a deeply contemplative stance and passionate fidelity to the discipline of discernment will uncover the new face of the living God hidden in the chaos of post-modern culture. Ultimately we ground our faith in God who promises to find us wherever we are.[53]

The kind of prophetic and contemplative orientation commended by Bechtle not only distinguishes religious life, but also offers implicitly a challenge to all baptized who are anointed to share in the prophetic office of the people of God.

Her statement clearly articulates the need to cultivate practices of discernment in the local church among the laity, clergy, and religious working together.

Parish Pastoral Councils

One could argue that looking at parish councils and lay involvement in ecclesial ministries and in apostolic action offers the most important way to determine whether the archdiocesan synod was implemented. *Lumen Gentium* challenged all the faithful to actively participate in the pastoral mission of the church. This seemed always to have been the measure used by O'Connor himself. At the end of the synod, the archbishop called on each parish to have an active parish council to implement the directives of the synod. He did everything in his power to foster active parish councils, short of mandating them (which was not canonically possible). The Office for Parish Councils, which at the time was headed by Msgr. William Belford with the assistance of Sr. Rosalie Kaley, S.C., devoted considerable time and attention to promoting this mandate, a seventy-six page handbook for the formation of parish councils, entitled *Parish and Parish Councils*, that offered concrete suggestions on how to start and maintain a parish council.

This handbook introduced a prayerful process of group discernment and decision making similar to that cultivated by the Sisters of Charity in the decades after Vatican II.

> A parish council is discerning. Its members participate effectively in policy-making process for the parish by bringing together the needs and the hopes of the parishioners and of the entire community (neighborhoods) in which they live. Through dialogue and deliberation, it merges the insights, the diverse experiences, the expertise and the faith of the councillors in order to provide vision and direction for the parish community. That vision finds expression in the priorities established and the broad policies adopted.[54]

Following a trend that emerged in the 1980s among parish pastoral councils, the handbook espoused the importance of consensus-building and working through different opinions by means of group discernment and decision making as a process, not in terms of the act of reaching a decision, following a majority rule approach found in *Robert's Rules of Order* and utilized in various civic organizations.[55] The document did not explicitly subscribe to a narrow approach to the work of the council that emphasized the decision-making authority of the priest as articulated in the consultative-only clause of canon law:

> The pastor/pastoral team ratifies the decisions of the council through his/their presence at the meetings and participation in the discussion and refinement of proposals. [Moreover,] since the pastor/pastoral team

is accountable to the Diocesan Bishop for the parish, and as part of the presbyterate is responsible for the spiritual life of each parishioner, councilors must be open to reconsideration of a decision in light of this responsibility.[56]

There are no channels offered in this document for recourse in cases when the pastor or pastoral team is not responsive to the decisions reached by the council.

Of utmost importance for the argument of this book, this handbook describes the parish council as prophetic. Here the handbook develops more broadly a theme introduced by Myles Bourke in his original draft of Cardinal Cooke's letter on the theological foundation for the council. The handbook reads,

> As a result of experiencing the fullness of God's Word, it [the council] brings a broader, more challenging vision to parish life. It strives to move outward to tackle some of the bigger issues within the Church and in the world, seeking to be a credible sign of concern for justice, peace, reconciliation and practical love. It is a group who are not afraid to challenge and take risks. . . . Council membership calls people to be sensitive to the anguish and pain of others and to respond in healing, reconciling ways.[57]

They do this by enabling all the members of the parish to become active participants in the mission and ministry of the parish community and the local church.

It is not simply the existence of the parish pastoral council that is the measure of the church's vitality in promoting the pastoral mission of the local church. A great deal of attention, however, was given to increasing the number of parish councils from the woeful 53 percent at the time of the synod to 70 and 80 percent and even higher at the end of O'Connor's tenure. Whether these councils were functioning well as collegial forums for discernment is the important question. To address that question the Office of Pastoral Research and Planning devised after the archdiocesan synod a Comprehensive Pastoral Report questionnaire that was to be filled out annually by each parish and signed by the pastor, vicars, deacons, pastoral assistants, school principal, director of religious education, parish council chairperson, and trustees. This form provided not only a record of the various kinds of pastoral practices and outreach taking place in the parish, but also promoted accountability. By 1998 there were 306 (78 percent) parish councils in existence, 12 (3 percent) in formation, and 39 (10 percent) with alternative structures and 6 (2 percent) are nonfunctioning and 27 (7 percent) without a council or alternative structure. This gives a total of 92 percent of the 399 Latin Rite parishes in the archdiocese. The director of the Office for Parish Councils at the time, Fr. Robert Aufieri, visited eighty-five councils, with thirty-five more visits planned.

At a deeper level, the very process of the synod itself offered a helpful resource for collective discernment about the signs of the times and the need to fashion a pastoral response. It allowed leaders to ask what top concerns and needs were not being met and to identify the major aspirations and laments in the community that could provide an impetus for a pastoral plan.

Cardinal Egan did not share O'Connor's zeal for parish pastoral councils. The following document was prepared during the first year of Egan's tenure as archbishop of New York:

> Following the 2nd Vatican Council, many Dioceses began to encourage the involvement of the laity in cooperation with the pastor. In the Archdiocese of New York, an Office for Parish Councils was established to offer guidelines. With the confirmation of John Cardinal O'Connor, a Synod recommended that every parish have a Parish Council or an alternative structure. A specific Office for Parish Councils no longer exists and the Parish Councils Handbook is no longer published by the Archdiocese. It is left to the prudential judgment of the pastor to decide the structure and workings of a Parish Council.[58]

When Cardinal Egan closed the Office for Parish Councils, he also disbanded the archdiocesan pastoral council.

It is one thing to count the number of parish pastoral councils, it is another to evaluate their vitality and effectiveness in promoting lay ministries and the mission of the parish. The same is true of the archdiocesan pastoral councils. Their effectiveness, if not their very existence, depends on the pastor and the bishop. This can lead to a great volatility in the effectiveness of councils and in the parish mission. Another factor contributing to the relative strength or weakness of a council depends on the people who are chosen to serve on the council and the training the pastor and councilors receive in fulfilling their roles. The archdiocese since Vatican II has offered various resources to help pastors and councilors: the parish council newsletter, the parish council handbook, and the possibility of pursuing some training at such places as the Center for Catholic Lay Leadership Formation, originally known as the South Bronx Pastoral Center.

The handbook recommended including in the parish bulletin (before parish websites became common practice) the names of members on the council, the agenda for forthcoming meetings, and the minutes from the previous meetings. The handbook also included a self-evaluation instrument for parish councils that encouraged them to rank various present realities in terms of always, sometimes, or never, and to identify future priorities in ranked importance: first, second, or third place. For example, under the category of "Discerning," one of the statements reads, "At PC meetings there is freedom to challenge and to be challenged, and freedom to dissent." Another one reads, "PC meetings are free from manipulation and domination by a few." And, "PC evaluates its past decisions." Under the category "Prophetic" it offers statements about whether the councilors have "a sense of the universal church," an operational knowledge of the teachings of Vatican II, and "a sense of the church in the archdiocese," and the need to discuss justice and peace issues as well as liturgical matters. Consistent with chapter two of *Lumen Gentium* it asks members to evaluate whether "religious, clergy, and laity work together as equal members," and even moving beyond this teaching incorporating the preferential option for the poor: "PC shows a concern for the poor, disadvantaged and alienated" both among members of the parish and those outside of the parish. It likewise promotes ecumenical and civic engagement. While the handbook generally and the self-evaluation form specifically encourage a visible presence of the council in the life of the parish, there is no clear mention of the need to offer opportunities for parish members (and potentially neighbors) to communicate with the pastor, pastoral team, and council members on an annual basis or on specific topics.

Even after Cardinal Egan closed the Office for Parish Councils and disbanded the archdiocesan pastoral council, many parish councils continued to thrive. Some parishes had developed the skills necessary to run effective council meetings with the pastor and pastoral team. One can find in every area of the archdiocese parishes with strong and sometimes distinctive local missions. For example, a tradition of open hospitality to lesbians, gays, bisexuals, and transgender people marked the parish missions of St. Francis Xavier in Chelsea and St. Joseph's Parish in Greenwich Village. Holy Trinity Church and Ascension Parish have had strong reputations as vibrant parishes with a special outreach to Latinos, together with professionals and university students and faculty. African Americans and recent African immigrants found their way to parishes in Harlem, the Bronx, and Manhattan. More recent immigrants from Vietnam, China, Japan, the Philippines, and Korea also discovered places of worship, community, and service in parishes in the archdiocese.

South Bronx People for Change and South Bronx Pastoral Center

What happened to the South Bronx People for Change? Two forces contributed to its decline and dissolution beginning in the mid-1980s; both merit comment. First, Cardinal O'Connor removed Neil Connolly from his post as pastor at St. Athanasius and as vicar of the South Bronx, and assigned him as pastor of St. Mary's on Grand Street on the Lower East Side of Manhattan. This occurred during the time when John Paul II and Cardinal Joseph Ratzinger were engaged in a coordinated effort to undermine the influence of liberation theology in Latin America and in other places around the world where its influence was being felt. Whatever O'Connor's motives were for reassigning Connolly, removing him in 1985 coincided with the criticism by some of the participatory style of lay leadership espoused in his vicariate and the kind of social action advanced by the People for Change, which reflected the larger theological dispute going on in the church.[59] This was precisely the moment when the theology of the people of God was being discredited in Central Europe by Ratzinger and other influential cardinals for being too easily politicized. With Connolly's reassignment, the work of People for Change was undermined. Fr. Louis Gigante, the new pastor of St. Athanasius, fired Kathy Osberger from her position as pastoral associate of the St. Athanasius Center.

Jesuit Dean Brackley, who had a doctoral degree in theology and worked closely with Connolly and Osberger with the People for Change, was reassigned by his Jesuits superiors in 1987 to academic work, after he was assigned to take a sabbatical for writing, further contributing to the declining synergism of the group. Even so, the local board and team remained active.

The work of People for Change continued until the early 1990s, but the end was hastened by a second decisive factor that came into play. Dynamic Lutheran pastor John Heinemeier, who had been a central figure in the formation of the East Brooklyn Churches in 1980, an affiliate of the Industrial Area Foundation (IAF), moved in 1983 to St. John's Lutheran Church in the Morrisania section of the South Bronx, a neighborhood with a predominantly black population. Heinemeier dedicated himself to connecting with people in the neighborhood. He also began collaborating with Ed Chambers, the close associate of Saul Alinsky with whom he had collaborated before in Brooklyn. Chambers's background made him particularly attuned to working with Catholic clergy and church members, but always alongside of people from other churches, faiths, and worldviews, and particularly with keen sensitivities to the concerns of the black community in situations of racial injustice and conflict. By 1985, Heinemier and Chambers had established South Bronx Churches as an IAF affiliate, with twenty-three Protestant congregations but not one Catholic parish.

Heinemeier and Chambers were convinced that they needed a genuinely ecumenical organization to be effective in the South Bronx. They needed Catholics involved, but they didn't want to alienate the People for Change or discredit their accomplishments. At one point in the mid-1980s, Chambers met with Neil Connolly to explore the possibility of this IAF group joining forces with the People for Change. Connolly was certainly open to having people associated with the People for Change approach Catholic pastors to enlist their involvement in the Heinemeier–Chambers effort, but this avenue was not pursued further. In Chambers's judgment the People for Change members were targeting Catholic parishes with large Latino populations and not effectively reaching out to Protestant churches, especially to predominantly black churches. Chambers stated the case sharply when he said "the Black community would have nothing to do with them [the People for Change], which really told us it wasn't broad-based. It was heavily Hispanic. . . . There was a real South American, Central American, constant overlay which just frightened the Blacks, just another Catholic thing. They did some good work. And in a vacuum, it looked pretty good."[60] This critical assessment has some merit, yet it overlooks the fact that black Catholics and people from the Caribbean were involved in People for Change, even though black Protestant churches were not.

The bottom line for Chambers was that if South Bronx Churches was going to be effective, it had to be ecumenical, with Protestant and Catholic support, and intercultural, with both Latinos and blacks. On this count, he was correct, and the inclusion of Jews and Muslims would also remain on the agenda. Beyond these ecumenical and intercultural issues Heinemeier was critical of the People for Change because it "didn't even have two-thirds of the Roman [Catholic] parishes in [its] organization. So that was silly on a power pattern. We were straight on that from the get-go."[61]

In response to this latter issue, Chambers invited organizer Jim Drake to come and work on garnering Catholic involvement in the South Bronx. Drake had worked closely with Cesar Chavez in California for seventeen years beginning in the 1960s and was the inspiration for the successful grape boycott in support of migrant farm workers. Drake started in April or May of 1986, about eight months after South Bronx Churches started, and was paid directly out of IAF funds to work on recruiting Catholic pastors. Over two months, he had ten or twelve meetings with pastors. They were invited to participate in ten-day training sessions to learn what they were about. The executive director of South Bronx People for Change also participated in one.

As this push was on to get Catholic pastors involved, Chambers said to the Protestant clergy, "we've got to be an ecumenical, Black, Hispanic, Catholic, Protestant operation. [Drake] did a masterful job getting the Catholics and getting in some of the lay people."[62] Four Catholic pastors and parishes initially joined South Bronx Churches, then four more, and by 1989 there were up to thirteen Catholic parishes involved. This was power-building and community-building on the model of the IAF. Effectiveness was weighed based on the ability to expand the number of groups in order to exercise more effective power in the social and political arena. South Bronx Churches was becoming increasingly ecumenical and interracial.

People for Change worked with different criteria for assessing effectiveness. They were building a faith community that focused on base communities, faith sharing that promoted a prophetic model of discipleship and mission, and community organizing on issues. They were building a community rooted especially in the Catholic parishes with an increasing number of Latinos as well as some African Americans and white ethnics. They also made efforts to reach out to Protestants, Jews, and also to people in the neighborhood with no faith traditions. Unlike South Bronx Churches, they were self-consciously forming a South Bronx style of a particular liberation vision of the church.

The interfaith and intercultural dynamics in the South Bronx were on some level wedge issues between the People for Change and South Bronx Churches, as well as with the Northwest Bronx Community and Clergy Coalition. All three efforts indicate a crucial reality: that all Catholic parishes need to promote and cultivate a close reading of the signs of the times in order to face the social, cultural, political realities on the ground, in their neighborhoods with their parishioners and neighbors; and they need to develop community organizing skills.

All three groups, People for Change, South Bronx Churches, and the Coalition, share these convictions. Specifically, all three groups share the most basic conviction that social analysis and power analysis are crucial parts of the equation when exploring economic and political issues involved in poverty, housing, employment, health care, and education. But what this tension between People for Change and South Bronx Churches reveals is that culture analysis is also of critical importance, not only for understanding distinctive groups, but also for working respectfully and collaboratively at intercultural crossroads. This is abundantly clear in the Bronx. Diverse forms of religious life, ritual practice, popular piety, music, food, and familial traditions are treasured by peoples from Puerto Rico, Dominican Republic, Cuba, Mexico, Colombia, and all the other Latin American and Afro-Caribbean immigrants; they in turn are neighbors to African American blacks, Africans, and also diverse Asian communities and cultures, such as the Filipino and Vietnamese, all living side by side with the various diminished European-based groups in the Bronx. People for Change, in practice, has the clearest sense of collaboration of laypeople with priests and women religious and brothers. Alinsky and the first generation of close followers tended to work with the established power brokers, with social and power analysis. They wanted a wider group of people involved in decision making, but there is no clear sense of the theological, cultural, or political vision undergirding this conviction.[63]

What happened to the South Bronx Pastoral Center, initiated, as we explored in the last chapter, by Frs. Bob Stern, Peter Gavin, and Neil Graham, joined by Sisters of Charity Nora Cunningham and Muriel Long, at Our Lady of Victory Parish? According to Dean Brackley, "the Pastoral Center eventually fished out its waters."[64] The stream of candidates for the program slowed to a trickle. When Robert Stern left, a new leader was chosen to lead the Center for Catholic Lay Leadership Formation, Rudy Vargas, who eventually moved on, even though he remains a key figure in Hispanic Education Advancement and leadership development in the archdiocese.

Northwest Bronx Community and Clergy Coalition

The Northwest Bronx Community and Clergy Coalition continued to build on the accomplishments of its first decade (1974–84) through the 1980s and 1990s. The ongoing collaboration of organizers, core leaders including clergy, and people in churches, apartment buildings, and neighborhoods generated enormous heat and light in the Northwest Bronx. For our purposes this energy can be identified with the prophetic activity of the people of God during a twilight period in sectors of the Archdiocese of New York.

The basic features of grassroots community organizing introduced in the Northwest Bronx at the inception of the coalition continued to operate during this phase. Coalition leaders gave increasing attention to cultivating and fine-tuning a dynamic combination of conflict and collaboration between the coalition and various power brokers in the borough and city, in ways that represented an evolution in the adversarial methods of Saul Alinsky.[65] While certain changes took place in the structure of the organization during this period, key ingredients in this community organizing method remained. Organizers and core leaders were encouraged to make contacts by means of conducting listening or door-knocking campaigns one-to-one, or door-to-door, and to meet in small groups in order to learn about the concerns of people in the neighborhoods and apartment buildings. Thanks to these efforts, called base-building, many new people joined the work of the coalition and became regular members of neighborhood and tenant associations on issues that interested them. Their concerns provided the impetus for individual organizers and leaders to conduct research on particular issues and collaborate with committees on these issues in neighborhood associations. At the coalition level, four neighborhood associations needed to commit to a project to establish coalition-wide standing committees devoted to an issue of concern. If the problems raised were substantive, these groups would "cut an issue" by working to identify and to pursue the most pressing issues that had been surfaced. In the area of housing, for instance, staff organizers conducted research into such things as contracts, titles, the policies and practices of corporations, and municipal, state, and federal laws in order to help bring into focus the nature and scope of the relevant problems and their underlying causes. These issues were discussed at meetings held at various levels of the organization: staff meetings, board meetings, committees devoted to particular issues, and general membership assemblies.

Equally important, these groups deliberated about possible targets, usually officials with institutional power, and various tactics like direct action or hits that might be used to voice grievances and demand accountability. These dramatic performances were used to bring officials back to negotiation.[66] Once an issue was clarified, a target identified, and a tactic chosen, there was a need to mobilize people in the neighborhood by distributing flyers in the neighborhood, apartments, churches, and community centers inviting people to attend an information meeting about this campaign issue. The purposes of these meetings were to raise awareness, explain complex issues, and rally support for public action.

Coalition organizers and core leaders also requested meetings with local leaders—such as landlords, executives of financial institutions, or elected officials. If local leaders resisted such meetings or were not engaging the issues being raised, conflict tactics were introduced such as demonstrations at offices or homes, or the convocation of a large public assembly requesting the attendance of officials so that members of the coalition could voice complaints, call for accountability, and demand public commitment to new policies. These various social actions aimed to promote negotiations and preferably collaboration and the building of alliances between coalition members with the institutional stakeholders in the community. Public discourse through dialogue is the basic medium; conflict and collaboration are the twin strategies that constitute what some have described as the agonistic character of democracy. This practice of holding elites accountable through the use of countervailing conflict and negotiating collaboration for the common good illustrates the prophetic dimension of civic life. Through this synergism, the coalition introduced a school for agonistic democracy and civic virtue.[67]

For roughly thirty years, from 1974 to 2004, the coalition operated as a federation of ten to twelve neighborhood associations. Each association had separate offices and staffs, which could function with about four people: a lead organizer, a tenant organizer who also worked with the board of the association, a full-time tenant organizer, and a youth organizer. It was costly, however, to maintain separate staffs and pay the rent and phone bills for separate offices, some of which were located close to one another. Mary Dailey, who worked as an organizer at the coalition for almost twenty years, the last ten as executive director, began during her last two years (2004–2005) to pair up these associations into regional areas in the interest of increased organizational efficiency and cost effectiveness.[68]

As was noted in Chapter 1, the coalition from its inception worked with largely Latino and black populations in the Northwest Bronx but had a disproportionately white staff of community organizers and board of directors. Julissa Reynoso highlights this in her 2006 study: "One internal issue that the leadership team has had to address is the adequacy of representation across racial and ethnic lines within the leadership of the organization."[69] In 2004, the governing bylaws of the coalition were changed to address this issue: "In electing the Board of Directors the general membership will strive to nominate members who represent the diversity of the broader community.... We choose to address issues that we believe promote social, economic, environmental, and racial justice for our families, our communities, and ourselves."[70]

Clergy and members from churches continued to play an important role in the work of the coalition during its second decade. Neighborhood organizations had clergy representatives, Catholic and/or Protestant, who participated in neighborhood associations and as members of the board of the coalition. A core group of clergy was, and remains, regularly active as members of the coalition board and committees, and wider clergy involvement has always been cultivated for public actions of the coalition. Clergy can thus mobilize the membership of their parishes and congregations by providing wide access through social justice preaching or through announcements, bulletins, or distributing flyers on issues of pressing neighborhood concern. Neighborhood association and coalition meetings often have taken place in churches, rectories, and parish schools. When there have been larger assemblies, there is regularly a prayer offered at the beginning of the meeting. In these prayers different faith traditions were drawn on to affirm God as source of human dignity and racial and economic justice, the common good, and the right of everyone to a home, a living wage, meaningful labor, safe neighborhoods, and all the basic ingredients needed for human flourishing. God was also invoked as the source of power and blessing in the struggle against destructive powers in the community.

The experience of the coalition corresponds well with sociologist Richard Wood's perceptive analysis. Wood contends that churches can legitimate and authorize public civic social engagement in ways that go beyond the narrow confines of a belief in religious personalism that accentuates individual engagement or other-worldly spiritually.[71] In doing so, these churches draw on prophetic traditions, traditions that justify the role of conflict in holding powerful elites in society accountable, while balancing such contestation with negotiation and compromise, thus helping religious members to combine standing firm with a realistic acceptance of the role of ambiguity in civic life.[72]

There is a danger that religious convictions and practices can be used to motivate public engagement in what sociologists call an instrumentalized manner, that is, without respecting the deeply held religious convictions of faith communities in a way that can serve as a critical check on the work of community organizing in civic action. This has not been an expressed concern in the coalition where many members maintain deep religious commitments that motivate their work for justice.[73] There are other risks and pitfalls for religious organizations in social life. Religious groups can be tempted to foster a rigid person-centered moralism or a therapeutic approach to religion that avoids conflict in the public realm.[74] On the other hand, certain issues that are debated among people of sincere faith— concerning birth control, abortion, and gay marriage, for example—are usually avoided in faith-based community organizing, or can be used to undermine broad-based community organizing.[75] Moreover, the high-profile involvement of clergy on boards, committees, and at public assemblies has the potential to undermine the development of lay leadership. Despite all these risks, the involvement of members of churches and clergy has lent religious and moral credibility, legitimacy, and faith-oriented passionate conviction to the coalition's work. Simultaneously, members who are not actively religious or have no religious background are welcomed and form civic bonds in the collective work of the coalition as a part of a pluralistic form of ethical democracy.

Clergy were especially involved in the work of neighborhood associations and the coalition during its first decade when apartment fires threatened the area and in the early1980s when drug abuse and violence plagued the Bronx. But during the coalition's second decade, clergy involvement fluctuated. Clergy regularly asked representatives from their community to come to board meetings on their behalf. Organizers learned to cajole the clergy to attend, but also recognized the many time pressures placed on them. Members of the coalition consistently invited and encouraged the involvement and leadership of the clergy, but the clergy were not always the main leaders or public face of the coalition. Rather it was a combination of community core leaders, board members, staff organizers (often in the background), with clergy as collaborators. This model of clergy involvement approximates the team approach spoken of by Neil Connolly when he started his work at St. Athanasius in the South Bronx and in the South Bronx People for Change. When South Bronx Churches, associated with the IAF, began their work in the Bronx, the central role played by the clergy as the public face of community organizing was emphasized. The coalition, by contrast, has tried to promote leadership at the grassroots level, including but not solely or primarily the clergy. Yet, by the end of the 1980s and the beginning of the 1990s, there was growing interest in promoting greater clergy and church involvement in the coalition. Sister Pat Dillon participated in an organizers-training session during this time with the PICO organization in California, which championed the importance of clergy involvement and returned wanting to promote clergy development at the coalition. During the 1990s, a series of coalition staff organizers were given the task of building the clergy base. This ultimately led to the formation of the clergy caucus. With this effort, the number of black and Latino clergy increased as well.

On matters of substance, the coalition's work on housing issues remained their signature concern during the decades of the 1980s and the 1990s (even to today in 2015 as will be indicated in Chapter 6) as they had been since the mid-1970s. But other grievances were also heard in the community, and these provoked other campaigns. During the 1980s and 1990s the coalition responded to complaints and fears surrounding the dramatic increase in the use of crack-cocaine and the presence of drug dealers in Bronx neighborhoods and apartment buildings, and the inadequate police response. Further, parents complained about school crowding and the declining quality of education, during a time when tax dollars were channeled into predominantly white and more affluent neighborhoods for better buildings, better teachers, better curriculum, and better after-school programs in the arts and athletic activities. There was an escalating call for more schools and better programming in the Bronx. It was difficult not to perceive this as symptomatic of economic injustice and racism suffered disproportionately by African Americans and by immigrant populations from the Caribbean and Latin America. The antidrug and proeducation campaigns of the coalition during this period were extremely important, but housing issues remained central and required continuous attention.

Margaret Groarke, coalition organizer and activist, now a political scientist, puts this period in context. "For the first ten years of the Coalition's history, reinvestment was the watchword—forcing banks and government to reinvest in the Bronx, to preserve and improve communities."[76] But the problems shifted during the 1980s and 1990s, which required new diagnoses and strategies.[77] By the end of the 1980s, a new pattern emerged: "affordability became the new watchword: reinvestment was futile if it made housing unaffordable to the current residents. NWBCCC organizers helped tenant associations fight . . . rent increases, and organized a campaign to demand changes in state housing law and policy to make major capital improvements more affordable to tenants."[78] This, it turns out, was but the tip of an iceberg. Following up on concerns raised by tenants, coalition organizers and the coalition's Reinvestment Committee discovered in the late 1980s that a large number of apartment buildings had major mortgages underwritten by the Federal Home Loan Mortgage Corporation, known as Freddie Mac. Freddie Mac was regularly giving loans for more than the properties were worth and engaging in widespread irresponsible lending practices in apartment building real estate in the Northwest Bronx area. This led to a protracted campaign against Freddie Mac executives, which the coalition ultimately won. Over the course of its first two decades, the members of the coalition had confronted a range of issues that undermined their communities' quality of life, formed bonds of solidarity and civic friendship among members, and engaged and challenged people in authority through strategies of conflict and negotiation.

Concluding Remarks

During an eclipse, the sun still shines; its light and power continue to have their effect, even if they are not fully perceptible. This chapter has used this metaphor to describe the eclipse of the people of God ecclesiology that occurred with the increasing influence of communion ecclesiology, especially as formulated and set into policy during the pontificates of John Paul II and Benedict XVI. The inspiration of the Spirit widely heralded as the source of the people of God ecclesiology was not extinguished but was restrained and restricted at the level of the universal church and, in particular, churches like the Archdiocese of New York. The impact of this eclipse on the church has been real, but there were laypeople, clergy, and bishops who continued to be inspired by the prophetic anointing that marks the church as people of God. This is manifest in countless ways, but here I have focused especially on how it is palpable in the advancement of local expressions of synodality and the church's role in advancing grassroots democracy.

Beginning in the mid-1980s, many Catholics perceived that there was an ecclesial impasse between communion ecclesiology and the people of God ecclesiology, or between the official curial version of communion ecclesiology and alternative variations within the church. During experiences of impasse, the idiom of lamentations becomes more pronounced. What can be learned from the laments of those in the church and in the world? What does this reveal about the relation between the Christian belief in the triune God and the ongoing challenge to be a prophetic people of God (as will be discussed in subsequent chapters)? These are questions that merit attention now.

Chapter 3

ECCLESIAL IMPASSE:
WHAT CAN WE LEARN FROM OUR LAMENTS?

"The resurrection of the church begins with lament."[1] This comment by a local priest in the aftermath of the Rwandan massacre of parishioners by parishioners invites reflection. In every generation there are believers—lay, religious, priests, and bishops—who grieve the current state of affairs in the church. Sometimes this is occasioned by traumatic violations, like the clergy sex abuse scandal, and at other times by spiritual and human needs and troubling signs of the times not being acknowledged or addressed by the community or church leaders. In our own day, discussion of grieving in the church has become commonplace.[2]

One might expect that such ecclesial laments would be a perennial topic of concern in ecclesiology and pastoral deliberations. In point of fact, however, many bishops, theologians, and pastoral ministers all too often prefer to accentuate inspiring images and stories of the church, while bemoaning the travail caused by personal sins. We are presented with the mystery and the beauty of the church, but rarely is attention given to the church's failures in living up to its identity and realizing its mission.

There are exceptions. One classic example is Antonio Rosmini's *Of the Five Wounds of the Holy Church* published in 1848.[3] This book challenged readers to reflect on some of the failures in the Italian church of his day by identifying them as the "open, gaping wounds in the mystical Body of Jesus Christ whence its life-blood oozes forth."[4] Rosmini mourns the loss of the church's vitality caused by internal divisions and weaknesses and by damaging external social and cultural movements and worldviews. This work illustrates how ecclesial laments can serve as a catalyst for a prophetic critique of the church and society, for church reform and renewal, and inspire the formation of new communities, practices, and forms of life.

In the post–Vatican II church, ecclesial laments have been particularly acute surrounding the implementation of practices of synodality, that is, the dialogical practices of communal discernment and decision making, especially but not exclusively as exercised in parish and diocesan pastoral councils, presbyteral councils, episcopal conferences, diocesan synods, and synods of bishops.[5] The stated intentions of these participatory structures of church deliberation as articulated in official documents and as expressed by testimonies from practitioners merit close scrutiny. However, it has become increasingly evident over the last thirty years that ascertaining and investigating the frustrations and failures encountered in ecclesial practices of communal discernment and decision making is at least as important for ecclesiology and pastoral practices as determining the intentions and achievements of these endeavors. In keeping with this growing realization, this chapter advances the claim that lamentations provide a particularly rich theological resource for reflecting on the frustrated intentions and thwarted aspirations of the church and a rationale for incorporating the lessons learned from laments in the study of ecclesiology and in pastoral practices. A phenomenology and hermeneutics of the intentions of the church's dialogical identity and mission finds its necessary counterpart in the study of laments in the church and the world.[6] I proceed by exploring how biblical, theological, and spiritual approaches to lamentations cumulatively provide a crucial resource for understanding ecclesial experiences of thwarted aspirations and intentions, and showing why we need rules for discerning ecclesial laments.

Ecclesial Impasse: Two Examples

Expressions of lamentation in the church on occasion surface deeper dynamics of ecclesial impasse.[7] Ecclesial impasse comprises situations of antithetical, and seemingly irreconcilable, viewpoints and practices. They frequently disclose contentious dialectical processes of doctrinal conflict associated with expanding social and cultural horizons, difficult conceptual negotiations and developments, collective conversion, and ecclesial reform.[8] Rather than being ridiculed or repressed, ecclesial laments and impasses are a social fact that merits special attention. Addressing lamentations requires not only fostering a heightened awareness of them, but also developing ways to interpret and assess them. This is especially important for ecclesiological method and for the discernment procedures employed in pastoral practices that pertain to the ongoing formation of the church's identity and mission.

Parishioners asked to give examples of collective laments they perceive in the church would undoubtedly include, in our time, a range of issues surrounding the sexual abuse of children by the clergy; but there would also be concerns raised about church teachings, policies, practices, and pastoral priorities viewed as out of touch with the convictions and aspirations of a majority or significant minorities of church members. These laments often point to deeper patterns of ecclesial impasse. Two widely discussed examples of ecclesial impasse in the wake of the Second Vatican Council can help us imagine the kinds of issues and dynamics that are involved.

The post–Vatican II period during the pontificates of John Paul II and Benedict XVI has been characterized by struggles between proponents of increased centralization in the exercise of church authority, and those cultivating the authority of the local church, as well as national and regional episcopal conferences. This ecclesial impasse about the relationship of the universal church and the local church is encapsulated in the exchange that took place from 1999 to 2001 between Cardinal Joseph Ratzinger, then prefect of the Congregation for the Doctrine of the Faith (CDF), and Cardinal Walter Kasper, who served as prefect of the Pontifical Council for Promoting Christian Unity from 2001 to 2010.

The formulation in the 1992 "Letter to the Bishops of the Catholic Church on Some Aspects of the Church Understood as Communion," issued by the CDF, which precipitated Kasper's intervention, reads, "in its essential mystery, the universal church is a reality ontologically and temporally prior to every individual church."[9] This formula, Kasper complained in 1999, "becomes thoroughly problematic if the universal church is being covertly identified with the Church of Rome, and de facto with the pope and the Curia. If that happens, the letter from the Congregation for the Doctrine of the Faith cannot be read as an aid in clarifying communion-ecclesiology, but as a dismissal of it, and as an attempt to restore Roman centralism."[10] The subsequent exchange between Ratzinger and Kasper indicates the depth of the impasse.[11]

The position articulated by Ratzinger reflects a theological paradigm associated with the theology of Henri de Lubac and Hans Urs von Balthasar that gained ascendance among many curial officials during the pontificates of John Paul II and Benedict XVI.[12] Kasper's position, which gives corrective attention to local churches, represents a contrasting approach associated with the ecclesiologies of Jean-Marie Tillard, Hervé Legrand, and Joseph Komanchak, to name but a few. Impasse is evident in the official limitations placed on synodal forms of decision making in synods of bishops and episcopal conferences, which papal and curial documents restricted to exercises of affective collegiality, but not effective collegiality, until quite recently with interventions from Pope Francis.[13] This contestation about the relationship of the universal and local churches reverberates in ecumenical dialogues Catholics are engaged in with the Orthodox, Anglicans, and Protestants.[14] This problem has also been experienced locally. Candidates for episcopal office during the pontificates of John Paul II and Benedict XVI were most often chosen based on their allegiance to the curial position on this disputed issue. Consequently, by design and unwittingly, there was frequently an imitation of papal and curial leadership styles by local ordinaries.

A second instance of impasse during roughly the same thirty-year period in the postconciliar church is at least as important as the first. The conflict centers on the reception of chapter two of the Dogmatic Constitution on the Church, *Lumen Gentium*. This section of *Lumen Gentium* gave prominence to the designation of the church as the people of God and the corresponding conviction that all baptized faithful are full and active participants in the nature and mission of the church.[15] This formulation amounted to an invitation to all the faithful to reclaim their baptismal inheritance by cultivating their own authority and agency based on their discernment of the faith of the church. Such an orientation expresses the prophetic character of ecclesial faith and offers the necessary counterpart to the sacramental character of ecclesial faith that is emphasized in communion ecclesiology.

In the aftermath of the council, this teaching of the people of God inspired individuals and local communities around the world to rethink their call to holiness and missionary engagement. Priests forged closer working relationships with their bishops on presbyteral councils, laypeople collaborated with priests and religious in the work of diocesan and parish councils, diocesan synods, and there were countless other opportunities for collective discernment and decision making in local churches and religious congregations. But several cardinals in Central Europe during the 1985 Extraordinary Synod sought to discredit this theology of the people of God and the various practices it inspired as being too sociological and democratic, too human and historical, and insufficiently mysterious and sacramental, placing at risk the clerical and hierarchical identity of the church.

The Final Report of the Extraordinary Synod said virtually nothing about the doctrine of the people of God, the category that had captivated the imaginations of so many people in the aftermath of Vatican II as a central framing motif of the achievement of the council.[16] Instead of trying to address the alleged—and disputed—problems introduced by the people of God motif by fashioning a deeper analysis and formulation, the Final Report simply avoided the topic, and established communion as the governing framework for the theology of the church and pastoral practice. In short, a perceived impasse between the people of God ecclesiology and an ecclesiology of communion profoundly shaped ecclesial policies and practices for over three decades before the election of Pope Francis.

These cases of impasse and lamentations, and others like them, are manifest at every level of the church. My aim here is to show how a theology of lamentations, and rules for discerning them, are needed in order to work our way through these contested matters.

A Rationale for Heeding Laments

The first step of my argument is to enlist a number of witnesses—scriptural, theological, and spiritual—to justify and advance cumulative arguments for why and how paying attention to ecclesial laments is important for ecclesiology and pastoral practice.

Scriptural Witnesses

The testimonies of lamentation in the scriptures provide the most prevalent biblical idiom refracted in numerous genres and reflective of various kinds of social dynamics and conflicts. The speech act and genre of lamentation in the Hebrew and Christian scriptures offer rich resources for individuals and groups seeking to respond to situations of conflict, frustration, and failure in personal and communal life. The particular literary form of lamentation finds expression in the full range of literary settings in the Hebrew scriptures: in the complaints of the Hebraic peoples and Israelites embedded in the grand narrative settings in the Torah, the historical books, and in prophetic literature. The largest repository of laments is found in the Psalms where they are combined with prayers of petition, repentance, and rededication, professions of trust, and expressions of gratitude and praise. In the aftermath of the Babylonian conquest and subsequent ascendance of the Hellenistic empire, laments reconstellated in shriller forms in later wisdom and apocalyptic traditions.

One frequent feature of lament that distinguishes it from the grand narratives, prophecies of consolation, and petitions, professions of trust, or expressions of gratitude, with which it is often accompanied, is *the cry for God to listen and respond*. Roughly a third of the lament psalms use this formula: "Give ear to my words, O Lord; give heed to my groaning. Listen to the sound of my cry, my King and my God, for to you I pray" (Ps 5:1).

At its most basic level, a lament offers testimony to personal and collective suffering in the form of complaint, grief, frustration, and despair. The motivation of the speech act that gives rise to this genre is not to express gratitude or worshipful awe, or even in its barest form to plead for help, which is a reflex step that is not always taken. At their core, laments express the pain of unfulfilled aspirations or intentions. The reasons for pain may be limitations or failings, personal or collective, singular or compounded, episodic or chronic, but whatever the cause (whether named or nameless, whether known or hidden to consciousness), the result is an ache, tension, rage, dissipation of energy, a numbness, all of which contribute to the state that Walter Brueggemann has aptly described as "disorientation."[17]

The driving forces behind the literary form of lament are, as Claus Westermann demonstrated over fifty years ago, two basic questions: why and how long?[18] Why is there this experience now of being lost in darkness, the absence of God's presence, seemingly abandoned by God (Ps 44:23), rejected (Ps 74:1), forgotten (Ps 44:24), and frustrated in bringing about God's purposes? As the psalmist writes, "Why, O Lord, do you stand far off? Why do you hide yourself in times of trouble?"(Ps 10:1). The second question is expressed with an equivalent sense of urgency: How long will this suffering go on? "How long will you be angry?" (Ps 79:5, 80:4, 85:5, 89:46). "How long . . . will you hide yourself?" (Ps 89:46). These two questions are more often implied than explicitly raised in the laments. And so too is the petition: "Do not be silent, O God of my praise" (Ps 109:1, 83:1).

The most important distinguishing structure of the lament is the complaint formula that involves a *triadic relationship*. First, there is the *I* or the *we* who laments; second, there is God as the one addressed; and third, there is the *other* often identified explicitly or by implication as an enemy who is accused of contributing to the reason for the lament.[19] The lament provides the occasion to struggle with the harsh reality of these relationships, and with the limited and distorted views of self, community, others, and even God revealed in situations of suffering.

Through the labor of lament, energy is activated in the lamenter in ways that can go undetected or be distorted in consciousness. At one level, the person or community confronts the experience of brokenness in situations of suffering, darkness, and disorientation. At another level, there is an attempt to negotiate the power differentials between the lamenter and God, and between the lamenter and the others—often identified as enemies, false witnesses, or accusers. The work of lamentation aims to reconceive and redistribute power between the one who laments and God, and between the one who laments and the others. The lamenter stands up to God not out of hubris, or to call into question God's transcendence, but to dare to pose liminal questions and to respond to the invitation to become a partner and collaborator with God in the midst of a suffering world. Simultaneously, the lamenter stands up to the others and calls into question destructive power dynamics by offering resistance and working to renegotiate the relations with authorities and along borders.[20] Ultimately, in all laments, there is taking place, above or below the surface, a trial where everyone is called to accountability, and no one escapes interrogation: God, the self, the community, and the others. The scrutiny of the exercise of power and the dissection of pain in the laments of the Hebrew scriptures can lead to blame of the self, and of one's enemies, and even God.

The lament provides a space and time in contemplation, in cult, and in community to be receptive to God's answers to the questions of why and how long in the face of impasse. The limitations and failings of persons and communities are exposed; questions of God's purposes, wrath, and mercy are raised; deeper fears and projections about the perceived enemy are allowed to surface.[21] And it is precisely here that the mystery of God, the hiddenness of God, and the eschatological character of the human person, the church, and the world are confronted. Laments serve as a furnace that release base ingredients of pity and anger, retribution and remorse. This caldron need not produce deadly toxins but can provide a crucible for compassion, where baser forms of pain yield purer forms of love-in-action and a truer, more purified understanding of the identities of self, others, and God.[22]

Are there instances of lamentations in the Christian scriptures stitched into the narrative fabrics of the stories of Jesus, his disciples, and the nascent church? One might be inclined to argue that "the New Testament is characterized by the absence of lament."[23] But closer examination suggests otherwise. Such an investigation consistently takes its bearings from the focal invocation of the lament psalm voiced by Jesus's cry on the cross in Mark and Matthew: "My God, my God, why have you abandoned me?" (echoing Ps 22:1–2).[24] No less pertinent is Paul's conviction that where there are the groans of human bodies, as of creation itself, with "sighs too deep for words," we discover the breath and voice of the Spirit at work, "searching everything, even the depths of God," and attesting to grief in the midst of precarious life alongside of pangs of new life emerging.[25] The new life issued forth in the resurrection of Jesus Christ and in the Pentecostal descent of the Spirit cancels neither the lament of the crucified Jesus nor the future of all lamentations.

In Luke's and Matthew's gospels, we also find Jesus expressing laments about people who have lost their way: "O Jerusalem, Jerusalem, killing the prophets and stoning those who are sent to you! How often would I have gathered your children as a hen gathers her brood under her wings, and you would not?" (Lk 13:34; Mt 23:37). And in Mark's gospel one can detect a lament in Jesus's reaction to the multitude longing to hear him teach: "he had compassion on them, because they were like sheep without a shepherd" (Mk 6:34; cf. Nm 27:17; 1 Kgs 22:17; Ez 34:5).

These two laments by Jesus insinuate the underlying and often implicit source of his own sense of mission: the laments of the people of God inspired him to teach in order to reveal a new vision of life, to touch so as to heal, to cast out demonic powers in order to free captives, and to share table fellowship with outcasts and sinners and by so doing to reveal God's compassion. Jesus's mission as herald of God's reign was his response to the laments of those overwhelmed by destructive powers. These are often imposed by those who exercise political, religious, economic, or social power on the poor, the marginalized, and the disrespected, but they frequently collaborate with patterns of self-loathing and self-destruction. Jesus establishes his mission to reach out to sufferers. The one who laments on the cross is suffering the consequences of responding to the laments of the people of God. The configuration of Jesus's identity and mission finds in his encounter with those who lament its deepest plot.

This narrative structure in the gospels establishes a framework for a series of specific laments voiced by the disciples of Jesus both during his lifetime and after his death and resurrection. Consistent with my overarching agenda, I will not attend to all the laments in the world of pain that must be placed at the foot of the cross. Rather I wish to concentrate on a set of laments among the followers of Jesus that bears on the identity and mission of the nascent church. In the New Testament, the formula of the lament in the Hebrew scriptures—why and how long—is not duplicated. But the struggle with the threefold power relation of lamenter, God, and the others is clearly in evidence. Let me recall several well-known examples.

Two laments came to define nascent Christianity as it emerged from the midst of Jewish and Hellenistic populations and cultures. On the one hand, the resistance by Jews to the message of the gospel of Jesus Christ was the source of Paul's lament "that I have great sorrow and unceasing anguish in my heart" (Rom 9:2), but also the occasion for him to learn that "the gifts and the call of God" to the Jews "are irrevocable."[26] The frequent and long-standing failure of Christians to learn from Paul has yielded the history of laments of Jews persecuted by Christians. On the other hand, Paul lamented Peter's betrayal of the truth of the gospel by yielding to the pressure of the Judaizers who insisted that Hellenists should follow the eating practices of Jews (Gal 2:13–16; cf. Acts 10:10–35). These laments disclose how Christians negotiated their own identity as aliens and sojourners amidst members of diverse cultures and religious traditions.[27] They also witness to the sinfulness of the church.[28]

Other scriptural testimonies suggest laments in the early church concerning who is to exercise authority and how it is to be exercised. One lament concerns privilege and jealousy among leaders in their desire for glory and power, as featured in the request of James and John to share in the heavenly glory of Christ and the reactions among the apostles (Mk 10:35–45). A second set of laments concerns the role of women in the community. The story of Martha grumbling to Jesus about Mary sitting at Jesus's feet and listening to him (Lk 10:38–42) has frequently been interpreted as the complaint of the activist against the contemplative, but it likewise implicates complaints about the roles of women as disciples and apostles and not just as hospitable hosts. This latter interpretation coincides with the grumbling about women speaking in church (see 1 Cor 14:34), daring to teach and claim authority among men, rather than remaining silent (1 Tm 2:12–15), and about women uncovering their heads as if they were created in the image and glory of God and not in the image and glory of man, her head (1 Cor 11:17; see Ephesians 5:22–24).

The lessons learned from these biblical laments often concern the Jewish and Christian dynamics of repentance and renewal. *Why do people lament?* The causes of pain are manifold. Laments frequently are traced back to the vestiges of idolatry and disordered loves. Laments are also often caused by frustration at human limitations, grief at the loss of life, human flourishing, and loving relationships, anger caused by experiences of conflict, or anguish at seemingly insurmountable situations of injustice. The biblical genre of lament often addresses the underlying problems in terms of human limitations and sin. *How long will this season of lament continue?* One view is that it continues until the individual or the group accepts their limitations, as well as repents of sinfulness, and rededicates themselves to God's covenant.[29] But laments are not only about personal conversion and reform. Lamenters are also challenged to reexamine their most basic convictions about who God is and how God works in the world, and about the need to confront situations of crisis and conflict, frustration and failure. Can we be receptive to new ways of reforming the community of faith and envisioning a more just world? These biblical witnesses attest that laments provide a process of purification on the way to a deeper wisdom about God, self, community, and others.

Augustine of Hippo

Recent findings occasioned by the retrieval of St. Augustine's *Enarrationes in Psalmos* confirm my main contention that we need to heed and discern the laments of the church.[30] In his meditation on Psalm 34 (35), Augustine offers this comment: "What is mourning for? [One] longs for what [one] does not posses."

> If you . . . want to be like [God], you will withdraw into the distance. If you are like him, be glad of it; if you are unlike him, groan over it, so that your groaning may arouse your desire, and your desire move you to groan the more. Then you will begin to draw near to him by your groaning, even though you have been heading in the opposite direction.[31]

For Augustine, the apostle Peter offers the most vivid illustration of lament and mirrors the experience of all Christians. In the words of Brian Brock, for Augustine, "lament is the expression of the pains of awaiting the eschaton."[32] Grief over the loss of earthly goods and the frustration of carnal desires must be weighed against the loss of heavenly goods.

Plenty of people . . . do grieve, and I grieve too, but I lament because they lament for the wrong reasons. [For instance,] someone who has lost a coin laments, but he or she raises no lament over the loss of faith. I weigh the coin against the faith, and my grief is keener over a person who grieves for the wrong reasons or does not grieve at all.[33]

Most importantly for my inquiry, Augustine is not simply concerned about personal laments. As Michael McCarthy has demonstrated, psalms of lament—or in a common translation, psalms of groaning—express for Augustine the voice of the church.[34] To quote Augustine, "if the psalm prays, you pray; if it groans, you groan . . . , for all [the psalms] written here are a mirror to us."[35] Groaning, more than praising or rejoicing, is the most frequent mood revealed in the psalms, which Augustine identifies with the church in the present.[36] In Augustine's time, there were plenty of reasons to lament. The church's challenges were emotionally charged and intellectually demanding. It was clear that the ecclesial body was not perfect, but rather a mixture of good and bad. As McCarthy explains, Augustine recognized that "to be a member of such a mixed body is to groan mightily at the obvious iniquities and imperfections that incorporation entails. To find oneself in such a body is to share in the laments so powerfully voiced by the Pslamist: 'My heart bellows its groans. All my desire is before you, Lord, and my groaning is not hidden from you' (Ps 37:9–10)."[37] Here Augustine confronts the mysterious and perplexing reality of the church, and by reflecting on the lament psalms, he "actively appropriates for the Church the groans which resound throughout the Psalter and indicates that, by lamenting with the Psalmist and reflecting deeply and continually on that affect, the Church comes to learn what it is, comes to be what it is."[38]

This argument about the ecclesiological significance and corporate labor of the church lamenting is rooted, for Augustine, in the belief that psalms are "the voice of the whole Christ, head and body, the one voice of the Incarnate Word speaking to, with, and within the Church."[39] In the words of McCarthy, "In order to understand the psalms, the hearer must already be situated in the ecclesial body. To see oneself in the psalm and be healed by it, one must see his or her own passion in the groans and lamentations voiced by the head on the cross."[40] Augustine's comments on the psalms of lament clearly have a Christological focus, but he does not overlook the Spirit of God at work in this genre. In his commentary on Psalm 26 (27), Augustine affirms that these laments are ours, yet not ours, but the

voice of the Spirit of God, because we would not be speaking these words if he did not inspire us; but it is not his, because he is not wretched, nor is he toiling. Yet theses are the groans of people who are wretched and toil. On the other hand, they are ours, because these words give expression to our misery; yet not ours, because our entitlement even to groan is the gift of God.[41]

It is particularly noteworthy that his *Enarrationes in Psalmos* cover over thirty years of Augustine's life (ca. 392–422), commencing shortly after he became a priest (in 391) and continuing on well after he became a bishop (in 396). His concentration on the performance and practical efficacy of the preacher's homily and the bishop/theologian's spiritual exegesis is important, so much so that McCarthy suggests Augustine appreciated that these performances make the church.[42] This is not just a rhetorical insight, although it is certainly that; but it also reflects Augustine's theology of revelation, priesthood, and episcopacy. The theologian's ecclesial task in biblical exegesis and preaching is here subsumed into the role of bishop. Priests and bishops join the great cloud of witnesses that includes apostles, martyrs, and ascetics, who testify to this revelatory psalm in their own suffering.[43] The voice of the whole body of Christ suffering, head and body, is heard in the psalms of lament and provides an interpretative framework for understanding the groaning of the church on its pilgrim journey. Augustine thus paves an important path for theological exegesis, priestly preaching, and episcopal teaching.

Here, however, I risk posing a question to the theology of Augustine. Does Augustine unwittingly fail to make room in his vision of the church for individuals and communities to express their own laments about everyday ecclesial and social life? Certainly for this great theological exegete, preacher, and bishop, heeding the laments of the ecclesial body is of utmost importance, as important as it is to explore present grief in relation to the dynamics of the scriptures. Yet does his theology create a public space for the people of God—not just the descendants of the apostles, martyrs, and ascetics, but all the faithful—to speak up for themselves and to voice their own laments? Are theologians, preachers, and bishops trained to attend in their pastoral practices to the living voice of the laments of the people of God? To put the matter in terms of church practices, is there a pastoral communal process for personal and communal laments to be articulated and heard in synods, dioceses, and parishes? This suggestion is consistent, I would argue, with the deepest convictions reflected in Augustine's ecclesiology of the groaning of the total Christ, but I wish to situate the role of the bishop or preacher or theologian within a wider ecclesial ambit in order to enable more effectively the performative, therapeutic, and pedagogical processes afforded by lamentations to take place.

Augustine's chief contribution is unassailable: a hermeneutics of ecclesial laments must be pursued in the context of a hermeneutics of the scriptures. Only in this way will we discern our way as church, creature of the Word, and as a living tradition of the pilgrim people, with the animating and transforming power of the Spirit, moving the church into the future. Augustine's way of interpreting laments cannot be repudiated; the central role of the bishop remains. But just as one might ask if it is even possible to imagine the synodal order fulfilling its mission, in response to laments, unless it is accompanied and led by the episcopal order, can the episcopal order fully interpret laments or the scriptures without the synodal order, where bishops, priests, religious, and lay people can voice their laments?

Constance Fitzgerald on John of the Cross

Constance Fitzgerald is widely recognized for her interpretation of the phenomenon of the dark night of the soul developed by John of the Cross in terms of the category of impasse.[44] In the process, she explores ways to negotiate the destructive, purifying, and regenerating patterns involved in these struggles. What she articulates bears a striking resemblance to the dynamics we have discovered in the biblical testimonies of lamentations. Among her most important achievements, Fitzgerald has demonstrated how impasses are not restricted to the personal province of one's individual spiritual life but extend and intersect with experiences of social impasse such as situations of oppression, prejudice, and ecclesial struggles for reform: "many of our societal experiences open into profound impasse, for which we are not educated."[45] In taking these steps, Fitzgerald's investigation of the field of impasse is coextensive with the field of ecclesial laments and thus directly relevant to ecclesiology.

Fitzgerald initiates her investigation by educing from the testimonies of individuals situated in diverse contexts a complex scene where individuals are forced to confront situations of impasse—personal, social, and ecclesial. In these circumstances one perceives that "there is no way out of, no way around, no rational escape from what imprisons one, no possibilities in the situation."[46] Her exploration begins by attending to the affections when facing impasse: an individual feels alone, rejected, powerless, misunderstood, and trapped. One faces the prospect of psychological disintegration, breakdown, and self-deception. There is often a depleted sense of worth and a diminished ability to recognize one's own achievements and contributions. We can draw the implications for communities and collective awareness: facing situations of ecclesial impasse, communities can question their own identity, direction, effectiveness, and value.

Next, following the lead of John of the Cross, Fitzgerald explores how impasse is a crucible for desire, reason, memory, and imagination. Like Augustine's treatment of psalms of lament, John of the Cross's consideration of dark night begins and ends with desire. Fitzgerald discovers in John of the Cross an interpretive framework for understanding the phenomenon of impasse in terms of "what kind [of] affective education is carried on by the Holy Spirit over a lifetime."[47] This pedagogy of the Spirit takes place for individuals and communities in circumstances where desire and the affections confront a dead end.

Situations of impasse force one to confront the limits of the powers of reason. Logic, analysis, and planning do not seem to help. The more one tries to find a rational escape, the more trapped one becomes. In this complex, one is pushed to the very limits of consciousness, where reason and desire are tested. Whether one holds firm to the results of reason with no clear breakthrough in sight or awaits something new and unexpected to take place, situations of impasse bring one to the threshold of consciousness, where one is left to search for a deeper order through the unconscious and the recesses of the affections.

During personal or communal periods of impasse, personal and institutional patterns predominate—Bernard Lonergan characterizes such periods as cycles of decline—and the memories that have long been the source of solace and orientation of self and community can betray and bedevil. Here John of the Cross teaches "the limiting and destructive power that memories [can] hold."[48] In Fitzgerald's words,

> What one remembers, how one remembers, how long one remembers is called into question. The past can seem a mockery or an illusion; the psychological and intellectual structures that have supported or held us together over a lifetime, 'the beacons by which we have set our course,' the certainties on which we have built our lives are seriously undermined or taken away.[49]

In the experience of dark night, now recognized as impasse, the sense of self and the perception of communal identity are called into question and can seem utterly annihilated. But this darkness and death can be the seedbed for hope. "For John of the Cross this experience signals that the memory is being deconstructed or dispossessed in a redemptive movement whereby the incredibly slow appropriation of theological hope gradually displaces all that impedes new vision, new possibility, the evolution of a transformed self that is freed from bondage to its confining or destructive past."[50] As Fitzgerald emphasizes, "the selfhood that is lost will never be regained and therein lies its hope. In this purification, the annulling of the memories, we are being dispossessed of the autonomous self, our achieved selfhood put together over a lifetime." Here she finds the basis of genuine theological hope for John of the Cross, as he writes, "Hope empties and withdraws the memory from all creature possessions, for as St. Paul says, hope is for what is not possessed. It withdraws the memory from what can be possessed and fixes it on what it hopes for. Hence only hope in God prepares the memory perfectly for union with [God]."[51] What Fitzgerald speaks of in terms of personal memory bears on the role of collective memory in communal life. If memories can be a source of genuine hope in the midst of darkness, nostalgia can hinder communities and guardians of memory from pursuing the hard labor involved in the purification of memories.

Impasse is also a crucible for the imagination. The social imaginary provided by ecclesial memory can be insufficient to address impasse and the signs of the times. Fitzgerald develops a diagnosis of the failure of imagination and its revitalization in John of the Cross. So we read,

> The negative situation constitutes a reverse pressure on imagination so that imagination is the only way to move more deeply into the experience. It is this "imaginative shock," or striking awareness that our categories do not fit our experience, that throws the intuitive, unconscious self into gear in quest of what the possibilities really are.[52]

When reason fails and imagination is in shock, God can work on the threshold of the unconscious to

> reveal new possibilities, beyond immediate vision. . . . It implies that the unexpected, the alternative, the new vision, is not given on demand but is beyond conscious, rational control. It is the fruit of unconscious processes in which the situation of impasse itself becomes the focus of contemplative reflection. Impasse can be the condition for creative growth and transformation *if* the experience of impasse is fully appropriated within one's heart and flesh with consciousness and consent.[53]

There are important personal and communal ramifications: facing situations of lamentation as experiences of impasse provide the fertile soil for the power of God to work in the imagination, if individuals or communities can let go of an imaginary they cannot sustain and can be receptive to new social imaginaries that can unleash fresh energies of life and action in apostolic mission.

In the dark night, one confronts the breakdown and failure of reason, memory, and imagination. Building on the important insights developed by Michael J. Buckley, Fitzgerald concludes that over time, one comes to realize that the desires and loves that inform one's cherished images and conceptions of God, and of how God operates with us, in the church, and in the world, are infected with strains of idolatry based on projections. These distortions can never satisfy, can never withstand the test of reality, and therefore need to be purified and freed through such experiences of negation.[54] In this way, through experiences of impasse, we can find passage to the intense furnace of laments that will destroy idols and distorted views of the self and community as it transforms our memories and imagination in the work of God.

Discerning Laments in Ecclesiology and Pastoral Practice

As I indicated in my introduction to this chapter, the customary way Catholic and other Christian theologians have reflected on the church's nature and mission is to consider certain motifs, whether biblical metaphors (body of Christ, temple of the Holy Spirit, people of God) or theological concepts (sacramental, communion, structured hierarchy, perfect society). Thus theologians delineate and illuminate the reality of the church as set forth in authoritative texts established by the intentions of ecclesial bodies.

In their quest for deeper understanding of the church's identity and mission, theologians have often turned to a phenomenological description of the church, broadly construed, guided by a hermeneutics of traditional texts and practices. In our own day in the Catholic tradition, these kinds of approaches have been reinforced, but also enriched and expanded by the contributions of twentieth-century proponents of transcendental Thomism (e.g., Karl Rahner, Bernard Lonergan, and Edward Schillebeeckx) and of *ressourcement* theology (e.g., Hans Urs von Balthasar and more recently Jean-Luc Marion's philosophy), in combination with historical and textual methods learned from biblical scholars and historical theologians. One can easily identify analogous illustrations of such efforts among Orthodox, Anglican, and Protestant theologians.

All this widely respected work has left its mark on the church's identity and practice. Christians have come to perceive in fresh ways the glory of God revealed in creation, in Jesus Christ, in the Eucharist, and in the church. This is what Hans Urs von Balthasar speaks of in terms of being transfixed and transformed by the perception of God's glory made manifest by means of the eyes of faith, and what Jean-Luc Marion would call instances of being bedazzled before a saturated phenomenon.

But for members of the church, being bedazzled does not simply entail being awestruck and entranced. They are just as often befuddled and bewildered. This means it is not enough for theologians and pastoral leaders to focus on a phenomenology and hermeneutics of the intentions of sacred texts and ecclesial authorities. It is not enough to ponder the rich recognition and reception of these texts by communities of faith. It is certainly not enough to assume that believers are to be transfixed by the idealized and harmonized forms culled from the scriptures, liturgies, conciliar texts that are then concretized in regulations and practices. It is equally important and necessary to discover ways to learn from the frictions, frustrations, and failures present in the church, and how these have thwarted the intentions and aims of the church, or how these difficulties may reveal deeper aspirations and hopes behind, within, and in front of our sacred texts and traditions. To heed and to respond to laments is the common and indispensable inspiration of prophetic critique, doctrinal development, and ecclesial reform in the church.

It is also not enough for individuals and groups merely to grow in awareness of laments in the church. In fact, to simply heighten the community's awareness of their laments can easily contribute to escalating frustration, anger, and cynicism. Unleashing laments could conceivably feed a mob mentality or breed venomous factions bent on destruction and denunciation with no clear vision of a future worth inhabiting. We only have to look to the contemporary political arena for evidence of this phenomenon. The last thing we need is to cultivate an ecclesial community of complainers who impugn the good will and character of others and foster hostility or pessimistic withdrawal. Instead, we need to develop a theology and hermeneutics of lamentation as an indispensable facet in ecclesiological method and in our pastoral practices by means of synodal processes of discernment. This means changing how we do ecclesiology and pastoral practice, but how?

What sense are we to make of our ecclesial laments? This challenge is reminiscent of Ignatius of Loyola's attention to experiences of desolation in the spiritual life and his efforts to advise strategic responses to them. Of first importance, he counseled people to develop the daily practice of heeding their consolations and desolations. The Rules for the Discernment of Spirits in the *Spiritual Exercises* provide an aid for growing in awareness and understanding of the various movements in the self in order to respond accordingly. Ignatius identified spiritual consolations as those times when our desires and passions are animated with and oriented by faith, hope, and love of God and everything in relation to God. He describes desolations in terms of "darkness of soul, turmoil within it, an impulse motion toward low and earthly things, or disquiet from various agitations and temptations, moving one toward lack of confidence, without hope, without love; finding oneself totally slothful, tepid, sad, and feeling separated from our Creator"[55]—characteristics similar to those of lamentations. When Ignatius ponders the possible reasons or motives for desolation, he identifies three: laxity in performing one's spiritual practices, a test of one's spiritual commitment, and an experience of one's poverty before God and one's radical dependency on God.[56]

Most intriguing for my inquiry is that while Ignatius originally identifies consolation with the efficacy and guidance of God and the good spirit, he subsequently qualifies this in the second set of rules, stating that "both the good angel and the bad can console the soul, for contrary ends: the good angel for the profit of the soul, that it may grow and rise from good to better; and the bad angel for the contrary, and later on to draw it to his damnable intention and malice."[57] Through his experiences at Manresa, Ignatius came to realize that one could have a deceptive sense of consolation, and this led him to develop a second set of rules for *greater discernment*.[58]

Interestingly, however, he fails to make the logically offsetting observation and qualification pertaining to desolations. Could it be possible that desolations have at times their impetus and motivation in good and holy desires and affections? Might they sometimes have their ultimate source in the Spirit of God groaning in the self, in the community, and in the world, accessing deeper unfulfilled desires and fostering greater imagination and generosity in response? Could it be that occasionally, not always, a believer, and by extension a community, might be in desolation, consonant with what we have identified as lamentation, not only because of sin and temptation, or solely because of one's radical poverty and dependency, but because of the agency of God advancing an unfinished work and new stage of development? If this is so, then one would need to follow through with a wider set of criteria for assessing desolations, for tracing them back to their sources, and for following them to where they might lead as suggested in the second set of rules.[59] As much as Ignatius's astute treatment of desolations overlaps with the analysis of lamentations as we have explored them, my consideration of the labor of God's Spirit in laments, the inverse inference not drawn by Ignatius, distinguishes the argument advanced here.

The most important repercussion of this insight into lamentations, following Ignatius's approach to desolations, is that there is a need for discernment of spirits in everyday life and especially when considering one's life choices. Ignatian discernment is not simply about personal asceticism but has crucial ramifications for discerning the apostolic mission of the church, both in ecclesiology and in pastoral practice. Peter Schineller has convincingly demonstrated that Ignatius during the period of his life when he crafted the *Exercises* was oriented by the image of soldier, as illustrated by his meditation on the two standards, where one must choose between following the standard of Jesus Christ or that of Lucifer. Subsequently, during the time when Ignatius formed a community and prepared *The Constitutions* with the help of his companions, the orienting metaphors in his writings shift to pilgrim and then to workers in the vineyard.[60] This represents a transition from a resolutely ascetic spirituality to a broader apostolic spirituality, which requires in turn an expanded criteriology for discernment.[61] In Schineller's words,

> In the process of discernment, when we are making choices regarding missions, there is an increased emphasis upon external factors, examination of the needs as uncovered in the historical situation. While prayerful listening to the interior movement of the Spirit (signs from heaven) remain constant, Ignatius puts more emphasis in the *Constitutions* on the circumstances, the objective conditions in the Lord's vineyard (signs of the times) and has us make decisions in light of that input.[62]

This larger framework is directly relevant to the discernment of desolations and lamentations, which can have everything to do with an apostolic, mission-oriented, spirituality. And as Jesuits have realized with ever-greater clarity since Vatican II, apostolic discernment must take place in common, in all kinds of communities, including with lay collaborators.[63]

At one of his lowest points in Manresa, Ignatius's desolation almost led him to take his own life. This is an important reminder that the dark undercurrents unleashed in laments, like those encountered in spiritual desolation, can be destructive for individuals, just as they can be for groups, if they are not expressed, addressed, and dealt with wisely. Just as spiritual desolation can unleash destructive dynamics in the self, where freedom is hindered and harm can be done, so too ecclesial lamentations can lead to the release of poison into the body politic, and vicious patterns of relationships can take hold.

As a result, I am proposing that the search for relevant theological methods and spiritual and pastoral processes be complemented by a quest for criteria of discernment that will enable us to heed, differentiate, and learn from laments that arise in the church, thus determining their significance and drawing on their energies positively into theology and into the pastoral life of the church. Communal laments, like personal desolation, can serve a diagnostic purpose in surfacing and analyzing potentially with great precision what problems need to be addressed, what desires and intentions need to be purified, and what new habits of mind and heart need to be learned.

To develop an ecclesiological method and pastoral process for discerning lamentations in the church would require determining the possible sources of these laments, the criteria for evaluating them, and delineating a range of responses to them. Here is not the place to pursue that agenda in any detail, but this much can be said. During this postconciliar period in the Catholic Church there have been times when frustrations and failures have arisen from conciliar texts not being implemented or synodal processes being restricted or not fully employed. Lamentations might reveal a deep longing to receive dimensions of a council or a synod that have been thwarted or undermined by policies and practices, by disciplinary codes introduced and implemented that may not reflect the deepest aspirations of the council. There may also be instances when testimonies of lament are disclosing new aspirations of the *sensus fidelium* of the church that build on what has previously been taught and practiced and bring into view a challenging new perception of the truth of the gospel. And, of course, as the scriptures, Augustine, John of the Cross, and Ignatius would all agree, laments can signal disorder and destructive dynamics at work in the church. Only by developing a heightened awareness of such lamentations and formulating rules for discernment can we hope to engage them authentically and wholesomely in the church.

Finally, one crucial conviction animates my proposal and offers a key to the orientation I am advocating. In advancing a contemporary theology of ecclesial lament, Augustine's Christological concentration on the groaning of the body, head, and members must be augmented with a complementary recognition that in laments we might hear the voice of the Spirit of God. For Christians, the laments of the Christian community and the countless forms of lament in a suffering world must not only be understood in the shadow of the cross of Jesus Christ and the crucified peoples, but also be understood in terms of the Spirit of God who searches the heart and "intercedes with sighs too deep for words" (Rom 8:22–23, 26). The groaning of laments can be an expression of the indwelling agency of the Spirit in a suffering church and world. People may not grasp the meaning of this groaning and may be clueless about how to offer a grace-filled response. But provided this groaning is not a "grieving of the Holy Spirit of God" that generates "bitterness and wrath and anger and wrangling and slander, together with all malice" (Eph 4:30–32), it can be the clarion call of the Spirit of God. Lamenting that is a work of the Spirit fosters compassion whereby lamenters become "kind to one another, tenderhearted, forgiving one another, as God in Christ has forgiven you" (Eph 4:32).

In the various schools of spiritual wisdom about the discernment of spirits, peace and joy and compassion are regarded as central signs of the work of the Spirit. But we need to be mindful that when there are cries too deep for words, there the agitating agency of the Spirit is at work, too. The lodestars in the process of discernment may be peace, joy, and compassion, but the energy fields that give birth to new galaxies and supernovas, new constellations in the church and in the world are laments. Cultivating a receptivity and attunement to laments is a work of prophetic obedience to the voice of the Spirit in the church and the world. A church that is prophetic is one that has learned how to be obedient to the voice of the Spirit in laments. This spiritual wisdom stands at the heart, the sacred heart, of Jesus's identity and mission.

Chapter 4

OBEDIENCE IN A DIALOGICAL CHURCH: TRINITARIAN REFLECTIONS

"If today you hear God's voice, harden not your hearts" (Ps 95:7–8). The psalmist makes this appeal by invoking the memory of the people called and chosen by God adrift in the wilderness. The book of Hebrews cites this passage twice (3:7, 15) as an admonition not to fall into disobedience, but instead to "be united by faith with those who listened" (4:2). How are Christians to understand a summons to listen to and obey God's voice within a community of faith that is caught up in the challenging dynamics of history, society, and the natural world?

This question about obedience requires special consideration in light of the fact that during the last half-century Catholic, Protestant, and Orthodox theologians and churches have often espoused a more dialogical approach both to the church and in the church's relations to other religions and other worldviews. How are we to understand the relation of obedience and dialogue?

For Catholics this question has become particularly vexing in light of what transpired at the Second Vatican Council and the changes that occurred in its aftermath. The council rejected a unilateral model of communication in the church, one that was identified with a triumphalistic, centralized, paternalistic, and clericalist vision of the exercise of authority and obedience, which had reached its apogee in the first half of the twentieth century and which was justified by a resolutely Christocentric ecclesiology. In its place, the council advanced a dialogical, collaborative, and collegial approach to life in the church and the world, which appealed to more pneumatological and self-consciously Trinitarian impulses in ecclesiology.[1] In the immediate aftermath of Vatican II, Catholics endeavored in many places to implement participatory forms of governance in the church associated with synodal and conciliar practices. Between the 1980s and the election of Pope Francis in 2013, these initial efforts and experiments in collaboration were undermined, or at least restricted, by the resurgence of a centralized, clerical, paternalistic vision of authority and obedience in the church, advanced in terms of an ecclesiology of communion that came to represent the church's official self-understanding for thirty years. Today, how obedience is to be understood in a dialogical church remains a disputed and unresolved issue among Catholics.

This chapter has four main sections. In the first section I describe various dimensions of the dialogical character of the church and situate obedience within those dimensions. The next section offers a Trinitarian reflection on listening and obedience as it has been developed in the theologies of Joseph Ratzinger, Hans Urs von Balthasar, and Walter Kasper. In the third section I will develop an alternative approach to the frequent focus on Jesus's obedience to the Father as depicted in the scriptures, which often serves to warrant the obedience of faith mediated by ordained ministers in the hierarchical church. The last section begins to draw some conclusions about obedience in a dialogical church in light of Trinitarian reflections on listening.

I begin by offering Thomas Aquinas's influential definition of obedience. He treats obedience as a part of justice, which is to give to another what is their due. For Thomas, obedience is based on a hierarchical assumption that inferiors give to superiors what is their due. In his words, "the higher must move the lower by their will in virtue of a divinely established authority." As a result, "inferiors are bound to obey superiors" (ST II-II, Q. 104, A. 1). He defines obedience "as a special virtue, [whose] specific object is an expressed or implied command, because the superior's will . . . is a tacit precept" (A. 2). Precept is a term used in legal contexts; Thomas in his theological arguments often uses legal idioms (for example, divine law is associated with scripture, the new law refers to grace, natural law identifies a perceived teleological order in nature). Of particular relevance for this investigation, he goes on to say that we are to obey God in all things, but not other superiors if they contradict God's will (AA. 5–6).

By way of contrast to Thomas's formulation, I will speak of obedience in terms of a set of interrelated actions that include three central movements: attentive listening to the presence and voice of the other, receptivity to this presence and voice, and a response. Obedience is thus a behavior specified by an act of attention to another person, an act of reception or recognition of the claim of the other, and an act of response.[2] The act of attention entails interested openness to the other. In a biblical idiom, this attentiveness is spoken of in terms of having "eyes to see and ears to hear" (disobedience is defined by the opposite, Rom 11:8, 28–32, Mk 8:18; cf. Is 6:9–10, Jer 5:21, Ez 12:2). The act of reception involves not only acknowledging the offer or the claim of the other, but also comprehending and incorporating the claim of the other into one's self, one's affections, and one's thoughts. Reception can lead to a responsive action in word and/or deed.[3] In sum, obedience entails attention, reception, and response. This definition of obedience can still be understood within the general framework of justice—giving to someone their due—as laid out by Aquinas, but his hierarchical assumption, inferior to superior, and his privileging a legal paradigm associated with the precept, I will argue must be judged as unnecessarily restrictive (limiting, constraining) and reductive (simplifying a phenomenon that is more complex).[4]

Where Is God's Voice Heard in a Dialogical Church?

Let me offer a modest prelude to a phenomenology of dialogue and obedience in the church. The phenomenon of dialogue and obedience in the church can be approached from three different vantage points. These three different perspectives reveal three spheres, domains, or fields within the one dialogical reality of the church. Dialogue takes place in all of these spheres, but certain dimensions of dialogue receive special attention depending on one's angle of vision.

The first sphere consists of a person's dialogical relationship with God that takes place within, and by means of, a community of believers through participation in Christian traditions and practices. People are invited into this dialogue of faith in numerous ways: through baptism and the Eucharist; through the celebration of feasts and seasons during the liturgical year (Advent, Christmas, Lent, Easter, Pentecost, Ascension); by reading scripture; through the community's profession of creedal faith; by means of personal and communal practices of prayer and meditation; and through the give and take associated with catechesis. The process of handing on the church's living tradition of faith takes place through this variety of dialogical practices.

By these means—ritual behavior, reading, meditation, and catechesis—a person has the opportunity to attentively listen, receive, and respond to the voice of God. This requires cultivating a dialogical imagination by participating in varied religious practices of communication. One is invited, for instance, to participate in the dialogue that takes place between the characters in a biblical story or between liturgical ministers and parishioners in a sacrament. These practices provide a venue that initiates a kind of dialogue between God and believers, where believers address God and they seek to hear God's voice in the scriptures and sacraments as well as in the voices of others in the church and in the world. Bishops and clergy by their offices, theologians by their calling, charism, and training, and all the faithful by their baptism are charged with fostering and protecting this dialogue of faith, each in their own way. They are to ensure that the voices of the apostles and other respected witnesses are remembered so that they may be heard again, as a potentially life-giving echo, so that the dynamism of the dialogue of faith may continue unhindered. They are also to pay special heed to the prayers of the faithful, whose aspirations and laments help constitute the living tradition of the pilgrim people of God. In this first sphere, then, obedience is centered on attentive listening and receptivity to the voice of God mediated through venerable traditions and practices of the church and carried on by all the faithful, which results in the responses of profession of faith and faith in action.

In a second sphere of communication within the church, conversation occurs among members of faith communities. These conversations take place in social settings, whether around informal prayer, meals, or celebrations, but also in various forms of ministry; religious education; works of mercy with the sick, the poor, the homeless, and the imprisoned; and in the kinds of work for justice and social transformation fostered by community organizing in the surrounding neighborhoods. In this sphere I am especially interested in deliberation about the mission and activities of the parish and diocese that takes place in councils, synods, and other forums. These particular conversations should ideally be places where open and honest dialogue occurs: where people learn to discern and deliberate about pastoral practices and priorities, the needs of the community and the neighborhood, and also honestly evaluate the activities of the parish or diocese and hold accountable people who exercise leadership roles in the community. In these settings people get to know each other and share their faith as it pertains to everyday life, their aspirations and hopes, frustrations and griefs. This is where the community and community leaders get to know each other's concerns. Fostering these connections should contribute to better mutual understanding and more focused decision making about the church's activities and mission outlook. Bishops cultivate such patterns of communication with the members of the local church by means of presbyteral councils, diocesan pastoral councils, diocesan synods, and other forums, among bishops at episcopal conferences, and with the bishop of Rome at synods of bishops. This is the sphere, especially in synodal and conciliar forums, where honest dialogue can take place between various sectors of the people of God, and individuals should be able to raise questions and concerns about pastoral priorities, the signs of the times, and official teachings.

The 1983 revision of the Code of Canon Law prescribed that free and honest conversations take place in these pastoral settings in synods and councils in parishes, dioceses, in episcopal conferences, and in synods of bishops, but stipulated that these conversations are consultative only, not genuinely decision making.[5] In Chapter 6 I will argue that the consultative-only clause is an unwarranted restriction of the baptismal calling and prophetic mission of all the faithful and the requirement of cooperation and mutual accountability in the church. Yet even if one works within the limits placed on the church by this clause, obedience in these pastoral contexts requires, in the interest of genuine collective discernment by the ordained and all the faithful, that people cultivate the skill of listening to various voices participating in the conversation. Obedience in a dialogical church requires nothing less. The escalation of a paternalistic style of clerical, episcopal, and papal authority during the pontificates of John Paul II and Benedict XVI undermined more robust synodal, collegial, collaborative, dialogical modalities of collective discernment and obedience in parishes, dioceses, and even in synods of bishops.[6] As a result, the promise of dialogue in the church was gravely threatened and eroded, and is only now being revived.

Whereas the first sphere focuses on taking part in the active dialogue of faith in and through traditions of ritualized practices, the second sphere highlights the exchange among participants in the dialogue of faith in everyday existence, wherein participants converse about how traditions and practices move and console, but also where beliefs and practices may elicit pain, doubt, and consternation. This living dialogue of faith among the faithful was a crucial ingredient in the genesis and evolution of traditions of belief and practices, beginning with biblical and ancient Christian documents and rituals, and has always been a part of the ongoing exercise of proclaiming the gospel, and of evaluating and developing official teaching in the church. Whereas the first sphere emphasizes the authority of traditions and official mediators and teachers, the second accentuates the contribution and authority of all the faithful in the dialogue of faith.

Can we not also speak at this second level of mutual obedience in the dialogue that takes place? Can bishops not be called to obey in some way the voice of the people of God, of all the faithful? "*Vox populorum est vox Dei*," "The voice of the people is the voice of God," is an old adage frequently cited in democracies. But the church is not a democracy, we are often told. Neither is the church a monarchy nor an oligarchy. Yet the claim "the voice of the people is the voice of God" is not far removed from another ancient legal precept, one often cited by canon lawyers and theologians who share certain democratic orientations: "*Quod omnes tangit, ab omnibus tractari et approbari debet*," which is translated, "What touches everyone should be discussed and approved by everyone."[7] Here the doctrine of the *sensus fidelium* is of decisive importance. The kind of discernment associated with obedience to God's presence and activity in the community is not by vote, not by consent, but rather by discerning the *sensus fidelium* receiving, actualizing, and developing the living tradition of faith as God's unfinished project unfolds in the midst of God's people and God's world.

The third sphere sheds light on marginalized voices, always an ingredient in the two previous spheres, as a constitutive domain in the phenomenon of dialogue in the church. In this sphere two questions are posed. First, whose voices have been a part of the dialogue of the church, but have been forgotten, excluded, muted, silenced, or repressed either in the first field of dialogue or in the second?[8] Second, whose voices at the borders of Christianity have been distorted or prevented from having a creative and constructive role in the dialogue that constitutes Christianity? In every generation, there are dissonant voices, critical voices, voices viewed as strange that are a legitimate part of the ecclesial dialogue but that have been ignored or drowned out both in traditions and practices (first sphere), and in the living practices of discernment (second sphere) in informal settings and official meetings in parishes, in diocesan settings, and larger ecclesial participatory structures. We are more mindful today of how gender, race, sexual identity, and economic and social status have affected and still influence not only the process of listening and receiving traditions and practices, but also the ability of some to speak forth and testify from their own experiences of the faith. The voices of members of marginalized and minority traditions can become muted, sometimes inaudible; and sometimes speakers and groups of speakers can be treated poorly, persecuted, and oppressed.

This struggle and failure to enter into dialogue also occurs at the borders of the church, in Christians' interaction with faiths and worldviews of other communities, be they Jews, Hindus, Buddhists, Muslims, animists, atheists, the heterodox, or the hyperorthodox. These struggles and failures take place not only in the context of high culture, but also popular culture and in global telecommunication. Dialogue within the church and at the borders of the church with other persons, or with groups that challenge and disorient, can be difficult, tentative, painful, seemingly impossible, and therefore avoided or postponed. There must be a place for obedience, discerning the voice of God and the other, in these challenging dialogical contexts. But what would it mean and how can one describe it? Are there ways to enlarge the conversation in order to incorporate and to be authentically affected by these voices as a part of what it means to be obedient to the voice of God?

I have attempted this descriptive analysis first in order to state matters prescinding from the passions that are often evoked by differing positions advanced by theologians and schools of thought. It is important to note that at its apex, the pre–Vatican II theology associated with the old Roman school, which was neoscholastic and informed the manualist tradition of theology, focused almost entirely on the first dimension or sphere of communication. If the second or third dimensions were discussed, it was at a spiritual and practical level, not as constitutive dimensions contributing to the dialogue of the church as collectively learning and teaching. The doctrine of the magisterium as the teaching church and the rest of the church as the learning church symbolized this manualist position.[9] The Second Vatican Council rejected this dichotomy between the magisterium as the teaching church and the faithful, including theologians, as the learning church. After the council, if we were to trace these three different dimensions of the one dialogical reality of the church, we would find that all theologians affirm all three. *Ressourcement* and other hermeneutically oriented theologians have given special attention to the first field but not without attending to the second field, and sporadically the third field as well. Theologians associated with mediating forms of Catholic theology, transcendental Thomists, correlation theologians, and revisionists, have sought to give greater attention to the second dimension relative to the first dimension, and many have attempted to incorporate the third dimension. Liberation and contextual theologians have given special attention to the third dimension, and have considered the first and second dimensions in light of the third.

From these various theological perspectives on dialogue in the church, there emerge various debates and tensions. One school of theology, sometimes described as a particular version of *ressourcement* theology, associated with official Roman or curial teaching during the pontificate of John Paul II and associated above all with the positions of Hans Urs von Balthasar and Joseph Ratzinger, has been the focal point of the debates between theological schools precisely on the nature of dialogue and obedience in the church. I will speak of this school of theology as the new Roman school, distinct yet in certain fundamental ways related to the nineteenth and early twentieth century old Roman school. The new Roman school emphasizes faithful obedience to the truth of the gospel as interpreted by the official teachings of the church in the dialogue of faith as the proper path of Christian discipleship, and it does so while it fights against a reductionistic view of the truth of the gospel, associated with secularism, relativism, and dissenting viewpoints in the church. This viewpoint not only affirms hierarchical authority, but accentuates it: papal and curial authority in relation to local churches, episcopal authority in local churches, and priestly authority in parishes. In the language of sociology, a descending model of power is operative in this theology; in the business world, it would be called a top-down management style. It is important to note that a Christological view of episcopal office, authority, and obedience and ordained priesthood undergirds this approach. Jesus's obedience to the Father is a central motif here, and though pneumatological considerations are increasingly included in this vision, and the doctrine of the triune God is invoked, it is still Christology that is central and governing in this approach to dialogue and obedience. This Christological framework is determinative not only for the theology of episcopal and priestly office, but also for papal primacy and the exercise of the Petrine ministry. This new Roman theology has fostered a strong centralized authority throughout the church, limited the scope of the exercise of episcopal collegiality, and questioned the principle of subsidiarity as it applies to the exercise of authority throughout the church. Little thought is given to broad consultation and collaboration with representatives of various sectors of the church, including the laity, throughout the episcopal exercise of the teaching office. Although this position does not self-consciously abide by the older dichotomy between the teaching church as the magisterium and the learning church, which is everyone else in the church, it is reminiscent of this position.

A second theological trajectory is often linked with various correlationist and hermeneutical approaches associated with heirs of the theologies of Karl Rahner, Bernard Lonergan, Edward Schillebeeckx, and Yves Congar, and offers an alternative vision to the *ressourcement* form of the new Roman school of theology that prevailed from the 1980s until 2013. Without denying episcopal and papal authority, this second orientation stresses that the entire church is a teaching church and a learning church. Its representatives therefore advocate for the entire people of God to learn how to listen to each other. They promote discerning the will of God by distinguishing the spirits in the church and world, by reading the signs of the times, and by collectively determining the mission of the church. Bishops in particular, it is said, cannot exercise their teaching ministry unless they consult and preferably collaborate in decision making with each other and with the laity, priests, and religious on matters of faith. This orientation shares the Trinitarian formulation of the previous approach; on this there is agreement in principle between the two trajectories of thought. But instead of emphasizing a certain kind of Christological approach to hierarchical authority, greater attention is given to the role of the Spirit, bestowed in baptism, who instills a *sensus fidei*, a perception or instinct of faith that informs the *sensus fidelium*, the sense of all the faithful. Those associated with this second trajectory that emphasizes the agency of the Spirit and the need to heed the *sensus fidei/sensus fidelium* promoted postconciliar experiments in collegial and collaborative deliberation in generating and developing church teaching to be renewed, so that new effective patterns of dialogue and communication could be found and established. Representatives of this approach also called for the application of the principle of subsidiarity developed in Catholic social teaching to matters of decision making in the church[10] as well as for much greater collaboration between officeholders and other ministers as equals in the church, with diverse responsibilities. Collegiality, consultation, subsidiarity, and collaboration require attention and receptivity to the voices of representatives of various sectors in the church.

The third theological trajectory is identified with a wide range of liberationist, contextualist, and postcolonialist approaches to theology. Theologians associated with this trajectory have a special interest in learning the vernacular and cultural idioms of local communities and heeding the voices of those previously muted or ignored: the poor, women and men regardless of their sexual orientations, people from racial and ethnic groups who have been marginalized, and those who practice and are receptive to the religious traditions of Asia, Africa, Latin America, and Native America. These theologians are often quite critical of abuses of power by those who hold offices of authority in the church and in society. Moreover, because of the long history and painful memories of exclusion and prejudice, people associated with this theological orientation are often suspicious of dialogical practices of discernment and decision making. This predisposition to suspicion is not necessarily a repudiation of dialogical practices as such but a call for courage and vigilance in working for genuinely deliberative bodies that are willing to confront and work against the pernicious power of prejudice and ideology, in the promotion of the fullness of life in the church and the world.

Where is God's voice heard in a dialogical church? As one step toward addressing that question, this chapter espouses a comprehensive approach to obedience in a dialogical church by advancing a Trinitarian approach to listening and reception. By so arguing, I want to affirm the importance of each of the three spheres as constitutive of dialogue in the church and by so doing to formulate a position that transcends the context of the debate between the corresponding three theological trajectories. Along with the proponents of *ressourcement*, and with members of other schools of theology, I believe that it is of paramount importance to cultivate the first sphere of dialogue as constitutive of Christian faith and life. I share the commitments associated with the second trajectory, especially the convictions concerning collegiality, subsidiarity, and collaboration in decision making. I believe it is incumbent among deliberative bodies in the church, consistent with those who concentrate on the third dimension of dialogue, to enlarge the conversation to heed the claims of previously excluded persons and groups, and to incorporate their voices into the church's living witness of faith. To say that God's voice can be heard at these various levels offers no particular help in determining how precisely the church is to discern God's purpose. This latter is a necessary but secondary question. To pave the way to take up that question, I want to rethink the entire issue at a more basic level, that is, in terms of how the triune God is understood, which theologically enables and requires us to reframe how we think about obedience in a dialogical church.

The Obedience of the Triune God

Jesus's obedience to the Father as depicted in the Gethsemane scene in the gospels (Mk 14:32–42; Mt 26:36–42; Lk 22:40–46; Jn 18:1) has usually provided one focal point and framework for developing the Christian theology of obedience. This approach has had an impact on understandings of obedience to God and derivatively to authority figures in the church, and by extension in social arenas—familial and political. There are, however, other ways of characterizing God's obedience depicted in the polyphony of scriptures, and I will examine a few of them in this chapter in the interest of advancing a more comprehensive way of construing obedience as a dimension of God's dialogical identity.

In twentieth-century theology, during the heyday of the biblical theology movement, the *speaking God* was often theologians' starting point. Biblical testimonies devoted to God's messages, promises, and directives received special attention. The *acting God* was understood in light of the *speaking God*. Word and action were understood as mutually interrelated and interpreting. When listening and receptivity were considered, it was the Son who was the focal point. Joseph Ratzinger and Hans Urs von Balthasar are key examples of Catholic theologians who have espoused a dialogical approach to Trinitarian relations and have emphasized the Father as the speaker and the Son as the obedient listener.

From early in his career, Joseph Ratzinger gave special attention to the dialogical character of creedal faith. In *Introduction to Christianity* he summarized his earliest convictions: "belief is the result of a dialogue, the expression of hearing, receiving, and answering which guides man through the exchanges of 'I' and 'You' to the 'We' of those who all believe in the same way.... If in the dialogic structure of faith an image of man is thus defined, we can add that it also brings to light an image of God."[11] This formulation written in the aftermath of Vatican II reflects Ratzinger's earliest work on Augustine: the heart of Jesus for Augustine inspires a dialogical anthropology and provides the foundation for his theology of the church as the house of God where one can find rest and a home.[12] One could argue that for Ratzinger the creedal dialogue comes to replace the office of prophecy that was recognized in the Old Testament as "the true voice of God" with Jesus as the fulfillment of the prophecies. "[P]rophetic criticism in the old sense of the word has spent itself.... The prophetic criticism in this extremely radical sense can never again exist because the proviso on which it was based no longer exists. The Church now possesses this absolute obstinacy of divine grace, God's salvific will as its essential element."[13]

Ratzinger finds the deepest rationale of the human person's and the church's dialogical identity in the Christian understanding of God: "There is a 'We' in God—the Fathers found it on the very first page of the Bible in the words, 'Let us make man' (Gen 1:26); there is an 'I' and a 'You' in him—the Fathers found it in the Psalms ("The Lord said to my lord': Ps. 110:1) as well as in Jesus' conversations with the Father. The discovery of the dialogue within God led to the assumption of the presence in God of an 'I' and a 'You', an element of relationship, a co-existent diversity and affinity, for which the concept '*persona*' absolutely dictated itself."[14] This personalist theme remained decisive even after Ratzinger became the prefect of the Congregation of the Doctrine of the Faith in 1981: "the center of the life and person of Jesus is his constant communication with the Father."[15] Informed by the theology of Maximus the Confessor and the Third Council of Constantinople, he finds that "Jesus' prayer on the Mount of Olives . . . expresses Jesus' unique relationship to God, . . . the inner life of the Word-made-man . . . [,] revealed to us in the sentence which remains the measure and model of all real prayer: 'Not what I will, but what thou will'" (Mk 14:36).[16] These themes are echoed again in his 2007 book on Jesus of Nazareth: "Jesus' teaching is not the product of human learning, of whatever kind. It originates from immediate contact with the Father, from 'face-to-face' dialogue—from the vision of the one who rests close to the Father's heart."[17] The source of Jesus's teaching is found in his obedience to the Father and reveals the dialogical character of God as the basis of filial communion. Ratzinger's comments in 2011 on Gethsemane, quoting Christoph Schönborn, follow Maximus: "the transition between the two wills [in Jesus] from opposition to union is accomplished through the sacrifice of obedience. In the agony of Gethsemane, this transition occurs."[18] In Ratzinger's words, "Thus the prayer 'not my will, but yours' (Lk 22:42) is truly the Son's prayer to the Father, through which the natural human will is completely subsumed into the 'I' of the Son. Indeed, the Son's whole being is expressed in the 'not I, but you'—in the total self-abandonment of the 'I' to the 'you' of God the Father. This same 'I' has subsumed and transformed humanity's resistance, so that we are all now present within the Son's obedience, we are all drawn into sonship."[19]

Hans Urs von Balthasar also contributed to a dialogical understanding of the human, God, and the church in a way that reflects his wide engagement with patristic literature, modern literature, philosophy, and theology, as well as aesthetic and drama theory. But in a special way, Balthasar's dialogical theology is marked by his early work published in 1941 on Maximus the Confessor, long before Ratzinger pursued this particular topic.[20] Balthasar came to conceive of the incarnation as the transition out of the monological sphere of sin into the dialogical sphere that is the realm of obedience. "The 'image' of God that Christ concretizes for us has its own dynamism which means that here we have someone who can speak and act with divine power and also suffer and die with human impotence. . . . [T]he one speaking with God's power and suffering with man's impotence does both things in accordance with the identical disposition: he does both things out of obedience."[21] Balthasar emphasizes that there can be no drama in salvation history without dialogue, but that dramatic action and plot are not reducible to dialogue. "God must allow his Son to become man so that there may be a genuine dialogue between God in heaven and God as a human being on earth, where freedom, love and obedience can unite."[22] Balthasar finds this dynamic in Thomas Aquinas's treatment of Christ's identity, "in the *processio* within the godhead, which constitutes the Son as the Father's dialogue partner, [which] is identical, in God's going-out-from-himself toward the world, with the *missio*, the sending of the Son to mankind. (The *missio* is completed by the sending of the Spirit into the world, proceeding from both Father and Son.)"[23] Jesus's dialogue with the Father and his dialogue with others is the dynamic field for the unfolding of Jesus's mission. But for Balthasar, Thomas's use of the scholastic principle that Jesus could learn from things, but not from other people (*Summa Theologiae*, Q. 9, A.4; Q. 12, AA. 2–3), violates his personalist conviction: "unless a child is awakened to I-consciousness through the instrumentality of a Thou, it cannot become a human child at all. Thomas' proposition is at odds with the logic of the Incarnation. . . . Nor does this apply only to the initial awakening of self-consciousness; it extends to the child's initiation into the world of spiritual tradition into which it has been born."[24]

Based on his convictions about dialogue, Balthasar develops an alternative approach to Trinitarian relations and consequently divine obedience in his doctrine of Trinitarian inversion. To complement the traditional ordering of the Father who sends the Son and the Spirit, he accentuates the role of the Spirit in the relation of the Father and the Son as "he is breathed forth from the one love of the Father and Son as the expression of the united freedom . . . ; but, at the same time, he is the objective witness to their difference-in-unity or unity-in-difference."[25] Thus, for Balthasar, "the Spirit takes over the function of presenting the obedient Son with the Father's will in the form of a rule that is unconditional and, in the case of the Son's suffering, even appears rigid and pitiless."[26] This enables Balthasar to conclude, "as an earthly man, [Jesus] is obedient to the Spirit; exalted, he breaths the Spirit into the world. So he can cause believers to share in both obeying the Spirit and communicating the spirit, essential roles for members of the Church of Jesus."[27] One may argue that this approach effectively casts the Spirit in a new role in the drama of salvation, and it cannot be denied that it opens up the imagination to other possibilities, but in the end Balthasar's rendering does not alter the substantive character of Jesus's obedience to the Father and its ecclesiological implications. Nevertheless, Balthasar recognizes in the three hypostases a paradox that merits equal weight: "the order of processions and the equal rank of the divine hypostases." He explains,

> We must on no account think that, because the Father is origin, he "commands" the other two; the Son and the Spirit are not, so to say, his obedient executors. The Son and the Spirit have proceeded from the Father coeternally with him. Therefore it retroactively affects the origin itself without neutralizing the order of origination. The Son's and Spirit's equality of rank with the Father gives them an equal share in the properties and modes of conduct of the one God; the hypostases determine in their *circumincessio* what God is and wills and does.[28]

The basic dialogical pattern we find in Ratzinger and Balthasar is also in evidence in the theology of Walter Kasper even though with distinctive characteristics. Consider this summary formulation articulated by Kasper, one that I believe is predominantly consistent with the positions of both Balthasar and Ratzinger:

> The divine persons are not only in dialogue, they *are* dialogue. The Father is a pure self-enunciation and address to the Son as his Word; the Son is a pure hearing and heeding of the Father and therefore pure fulfillment

of his mission; the Holy Spirit is pure reception, pure gift. These personal relations are reciprocal but they are not interchangeable. The Father alone speaks, the Son responds in obedience; the Father, through the Son and with the Son, is the giver, the Holy Spirit is pure recipient.[29]

From where do these dialogical distinctions Kasper advances come? He acknowledges that they offer a modern interpretation of older classical treatments of the immanent Trinity: the Father as unbegotten, the source, the Son as begotten and also the one who begets, with the Father, the Spirit who is receptive. This formula can be traced back to the neoscholastic manualist tradition, which distinguished the paternity of God as source in terms of activity, and when describing the two processions in the Trinity, filiation is spoken of in terms of being active and passive, and spiration in terms of being purely passive.[30] This stance reflects Eastern and Western patristic theology of God the Father as the original cause (monarchy) or source, but it embodies the Western doctrine of the filioque in which the Sprit comes from the Father and the Son, rather than maintaining, as the East does, the monarchy of God as source.[31] The use of the distinction of active and passive in Trinitarian theology can also be found in the work of Thomas Aquinas. In the *Summa Theologiae*, we read, "Origin has in God an active and passive signification—active, as generation is attributed to the Father, and spiration, taken for the notional act, is attributed to the Father and the Son; passive, as nativity is attributed to the Son, and procession to the Holy Spirit" (I, Q. 41, A. 4). Thus for Thomas, the Father is only active, the Son active and passive, and the Spirit, only passive. Transposed into a dialogical framework this justifies the traditional emphasis on the obedience of the Son and the passivity of the Spirit.

There is a problem, however, with Kasper's transposition of classical Trinitarian distinctions into a dialogical framework. His approach establishes a strict correspondence between each of the divine persons and a distinct facet of dialogue, based on the relations of origins in the immanent Trinity. This deductive approach distorts the character of dialogue and phenomenon of obedience in the divine reality; it does so by privileging certain scriptural passages and neglecting others in a narration of the Trinitarian drama that concentrates on the Son's obedience to the Father and casts the Spirit in a passive role rather than as an active agent. Besides presenting problems for the Christian construal of God, this manner of proceeding lends itself to a paternalistic and hierarchical approach to obedience in the exercise of authority in the church,[32] something that is mitigated to a degree in Kasper's own ecclesiology.[33]

An Alternative Proposal

As an alternative to Kasper's interpretation of the dialogical character of God, I propose to refigure his portrait of God's communicative identity by accentuating other resources in the scriptures that illustrate my broader definition of obedience as attending (attentive listening), receiving (including the process of recognition), and responding, which undercuts paternalistic and hierarchical (subordinationist) assumptions at work in traditional interpretations. My argument is that obedience is common among, yet distinctively manifested in, the full, triune identity of God as revealed in the economy of salvation in its mutual and reciprocal activities.[34] I do not wish to concentrate on the Trinitarian drama of the Son's obedience to the Father, illustrated by Ratzinger and Balthasar as a prism of communion, and of hypostatic union of the divine and the human in light of the Chalcedonian Christology of Maximus the Confessor, a view that has certain affinities with the position of Kathryn Tanner. Instead, I propose giving precedence to the voice of the Spirit of God detected in the groaning of the created world and in the aspirations and lamentations of humans in history. My chosen avenue of approach brings into clearer focus the prophetic character of Jesus's messianic identity and the church, without delineating here how such an approach can and must be drawn from and integrated into an incarnational, Nicene and Chalcedonian approach. My argument that the Spirit provides a crucial key to unlocking the mystery of obedience may be different from Kathryn Tanner's focus on Christ as the key, but there are important areas of convergence concerning the anthropological, ecclesial, and political repercussions of our respective positions.[35]

My commitment to follow the lead of the Spirit's voice perceived in aspirations and lamentations paves the way for considering recent developments in pneumatology. By pursuing the Spirit at work, especially amidst human aspirations and laments, one can more fully accept and judiciously assert, on the one hand, the prophetic identity and mission of Jesus the Christ and the church often associated with the people of God ecclesiology of Vatican II and liberation and political theologies, and, on the other hand, a wider range of developments in Spirit Christology and a more robust pneumatic approach to the nature and mission of the church. There is a further advantage to pursuing the Spirit's work by tracking the groaning of the Spirit in creation, which corresponds with new efforts in environmental ethics, ecology, and evolution (for example, in the recent work of Elizabeth Johnson and Denis Edwards).[36] In more general terms, this pneumatological orientation fosters receptivity to fresh approaches to the biblical materials, diverse positions associated with ecumenical deliberations about Western and Eastern traditions, and developments in Pentecostal traditions.

Giving prominence to the theology of the Spirit of God in considering the self-communication of God and the work of divine obedience aims to foster the recovery of underappreciated biblical texts in the pursuit of a fuller understanding of God's identity and mission, which will in the process enable us to rethink the dynamics of obedience in a dialogical church. This phase of my argument takes its lead from the text in Paul's *Letter to the Romans* that draws attention to the labor pains of all creation suffering from the futility and constraint of finitude and contingency, and the pain of human suffering from finitude and sin. Paul speaks of the moaning of creation and the mourning of humanity in conjunction with the

Spirit who helps bring to articulation "the sighs that are too deep for words" (Rom 8:18–39, at 8:26). "We know that the whole creation has been groaning in labor pains until now; and not only creation, but we ourselves, who have the first fruits of the Spirit groan inwardly while we wait for adoption, the redemption of our bodies" (Rom 8:22–23). "God who searches the heart, knows what is the mind of the Spirit, because the Spirit intercedes . . . according to the will of God" (Rom 8:27, cf. 1 Cor 2:10). Paul's statements in Romans evokes a passage from *Exodus* that speaks of the groaning of the sons and daughters of Israel who cry out to God, and God takes notice of them (Ex 2:23–24; cf. Ex 6:5), a passage in Job that describes the earth crying out (31:38–40), and more obliquely the howling wind of God whirling in the midst of chaos over the waters (Gen. 1:1–2).[37]

The Obedience of the Father

It is widely acknowledged that the earliest traditions that name and narrate the identity of God in the Hebrew Bible are those surrounding the Exodus event. The creation myth and the ancestral legends, scholars widely agree, were written centuries later than these foundational testimonies to the Exodus in the history of the Israelites, even though it introduces the first book of these scriptures.[38] My argument about the obedience of God in the Hebrew Bible finds its firmest basis in the Exodus traditions that reverberate through many later layers of scriptural tradition, and that frame and shape these subsequent traditions. A derivative and secondary argument can also be advanced about the obedience of God in the later creation myth.

When considering the self-communication of God, Christians have followed the heritage of ancient Israel by beginning with the sentence from the Genesis myth of creation: "And God said 'Let there be light,' and there was light" (1:3). This formulation has become the basis for asserting that God, the source without origin, speaks forth to create the world. This God who speaks and thereby creates has many names in the scriptures. Some are associated with the presence and activity of God in terms of Sophia as creation's architect or as a mother who gives birth and nurtures.[39] But this God who speaks and creates has often become identified for Christians, too often in a restrictive way, as the Father who not only creates, but also generates a Word that in time takes bodily form in Jesus of Nazareth.[40] Without discrediting the interpretation of God as the one who speaks the Word and thus creates the world, I am suggesting that Christians need to acknowledge at the same time that the Spirit of God is active at the beginning of creation (Gn 1:2) in the image of the wind of God that hovers over chaos, the void, and turbulent waters. In the midst of this creative energy field, the wind and breath of God participate in the divine creative vortex of the seas, in the atmosphere and air, and in God's spirit that breathes life into human form. Here the creative source, the Spirit of life and order, manifests a deep attentiveness, receptivity, and responsiveness to the void and chaos of a disordered world and lifeless particles of dirt. Here, one might affirm, the work of evolution begins. Here, the Spirit depicted as the wind and breath of God is neither a passive third nor reducible to the bond of communion between the Father and the Son, but is the active agency of God present in a chaotic world.

In the interest of heeding the voice of the Spirit in a world of woe, I am proposing that we do not start with the commanding voice of a divine source who gives life and establishes order, who invites collaboration and promises loyalty. Instead I suggest we begin with the obedience of God who is always ready to attend, receive, and respond to the moaning of the cosmos and the mourning of creatures. While the God of the Israelites in the ancient Near East was given many names, the one who became known as creator and covenant maker has, in certain texts and at certain times, been named and narrated among Jews and Christians as Father. I am recommending that we make room in the Catholic imagination of faith to recognize that God the Father obeys. I am convinced, based on my phenomenological description of obedience, that one has reason to say that God the Father attentively listens, receives, and responds to the voice of the Spirit that groans in creation and is expressed in human aspirations and laments. Even though I believe we need to expand our active vocabulary in liturgy, doctrine, and in everyday life to incorporate female discourse into our theological imagination, I am here accentuating the obedience of the Father to challenge a certain paternalistic and hierarchical subordinationism in our theological discourse.

The most basic warrant for the claim that God—who is identified as the source of all, the one Christians frequently, but by no means only addressed as Father—is obedient, is based on the conviction of Paul that the Spirit of God can be heard in the cries and longings of the human heart. This, too, is the pneumatological wellspring of a theology of lamentations. Seen through this lens, the great acts and words of God in protecting, forgiving, liberating, and bringing forth justice and life are the divine response to human cries that are sometimes too deep for words. The obedience—that is, the attentive listening and responsiveness—of the Father comes to expression in the founding story of Moses in Exodus: God says to Moses: "I have observed the misery of my people who are in Egypt; I have heard their cry on account of their taskmasters. Indeed, I know their sufferings, and I have come down to deliver them from the Egyptians. . . . The cry of the Israelites has now come to me" (Ex 3:7–9). God's listening attention and receptive response to human voices comes to define the Exodus experience. In Numbers we read, "When we cried to the Lord, he heard our voice and sent an angel and brought us out of Egypt" (20:16). In Deuteronomy, "When the Egyptians treated us harshly and afflicted us, . . . we cried to the Lord, the God of our ancestors, the Lord heard our voice and saw our affliction, our toil, and our oppression" (26:5–10, at 6–7). Jeremiah echoes this ancient wisdom when he prophecies to those in exile during the Babylonian captivity: "For surely I know the plans I have for you, says the Lord, plans for your welfare and not for harm, to give you a future with hope. When you call upon me and come and pray to me, I . . . hear you" (Jer 29:11–14, at 11–12). God hears and responds to the cries of suffering humanity in their everyday lives, and especially those who are poor, marginalized, forgotten, and silenced. The psalms give abundant testimony to the belief that God hears the aspirations of the human heart, the cries of those who suffer unjustly, those who suffer from their own finitude and sin, those who suffer at the hands of the powers of death and destruction (e.g., Ps 6:9 and numerous other psalms).[41]

To speak of the obedience of God or the obedience of the Father gives a fresh expression to the central motif in Abraham Heschel's work on the prophets, where he declares that "the people of Israel groaned under their bondage in Egypt and cried out for help . . . and God heard their groaning."[42] In short, "Israel's suffering is God's grief."[43] This is the basis for Heschel's portrayal of God as one with feeling or sympathy for those who grieve, which he develops in terms of the prophetic theology of God's pathos.[44] "Th[e] notion that God can be intimately affected, that He possesses not merely intelligence and will, but also pathos, basically defines the prophetic consciousness of God."[45] Does this not provide the impetus to consider the obedience of God the source, creator, or Father in terms of God's compassionate self-emptying and passionate engagement with life in the cosmos and in human history? The kenosis of the Father is manifested in God's obedience to the groaning of creation and human laments.

For Christians this approach to the obedience of the Father to the voice of the Spirit contributes to a further discovery. God the Father not only obeys the Spirit perceived in creation's moaning and in expressions of human heartache; also, the Father obeys the Son. The Father heeds and hears the Son, just as the Father hears all his daughters and sons in their travail and aspirations given utterance by the Spirit.

The Obedience of Jesus

Selected passages in the Christian scriptures attest that Jesus of Nazareth, the one identified as prophet, proclaimed as messianic Son of God, and worshipped and honored as the Word made flesh, is *also* called to be obedient to God, that is, to hear, receive, and respond. The response of the Father and the Son in words and actions to the mourning of humanity and the groaning of creation is their obedient response to the intercessions of the Spirit. The Son of God not only obeys the Father, but also heeds, receives, and responds to the voice of the Spirit in the world of suffering and longing. The Son comes to realize his identity and mission by means of obedience to the Spirit perceived in the voices of laments as much as in the call of the Father who sends him to advance God's reign.

The gospels repeatedly proclaim that Jesus is the one who speaks with power and acts with power. He is the great teacher, the itinerant storyteller who can grab your ear and tug at your heart. He is the healer and exorcist who talks back and acts up against destructive personal and social powers, and is not afraid to confront power with power. Even when Jesus drinks and eats with his newly found friends, the power of his words and deeds are manifest. But one must ponder carefully this fact also suggested in the gospel narratives: the powerful words and the powerful deeds of Jesus are funded by an equally powerful listening mind and heart. Jesus speaks with power. Jesus acts with power. So, too, Jesus *hears* with power those to whom he is sent to announce the reign of God, and by so hearing, he cannot help but speak and act. Jesus's obedience to the Spirit is here made manifest. This brings us back to the bestowal of God's Spirit in the anointing of Jesus in his baptism that leads him to the proclamation of justice, mercy, and God's reign (Mk 1:8 and parallels; cf. Jl 2:28–29; Mt 12:18 quoting Is 42:1).

Luke's gospel provides the most pronounced version of this insight, but the entire symphony of New Testament voices sound the motif: Jesus has been inspired by the voice of the Spirit in the people who suffer, struggle, and fight to bring some order out of chaos, to make ends meet, and who find it difficult to hope. It is the Spirit that leads Jesus into the wilderness after his baptism to wrestle with the devil about what will orient his unfolding identity and mission (Lk 4:1). Returning from this struggle, Jesus goes to a synagogue in Nazareth and reads a passage from Isaiah. Jesus proclaims that the Spirit has anointed and sent the servant, the prophet, the one identified in the gospel tradition with Jesus, to listen, heed, and respond to the poor, captives, and the blind (Lk 4:18–21 quoting Is 61:1–2). To further develop this line of thinking by drawing on Paul's insight, the Spirit gives utterance in the cries of the poor, the captives, and the blind; and it is not only the divine source who sends Jesus to respond to these cries, Jesus hears these cries too. And by hearing the travails of those who suffer and the deep desires of those who struggle, whether on the road or in the village, whether sharing a meal or sharing a life story, Jesus becomes who he is; that is, it is *by hearing* that his identity and mission become clear. In other words, Jesus's obedience to the Father in the gospel narratives as one sent is profoundly connected to Jesus's deep attentiveness, receptivity, and responsiveness to the voice of the Spirit in the aspirations and lamentations of those around him. It is this receptivity and responsiveness—to the voice of the Spirit in those who struggle and to the source, whom Jesus calls Abba, who too hears the cries of aspiring and suffering humanity—that compels Jesus in his mission. It is this attentiveness, receptivity, and responsiveness that lead him into more public and more dangerous conflicts for the sake of those he has heard.

The dynamics of Jesus's life as depicted in the gospels leads him to confront his destiny in the garden of Gethsemane, which marks the first scene of the passion narrative. To advance my argument, there is no need to minimize the importance of the dialogue of the Son and the Father in these pivotal gospel scenes. "I am deeply grieved, even to death . . . ; Abba, Father, for you all things are possible; remove this cup from me" (Mk 14:34, 36; Mt 26:38–39; Lk 22:42). As important as this depiction of a dialogue of Father and Son is, it seems theologically warranted and now more compelling to situate this decisive moment of the unfolding identity and mission of Jesus in relation to his being attentive, receptive, and responsive to the Spirit as well. Gethsemane dramatizes that the one who is called and responds to the voice of the Spirit in the aspirations and sufferings of those who are overwhelmed by destructive powers must also face their fate. In Gethsemane, as on the cross, Jesus echoes psalms of lament (Pss 42–43 and 22) that provide a litany of people who struggle with their fate.[46] Jesus shares in the grief and laments of those he came to serve. And just as many who lament confess that God hears and responds in ways not always comprehended, one cannot help but affirm that the Father also obeys the Son by listening, receiving, and responding. As we read in the story of the raising of Lazarus in John's gospel, "Father, I thank you for having heard me. I know that you always hear me" (11:41).

"Your will be done." The Father's will is invoked in one version of the Our Father: "Your kingdom come, your will be done" (the couplet in Mt 6:10 is not repeated in Lk 11:2–4, but only "your kingdom come"). And in the Gethsemane scene we read, "remove this cup from me; yet, not what I want, but what you want" (Mk 14:36; Mt 26:39; Lk 22:42). Instead of interpreting these references in terms of submitting to some predetermined plan of God the Father, it seems more fitting to think of this moment in terms of Jesus's surrender understood as detachment, indifference, or what Stoics and certain early theologians identified with *apatheia*. Jesus embodies the beatitude of the pure of heart by giving up trying to control his own destiny. Let God's kingdom come, he prays, and let me not be destroyed in the midst of my own laments.

In the gospel narratives, the crucifixion is the ultimate symbol of Jesus's obedience to the Father and to the Spirit, but it also turns our attention back to the obedience of the Father and the Spirit. Jesus's cry on the cross is but one more voice in the crowd crying out to the Father, who attends and does receive, who hears the Spirit's voice echoed in the cry of the Son, and who obediently responds.[47] During the passion and on the cross, Jesus's cry too deep for words testifies to the obedience of the Spirit, who gives voice to the human pain of betrayal, violence, and destruction. The resurrection of Jesus bears witness once again, but this time decisively and in a new way, to the obedience of the Father to the cries of suffering humanity. Likewise, the death and resurrection of Jesus is the testimony of the life-giving Spirit being bestowed in obedient response to those who continue to struggle against the forces of destruction and death. Forgiveness, reconciliation, healing, and new life are brought about through hearing and by receiving the cries given voice in and through the mutual obedience of the Father, Son, and Spirit.

Based on this interpretation of the obedience of Jesus in the gospel narratives, let me comment briefly on two other texts that speak of Jesus and obedience. In the *Letter to the Hebrews* Jesus is presented as the model, the pioneer, and indeed the perfecter of faith (Heb 12:2). This is illustrated in his portrayal as one who "in the days of his flesh . . . offered up prayers and supplications, with loud cries and tears, to the one who was able to save him from death and he was heard because of his reverent submission. Although he was a Son, he learned obedience through what he suffered" (Heb 5:8), and through this suffering he was transformed into the very compassion and mercy of God toward those who suffer. This Jesus is perfected and "became the source of eternal salvation for all who obey him" (Heb 5:9). Jesus obeys through suffering and then his fellow sufferers are to obey him because he understands and is united in their suffering. The connection to older Jewish, Greek, and Roman traditions about learning (*paideia*) through suffering should not be lost sight of or minimized.[48]

Alongside of the Jewish tradition of lamentations must be placed the Greco–Roman heritage of tragedy. But in *Hebrews* this received wisdom is reconfigured in terms of Jesus's life. The *Hebrews* passage recalls the Gethsemane scene, with personal betrayals and denials, and religious and political consequences in the offing. It is not difficult to place Jesus in Gethsemane as the righteous sufferer who offers "prayers and supplications, with loud cries and tears, to the one who was able to save him from death, and he was heard because of his reverent submission" (Heb 5:7).[49] But Jesus's submission to the will of God, even in this text, stretches back to the beginning of his career and his life, indicated by the quote "See God, I have come to do your will, O God" (Ps 40:8; Heb 10:5–7). This passage suggests that Jesus's education in obedience through suffering takes place throughout his life and concerns his own personal and institutional relations, which, in turn, are associated with his compassion and mercy toward, and his solidarity with, all those others who suffer. By siding with the outcast, he becomes an outcast. By reaching out to those who have fallen through the cracks, he is cast into oblivion on the cross.

The second text is Paul's great hymn in the *Letter to the Philippians*. Jesus Christ is described in opposition to Adam's act of disobedience in eating the forbidden fruit so as to elevate himself, which led to his demise; rather Jesus "humbled himself and became obedient to the point of death," and in return God exalts him (Phil 2:8; cf. Rom 5:19). Paul in the letter to the *Romans* argues that through Jesus Christ "we have received grace and apostleship to bring about the obedience of faith" (ὑπακοὴν πίστεως, Rom 1:5, 16:26; 2 Cor 10:1–18, at 5–6). This faith comes from hearing (πίστις ἐξ ἀκοῆς, Rom 10:17), which is testified to by the true apostles (2 Cor 10:1–18, at 5–6). This obedience of faith should lead one to present his or her body as a living sacrifice in worship of God and not to be "conformed to this world, but be transformed by the renewing of your minds, so that you may discern what is the will of God" (Rom 12:1–2). As in the case with the *Letter to the Hebrews*, the burden of my claim about a Trinitarian obedience is that one can affirm what is being said about the obedience of the Son to the Father, the connection between Jesus's obedience in suffering, the obedience of faith, and the obedience to the true apostle, and still set this way of speaking and thinking within this larger Trinitarian vision, that incorporates obedience to the Spirit.[50]

The Obedience of the Spirit

The Spirit's obedience to the Father is a concept that flows from the biblical affirmation that God sends forth the Spirit into the world to give voice to aspiring and lamenting humans and a weary and wounded world. God as primal source commissions the Spirit to communicate. On this view, the doctrine of the monarchy of the Father need not issue forth in a hierarchical or subordinationist approach to obedience, casting the Spirit in a passive role that reflects a distorted understanding of reception. Instead, we discover a doctrine of the monarchy of the Father within the doctrine of the Trinity as mutual, reciprocal, or as tradition puts it, perichoretic.

This particular approach to the Spirit's obedience to the Father in the mission to give expression to suffering, longing, and destruction must be combined with traditional claims about the Spirit's mission in the lives of individuals and in the life of the church; in other words, it must be integrated both anthropologically and ecclesiologically.

It is customary in Jewish and Christian literature to give precedence to the role of the Spirit of God in the charismatic inspiration given to individuals or groups called to communicate a divine word of judgment or consolation for the good of the community. This is a communal, and, for Christians, ecclesiological conviction. One can infer here that the Spirit of God is obedient to God the source in fulfilling the mission of being sent and in conveying a divine message to inspired spokespersons. In turn, the Spirit is said to be at work in the act of heeding, receiving, and responding to the inspired message, and more broadly as the source of faith, sanctification, and holiness in the lives of individuals. The corresponding inference can be made that the Spirit is obedient to God by enabling obedience in believers. The ecclesiological aspects of these claims are based on Paul's treatment of the charismatic gifts of the Spirit (1 Cor 12:8–10) and the roles of apostles, prophets, teachers, those who work with special powers, healers, helpers, leaders, and people who speak in tongues (1 Cor 12:28). The anthropological aspects are accentuated in Paul's treatment of the charismatic gift of love, and by extension faith and hope (1 Cor 13), the fruits of the Spirit (Galatians 5:22–23), and the Spirit's gift of freedom (2 Cor 3:17).[51] The Spirit is sent by God and is obedient to God, which results in people receiving and freely witnessing to the truth in personal and ecclesial word and deed, in discourse and symbolic action. Among theologians, the anthropological approach to the fruits of the Spirit associated with personal sanctification and holiness has at times failed to include the sense of mission given to church leaders. A hallmark of the corrective contribution of Yves Congar is his argument that a pneumatological anthropology and a pneumatological ecclesiology must be integrated.[52] Further advancing Congar's arguments, I am accentuating the Spirit's obedience to God the Father in the mission of interceding on behalf of suffering humanity and the damaged cosmos, as an act of equal significance to any inspired message given and received, and as important as any claim associated with a pneumatological anthropology and pneumatological ecclesiology.

Biblical scholar John Levison has recently advanced a highly regarded argument that in the Hebrew scriptures, one should not dichotomize the Spirit as life principle and the Spirit as charismatic endowment. These traits of the Spirit should be seen as continuous and related.[53] Levison's argument lends additional support to the theological argument I am making. God breathes life into the dust of the earth (Gn 2:7), and is the source of life, understanding, and wisdom made manifest in people who live in the shadow of death and before the ash heap (Jb 34:14–15).[54] Levison resists the common practice of reading earlier statements about the spirit of

God in the Hebrew Bible in light of later theologies of the Spirit of God that accentuate the charismatic Spirit. Even the prophetic claim of Micah about being filled with spirit, power, justice, and might, he argues, need not be viewed primarily or reductively as a supernatural pneumatic endowment in contrast to a human ability, but can be seen rather as "an expansiveness of the spirit within" that stands against life-harming false prophets.[55] As Levison concludes in his treatment of Israelite literature, "The spirit given at birth was considered no less divine, no less the spirit of God, than the spirit understood as a subsequent, charismatic endowment."[56] Wisdom, knowledge, and insight are manifestations of spirit, human and divine. My argument extends Levison's insight: the presence of the spirit of life and power can be understood as a human and divine response to the diminishment of life and the threat of death that we associate with lamentations. The mission of the Spirit is encapsulated in the creed as the giver of life. The Spirit of life, given in creation, generates restored life, reconciled life, a life of freedom, and a life of love.

Trinitarian Summary

The bestowal of the pentecostal gift of the Spirit beyond the borders of the Jewish Christian community offers one among a cluster of New Testament examples of the catholicity of the Trinity in obedience, in word, and in deed. The Father knows no partiality when listening to the groans of creation and the sounds of suffering and aspiring humanity; God listens wherever these arise in the created world, from whatever nation, tribe, race, or ethnic group. Likewise, Jesus holds no one back who wants to speak to him, whatever the condition of their body, age, gender, or racial–ethnic group. In fact, Jesus seeks out those marginalized Israelites whose cries have not yet been heard and those whose stories have not yet been received. In the unique case of the Canaanite woman who cries out to Jesus on behalf of her wailing daughter, begging him to pay attention, receive, and respond to her lament, he initially demurs because of his mission to the "lost sheep of Israel"; but Jesus ultimately obliges and by so doing realizes further dimensions of his mission (Mt 15:21–28). As attested in scripture and in the life of the church, the Spirit is present in the efforts of individuals and groups to realize their own voices and to combine the voices of different tongues together. The Trinity is catholic in obedience, word, and deed. And so we detect the Trinitarian mystery, as Source, Word, and Spirit at work in the diversity of human cultures, in the particularity of the pain and joy and achievements of individuals, and in the wild diversity of ecosystems and evolutionary processes. Catholicity and individuation are aspects of this same Trinitarian mystery, honored in the work of creation, in Jesus's ministry, and in the Spirit's role in the formation of personal and communal identity and mission.

The diverse biblical testimonies conveying God's heeding, receiving, and responding merit attention in the various traditions in Trinitarian theology.[57] The action of the triune God in creation and redemption is in response to a shared attending and receptivity as distinctively expressed in the primary language of faith.

In the Trinity, mutual hearing and receptivity is the basis for mutual speaking and acting. This obedient receptivity is not a defect or deficiency but is a perfection that is a part of every act of communication, every dialogical encounter.[58] A dialogical and communicative understanding of the Trinity that confesses the triune God who hears and receives honors, and does fuller justice to, the identity and mission of God as revealed in the scriptures and attested to by the living faith of the church in liturgy and in daily life.

My proposal emphasizes the obedience of the triune God, and, by so doing, accentuates the compassionate *kenosis* of God in heeding, receiving, and responding to the groans of creation and to human longings and laments. This proposal, or any proposal commending a Trinitarian approach to obedience, must be judged according to the strength of its theological, including scriptural, warrants. The fact that my innovative approach to obedience in terms of attentiveness, receptivity, and responsiveness in the triune God has emerged in the sociopolitical and ecclesial context of the early twenty-first century certainly contextualizes my interrogation and interpretation of classic biblical and theological texts. This context does not discredit my argument; yet the doctrinal matter must ultimately be adjudicated in terms of biblical witnesses, the creeds, liturgical traditions, and the living and ongoing tradition of the church.[59]

The Obedient Church after the Image of the Triune God?

What does it mean for the church to be an icon of the Trinity, a sacrament of the triune communion of persons, of communion with God and others? Does it contribute anything to an understanding of dialogue and obedience in the church to consider this larger mystery of dialogue and obedience in the economic Trinity? Here we must proceed cautiously.

It must first be acknowledged what we cannot do and what we should try to avoid. First, we cannot deduce the identity or mission of the church from the doctrine of the Trinity in a strictly *scientific* manner. To do so would betray an idealist approach to reality of the church as the realization of the divine idea, which although provocative would fail to recognize the way these ideas function in the social and cultural linguistic worlds.

Second, we have to address the risk, or perhaps more adequately, the inevitability, of projection in the doctrine of Trinity and in ecclesiology. Do we make God in our own image, and if so, to what degree, projecting onto the triune God the ideal (utopian) image of a reigning ideology and its corresponding social–political–ecclesial structures? The counterargument has also been made that an emphasis on the reality and unity of God can be used to resist existing ideologies or structures, or "to undermine or legitimate hierarchical and absolutist forms of government."[60]

I have also underscored the fact that the two diverging trajectories (one more hierarchical and centralizing and the other more communal and decentralizing) in their approaches to dialogue and obedience in the church both accentuate the importance of a Trinitarian theological frame of reference and the significance of pneumatology. However, the discourse of the former addresses dialogue and obedience to emphasize the importance of promoting unity in diversity, an ordered, centered communion. The latter approach highlights how the advocacy and recognition of diversity contributes to an enriched, porous, polycentric unity that thrives in a dynamic energy field. Now clearly we can only think of God in terms of human analogies, and when someone in any era seeks to retrieve older, forgotten analogies, or to develop innovations or creative reformulations, they cannot help but be influenced by reigning presuppositions of the day. This has always been the case. Whether one analogy is more driven by a personally interested and invested projection (in the interest of advocacy) than another may be hard to determine. What can be evaluated is whether the analogy is warranted in terms of biblical teachings, ongoing tradition, and the sense of the faithful.

Is there a particularly pernicious and problematic form of projection that must be rejected? One might argue, as Karen Kilby does, that this is the case when "what is projected onto God is immediately reflected back onto the world, [or in this case, the church], and this reverse projection is said to be what is in fact *important* about the doctrine."[61] But it is also the case that when theologians have developed a certain approach to the church, or society for that matter, they have striven to avoid projection and solipsism by drawing from biblical and traditional materials from Christology and pneumatology as warrants and backings for their positions.

This issue of projection pertains to the topic of obedience. Why were the Trinitarian dimensions of God's heeding, receiving, and responding that I have identified with obedience apparently historically overlooked? Some might wonder whether they indeed have been. But even if theologians did acknowledge that God heeds, receives, and responds in earlier periods, the church never fully integrated this truth into the doctrine of God or thought through the implications of these convictions for the church. Without belaboring the point, could it be that received social practices, structures, and corresponding ideologies that inform historical Western views of authority have unduly restricted our reading of the scriptural witness about God and the church? To this must be added the philosophical predispositions inherited from Greek and Latin cultures about the inferiority of receptivity as contrasted to activity, filtered and shaped by the church's reading of the Hebrew and Christian scriptures.

In the end, one must recognize that any articulation of a doctrine of the Trinity is based on human analogies. And in using analogies, which highlight similarities, we must simultaneously acknowledge the nonidentity, the dissimilarity, between the image or concept drawn from human experience and God, the always greater and always more. In addition, in affirming that the church is an icon of the Trinity, after the *imago trinitatis*, a sacrament of the triune communion of persons, we have a double nonidentity to acknowledge and confess: in the use of human images and concepts of God, and in using the analogy of the Trinity in ecclesiology.[62]

But once we have acknowledged that throughout personal and communal life, one will inevitably be involved in projections to some degree, one can only hope that one, and one's community, will continually be led toward a purification of these projections in a movement toward greater purity of heart and clarity of vision.[63] After we have stated all the caveats and established the conditions, I believe we are required to go on to explore the analogy between the Trinity and the church. In the final analysis, how one construes the identity and mission of God is reflected in how one construes the identity and mission of the church. This is also true for the obedience of the triune God and obedience among members in the church.

I have been contending that we must move beyond a Christomonist approach to obedience in order to affirm the obedience of the triune God. Based on that conviction, I now wish to argue that this Trinitarian approach to attentiveness, receptivity, and responsiveness should affect how one understands and lives out a life of obedience as a Christian in the church and world. How does one affect the other? There is no deduction or causal connection between one particular theology of God and a specific theology of the church. Rather, there are elective affinities between one's understanding of God and one's construal of the church. One can search for coherence and fittingness, for an affective, rational, aesthetic, and moral power and persuasiveness that connects our theology of God and theology of the church, and that draws the church to be true to God's identity in what it says and does.

A dialogical approach to Trinitarian theology and the obedience of the triune God offers an appropriate justification for affirming and integrating the three spheres initially delineated in this chapter concerning the phenomenon of dialogue in the church. At one level this is about the personal and collective process of dialogue and communication involved in the church as learning and teaching. Accordingly, first is recognized the importance of the primary language of faith, the biblical, liturgical, and creedal traditions and practices in the dialogue of faith, and the legitimate authorities in the church, ordained and nonordained. At the same time, secondly, the exercise of church authority in these ordained offices and nonordained ministries can only be properly understood in terms of the relational character of these offices and ministries among all the faithful, and by means of a fuller development of the practices of collegiality, subsidiarity, consultation, and collaboration. All of this fosters and promotes listening and receiving the groaning of creation and the aspirations and lamentations of humans at every level of the church. And third, in this process of actualizing the authority of all believers, special attention must be given to marginalized and muted voices within the church, and those who live at the borders in our world.[64] This polycentric view of obedience and consequently of authority offers an alternative to a centralizing view, a more theologically appropriate one that can better account for the dynamic balance between the universal church and local churches.

Can one affirm this polycentric approach to dialogue in the church without this particular Trinitarian approach to obedience? Yes, certainly one can. In fact, one could draw on a Christ-centered approach or a Spirit-centered approach. But I am convinced that one would be more inclined to emphasize one sphere of dialogue in the church at the expense of another sphere without a fully developed Trinitarian theology in keeping with the scriptural texts and theological arguments explored here. I believe that ultimately how one construes the identity and mission of God must inspire and govern one's understanding of the church's identity and mission.

Finally, we need to explore how this triune obedience not only informs the Christian understanding of faith, but also the path to holiness that includes works of mercy and work for justice. Thus, a Trinitarian approach to obedience can foster a Trinitarian spirituality that cultivates an attentive and a receptive mind and heart. In the end, to honor and glorify the triune God, one must obey. But this does not lead one to a narrow and scrupulous approach to Christian traditions and practices and to authoritarianism. Rather it finds in traditions and practices the entrance into a rich dialogue of faith, friendship, service, and life, where the voice of God is heard, if one is only attentive, receptive, and responsive.

"If today you hear God's voice, harden not your hearts" (Ps 95:7–8).

Chapter 5

What Does Prophetic Obedience Require?

The previous chapter advanced a Christian understanding of obedience in terms of a dialogical vision of the church in relation to a theology of the triune God. The current chapter develops this argument in terms of the prophetic character of all Christian believers as disciples of Jesus of Nazareth, who is portrayed in the gospels as the decisive prophet, anointed with God's Spirit, whose full identity is revealed as messianic son of God, suffering servant, and word and wisdom incarnate.

To say that all Christians individually and collectively have received an anointing, calling, and mission to live a life of prophetic discipleship is not to suggest that all Christians are mandated to act like classic prophets of the Hebrew Bible, such as Jeremiah or Isaiah, Amos or Hosea, or like those rare individuals in the history of Christianity who have received special prophetic charisms, messages, and visions. Nor am I suggesting that the prophetic anointing shared by all Christians is the same as, or discredits, the teaching office or what is officially designated the magisterium of the bishops, which Vatican II identifies as the way bishops participate in the prophetic office.[1] Rather, the anointing of the Spirit through baptism provides not only a blessing, but also a gift of the Spirit that is manifested in the life of all the faithful, whether lay or ordained, in numerous ways. Specifically, the anointing of the Spirit that is the source of the prophetic office is expressed in certain modes of action and character traits that are shared by all the faithful, operative or realized by the prophetic people of God in different ways depending on different human capabilities, charisms, and callings.

The burden of proof for my argument is to bring into clear relief certain distinctive features associated with the prophetic character of Christian life, features that are vitally important for the faith development and vocation of individual Christians, and for the identity and mission of the church. Christians may be reluctant to think of themselves as prophetic disciples of Jesus for any number of reasons. Such a description may seem eccentric, pretentious, or outdated; it can also seem difficult or frightening. My argument is, however, that the traits associated with prophetic discipleship are made manifest in the process of living a life of prophetic obedience, a pattern of life that should distinguish every individual Christian and Christian church.

The fresh recognition of the prophetic identity and mission of the people of God is a seed that was planted for Catholics by the teachings of Vatican II. My aim in this chapter is to affirm, advance, and help deepen and develop that teaching.

My hope is that this seed of the council may, like the mustard seed of the gospels, continue to take firm root and grow abundantly. Here I take my bearings, just as the council did, by following the lights offered by the Hebrew and Christian scriptures. I thus begin this chapter by recalling a few biblical traditions that have inspired the vision of the prophetic character and mission of the people of God.

A foundational text is the book of Deuteronomy that depicts Moses as the paradigmatic prophet: "Never since has there arisen a prophet in Israel like Moses, whom the Lord knew face to face" (34:10–11, 18:18–23). This depiction of Moses with his face-to-face intimacy with God offers a counterpoint to the episode in the book of Exodus that narrates Moses's initial encounter with God at the burning bush, where Moses hides his face out of fear (2:23–4:17). In the Exodus text, Moses learns from God to heed the laments and aspirations of God's people and to receive and convey God's message that will address their plight. God's summons to heed the people's laments and to convey God's message distinguishes the prophetic mission of Moses.

A prophetic summons for all of God's people surfaces in an unusual story about Moses. In the book of Numbers the prototypical prophet Moses is depicted as weary with the duties of his calling and mission (11:16–25). God directs Moses to reach out to others in the community to share in his prophetic vocation. Moses draws a group of seventy elders together into the Tent of Meeting. In this assembly God's spirit of prophecy, earlier bestowed on Moses, is shared with the elders. They are called on to "bear the burden of the people" along with Moses and to assist him, and under the influence of this charismatic gift to exercise prophecy, personally and collectively.

As the story is told, two figures at the margins of the group, Eldad and Medad, did not enter the tent, but nevertheless received a share of the spirit's inspiration and accordingly began to act in a prophetic manner (which likely means in this context they engaged in ecstatic behavior in word and action). Their behavior was met with a protest by the "inner circle" of prophets who were present at the prophetic installation and anointing. They complained to Moses and demanded that these would-be prophets be silenced. Moses responded: "Are you jealous for my sake? Would that all the Lord's people were prophets, that the Lord would put his spirit upon them" (Nm 11:28–29). This can be called Moses's petition: let all of God's people receive the spirit of prophecy. As Moses's words affirm, such an outcome would neither undermine Moses's calling and mission nor that of the elders, but would call forth a new level of prophetic vocation and mission among all of God's people.

Moses's petition that the Lord's spirit be given to all of God's people so that they might all be prophets receives one especially noteworthy response from God, conveyed to the postexilic prophet Joel.[2] Set in a time of crisis occasioned by an ecological disaster—locust infestation and drought in Judah during the Persian period and all the economic hardship that accompanies such occurrences—Joel calls for public liturgical acts of lament and repentance. It is in this setting that Joel receives a consoling word from God; Joel prophesies to the people mercy, ecological renewal, and economic recovery, and with a singular prophetic utterance declares,

"I will pour out my spirit upon all flesh and your sons and your daughters will prophesy, your old men shall dream dreams, and your young men shall see visions. Even on the male and female slaves, in those days, I will pour out my spirit" (Jl 2:28). For Joel the bestowal on all flesh most likely means all Jewish flesh, but for subsequent generations, the echo of this prophecy was received as an announcement of a bestowal of God's spirit on the people of all tribes and nations.

In the Pentecost narrative found in the Acts of the Apostles, Peter declares that this passage from Joel is being fulfilled in their midst with the bestowal of God's Spirit on all nations (2:17–18). The descent of God's Spirit at Pentecost joins the resurrection of the crucified Jesus for the author of Luke-Acts, as for the apostle Paul in his letters, as a sign of the messianic age being ushered in as Jewish and Gentile followers of Jesus share in the anointing of God's Spirit. This story of the Spirit at the beginning of the Acts of the Apostles has been crafted to mirror the beginning of the gospel of Luke, in which Jesus reads from the prophet Isaiah in his first public act in the synagogue at Nazareth and takes upon himself the prophetic mantle. "The Spirit of the Lord is upon me, because he has anointed me to bring good news to the poor. He has sent me to proclaim release to the captives and recovery of sight to the blind, to let the oppressed go free, to proclaim the year of the Lord's favor" (Lk 4:18–19, alluding to Is 61:1, 2, 58:6). Jesus takes upon himself the prophetic mantle as he announces to his audience, "Today this scripture has been fulfilled in your hearing" (Lk 4:21). In the New Testament traditions, the disciples of Jesus come to share in this same Spirit of prophecy and are called to carry on Jesus's mission.

Pope John XXIII prayed that the council he convoked would be a new Pentecost in the life of the church.[3] This prayer became policy in one of many passages in *Lumen Gentium* (cited as LG) that recalls the event of Pentecost in the Acts of the Apostles that cites Joel and evokes the recollection of Moses's plea in Numbers. The prophetic identity and mission of Jesus Christ is to be carried out not only by bishops, but also by all the baptized. "Christ is the great prophet who proclaimed the kingdom of the Father both by the testimony of his life and by the power of his word. Until the full manifestation of his glory, he fulfills this prophetic office, not only through the hierarchy who teach in his name and by his power but also through the laity" (LG, 35). This prophetic anointing is made manifest in the "appreciation of the faith (*sensus fidei*) and the grace of the word" in everyday life in family and society through "continual conversion" and by means of "struggling against the rulers, against the authorities, against the cosmic powers of this present darkness, against the spiritual forces of evil" (LG, 35; Eph 6:12).[4]

This chapter offers a constructive argument about the significance of this prophetic anointing of all the faithful. By drawing on two basic dimensions of prophecy, I will explore five characteristics of prophetic discipleship that contribute to a sense of personal vocation and collective mission. Before exploring these dimensions and characteristics of prophecy, it might be helpful to consider three sources of resistance to such a prophetic orientation.

Sources of Resistance to the
Prophetic Character of All Believers

Incarnational Christologies

There are three contemporary sources of resistance to the prophetic character of discipleship and the church that merit our attention.[5] The first is associated with the critical reaction to modern attempts to recover the prophetic character of Jesus's ministry and mission, either as this has been advanced through historical–critical biblical studies' quest to reconstruct the various strata of gospel traditions and the Jesus of history or through rhetorical or narrative critics' efforts to gain a deeper appreciation of the prophetic character of the identity of Jesus Christ as it is presented in the canonical gospels. Frequently the interest in the reconstruction of the history of Jesus is traced back to the turn of the century efforts of Johannes Weiss (1863–1914) in his book *Jesus' Proclamation of the Kingdom of God* to recover the eschatological and specifically apocalyptic character of Jesus's ministry.[6] Weiss accentuated Jesus's message of God's reign to a religious community in crisis, in a conflictual social world on the threshold of disaster under the military power of the Roman Empire. Weiss offered an alternative, on the one hand, to nineteenth-century liberal and romantic portrayals of Jesus's life that reflected the dominant cultural *zeitgeist*, and, on the other, to the long-standing traditional understanding of Jesus as the God-man, the Word made flesh derived from incarnational and sapiential motifs in the New Testament, which set the stage for subsequent debates that led to the creedal Christologies of the councils of Nicaea and Chalcedon.

Motivated by a desire to recover the Jesus of history, scholars analyzed Jesus's teachings, healings, exorcisms, and table fellowship in the synoptic gospels. They generated elaborate theories to identify authentic material from the earliest strata of the gospel traditions by positing various layers of oral and literary tradition that corresponded to distinctive stages in the life of the nascent Jesus movement and Christian community. Jesus's engagement with his religious and political contemporaries also received increasing scrutiny throughout the twentieth century. These efforts were combined with increasing attention to the eschatological character of Jesus's message in relation to prophetic and apocalyptic literatures.

A formidable tradition of Protestant biblical scholarship on the prophetic identity of Jesus extends from the work of Johannes Weiss in the nineteenth century, to the second half of the twentieth century with E. P. Sanders, and more recently to scholars such as Dale C. Anderson and N. T. Wright.[7] The result has been an understanding of Jesus's words and actions situated in the context of the Roman Empire and Second Temple Judaism, amidst religious groups ranging from temple priests, scribes, and Pharisees, to Essenes and Zealots, and people representing diverse economic strata, which has cumulatively given prominence to Jesus's prophetic identity.[8] Catholic biblical scholars and systematic theologians have likewise contributed to these developments. John Meier, Ben F. Meyer, Adela Yarbo Collins, Elisabeth Schüssler Fiorenza, and Luke Timothy Johnson have all pursued this line of inquiry in North

America.[9] Catholic systematic theologian Edward Schillebeeckx is among the most widely recognized for his explorations of the implications of this prophetic under-standing of Jesus's identity and mission for the disciples of Jesus and the church,[10] but even Karl Rahner and Yves Congar gave special attention to the importance of the prophetic identity and mission of Jesus of Nazareth.[11] Most recently, Sandra Schnei-ders, a scholar of biblical studies and Christian spirituality, has become one of the most articulate and widely read interpreters of the prophetic identity of Jesus, which she has explored in relation to the prophetic calling of baptized Christians and vowed religious in particular. We will return to her contribution below.

Some have viewed this attention to the prophetic and apocalyptic character of Jesus's teachings and actions as a threat and distraction to the New Testament confession of Jesus as messiah, Son of God, and the Word made flesh, the confession that ultimately supported the Nicene articulation of the identity of Jesus Christ as one in being with God the Father, and the Chalcedonian formulation that Jesus Christ has two natures, fully divine and fully human, united in one person (hypos-tasis). This line of critique raises enormous questions about how one envisions the relationship of efforts to acknowledge the significance of Jesus's prophetic character based on historical and literary-critical research, on the one hand, in relation to the various Christologies in the New Testament canon and the creedal faith of the church, on the other. I contend, however, that there is no need to set a prophetic approach to Jesus's identity and mission over against other New Testament themes or creedal confessions. Rather, in line with respected twentieth- and twenty-first century scholarship, I wish to advance the paramount significance of prophetic factors at work in the life of Jesus and his followers.

It is commonplace for theologians today to explore the classic Christologies of Athanasius, Augustine, and Thomas Aquinas, as well as those of the Cappadocian theologians (Gregory of Nazianzen, Gregory of Nyssa, and Basil of Caesarea), Cyril of Alexandria, and Maximus the Confessor seeking deeper theological interpreta-tions of the Nicene and Chalcedonian faith of the church. Such efforts regularly criticize or ignore the significance of the prophetic identity and mission of Jesus and the church marked by religious and political conflict. Works by Hans Urs von Balthasar[12] and Joseph Ratzinger[13] in Catholic circles are emblematic of this position. Current Chalcedonian understandings of Jesus Christ frequently avoid prophetic approaches because they do not accentuate the divine character of Jesus's identity and mission, the sacrificial and atoning character of his death, and the divine character of the church, the sacraments, and the church's mission. As a result, prophetic and Chalcedonian styles of discipleship and spirituality are regularly set in opposition. Setting up such an opposition, in my opinion, offers a restrictive and defective approach to biblical interpretation and the Christian faith. Theologians need to help members of the Christian church find ways to bridge this divide, rather than simply privilege later or earlier gospel sources and Christological formulas. The union of the divine and the human in the person of Jesus of Nazareth, and Jesus's receptivity to God's Spirit in his life and ministry as displayed in the gospel traditions, should find their fullest expression in a theology that embraces and accentuates Jesus's prophetic identity. Such an acknowledgment of the prophetic character of Jesus's identity and mission can, and should, be combined with Nicene and Chalcedonian Christologies for a full confession of faith and for the sake of the ongoing quest for a deeper understanding of faith in order to advance a more adequate Christology, pneumatology, and ecclesiology.

Communion Ecclesiology

A second source of resistance to a prophetic approach to individual believers and the church has been associated with the official program of communion ecclesiology that was advanced during the pontificates of John Paul II and Benedict XVI. This is so despite the fact that John Paul II's first encyclical, *Redemptor Hominis* (1979), emphasized that "The sharing in the prophetic office of Christ himself shapes the life of the whole of the Church in her fundamental dimension. A particular share in this office belongs to the pastors of the Church, who teach and continually and in various ways proclaim and transmit the doctrine concerning the Christian faith and morals."[14] As explored in the first two chapters, communion ecclesiology in certain ways eclipsed and restricted, without destroying or denying, the prophetic character of the people of God in the church as full participants in the life and ministry of the church, and as active leaders and agents in the church's mission in the church and the world. The official ecclesiology of communion, which became increasingly accentuated between 1978 and 2013, advanced a theological and epistemological frame that focused attention on certain doctrinal convictions and practices, and left other doctrinal and practical elements out of focus or out of the picture entirely.[15] By so doing the official theological program of communion contributed to greater divisiveness and polarization in the church, perhaps especially in the United States, and left little room for open discussion and debate among representatives of the plurality of theological schools. An open approach to synodality, conciliarity, and collegiality in the church was restricted and undermined, in order to foster church unity by means of a centralized church order marked by clericalism and paternalism.

While many may, for good reason, think of these tendencies as particularly Roman Catholic, they are also associated with the widespread adoption of communion ecclesiology in Orthodox and Anglican churches, as well as by some Lutheran, Reformed, and Evangelical churches, through the ecumenical cross-fertilization fostered by bilateral and multilateral dialogues and joint documents. The basic problems raised by the current predominance of an ecclesiology of communion, which has undermined the further development of the prophetic character of discipleship and the church, are not unrelated to Paul Tillich's now dated argument, which has an even older lineage: that there exists an incarnational, sacramental, and institutional "Catholic substance," which stands in tension with a Spirit-oriented and reformed-minded, "Protestant principle."[16] Tillich's formulation of this tension in terms of differences between Catholic and Protestant theologies fails to go deep enough, or back far enough historically to medieval and ancient materials, to uncover how this dynamic is operative in the Christian scriptures' portrayal of the identity and mission of Jesus Christ and the Spirit, in the tradition of prophecy in the Hebrew and Christian scriptures, and in the reception of these traditions throughout Christian history.

The problems raised by the official communion ecclesiology do not lie as much in what communion ecclesiology affirms of the sacramental, incarnational, and Trinitarian dimensions of the church as in what it denies, obscures, and excludes. Its particular vision of ecclesial communion eclipses, diminishes, and thereby undermines the prophetic mission-oriented character of the faith of individuals and communities by resurfacing a paternalistic and clericalist style of episcopal and priestly leadership in the liturgical, ministerial, and organizational life of the church, which has proven divisive and demoralizing. In this period, the nascent development of lay ecclesial leadership and ministries, and of synodal and conciliar forms of group discernment in parishes and dioceses and in episcopal conferences and in synods of bishops, has frequently been inhibited or subverted. The official communion ecclesiology has been particularly divisive in moral and political areas when its legitimate advocacy of charitable activities, the works of mercy that are a crucial part of the church's mission, has been combined with criticisms of work for justice connected with liberation theology's advocacy of the church's mission to the poor through work for economic, racial, and gender justice, and in the promotion of grassroots democracy.

The official communion ecclesiology, moreover, has been aligned with the defense of the truth of the gospel and the power of reason to comprehend order in the cosmos and the natural law, against modern and postmodern distortions of relativism by John Paul II, above all in *Veritatis Splendor* and *Fides et Ratio*,[17] and in various writings by Joseph Ratzinger/Benedict XVI.[18] These popes' defense of reason has been sometimes associated with a neo-scholastic interpretation of reason and nature.[19] The challenge posed by this approach to reason is that it perceives an order *in* reality but risks imposing an order *on* reality at the expense of *facing reality* honestly, *embracing reality*, and at times *struggling against reality* as dominating forces operate to suppress reality in its historical unfolding and in all its irrepressible refractoriness. The result is failure to leave ample room for the use of critical reason, for integrating the creative and productive imagination into reasoning, and for effectively employing practical reason in *engaging reality*.[20]

In the face of these divisive dynamics, the challenge before us is to reclaim the prophetic character of the life of faith and to foster prophetic communities. Only then will we be poised to discover a new and more multivalent approach to communion, charity, and reason that integrates genuine prophetic witness in word and action.

Divergent Impulses in Vatican II Documents

A third challenge to advancing the prophetic character of all the faithful and the church arises from a set of technical issues involved in interpreting and weighing those documents of Vatican II that address the prophetic character of all the faithful, which includes bishops, clergy, and the laity, and the teaching office of bishops, which is a distinctive way that bishops participate in the prophetic character of all the faithful. These issues are embedded in a larger set of topics pertaining to the ways the threefold office of Christ as priest, prophet, and king was invoked during the council and utilized in pivotal documents on the church, the bishops, priests, and the laity.[21]

As described in earlier chapters, the council asserted that through baptism all the faithful share in the three messianic offices of Jesus Christ, at the same time it stated that through ordination there is established the ministerial and hierarchical priesthood and episcopacy but that priests and bishops participate in these offices in an essentially different way.[22] The Decree on the Laity (*Apostolicam Actuositatem* [cited as AA]) puts it this way: "To the apostles and their successors, Christ has entrusted the office of teaching, sanctifying, and governing (*munus docendi, santificandi et regendi*) in his name and by his power. Laypeople, sharing in the priestly, prophetic, and kingly offices (*muneris sancerdotalis, prophetici et regalis Christi participes*) play their part in the mission of the whole people of God in the church and in the world" (AA, 2).[23] I wish to highlight selected textual issues pertaining to the prophetic office.

A pivotal formulation is found in *Lumen Gentium*, which I will cite at length, followed by a few observations and questions.

> The holy people of God shares also in Christ's prophetic office; it spreads abroad a living witness to him, especially by a life of faith and love and by offering to God a sacrifice of praise, the fruit of lips confessing him name (see Heb 13:15). The whole body of the faithful who have received an anointing, which comes from the holy one (see 1 Jn 2:20 and 27), cannot be mistaken in belief. It shows this characteristic through the entire people's supernatural sense of the faith, when "from the bishops to the last of the faithful," it manifests a universal consensus in matters of faith and morals. By this sense, aroused and sustained by the Spirit of truth, the people of God, guided by the sacred magisterium which it faithfully obeys, receives not the word of human beings, but truly the word of God (see 1 Th 2:13), "the faith once for all delivered to the saints" (Jude 3). The people unfailingly adheres to this faith, penetrates it more deeply through right judgment, and applies it more fully in daily life. (LG 12)[24]

This text asserts the prophetic character of the messianic anointing of Jesus Christ and identifies the prophetic office of Christ with the prophetic office of the faithful and specifically with the mission to witness in word and in deed. This emphasis on receiving and witnessing to the Word of God is a central prophetic motif, but, as I will argue, it offers a limited understanding of the prophetic charism, or anointing, as this appears in the accounts of the prophets of the Hebrew scriptures, and in the narratives of Jesus of Nazareth, his disciples, and the church. The text goes on to associate the prophetic office with the supernatural sense of the faith, which is present in individual believers, but it is also identified in the text with the supernatural sense of the faith of all the people.

I would like to introduce three lines of inquiry in this regard. A first pertains to the claim that the sense of the faith is associated with the prophetic office not only as the source of the capacity to recognize the abiding faith of the church, but also as a source for recognizing authentic doctrinal development, as believers penetrate the faith more deeply and through right judgment apply it to daily life. Does this sense of the faith and sense of the faithful serve as a source and also a developing norm, one that must be continually discerned in the church?

A second question is this: does participation in the prophetic office provide the basis for *consensus fidelium*? The text asserts as much. Yet, manifestations of the prophetic office are regularly associated with the opposite of consensus—with contestation, dissensus, protest, and denunciation. Is sufficient attention given here to the role of conflict and struggle in the church and in society, that is, to what could be called the agonistic dimensions of communal existence? The text affirms a connection between the prophetic office of the faithful and their sense of the faith as the source and criterion by which the people of God "cannot be mistaken in belief," which, in turn, leads to a consensus of faith. But does this text give sufficient attention to the prophetic task of testing and discerning the truth of faith while seeking and struggling to clarify the truth in the midst of the church and the world? Ultimately it is the Spirit's anointing that provides the basis for any genuine consensus, but this anointing can likewise manifest itself in conflict, which is why discerning and testing are required.

A third question pertains to the phrase that reads, "this sense [of faith], aroused and sustained by the Spirit of truth, the people of God, guided by the sacred magisterium which it faithfully obeys (*sub ductu sacri magisterii, cui fideliter obsequens*), receives not the word of human beings, but truly the word of God" (LG, 12). Who do the anointed people of God that share in the prophetic office obey? The text appears unambiguous: the faithful obey or are respectfully receptive to the teachings of the magisterium. But is this deference to religious authorities consistent with the prophetic office as we discover it exercised in the Hebrew and Christian scriptures? Or does the prophetic office of all the faithful acknowledge the teaching and governing authorities in the church, ordained and nonordained, to the extent they authentically and authoritatively witness to the sense of the faith of the faithful? This question provides ample reason for exploring the participation of all the faithful people of God in the prophetic office in terms of prophetic obedience, since it is through the exercise of prophetic obedience that the faithful receive God's word in the entire church.

Two Frames for Understanding Prophecy

It has been customary in the study of prophetic discourse in the Hebrew and Christian scriptures to characterize the nature of prophecy as a word or message given by God that is received by a prophet, which is then communicated by proclamation (word) or witness (in word or action). This kind of approach to prophecy is in evidence in the documents of the Second Vatican Council and is a significant part of its renewed approach to the scriptures. The council documents avoid the terse and dry propositional approach to revelation associated with neoscholastic manuals of theology. Instead Vatican II constitutions, decrees, and declarations espouse a vibrant rhetorical approach to revelation, one that cultivates an appreciation of the scriptures that respects the diversity of literary forms and historical contexts operative in the history of biblical traditions within a salvation history framework. This approach to the character of prophecy, as word received and witness given, enables theologically focused and flexible analysis of diverse biblical literary forms and of the history of Christian prophecy since the apostolic period. This orientation has remained the dominant framework for understanding prophetic discourse in official church teachings and among various theologians since the council.

In the aftermath of the council, however, numerous attempts have been made in biblical studies to deepen the understanding of the complex social, intercultural, and historical contexts of prophetic discourse in its inception[25]—with testimonies attributed to ecstatic groups and individual figures—and in its tradition history. Moreover, considerable attention has been given to the history of effects and history of receptions of prophetic discourse not only in the Global North, but also in post-colonial situations in the Southern Hemisphere and among refugees and immigrant populations around the world. There have also been countless efforts to wrestle with the complex literary and rhetorical dynamics at work in specific prophetic literary works and in the canonical scriptures more broadly. The coherence and harmonic convergence assumed and fostered by this dominant framework—word received, witness given—can have difficulty accounting for the contested character of these texts and the ways they have been utilized in communities with multiple intercultural dynamics of discourse and power. There are many sources of wisdom, courage, and frustrating conundrums to be gleaned from the prophetic literature, all of which have genuine significance for endeavors to explore the prophetic character of personal and ecclesial existence. The prophetic motifs drawn on in the documents of Vatican II and in the theologies that contributed to them and were nurtured by them have barely scratched the surface.

In an attempt to acknowledge and honor the diverse methodological options operative in contemporary biblical studies as well as in theology, I am proposing that the long-standing framework, word received and witness given, does not give sufficient attention to other important features of the prophetic phenomenon and prophetic discourse, and consequently needs to be augmented with another framework. This modest proposal aims to be compatible with diverse methodological options, which often stand in tension with, if not in explicit opposition to, one another. It is introduced in the interest of offering a wider approach to the prophetic character of individuals and communities that will be theologically accessible to diverse scholarly, ecclesial, and social audiences.

*Word Received, Witness Given: The
Dominant Framework*

As noted, the primary theological framework or schema for understanding prophecy has been in terms of the reception of a word or message from God, which is communicated by means of proclamation and witness in word and action. John J. Collins provides the simple rationale for why this framework has been so influential: "The word prophecy comes from the Greek *prophētēs*, 'proclaimer,' and refers to one who speaks on behalf of a god or goddess. The roles of such spokesmen or spokeswomen vary from one culture to another, and various terms are used to describe them. Prophets typically receive their revelations in a state of ecstasy, either by seeing visions or by direct inspiration."[26] Walter Brueggemann urges the acknowledgment of diverse manifestations of the phenomenon of prophecy in Israel and the inevitability of missing details in any general formulation. Yet his own working description of the nature of prophecy confirms the primacy of this framework: "Prophecy as a mode of mediation begins in the inexplicable appearance of individual persons who claim to speak Yahweh's revelatory word, and who are accepted by some as being indeed carriers of such a revelatory word."[27]

This prophetic message is described in terms of receiving a word, a vision, a thought, some special perception or awareness. The prophetic call to witness in word and deed is correlative to the message received. The message is often specified in terms of prophetic denunciation or consolation: destabilizing or validating political or religious leadership, cultic practices, or scribal traditions; challenging audiences to rededicate themselves to singular devotion to God (the *Shema*), the Torah, or some specific tradition. This particular formula is largely indebted to patterns found in the classical period of prophecy associated with the major prophets (Amos, Hosea, Micah, Isaiah, Jeremiah, Ezekiel, Jonah), and less so with the earlier, sometimes called primitive, tradition associated with the Deuteronomistic history, traditionally known as the Former Prophets, as found in the books of Joshua, Judges, Samuel, and Kings.[28] This schema provided the operative frame for major mid-twentieth century Catholic theologians, including Karl Rahner, Yves Congar, Joseph Ratzinger, and Hans Urs von Balthasar.[29]

*Heeding the Spirit in Laments and Aspirations:
An Alternative Framework*

There is an alternative framework for considering prophetic discourse, one that can be detected within prophetic literature in the scriptures, and that corresponds to my earlier argument concerning lamentations. This alternative framework intersects and is intertwined with the primary framework. It illumines an equally basic, interdependent, and at times prior summons received by the prophet. The prophet is called on to face reality, bear the burdens of this reality, and engage this reality.[30]

In this schema, communication is not initially by means of a word or message received, but through the wailing of the Spirit heard in vulnerable and grieving people suffering from the ravages of personal and social sin and difficult contingencies of life, and the clamoring of the Spirit in the created world abused by the negative consequences of sin and affected by the calamities of cosmic history. Without denying the periodic use of pneumatic themes in classic prophetic literature in the Hebrew Bible beginning in the eighth century BCE, this alternative framework likewise acknowledges the stress on the agency of the spirit of Yahweh associated with individual and group experiences of trances, mental dissociation, charismatic powers, and wonder working as found in older prophetic materials in the historical books.[31] As Joseph Blenkinsopp insists, the older and newer prophetic traditions in the Hebrew Bible should not be dichotomized or separated.[32] Acknowledging this alternative framework decenters the typical prophetic discourse paradigm, and expands the semantic field and narrative configurations for construing the ways the Spirit of God and the Word of God are depicted in the scriptures and in theology, beyond a divine word given and message received. Most importantly, the two frameworks can work in tandem as laments and aspirations are engaged in relation to a message received and witness given. For Christian theology, this new framework places the identity and mission of the Spirit at the heart of the identity and mission of Jesus, prophet, Word made flesh, in relation to God, the source, the one addressed as Father, Abba.

What commands our attention in this dual orientation is that the prophet is beckoned to perceive, listen, and empathize from God's point of view, to participate in God's solidarity with a people and the created world in complex religious, social, and political situations, and from this vantage point to speak out in God's name to and for these people and the damaged world, and against destructive powers, in the interest of fuller life. The sources of laments are myriad, but laments are always sites of conflict between powers intent on destruction and desires and aspirations striving for flourishing, and for the fullness of life and relationships that yield love and reconciliation in truth. Biblical scholars such as David Aune give a great deal of attention to the literary forms of prophetic utterance—judgment, salvation, assurance, admonition, and trial,[33] but this equally basic struggle for life over death is always a focal point for the divine calling of the prophet and derivatively of all God's prophetic people.

This alternative framework incorporates important contributions made by Martin Buber, Abraham Joshua Heschel, and Walter Brueggemann. For Buber, "out of the depth of the community's suffering there arises the conception of God as 'the God of sufferers.'"[34] This is the basic impulse of prophetic faith and discourse. Heschel speaks of a prophet's identification with the pathos of God and the laments of the people of God through the realization that "Israel's suffering is God's grief."[35] For Brueggemann prophetic criticism takes place in situations of crisis and "begins in the capacity to grieve," while the prophetic challenge is to energize through a work of the imagination that evokes repentance, courage, resistance, and hope.[36] Almost two decades later he described the situation of the prophets in this way:

> Prophets characteristically perceive their time and place as a circumstance of crisis, a context in which dangers are great and life-or-death decisions must be made. Or perhaps it is better to say that the appearance and utterances of the prophets *evokes* [sic] a crisis circumstance where none had been perceived previously. That is, the prophets not only respond to crisis, but by their abrupt utterance, they generate crisis. . . . They speak in images and metaphors that aim to disrupt, destabilize, and invite to alternative perception of reality [specifically through] the power of imagination . . . to construe, picture, and imagine reality outside of the dominant portrayals of reality that have been taken as givens.[37]

In her most recent work, Sandra Schneiders has built on Brueggeman's insights, explicitly arguing that "prophetic witness . . . involves two interrelated moments."

> First, by public lament the prophets try to pierce the numbness, the "royal consciousness," the sense that things have to be the way they are, which oppressed regimes generate to legitimate the domination system. . . . Second, the prophets strive to energize hope against the helpless despair of the people who succumb to this "royal consciousness" which makes the oppressive status quo, no matter how unjust, appear to be "the only game in town."[38]

Schneider's delineation of two dimensions of prophecy is similar to the two frameworks I have developed, but there are differences. She emphasizes the active role of the prophet as one who laments (which corresponds to the classical view of prophetic denunciation) and the active role of the prophet as one who energizes hope (which corresponds to the classical view of prophetic proclamation). By contrast, my two frameworks are intended to differentiate the obedience of the prophet to the laments of people and the groaning of creation, and the obedience of the prophets to the message of denunciation and consolation as a word and imagined vision conveyed by means of proclamation and witness. The word-centered approach emphasizes the vertical axis of prophetic obedience to God's transcendent message, whereas a horizontal axis predominates in the lament-centered approach. Together, these two approaches contribute to a richer comprehension of prophetic obedience, inviting a fuller understanding of the nature of prophetic discipleship, vocation, and sense of mission. At the heart of this approach to prophecy is an appreciation of Jesus's prophetic calling and mission as responsiveness both to the laments of others and to a message that announces the power of God to give life and to overcome destruction and death.

What Prophetic Obedience Requires

Drawing on these two complementary frameworks for understanding prophecy, I wish to delineate distinctive features of prophetic discipleship in terms of the constitutive ingredients involved in prophetic obedience. I am concentrating on the obedience of the prophets because I am interested in highlighting how one lives the life of prophetic discipleship by identifying the traits, practices, and orientations that distinguish such a life. I will not explore here all the commonly identified qualities, convictions, and agendas associated with prophecy. The traits that I will consider all find their source and significance in prophetic figures and writings in the Hebrew and Christian scriptures, and I am particularly interested in interpreting them through the prism provided by key motifs from the documents of Vatican II that bear on the prophetic anointing and mandate shared in myriad ways by all the faithful. I take this approach in the interest of deepening and developing this cherished retrieval achieved at Vatican II.

What differentiates the prophetic character of obedience from the basic understanding of Christian obedience? We can begin by considering a common-sense understanding of obedience that entails one person's complying with the will of another who is in a position of power and authority—be it parental, social, political, or religious. Jews, Christians, and Muslims speak of obedience to God's will as it is mediated by the dictates of texts and codified practices as interpreted by religious leaders, by conscience, or through other forms of mystical or communal experiences.

Christian obedience understood in terms of the primary schema entails submitting to God, who communicates God's purposes and desires through a word proclaimed and interpreted by designated charismatic or institutional leadership. These leaders are named in the Pauline tradition as prophets, apostles, and teachers (1 Cor 12:28). Over the first three centuries in the Common Era the emerging church identified certain leaders as overseers (*episkope*), commissioned as teachers and guardians of the apostolic heritage of faith against false teachers (associated, for example, with Gnosticism and the prophetic movement called Montanism).[39] These overseers were ordained presbyter-bishops and identified as apostolic teachers.[40] Bishops came to be associated with the magisterium or the so-called teaching office of bishops, and Vatican II correlated this office with the exercise of the prophetic office of Jesus Christ.

Christian obedience within this frame of reference thus corresponds to the reception of, and adherence to, a revealed word of God as it is communicated through officially recognized channels in the church, namely, scriptures, creeds, and the authoritative teachings of bishops. This form of obedience also acknowledges a place for personal receptivity and deference to God's communication of God's word through mystical experiences and/or one's conscience, for the sake of one's own vocation and sometimes for the good of the church and the world.[41]

Very important for the argument being advanced here, Justin Martyr and Irenaeus, following the Pentecost tradition found in the Acts of the Apostles, assert that the gift of the Spirit, associated with the prophetic charism, and the prophetic recognition of the apostolic Word of God, has been handed on from Jews to the Christian faithful, and is active in the church's discerning of the truth of the gospel and the mission of the church.[42] Following this line of thought, later theologians have argued that all the faithful receive a prophetic gift and have a certain role as bearers and guardians of the apostolic heritage against false prophets. So, in the nineteenth century, John Henry Newman and Orthodox theologian Alekei Khomiakov drew special attention to the role of the lay faithful as crucial guardians of the faith received, a role they regarded as a manifestation of the prophetic office shared by the entire church.[43] Thus it is not only bishops who safeguard or who hold members of the church accountable for maintaining the living apostolic heritage. The laity, also anointed by the Spirit, must cultivate their own prophetic practices of guardianship and calling to accountability. Thus, all of the faithful join the bishops and theologians in the prophetic task of applying and developing deeper insight into the gift of faith they share.[44] The prophetic office places a responsibility on each individual believer to exercise obedience by receiving and witnessing to the Word of God handed on by the entire apostolic church community, under the apostolic leadership of the episcopacy. The gift of this prophetic office with its summons to prophetic obedience also serves as the impetus and rationale for collaboration among the laity, bishops, and theologians in discerning the faith of the church and the church's mission.

Turning to the second framework of the prophetic office that I have identified, Christian obedience further requires heeding, receiving, and responding to the voice of the Spirit in the aspirations and laments of God's people and God's created world. Looking at obedience in this way makes explicit what is implied in the first framework, by drawing attention to the variety of ways God's self-communication occurs beyond proclamation and witness in word and sacrament and official leadership. To be attentive and receptive to officially recognized texts, practices, and designated leaders, it becomes clear, is necessary but not sufficient. One must also heed, receive, and respond to the aspirations and laments discovered in oneself; in the various communities of which we are a part; and in the world's social, political, economic, and environmental realms. God's self-communication is thus encountered in the I, the we, and the globe.[45] In particular, attentiveness to laments as a medium of the voice of the Spirit heightens one's consciousness of interruptions in ecclesial tradition, in turn making the role of critical questions and resistance to various official norms religiously meaningful. In this regard, prophetic obedience entails a process of discerning the soundings of Word and Spirit in order to reach judgments and make decisions about what is true and righteous about one's stance in the world. Prophetic obedience as discernment entails cultivating attentiveness, receptivity, and deliberative responsiveness to the various voices and claims within this web of relations.

By the end of the twentieth century it was more common, if still contested, to contrast a hierarchical, patriarchal, and paternalistic model of authority and obedience with a more egalitarian and dialogical model. The former has been associated with the exercise of power over other people, a hierarchical teaching church and the taught lay members of the church, and the latter approach identified with the empowerment of members to freely advance the church's mission. As Sandra Schneiders points out, many twentieth-century events contributed to the reconsideration of authority and obedience: the atrocities of Nazi Germany and manifestation of authoritarian personalities in various forms of modern totalitarianism; the civil rights movement, the feminist movement, the anti–Vietnam War movement, liberation theologies, and in the midst of all of these, an escalating critique of hierarchical triumphalism and clericalism in the Catholic Church during the post–Vatican II era.[46]

After Vatican II, vowed male and female religious were called upon to reflect on the practice of the vow of obedience in their personal lives, and in the lives of their religious congregations. Before the council, vowed religious were widely regarded as having a higher calling than the laity, their dedication to the counsels of perfection through poverty, chastity, and obedience making them different in kind from the lay faithful who were called, simply, to "the obedience of faith."[47] Vatican II's affirmation of the universal call to holiness challenged this long-held framework for differentiating vowed religious and the laity. There slowly emerged the realization that the personal and collective discernment processes of vowed religious were comparable to practices of laypeople engaged in the church's apostolic mission by promoting works of mercy and work for justice, and in many forms of lay ecclesial ministry. This new awareness led many to join a rallying cry for the liberation of the laity from paternalism and clericalism.[48]

Sandra Schneiders has emphasized the prophetic character of the religious lifeform as distinct from that of all the faithful. She concludes from her study of the Christian scriptures that the early followers of Jesus understood him as a prophet, amidst the many other claims made about him, and that the disciples are portrayed as people summoned to live in a similarly prophetic manner. Schneiders articulates this point employing the primary framework of prophecy as word received and witness given.

> The itinerant band of followers who accompanied Jesus during his public life and were commissioned by him after his Resurrection to continue his mission were initiated into Jesus' own prophetic ministry by Jesus himself. Many ministries of the word, such as apostleship, evangelization, and teaching developed in the early Church and there was much overlapping among them. All of them had a prophetic dimension though each was specified by distinctive goals. . . . Religious Life, as the lifeform most closely modeled on that of Jesus's original itinerant band, also involves participation in these various forms of ministry of the word. But I want to suggest that one of those ministries, prophecy, is central to and defining of the Religious lifeform as it was of Jesus' pre-Easter ministerial life.[49]

For Schneiders, prophetic obedience is a defining characteristic of the prophetic vocation, charism, and spirituality that shapes the lifeform of religious congregations of women and men.[50] She is not the only scholar to make such a claim, and, in fact, this is a conviction voiced by Pope Francis; but hers is the most developed form of the argument at present.[51] It needs to be clearly understood, however, that Schneiders likewise recognizes the prophetic character of all the faithful, as does Pope Francis.

> As a Christian lifeform Religious Life must be understood first and fore-most, as sharing the common Christian heritage which is distinct and recognizable without claiming to be either separate or superior. . . . All Christians, by baptism, are incorporated into Christ and share in his identity as Son of God and his mission as prophet, priest, and king. . . . Individual Christians live this identity and mission in different ways, but the differences consist more in the way they constellate, emphasize, and witness publicly to the various dimensions of this universal Christian vocation, rather than in the presence of specific elements in some voca-tions and their absence in others.[52]

In keeping with Schneiders's differentiated viewpoint, but in contrast to her concentration on religious life, I am drawing out the implications of the prophetic character of all the faithful and the importance of prophetic obedience for the faithful in personal and communal discernment, particularly as these are manifested in the local church through participatory structures of governance—councils and synods, and through the local church's involvement in advancing grassroots democ-racy. Prophetic obedience differentiates a self-consciously missionary form of discipleship. This missionary form pertains not only or primarily to vowed members of religious congregations—even though in their resolute mission orientations, these men and women no doubt provide some of its most inspiring illustrations—but to all the faithful.

It is precisely this feature of the prophetic office of all the faithful that merits much greater attention in Catholic teachings and practice. The official commu-nion ecclesiology of the Catholic Church has privileged the prophetic office of the episcopacy in teaching as this correlates with prophetic obedience by the people of God to the bishops' teaching (LG, 12). This approach to the prophetic charism and prophetic obedience is at the expense of a broader understanding of the prophetic obedience of all the faithful involved in the process of personal and collective discernment and deliberation. In fact, far more attention needs to be given to how the universal call to prophetic obedience, witness, and authoritative guardianship of the faith is practiced by all the faithful, by theologians, and by bishops personally and collectively. This is one facet of the challenge of clarifying the meaning and practice of prophetic obedience amidst multiple voices in the church and world.

I will now attempt to describe prophetic discipleship and prophetic obedience in terms of the following traits that are shared by all the baptized. Together, these traits identify what Pope Francis had called missionary discipleship. Prophetic discipleship and prophetic obedience distinguish all the baptized people of God, whether lay or ordained. They mark the prophetic office of all the faithful people. There also exist certain more-specific prophetic charisms and offices in the church. Everyone is called to share in the priestly, prophetic, and kingly offices of Jesus Christ through mission in daily life, but not all have a particular prophetic ministry—whether the teaching office of the bishops, the professional teaching function of theologians, or the role of prophetic discernment exercised by lay ecclesial ministries and designated lay leaders in the church or in civil society. All leaders in these specific prophetic roles are duty bound not only to consult the faithful, but also to be in active relationship with them—in worship, as collaborators in works of mercy and work for justice, and in the variety of evangelical missionary activities. The traits that I will differentiate below are shared by all the baptized and should inform their mission in daily life, but certain special prophetic offices, functions, and messages carry with them a burden of collaborative leadership with, and for, all the faithful and accountable to them.

Discernment as the Decisive Dimension

Prophets practice discernment about their calling and mission in relation to the concrete conditions of religious, social, and political life. Of course, people in every walk of life practice discernment as they make decisions large or small. But I am suggesting that the term *prophetic obedience* differentiates a personal and collective process of discernment whereby individuals or groups reach judgments and decisions that bear on the mystical and political, the sacramental and the social character of Christian life.

The topic of discernment in Christianity has a long history of interpretation in numerous influential scriptural, theological, and philosophical sources. I will highlight the importance of prophetic discernment in Hebrew and Christian scriptures, most prominently in efforts to distinguish true from false prophets and true from false prophecies. Early Christian authors who considered "the discernment of spirits" (1 Cor 12:10), as Paul commended, did not always make this connection with prophecy. I will thus comment briefly on various traditions that have contributed to the Christian understanding of discernment, including those that do not speak about discernment in terms of prophecy, in the interest of arguing that these diverse trajectories of thought can contribute to a fuller approach to prophetic obedience.

According to scripture scholar Joseph Blenkinsopp, the need to differentiate between true and false prophets arose at times when prophecy became associated with violence, warfare, and religious crusades. The ideological distortion of prophecy in various times and places gave rise to the need to determine what is socially acceptable and religiously legitimate by means of "a 'discerning of spirits' by the society or that segment of it addressed by the prophet."[53]

In his book *Prophecy and Discernment* R. W. L. Moberly investigates key scriptural passages in search of criteria for critically discerning prophetic authenticity. He identifies these criteria by examining five examples of biblical prophets engaged in discernment. First, Jeremiah discerns that the prophets of Samaria are false for three reasons: (1) their lack of moral integrity, (2) their failure to bring about genuine conversion to God, and (3) the realization that the alleged prophet's message is his or her own and not one received from "the council of the Lord" (23:9–22).[54] Second, the prophet Micaiah ben Imlah advises the king contrary to the views of four hundred prophets in 1 Kings (22:1–38) and exemplifies the application of the criteria of discernment. The moral integrity and courage of the prophet reveal receptivity to "the council of the Lord," which results in ultimate, if dubious, effectiveness. Third, Moberly contrasts Elisha's ability, in the midst of historical ambiguity, to discern that he will succeed Elijah (2 Kings 2:1–18), with Balaam who struggles to discern (Nm 22:1–35).[55] In the New Testament, Moberly considers, fourth, the text from the First Letter of John: "Do not believe every spirit, but test the spirits to see whether they are from God; for many false prophets have gone out into the world" (1 Jn 4); and, fifth, from Paul's First Letter to the Thessalonians: "Do not quench the Spirit. Do not despise the words of prophets, but test everything; hold fast to what is good; abstain from every form of evil" (5:19–22). Based on his study of these texts, Moberly draws the conclusion that "for the (would-be) prophet there are two prime criteria of discernment: on the one hand, disposition, character, and lifestyle; on the other hand, a message whose content and searching [. . .] reflect God's priorities and seek to engender unreserved engagement with God."[56]

Moberly concludes his study by acknowledging that there may be difficulties with these criteria: they may be too vague; run the risk of moral rigorism; offer few resources for "discerning speech for God in those of other faiths or no faith"; and provide few resources for those struggling to face chronic and new challenges associated with discrimination based on race, gender, and sexual orientation, and the transgenerational problems of poverty.[57] Had Moberly incorporated the alternate framework for identifying prophecy I have proposed, which requires heeding, receiving, and responding to the voice of the Spirit in the laments of suffering humanity and a damaged world, he could have accessed one of the distinctive features of prophetic discourse and action to advance his argument about the need to face, embrace, and engage these realities. Nevertheless, Moberly's conclusion that the need for discernment remains real, even though the results are not guaranteed, is entirely consistent with both frameworks for prophecy as I have delineated them here.[58]

The Christian understanding of prophetic discernment is deepened by considering a larger set of issues pertaining to Paul's use of the formula "discernment of spirits" (1 Cor 12:10) and the use of the Greek term διάκρισις (*diákrisis*)and the correlative Latin term *discretio* by theologians and ascetics in early Christianity. Joseph Lienhard analyzes the term *discernment of spirits* in exegetical commentaries on Paul's writings and in ascetical writings in Greek and Latin patristic literature. There the phrase is identified with a gift given to clergy or monks seeking, not to distinguish true from false prophets, but rather to perceive the influence of the good spirit over against evil spirits associated with the demonic, evil spirits that in the ascetical tradition eventually became associated or identified with the passions.[59] Lienhard detects no criteria for distinguishing the spirits in this exegetical literature. Rather he finds attention given to the mental or psychological experiences of calm and freedom in Origen, joy and confidence in Athanasius, the absence of doubt in Pachomius, and consolation resulting in love in Diadochus. "For the [Sayings of the Desert Fathers] *Apothegmata partum*, Cassian, and Benedict, discernment (not discernment of spirits) is a form of superior insight exercised in acting and deciding."[60] Although there is no apparent direct connection in this literature to discriminating between true and false prophets, the issue remains one of judgment and decision exercised by individuals and communities. The source of falsehood and deception might have shifted from an external source—the false prophet—to internal sources working through spiritual and personal powers, moral and psychological, but the decisive issue remains one of determining how to weigh evidence in matters that require discernment, even in the midst of disturbances, darkness, conflict, and ambiguity.

In *Discernment in the Desert Fathers*, Antony D. Rich traces how the Greek and Latin terms for discernment are used in the Septuagint, the Apocrypha, the New Testament, in Neo-Platonism, and in Origen's writings. Rich's aim is to lay the groundwork for clarifying the development of the meaning of discernment in the influential works of Evagrius Ponticus, John Cassian, and the the Sayings of the Desert Fathers.[61] He reaches the conclusion that "the term διάκρισις [*discretio* in Latin] among the Egyptian monks was a development of the biblical charism of διάκρισις πνευμάτων [discernment of spirits] *and* the wider concept of διάκρισις found in Scripture generally."[62] In Evagrius as in Athanasius, discernment of spirits is associated with wrestling with particular evil thoughts that have their source in particular evil spirits.[63] Cassian is credited with deepening and systematizing the Christian treatment of discernment.[64] There is a gradual move in Egyptian monasticism from speaking about discernment of spirits to treating discernment as an intellectual faculty of the soul or as practical wisdom (*phronesis*, prudence) associated with judgment. Though Lienhard's and Rich's studies make no reference to distinguishing true and false prophets, they surface pertinent issues by focusing on the role of rational insights and affective orientations in the struggle to discern between the divine life-giving spirit and destructive spirits in a discriminating manner that draws on practical wisdom associated with *phronesis* and prudence. These claims can contribute to a richer understanding of prophetic discernment and obedience.

The contribution of Ignatius of Loyola, widely recognized for developing the influential Rules for the Discernment of Spirits in his *Spiritual Exercises*, merits special attention. For Ignatius, discernment of spirits entails differentiating the calming, energizing, and encouraging power of spiritual consolation in human consciousness from the agitating and dissipating power of spiritual desolation. Consoling aspirations that are motivated by the love of God, or by hope, faith, and joy, can fruitfully inform one's life choices, just as frustrations, darkness, and turmoil can result in disorientation, disturbances, and compulsions that lead one away from God and the ways of love. The importance of cultivating an awareness and an understanding of affective movements of consolation and desolation in order to make wise decisions about major life choices and in everyday life motivated Ignatius to develop two sets of Rules for the Discernment of Spirits.

Although Ignatius never wrote about discernment in terms of prophetic obedience, it is not too difficult to consider how this theme is suggested in key moments in the *Spiritual Exercises* such as the Principle and Foundation (no. 23); The Call of the King (no. 91); the Two Standards (nos. 136–48); the Three Ways of Being Humble (nos. 165–67); Making an Election (nos. 169–89); and the Rules for Thinking, Judging, and Feeling with the Church (nos. 352–70). Such practices of meditation and contemplation can lead to radical commitments consistent with what many would describe as a prophetic way of life.

Although prophetic obedience or, interestingly, even the term *obedience* is not used in Ignatius's *Exercises*, the vow of obedience was explicitly treated in *The Constitutions of the Society of Jesus*, which he crafted.[65] There we read, "All should keep their resolution firm to observe obedience and to distinguish themselves in it, not only in the matters of obligation but also in the others, even though nothing else is perceived except the indication of the superior's will without an expressed command."[66] Obedience is practiced for the sake of "God our Creator and Lord" by observing the constitutions and obeying the command of the Pope and the superiors of the society "as if it were coming from Christ our Savior, since we are practicing the obedience to one in His place and because of love and reverence for Him" (no. 547). One is urged to "renounc[e] with blind obedience any contrary opinion and judgment of our own in all things which the superior commands and in which some species of sin cannot be judged to be present" (no. 547).[67]

Thus far, I have been searching for connections between prophecy and discernment as a decisive characteristic of what I am describing as prophetic obedience. The scriptural basis is substantive, but early Christian monks, ascetics, and theologians wrote of discernment or discernment of spirits without explicit reference to prophecy. These contrasting formulations and their diverse sources need not be judged antithetical, but rather as mutually enriching for a constructive formulation of discernment in relation to prophetic obedience.

A further contribution is offered by the renewed attention to communal modes of discernment among Jesuits under the influence of Vatican II. Beginning in the 1970s and following the lead of Pedro Arrupe, who at the time was superior general, Jesuits began to consider how Ignatius's Rules of Discernment could be applied in communal contexts. This effort corresponds with similar efforts among other congregations of religious life, particularly by congregations of women religious, for example, the Adrian Dominicans and the Sisters of Charity, who were at the forefront of developing communal models of discernment in the United States.[68] Writing in the early 1970s, George Ganss dramatically describes that shift in the church and in the Jesuits: "The Church—and consequently every diocese and religious institute within her—is now passing through a transition as momentous as that of the Reformation and the Council of Trent. She is moving from an era of authoritarianism, when most of the impulses came from the top downward in her no less than in the civil commonwealths under absolute monarchs, to an epoch far more democratic, when most of the ideas and initiatives are coming from the members upward. . . . One manifestation of this trend toward increasingly democratic procedures in the Church is the growing use of 'communal discernment'—which in turn further stimulates democratization."[69]

Jesuit Dean Brackley, whose life and work were introduced in earlier chapters, reinterpreted Ignatius's *Exercises* in *The Call to Discernment in Troubled Times*, based on his own involvement in work for social justice and the cultivation of diverse cultural traditions through parish-based ministry in New York, and eventually in El Salvador in a university setting.[70] Nowhere in this book is obedience mentioned. Yet he speaks about Ignatius commending the importance of heeding affectivity in discernment, alongside of using reason in being responsive to the call of God in making life decisions. Brackley links this closely with the agency of the Spirit in prophetic discipleship, contending that "the work of the Holy Spirit—the Spirit that filled Jesus and all genuine prophets—has been chronically undervalued in Western Christianity, and Western culture has frequently denied the disclosive power of affectivity. Against this background, the [recent] rehabilitation of the second method [that follows affective movements of consolation and desolation] is certainly welcome. Ignatius considered it more reliable than the way of reason [alone]."[71] Brackley later comments,

> The Spirit that consoles is a prophetic spirit. The prophets of Israel were inspired (consoled) to denounce injustice and announce the coming of justice and peace. Jesus applied Isaiah's oracle to himself: "The Spirit of the Lord is upon me, because he has anointed me to bring good news to the poor" (Luke 4:18; cf. 3:22). This same Spirit now consoles Christ's disciples, inspiring them to speak and act for justice.[72]

Brackley's argument provides a crucial ingredient as we proceed.

Brackley's formula highlights only half the story: the prophetic Spirit is not only detected at work in moments of consolation, but also, as I have argued beginning in Chapter 3, in moments of desolation and agonistic struggle. This is why there is a need to heed the voice of the Spirit not only in consoling aspirations, but also in the desolation of the laments and struggles of people and a damaged world. Not every aspiration and every lament can be transposed into the key of Ignatian consolation and desolation, and this is another reason why these aspirations and laments call for prophetic discernment at personal and communal levels. As Ignatius concedes, there can be false lights in consolation, to which it should be added that God can be at work in the darkness and conflict associated with lamentations.

The prominence given to attending to consolation and desolation in the discernment of spirits by Ignatius of Loyola and his later followers can be reformulated into a precept I have learned from colleagues in Germany and Austria: "passionate engagements and disturbances take precedence."[73] This is true in the personal and communal discernment that shapes a life of prophetic discipleship and mission.

Prophetic Obedience Is Not Blind Obedience

Sandra Schneiders introduces our second trait: "Discernment based on attentive listening, not submission to the will of another, is the essence of prophetic obedience."[74] Some may wish to argue that there are cases when prophetic obedience includes submission to the will of another, not only obedience to God mediated through a personal discerning process that includes the exercise of conscience, but also the submission to a religious officeholder such as a bishop, provincial, or local religious leader. But as Schneiders argues, prophetic obedience cannot be blind obedience. "There is no avoiding the challenge and the obligation of discernment, and 'blind obedience,' that is, uncritical submission to power, is neither discernment nor obedience—nor can it ever be a substitute for either."[75] This is true not only for vowed religious, but for all the faithful.

Following Schneiders's lead, what more might one say about prophetic obedience as the antithesis of blind obedience? Early Christian approaches to obedience to hierarchical leadership in the Christian church and in society were influenced by ancient Jewish, Greek, and Roman civilizations, and these influences find some expression in calls for unhesitating obedience in the New Testament. Paul's letter to the Romans states, "Let every person be subject to governing authorities; for there is no authority except from God, and those authorities that exist have been instituted by God. Therefore whoever resists authority resists what God has appointed, and those who resist will incur judgment" (13:1–2). Deutero-Pauline letters insist that "wives be submissive to your husbands as you do to the Lord" (Eph 5:22; Col 3:18). In 1 Peter we read, "servants be submissive to your masters" (2:18). These indications of civic, familial, gender, and ultimately racial forms of subservience reflect hierarchical forms of social relationship that also shaped the understanding of obedience in the Christian church. Such passages must ultimately be considered in relation to Jesus's prophetically critical stance toward certain priestly, religious, and civic institutions and modes of authority.

The statement commending blind obedience to religious superiors found in the constitutions of the Society of Jesus, a formulation also associated with the vow of obedience made by men and women religious in cloistered and apostolic life, offers a particularly stark expression. Though the term *blind obedience* is not widespread in early Christianity, unhesitating obedience to religious superiors is commonplace in classic formulas from ascetic monastic communities dating back to the fourth and fifth centuries. In practicing discernment, novices in religious communities were trained to cultivate humility and indifference by being obedient to religious superiors in the religious community. The Egyptian monks taught that one learns the ways of discernment by being obedient to elders in the religious community. Anthony Rich explains that for John Cassian, "within a monastery monks were not allowed to direct their own lives or those of others until they had been accomplished in practical disciplines and learnt obedience and humility."[76] Novices and disciples learned discretion initially by not trusting their own personal judgment and discernment, but rather relying on the discretion of elders. One thereby resists vicious inclinations within the self and diabolic temptations from without, which, under certain circumstances, can be manifested as an angel of light (2 Cor 11:14). This sometimes entails extreme forms of obedience. "Novices were required to gain permission to carry out even the most trivial actions and would, as if commanded by God himself, attempt impossible or futile tasks without hesitation if asked to do so."[77] As Rich illustrates, "a teacher often tested the extent to which a disciple had renounced self-will by instructing him to do bizarre things, even to break [religious] disciplines."[78] Such a high regard for obedience in religious life, even if not as extreme in formulation, finds classic expression in *The Rule of St. Benedict* and *The Rule of St. Augustine*. These traditions laid the groundwork for the understanding of the religious vows of obedience, poverty, and chastity as these shaped later traditions of religious congregations.

By contrast, prophets are frequently portrayed as critics of religious and political authority, and prophetic obedience as the antithesis of blind obedience. Following the teachings of the Hebrew scriptures, prophets are described as critics of institutional intransigence, moral and legal scrupulosity, and sacramental formalism in situations of idolatry and injustice. In the twentieth century, and for Catholics especially after Vatican II, this understanding undergirded prophetic impulses to criticize ecclesial triumphalism, paternalism, clericalism, and various forms of privilege associated with differences in race, gender, and sexual orientation. The Jesuits, in particular, wrestled with the ways that following the call for blind obedience in their constitution may run the risk of relinquishing the "judgment, responsibility, and initiative" required of discernment, and undermining the legitimate use of human reason and freedom in decision making by conceding control to authority figures, doctrines, norms, or structures.[79] This became a common topic of concern among congregations of religious women and men after the council.

While we think of blind obedience to individual authorities or external norms, there is a collectivist corollary in which blind obedience entails succumbing to a mob mentality, where one follows a group without thinking for oneself and standing up for one's own convictions. Prophets are thus identified with taking stands against religious and civic leaders but also against power elites and mob rule that exercises destructive powers.[80]

Yet the exercise of prophetic obedience is not antithetical to the exercise of leadership and authority in religious and civic communities. Prophecy and priesthood are sometimes placed in opposition, yet prophetic figures like Jeremiah and

Ezekiel were themselves priests. Prophetic people of conscience have been wise counselors to political and social leaders and collaborators in communities, but they are also people who offer reality checks, and are not afraid to raise difficult questions or offer criticisms based on their perceptions of unacknowledged problems or the abuse of power.[81]

Individuals and communities who have cultivated prophetic obedience can be wise advisors and collaborators with people who choose to exercise authority and leadership in relational ways. Prophetic obedience, thus, is the antithesis of blind obedience to institutional authorities in the church and in society. And yet, as we will explore below, it is not that prophetic discipleship eschews traditions and authorities; rather it requires a discerning posture toward them.

Prophetic disciples must also always be vigilant against a mob mentality associated with certain forms of social or religious collectivism or communitarianism. Prophetic obedience cannot be reduced to *vox populorum est vox Dei* understood in terms of majority rule, poll results, or even a model of consensus that offers no role for a loyal opposition and the dissenter.[82] Ecclesial synods and councils and democratic civic deliberations must always be on guard against a mob mentality that hinders the time needed for reason and passions to be clarified and plans of actions to be chosen wisely. In the final analysis prophetic obedience must stand the test of communal discernment.[83]

Prophetic obedience by means of personal and communal discernment requires particular attentiveness to individuals and groups whose voices and points of view have not been recognized. This will entail situations of conflict and struggle. In this vein, certain contemporary political theorists, such as Judith Butler and Bonnie Honig, have advanced an agonistic approach to democracy. In the words of Honig, an agonistic approach to democracy is based on a politics of lamentation, which does not succumb to the lamentation of politics, but rather engages in forms of communicative action in the struggle of democratic societies that make room for contentious debate and protest in the midst of advancing consensus building.[84] Prophetic discipleship and obedience, likewise, acknowledge the agonistic character of synodality in the church and democracy in society. Prophetic obedience leads to honesty about situations of conflict and accountability amidst efforts to work for consensus, and a perspective that is attuned to the role of differentiated consensus and dissensus in religious life and civil society.

A Prophetic Sense of Faith

In the teachings of Vatican II, the doctrines of the *sensus fidei* and the *sensus fidelium* are explicitly connected to a prophetic approach to personal discipleship and ecclesial communities.[85] As we have previously explored, *Lumen Gentium* (LG, 12) asserts that all those baptized participate, through the anointing of the Spirit, in the prophetic office of Jesus Christ. This prophetic office is particularly identified with the individual sense of the faith and the communal sense of the faithful, which provides the basis for consensus of the faithful.

The prophetic character of the *sensus fidei* and the *sensues fidelium* has usually and for good reason been advanced solely in terms of the primary schema for understanding prophecy: word received and witness given. In keeping with my proposal, however, I am arguing that the sense of the faith and the sense of the faithful are provided stronger biblical, theological, and practical moorings by including the alternative framework that requires attentive and receptive responses to the laments and aspirations of the people of God and the groaning of a damaged world.

Following the analysis of Ormond Rush and augmented by the work of John Burkhard, one can best describe the sense of the faith (*sensus fidei*) as the reception and apprehension of the apostolic faith by individuals made possible by the anointing of the Spirit of God in baptism.[86] This faith empowers prophetic discernment and obedience through the active imagination exploring how the reception of the gospel can have an impact on everyday existence and practice. This sense of the faith, following the primary schema, leads individuals to discern the truth of the gospel in their everyday lives. In keeping with the alternative framework, this entails attentiveness to the role of laments in personal, communal, and larger social and environmental dimensions of the life of faith. The prophetic apprehension of faith entails not only understanding, interpreting, and applying the faith professed, as Ormond Rush cogently argues, but also an awareness of how this faith is understood, interpreted, and applied in light of deeper and as yet undeveloped dimensions of the faith that may be detected in lamentations and in inchoate and deeply held, and yet unfulfilled, aspirations.[87]

The sense of the faithful is the collective recognition and reception of the faith through communal processes of discernment that is, following Rush again, evaluative and approbative, by which he means sanctioned by the community of faith. The sense of the faithful may be inchoate and at times implicit in the life of the church. However, it can become explicit by means of communal processes of discernment and the formation of emerging consensus.[88] If, as I have argued, prophetic obedience is the mark of an individual's maturing sense of the faith, the community's prophetic obedience requires collective processes of discernment of the faith and its practical implications. This is not simply a matter of articulating and witnessing to the faith of the church that is already professed. It also requires heeding the laments and aspirations of the people of God who share in this prophetic charism, not only practicing Catholics or Christians, but also "inactive, lapsed, marginalized, and disaffected Catholics" who "raise questions that may be a genuine call to greater fidelity to the Christian life."[89] The prophetic sense of the faith shared by all the faithful through baptism is emerging and maturing, and remains operative even when problems or troubling experiences arise in one's personal life or in the Christian church.

This understanding of divergence of opinion, or *dissensus*, among the faithful and with those on the margins of the faith community complicates efforts to commend and theorize the role of consensus in communal discernment. In fact, all that can be hoped for within the church, in ecumenical exchanges, and in the church's involvement in public life is a "differentiated consensus" that leaves room for critical prophetic dissent (*dissensus*) representing marginal, minority, peripheral voices and traditions.[90] Here I am in agreement with Rush's judgment that the sense of the faithful cannot be reduced to the sort of agreement imaged in Hans Georg Gadamer's metaphor of a "fusion of horizons" but must also embrace the dissensus suggested by Hans Robert Jauss's conception of a "differentiation of horizons."[91] It is invariably through such a differentiation of horizons that personal and communal conversions take place, between people with different worldviews and cultures reflective of different parts of the world, and composed of different groups based on race, ethnicity, class, gender, and sexual orientation. Pursuing this differentiation of horizons requires that positions and power relations be periodically renegotiated, and communal relations modified in the ongoing process of forming individuals and communities.

Heeding laments in the sense of the faith and in the sense of the faithful is not only correlated with a saving message to suffering people and to a creation damaged by human sin and the contingencies of existence. Heeding laments also helps disclose the struggle among the people of God to articulate authentically and witness honestly to the ongoing processes of clarifying the sense of the faith involved in the work of reception. In other words, the struggles of individuals and communities with the very substance of the faith can also be a part of the prophetic legacy working itself out in history. The laments and unrealized aspirations of the people of God can disclose the need for more fully receiving the testimony of faith in truth and in deed, but they can also reveal shortcomings and limitations of the Word received and ongoing and unfinished processes at work in the traditions of the faith community.

This position is reinforced by Karl Rahner's writings on the role of conflicts in the history of dogma and the future of theology, and by the testimony of countless theologians who have struggled with official teachings of the church.[92] To be quite concrete, consider the oft-repeated laments of the US faithful surrounding birth control, the failure of Catholic bishops and priests to speak out often enough prophetically against racism, or papal and curial resistance to open dialogue about the role of women in the church, about people with diverse sexual orientations, and about the various ways that religious pluralism enriches and influences people of Christian faith. The cacophony in the church on these issues needs to be understood in terms of the exercise of the prophetic office in the church, not only as a message faithfully received and witness given, but also in terms of the crucible of lamentations and aspirations in the agonistic transmission of the living faith of the church. This is precisely why the two prophetic frameworks must work in tandem both in ecclesiology and in the pastoral practices of the church.

Discerning Signs of the Times

Prophetic obedience requires discernment of the signs of the times. This formulation was one of the most important motifs in the documents of Vatican II. This Matthean turn of phrase (16:1–4) was commended at the council in four texts, most prominently in *Gaudium et Spes* (cited as GS).[93] The council documents did not explicitly link prophecy with the need to discern the signs of the times, but, as we will explore below, Marie-Dominique Chenu, one of the key theological experts involved in drafting these particular documents, perceived the connection. Prophets in the scriptures and throughout history have drawn attention to important signs of the times. In the aftermath of the council, the call to heed the signs of the times became associated with the rallying cry for greater interdisciplinary social analyses. These approaches were soon called into question by a few influential theologians for being sociologically reductionist and insufficiently theological.[94] Yet this allegation did not undermine the growing awareness in the church that to discern the signs of the times is properly identified with the prophetic charism and the prophetic character of discipleship and the church.

When the Matthean expression was initially introduced in the conciliar draft of *Gaudium et Spes*, some raised concerns about its precise meaning and suitability. The term had gained some currency among Protestants in the nineteenth century and Catholics in the twentieth century.[95] John XXIII's 1963 encyclical *Pacem in Terris* captured its meaning with a section subtitled "characteristics of the present day" in which he identified expressions of the signs of the times in the labor movement, the women's movement, and challenges posed to colonialism (nos. 39–43). Pope John used "Signs of the Times" as a subtitle in a later section that treated promising indications that in situations of conflict, nations and groups were pursuing negotiations rather than violence and warfare (nos. 126–29).

Historical theologian Marie-Dominique Chenu, an expert in the work of Thomas Aquinas and a proponent of the social activism associated with the "see, judge, and act" method of Joseph Cardijn's version of Catholic Action, came to play a pivotal role in the discussion on the signs of the times in the commission that drafted *Gaudium et Spes*.[96] Despite concerns raised by bishops, by theological experts not on that particular commission, and by ecumenical observers, the expression made its way into the conciliar document.[97] The text reads, "In every age, the church carries the responsibility of reading the signs of the times and of interpreting them in the light of the gospel, if it is to carry out its task" (GS, 4). In every generation, this responsibility requires that the church communicate with people about their yearnings and concerns about dramatic developments in history. This agenda is closely identified with the need for discernment. "The people of God believes that it is led by the Spirit of the Lord who fills the whole world. Impelled by that faith, they try to discern the true signs of God's presence and purpose in the events, the needs and the desires which it shares with the rest of humanity" (GS, 11). Later the document explains who is involved in this discernment: "With the help of the holy Spirit, it is the task of the whole people of God, particularly of its pastors and theologians, to listen to and distinguish the many voices of our times and to interpret them in the light of God's word"(GS, 44). The Decree on the Ministry and Life of Priests (*Presbyterorum Ordinis* [cited as PO]) drew out the implication of this logic for local clergy who are urged to "be willing to listen to lay people, give brotherly consideration to their wishes, and recognize their experience and competence in the different fields of human activity. In this way they will be able to recognize along with them the signs of the times" (PO, 9). This requires "testing the spirits to discover if they be of God" (PO, 9). This particular conciliar text thus juxtaposes and indeed links the phrase *signs of the times* with the need to test the spirits associated with prophetic discernment (1 Jn 4:1, cf. 1 Thes 5:20–21).

After the council, Chenu drew explicit attention to the prophetic character of assessing the signs of the times by people who are "realists" immersed in history and struggling to engage reality.

> In humanity's progress forward, the significance of these characteristic events is first perceived clearly by men [and women] who are so immersed in their community that they read its destiny by a full intuitive grasp of each succeeding generation. These prophets do not accomplish this by carefully thought-out analyses, but by a deep-rooted communion with the hopes of these people. The "signs" are the focal points for their perception. They will be primary elements through which these prophets will offer their testimony. . . . In all these cases, the prophet is more of a realist than the scholar because he reads into history. He sees the signs of the times that lie beyond simple statements of principle.[98]

As Chenu expresses so clearly, prophetic attentiveness to the signs of the times and the aspirations of the people of God demands people who are realists. Three theologians have called for a similar kind of awareness in the wake of Chenu's work. Most closely affiliated with Chenu is Edward Schillebeeckx, a fellow Dominican, student of St. Thomas Aquinas, and fellow expert at the council, who at one point in his career after the council called for disciples of Jesus to wrestle with "the refractoriness of reality." This refractoriness comes to light when people attend to negative contrast experiences, a philosophical corollary to the discourse of lamentation. Negative contrast experiences elicit questions about the way reality is interpreted in society and in the church and can elicit prophetic resistance when these interpretations are not engaging reality in the interest of promoting human wholeness.[99]

Ignacio Ellacuría offered his own summons for Christians to face reality based on his experience in El Salvador; his thought, as well, can be brought to bear on our approach to the task of discerning the signs of the times. In the words of Ellacuría, "Confronting . . . reality has a threefold dimension: (1) becoming aware of the weight of reality; (2) taking up the weight of reality; and (3) taking charge of the weight of reality."[100] To do this, individuals and communities must develop (1) a cognitive awareness of the complexity of reality, (2) an ethical responsibility toward reality, and (3) a praxis-oriented intelligence necessary to confront and engage reality. Reality is weighty for Ellacuría not only because it cannot be faced in an idealistic manner or by imposing a meaning on it, but also because of its materiality, its historical character, its complexity and density, and because it is both graced and sinful.[101]

Based on this orientation to facing reality, Ellacuría developed a Christian theology of utopia and propheticism. The prophetic approach requires being located in the proper place—"if it is to be realistic and fruitful, [one] must be situated in precise geo-socio-temporal coordinates."[102] Ellacuría distinguishes propheticism (*profetismo*) and prophecy (*lo profética*), which certain commentators explain in this way: "Propheticism implies something beyond the discrete word or act of prophecy; it refers to an integrated and integrating vision, a structuring principle, a way of life."[103] The historical reality of Latin America provided a *topos* for Ellacuria's approach to propheticism and utopia. While utopias are often understood as an ideal place set in opposition to a difficult and corrupt place and space, for Ellacuría the Christian utopia provides a horizon, an imaginative framework, or a "social imaginary," to use Charles Taylor's formulation, within which historical reality can unfold through praxis. Utopia is not a place that is never realized, but rather a place that is historically coming into existence. Though there are times when Ellacuría appears nearly to identify the reign of God with this utopia, he keeps them distinct. As Michael Lee explains, "Despite this ambiguity, it seems that Ellacuría names as utopia that Christian imagination, rooted in revelation and the tradition, which attempts to name and identify the contours of the Reign without equating that imagination with the actual Reign of God. . . . [T]he concretizing (*concreción*) of utopia is the historicizing of the Reign of God, an activity that occurs in both hearts and structures."[104] This concretizing process always involves the struggle of facing reality, mindful of the power dynamics involved.

More recently Hans-Joachim Sander, in his commentary on *Gaudium et Spes*, has advanced a theology of the signs of the times reformulated in light of the theories of contemporary French philosophers, especially Michel Foucault's views on "*heterotopie*"—the place of the other.[105] Sander's approach acknowledges the agonistic struggle involved in creating space for nondominating power dynamics to operate in diverse social situations. *Heterotopie*, the place of the other, for Sander provides a necessary vantage point to assess the diversity of the signs of the times in the plurality of local churches vis-à-vis the new awareness of the world church and the challenge of creating strategies that can address shifting situations and institutions. Taking this heterotopic perspective can provide imaginative strategies for offering resistance, promoting change, and creating the conditions for vigilance and hope. Such a heterotopian theology of the signs of the times admits what Zygmunt Bauman calls the precarious liquidity of the present, the relativity, in the globalized church. Sander argues that there is a need for "a change of place" from a utopian theology that tries to escape this precarious liquidity by offering an inflexible apocalypse, to a heterotopian theology of the signs of the times, which admits no power over time. Such "heterotopian places reveal mechanisms of exclusion and practices of discipline and in doing so, relativize utopian power-claims . . . [Consequently] one is compelled suddenly to realize a precarious presence that one can simply

not avoid."[106] This intervention by Sander offers, I believe, a trajectory of imagination, thought, and action that intersects with, rather than repudiates, Ellacuría's
approach to propheticism and utopia. Sander, like Ellacuría, works to develop more
textured and complex theoretical approaches to the plurality of times and spaces.
This is precisely what is required to more adequately assess shifting patterns of
religious involvement in the ongoing challenges facing refugees and migrants, in
the residual effects of colonialism and empire building, in the legacy of slavery, in
sexism, in heteronormativity, and in various forms of corruption and diversion in
the church—triumphalism, paternalism, and clericalism.

A Commitment to Mission as Prophetic Dialogue

The mission of the prophet is not usually associated with dialogue. More often
it is associated with a prophetic diatribe, which is hard to imagine as a conversation
starter. At its most belligerent, the prophetic tradition represents hostility toward
the nations and the outsider, which can be associated with the following ideology:
"Yahweh intends to displace and destroy the 'seven nations' in order to make room
for Israel in 'the land of promise.'"[107] This trope is exemplified in the traditions of
Deuteronomy (12:29–30; cf. Deut 4:38, 7:22, 8:20, 11:23) but also is found, as
Brueggemann has argued, in the Moses-Joshua-Deuteronomy traditions. Such a
model of royal sovereignty is not unheard of in Christian circles; it certainly flourished under the banner of the Constantinian Empire.

A variant tradition in the Hebrew scriptures paves a way for a theology of
mission in its outreach to other nations (see Gn 12–36; Ex 19:5–6; Is 42:6–7,
49:6–9). According to this trajectory, the nations can be blessed and join in praise
and obedience of God with Israel (such as Is 2:2–5; cf. Mi 4:1–4).

In the Christian scriptures, Jesus fulfills a prophetic mission by calling people
to judgment—"The time is fulfilled, and the kingdom of God has come near,
repent, and believe in the good news" (Mk 1:15). Jesus's primary audience is
Jewish and the prophetic mandate here is clear: adhere to the covenant and the
Torah. Yet Jesus's primary prophetic message about God's reign is not diatribe.
Rather he is often depicted as a prophet-like figure anointed by the Spirit to
listen to those lamenting and those aspiring for more. His parables, aphorisms,
and behavior embody Jesus's response to these laments and aspirations in the form
of a prophetic message, but the message is often delivered in a dialogical idiom
and style. His parables and aphorisms, even when they have prophetic rhetorical
punch, seem part of a conversation. So, for example, the lawyer asks Jesus, "good
teacher . . . what must I do to inherit eternal life?" (Lk 18:18). Jesus offers the
textbook prophetic answer: "love the Lord your God with all your heart, and
with all your soul, and with all your strength, and with all your mind, and your
neighbor as yourself" (Lk 10:27). The questioner asks a further question: who is
my neighbor? And Jesus again responds, by telling the story of hospitality to the
outsider, someone from another nation, racial group, ethnic community. Religious

officials and elites fall short in the story, but the Samaritan exemplifies someone living out the heart of the gospel.

Jesus's dialogical style can also be heard in many gospel parables and aphorisms. In these prophetic exchanges he often challenges people's expectations and their priorities. What's last is first, the outsiders should be welcomed inside, it is not something outside you that you eat that defiles you but what comes out of you. This is classic prophetic wisdom, but in dialogical form. Jesus's sage prophetic interventions are embodied in deed as well as in word: it is Jesus's table fellowship with the outcasts and public sinners that most clearly embodies Jesus's dialogical style of prophetic mission.

I have mentioned these contrasting scriptural impulses in our understanding of the mission of the prophet in order to offer a preliminary justification for speaking about mission in terms of prophetic dialogue. My inspiration for this line of argument comes from the Divine Word Missionaries (*Societas Verbi Divini* [SVD]), the world's largest congregation of male religious engaged in missionary work, who came to think of their work in terms of prophetic dialogue. This collective conviction has been articulated and further developed by Stephen Bevans and Roger Schroeder, both members of the SVD congregation. Their work follows the Fifteenth General Chapter of the SVD completed in July 2000.[108] The SVD's formulations draw especially from the primary framework for understanding prophecy in terms of a message received and witness given. However, I believe that we can also detect in their proposals the second framework, heeding the Spirit in the laments and unfulfilled aspirations of people and the world, which offers a complementary schema for articulating more comprehensively the dialogical character of mission that they develop.

The SVD chapter delegates identified four missionary situations that called for prophetic dialogue as characterizing the *ad gentes* missionary charism: "primary evangelization and re-evangelization, commitment to the poor and marginalized, cross-cultural witness, and interreligious understanding" (no. 52; cf. no. 76). Choosing not to speak of the frontiers of mission, which can imply colonialist aspirations, the delegates came to speak of four missionary situations of dialogue. Dialogue, they perceived, privileges forging relationships in mission rather than focusing solely on proclamation of the gospel or evangelization. Missionaries enter into dialogue as companions with others on the journey of life in a suffering world, in "solidarity, respect, and love" (GS, 3), not as people with the answers. "Limited as we are by our personal and cultural viewpoints, none of us has attained the whole truth contained in God and revealed fully in Christ. In dialogue we search together for this truth" (SVD, no. 53). Acknowledging their own sinfulness and need for ongoing conversion, the delegates also affirm that, "we witness to God's love by sharing our own convictions boldly and honestly, especially where that love has been obscured by prejudice, violence, and hate." But why call this dialogue prophetic? "It is clear that we do not dialogue from a neutral position, but out of our own faith. Together with our dialogue partners we hope to hear the voice of the Spirit of God calling us forward, and in this way our dialogue can become prophetic" (SVD, no. 54).

The Divine Word Missionaries underscore the importance of communal discernment in this process, and the need to heed the voice of the Spirit. As their document states,

> It is true that the Spirit often speaks through the creative insights of individuals, but we are convinced that such intuitions need to be tested in community, where our charism and tradition can be brought into the discernment process. Obviously the struggle involved in striking a balance between individual and communal discernment will remain. But communal deliberations, both within our religious community and with the people we serve, do often become the real touchstone of a Spirit-inspired insight (no. 7).

Here one detects a vision of prophetic obedience: "we need to continue to listen to the Spirit so as to know and do the will of the triune God. We are convinced that when we enter into dialogue with others, we surrender ourselves to God" (SVD, no. 109).

Bevans and Schroeder develop this model by speaking of six facets of mission: "the various elements involved in an understanding of mission today—witness and proclamation, liturgical action and contemplation, inculturation, interreligious dialogue, working for justice and commitment to reconciliation—all contribute to a missionary practice that is both dialogical and prophetic, faithful to contemporary context as well as the constants of Christian faith."[109] They explain, "Mission is dialogue. It takes people where they are; it is open to their traditions and culture and experience; it recognizes the validity of their own religious existence and the integrity of their own religious ends. But it is *prophetic* dialogue because it calls people beyond; it calls people to conversion; it calls people to deeper and fuller truth that can only be found in communion with dialogue's trinitarian ground."[110] "Mission must by all means be dialogical, since it is nothing else finally than the participation in the dialogical nature of the triune, missionary God. But it must be prophetic as well, since, at bottom, there can be no real dialogue when truth is not expressed and clearly articulated."[111]

Conclusion

These five characteristic traits—discernment, no blind obedience, *sensus fidei*, signs of the times, and mission as prophetic dialogue—can be self-consciously promoted by Christians without any explicit reference to prophecy or prophetic obedience. Yet their context of origins is most explicitly found among the prophets in the Hebrew and Christian scriptures and exemplified by the prophetic mission of Jesus and his summons to a prophetic form of discipleship. The question remains, how are these various characteristics of prophetic obedience practically manifested in mission-oriented communities and in local contexts? In the next chapter, I will elaborate two examples from the New York area; one builds on an example from Chapters 1 and 2, and the second example is from the Diocese of Brooklyn, New York.

Chapter 6

Prophetic Obedience in Practice

This chapter will explore how the features of prophetic obedience delineated in Chapter 5 are operative in social practices of the local church in the New York area. One example is provided by recent efforts of the Northwest Bronx Community and Clergy Coalition, a community organizing association introduced in Chapters 1 and 2. The second example features parish pastoral councils and planning in the Diocese of Brooklyn.

Numerous scholars and practitioners have written about community organizing and parish pastoral councils and other forms of participatory structures of governance in the church. Some have addressed selected theological and ethical dimensions of community organizing; others considered official teachings of the Catholic Church or other Christian traditions as these justify various councils and synods.[1] My more narrowly focused aim here is simply to demonstrate that the practices associated with these two participatory structures of decision making can be understood in terms of traits associated with prophetic obedience. I will also consider how specific dimensions of prophetic obedience raise new questions about these practices and their justification.

In these two examples, we will see ways that prophetic discipleship and obedience advance, in the first instance, grassroots democracy and in the second case local forms of synodality, illustrated here by parish pastoral councils. We will observe roughly similar practices promoting notably different missions. Yet, as we will also see, there can be a synergism between parish pastoral councils that foster grassroots synodality and broad-based community organizing for grassroots democracy.

Prophetic Obedience in Community Organizing

Chapter 1 described the inception of the Northwest Bronx Community and Clergy Coalition forty years ago. Here I will explore recent community organizing campaigns of the coalition to illustrate the characteristics of prophetic obedience in action.[2] Prophetic obedience, as I am using it here, is distinguished by the cultivation of personal and collective discernment through dialogical practices.[3]

The first principle and one of the initial steps involved in community organizing is dialogue fostered by *one-on-one* or *door-to-door* listening campaigns.[4] This principle of community organizing corresponds to what I have identified as a key practice entailed in prophetic obedience—listening to the aspirations and laments of individuals and groups as expressions of the voice of the Spirit of God. This religious formulation is consistent with the advice Saul Alinsky offered community organizers in a secular idiom: "The first thing you've got to do in a community is listen, not talk, and learn to eat, sleep, breathe only one thing: the problems and aspirations of the community."[5] For Alinsky, such conversations help bring into focus people's self-interests. Learning about someone's background and what they do for a living inevitably leads to a discussion about their interests; what motivates them; and their anxieties, concerns, and troubles. One-on-one listening campaigns offer opportunities for community leaders, clergy, and organizers to expand the field of discernment by not only surfacing self-interests, but by identifying how individual self-interests can lead to uncovering collective interests and the common goods needed for human flourishing.[6]

These one-on-ones surface two traits of prophetic obedience: the need to identify personal and communal laments and the opportunity to identify important signs of the times, as laments shed light on social, historical, and institutional realities that often intersect with municipal, state, national, and global trends and dynamics. One-on-ones provide ground-level first steps toward building coalitions of people that can be mobilized to stand against destructive powers and dynamics in the community, and can engage in public, collective action for justice and social transformation.

Collective discernment in community organizing is a long-term process with many steps. Listening campaigns are an early step that prepares key members of the coalition, staff organizers, and core leaders to engage in what is called cutting an issue. This entails identifying shared concerns among participants in listening campaigns. To bring issues into actionable focus, community organizing staff and coalition leaders must next conduct research about the nature of the problem and begin to explore possible responses. This phase includes reaching out to people involved in government, unions, and local interested groups, as organizing leaders begin to identify a campaign issue with a concrete objective and attainable goal. Once leadership has identified an issue and course of action, another round of listening sessions by one-on-ones or small group meetings may take place to invite reactions and measure the level of community support for participation in the course of action.

In the process of more sharply focusing an issue, a reasonable objective, and an actionable goal based on research and discussion, organizing leaders identify individuals responsible for the problem being addressed. The leadership team's next move is to determine which individual or individuals should be engaged through collective action. Alinsky spoke about this step in terms of identifying a *target* at which the group rhetorically takes aim. The point of identifying a *target* is to determine who is the most reasonable person to be held accountable and with whom to negotiate. In terms of the framework provided by prophetic obedience, the organization is seeking a pivotal person who exercises power over people, or an individual who represents an administrative collectivity exercising power and authority over people. In the prophetic formula we have used, the demand for accountability and negotiation represents a rejection of blind obedience to, or compliance with, either individual authorities or an administrative collective acting as a mob.

Next a public forum must be created in which individuals and institutions can be held responsible for actions that are adversely affecting members of the community. Accountability sessions are meetings in which members of the community can voice their complaints about how they have been treated by persons in authority. Accountability sessions may be employed to generate a change in a leader or an administrative group, to promote negotiation on disputed issues, or to publicly symbolize the resolution of a conflict.[7]

One-on-one campaigns conducted in the neighborhoods of the Bronx regularly surface laments about housing, unemployment and low wage jobs, about the quality of the education of young people, about policing practices toward people of color, especially men, and about a variety of health-related issues, not only health care insurance, but also the high incidences of asthma, high blood pressure, and diabetes among residents caused in part by the poor availability of healthy food in stores and restaurants in areas identified as food deserts, and by environmental problems that adversely affect the population. Such litanies of laments reflect chronic problems associated with transgenerational poverty in communities like the Bronx, with a high percentage of first and second generations, and immigrant families of color from the countries of the Caribbean, Latin America, Africa, and Asia. Stated differently, these grievances reflect the intersections of economic injustice, racism, and the legacy of colonialism.

For coalition members, the many issues faced by the people of the Bronx have provided a school for learning the skills of prophetic obedience in the promotion of grassroots democracy. These include training in conducting listening campaigns, discerning local signs of the times pertaining to pressing issues, discerning a particular issue that is actionable, discerning by way of imagining possible strategies for moving the issue forward, and holding accountable people in authority with power. People also must cultivate the abilities to resist and counter the cynicism and apathy that beset the masses of people who have given up hope for any positive change. In these and in other ways, such campaigns or missions bear the marks of prophetic dialogue.

One recent example of a Bronx community's prophetic discernment and action is provided by the story of the Coalition's two-decade struggle to address the problems raised by the long-vacant Kingsbridge Armory. The armory is a huge building, a historical landmark that incorporates Romanesque features. It was built in the first decade of the twentieth century as the residence of the Eighth Regiment of the National Guard and was used for that purpose until 1996, when it became vacant. Over the years since, it had intermittently been used for public exhibitions, as a boxing arena, as a film set for a major movie, as a stage for a music video, and as a homeless shelter, but most of the time it sat vacant. Beginning in 1994, the Coalition entered into dialogue with people in the neighborhood to provide them an opportunity to voice their concerns about the dormant armory. Residents came together and began to dream about how that space could be used with the needs of the community in mind. A recurring topic of discussion was the chronic problem of school crowding and whether the amory could be used for educational purposes.

A number of proposals were advanced between 1994 and 2008 by developers about how to use the armory property. But through the local leadership of the coalition, and a process of dialogical discernment among laity and clergy together, an active group of people from the neighborhood reached the collective decision to resist efforts that did not take adequately into account the needs of the surrounding community. In 2008, as new proposals to repurpose the armory surfaced, the Northwest Bronx Community and Clergy Coalition joined nineteen (eventually twenty-four) churches, including Catholic parishes Our Lady of Angels, St. Nicholas of Tolentine, and St. Simon Stock, and Lutheran, Reformed, Methodist, and Pentecostal congregations, as well as labor organizations and other tenement and education associations, to form the Kingsbridge Armory Redevelopment Alliance (KARA). KARA's purpose was to promote dialogue and collective deliberation about what neighborhood residents felt and thought should be included in the design of a community benefits agreement (CBA) to be negotiated with any armory developer in return for the financial subsidies received by the developer. Once a plan and strategy emerged, KARA exercised the community's collective power with economic and political elites by means of public prayer rallies, meetings with elected officials, and through attempts to meet with developers. In the end, KARA's community-based resistance to economic and political elites' intent on acting without the consent of local residents prevailed.

The community's efforts entered a new phase when Mayor Michael Bloomberg invited proposals for the redevelopment of the armory. By 2008, Bloomberg was poised to approve an agreement with Related Companies to redevelop the armory into a big-box shopping mall with a promised investment into the surrounding community of $310 million. The coalition, as a participant in KARA, helped spearhead concerted resistance to the Related plan because the developers were unwilling to negotiate a CBA with KARA. Furthermore, Related's plan offered only minimum wage jobs, was focused on cultivating a customer base outside the Northwest Bronx, which involved plans to expand neighborhood streets for delivery trucks and suburban customers, and exhibited little concern about the economic needs of local residents or about disrupting the communal cultures of the neighborhood.

The City of New York's Planning Commission approved the project in 2009, but in response to public protests and concerted pressure from the Coalition and KARA, the City Council in 2010 rejected the proposal 45–1. When the mayor vetoed this decision, the council overrode the veto (48–1). This was a great victory for the coalition, KARA, and grassroots democracy. The outcome testified to the positive results of the slow labor of dialogue and deliberation in the development of a cogent plan of social action, and countless hours of accountability sessions with elected officials, as well as patient work with affiliated members as they developed the skills of being community leaders and active citizens. To use the sociological language of Richard Wood, the Kingsbridge Armory effort demonstrates the power that religious institutions can exert in the development of social capital in the public realm through community organizing.[8] Or, in the idiom of the democratic theory of Jeffrey Stout, it shows the viability of grassroots democracy against vested interests and power structures.[9] In keeping with political theologians like Luke Bretherton, it demonstrates the power of communities of faith to engage in faithful witness for justice in the secular arena.[10] And for a politically engaged ecclesiology, this Bronx campaign illustrates how prophetic obedience is practiced by means of dialogue, protest, and negotiation in the promotion of economic justice.

The defeat of the Bloomberg's Bronx redevelopment plan had remarkable ripple effects. Most prominently, it sparked a citywide campaign in all five boroughs to advance living-wage legislation for large taxpayer-subsidized development projects. During the next two years, the Coalition and KARA joined forces with religious, labor, and other community organizing groups to promote this living-wage legislation. Major rallies with religious leaders and elected officials took place in the Riverside Church and in front of City Hall. The Fair Wages for New Yorkers Act was passed by the City Council in February 2012, requiring all city-subsidized building projects to guarantee that all workers be paid $10 per hour with at least $1.50 of benefits, or $11.50 per hour without benefits. As significant as this achievement was, during the process, labor union leaders and Christine Quinn, the head of the City Council, entered into backroom negotiations and reached a compromise without the full and active participation of the coalition and other local organizations that were advocating for a living-wage ordinance. The approved legislation was thus a bittersweet victory for many core leaders of the Coalition, for it failed to live up to the promise of the original living-wage campaign. Again Mayor Bloomberg vetoed the bill, and once again, in June of 2012, his veto was overridden (46–5). Two years later, on September 30, 2014, now-Mayor Bill de Blasio offered a partial remedy to the flawed legislation by signing an executive order that raised the minimum hourly wage for this same group to $13.30, an increase that went beyond the Quinn and union leaders' compromise, but that was still shy of the $15 an hour sought by many advocates.

The next phase of the Kingsbridge campaign began in 2012 when bidding was reopened for new proposals for repurposing the armory. The Coalition, as a key partner with KARA, brought people from the neighborhood to gather in small groups for conversations about what elements to include in the CBA that would be negotiated with any company submitting a redevelopment plan. These conversations combined real vision with the fits and starts of small group meetings. After negotiations that took place over four months, the project was ultimately awarded to the Kingsbridge National Ice Center Partners (KNIC), to develop a five thousand–seat ice hockey arena with nine rinks. KNIC then entered into negotiation concerning a CBA with representatives of the KARA-affiliated churches and associations.

As chosen representatives of the twenty-four neighborhood organizations involved in KARA, three key people, coalition board president Desiree Pilgrim

Hunter, core leader Alice McIntosh, and Pastor Que English from the Bronx Christian Fellowship, all three women of color, negotiated a CBA with the new developer. This legally binding agreement committed the new owners to provide many benefits to the community: living-wage jobs for all employees, preferential hiring to local residents, a commitment to procure between 25 and 50 percent of the goods and services to be used from Bronx businesses, over fifty thousand square feet of community space for public usage, free access for schools and kids, and a plan to upgrade the building to the highest level of green infrastructure.

This agreement represents a new kind of partnership being formed in local communities, wherein residents, people in business, and elected officials reach agreements for the common good of the community.[11] In April 2013, Bloomberg and the developer announced an agreement on final terms that included the negotiated CBA. On December 10, 2013, the New York City Council approved the agreement. The coalition's twenty-year campaign had resulted in a major victory with the collaboration of the KNIC developer, the mayor, and the City Council. What KNIC and KARA agreed to must now be vigilantly monitored to make sure commitments are kept and, if they are not, that legal action is taken.

For the Coalition, the CBA with KNIC was a dramatic achievement. It has also been a prelude to an even more ambitious effort, now under way in the Bronx, to promote economic democracy through the establishment of worker cooperatives. To this end, Nick Iuviene, a former coalition organizer, with the collaboration of long-time Coalition leader Yorman Nuñez and the Massachusetts Institute of Technology Community Innovators Lab, have pioneered a project called the Bronx Cooperative Development Initiative.[12] This project takes its inspiration from the Mondragon Corporation in the Basque region of Spain, started by a parish priest, José María Arizmendiarrieta. In the 1940s, this priest sought to implement principles of Catholic social teaching by developing a worker cooperative that initially manufactured paraffin heaters but eventually expanded to become the largest and leading business group in the Basque Region in four areas: finance; industry; retail; and knowledge by means of research centers, a university, and vocational and training centers.[13] There have been other similar efforts in the United States: one example is the Evergreen Initiative in Cleveland, Ohio; in addition, the Bronx is the home of the country's largest health care cooperative, Cooperative Home Care Associates.[14]

Significantly for the argument of this chapter, the coalition's involvement in promoting economic democracy has required community members to revisit their aspirations for economic sustainability in the Bronx and to examine more deeply their lamentations about ways these aspirations have been thwarted—and the reasons why. This grounding in aspirations and laments always takes place through one-on-one and small group dialogue. These dialogues open doors to deeper analysis, reflection, discernment of the signs of the times, and examination of the social dynamics that contribute to transgenerational poverty in the Bronx. A pilot group of coalition members working on economic democracy formulated the project's guiding values and vision this way:

> Our community is rich in assets and our people are resilient, hard-working, and innovative. We reject the idea that resources are scarce. Instead they have been taken from the marginalized many and are hoarded by the privileged few. We must exercise our collective, creative imagination to design an economy that sustains and builds upon that abundance for the holistic health and wellness of our community, now and for the future.

It is no longer sufficient, they continue, to "focus . . . only on *responding* to short-term recurring problems;" there is a need "to deepen . . . and widen . . . our approach by *creating* long-term solutions that put greater emphasis on several values that reflect the identity and aspirations of the people of the Bronx community."[15]

In the vocabulary of my argument, the prophetic obedience that this project embodies does not simply require, and is not accomplished simply by, denunciations of injustice. Rather, it demands diligent, detailed research into the institutional, communal, and personal assets of local communities, and the lending of creative imagination and skills to build relationships that can create new opportunities for genuine social transformation.

The coalition's latest project may appear to be setting unrealistic goals: won't a campaign for *economic democracy* only create false hopes and compound disappointments and frustrations? There is no doubt that this agenda requires stretching the social imaginary of the community to envision future economic arrangements that can confront the basic causes of social laments and that it requires the tenacity to work toward short- and long-term goals that will be difficult to achieve. Moreover, addressing any social problem in the Bronx through prophetic organizing requires brutal honesty about the difficulties and pitfalls involved. Developing the required leadership skills takes time, learning through missteps, and mutual accountability through feedback. Core group meetings and public assemblies can be effective and energizing, but there are times when these are difficult and not in all ways well organized or executed, when people make long-winded statements, their statements are unfocused, or the group's concentration is waning. At its best, the coalition functions as a school of continuing education in grassroots democracy and prophetic obedience, for learning the skills of public discourse and public action in a context where everyone around the table is held accountable for what they say and what they do. This requires discipline and practice. It also requires fortitude, a persistent willingness to try to learn from mistakes and failures, and to begin again.

Further Observations and Reflections

Broad-based community organizing is a school for laments, anger, solidarity, conflict, negotiation, and courage. People are given opportunities to name their own laments and listen to those of others. Community organizing teaches that there is a constructive, life-giving role for grief, anger, and conflict in community relationships, and in the promotion of justice, social responsibility, and mutual respect. Sadly, these are lessons rarely taught in churches and schools, where the role of grief and anger in the cultivation of courage and hope is rarely explored, and where, too often, compliance, meekness, and conflict aversion remain the predominant curriculum.[16]

One key trait of prophetic obedience is that it is contrary to blind obedience, either to authorities or to mob rule. In this sense, the notion of prophetic obedience extends traditional religious definitions of obedience to incorporate the need for individuals and groups to stand up and speak out for their own positions in their communities, and potentially against political and economic structures and authorities that undermine their agency and flourishing. Prophetic obedience also entails a willingness to stand on one's own or with a minority opinion on matters of justice. Prophetic obedience often demands taking a stand against elites in the interest of advancing justice, but it can also require disagreeing with other members of the prophetic community over social goals or means of advancing them. In these contexts, anger and laments can give rise to conflict, contestation, and protest, while ruling out abusive behavior. Community organizing aims ultimately at building relationships and forging partnerships between grassroots community members and other political and economic actors, and doing this requires negotiation in the interest of coalition-building and the formation of consensus. But too quickly accentuating the need for consensus can cloak underlying *dissensus*. Grassroots democratic communities must continually work to find ways to move forward by building differentiated consensus, which can also acknowledge and respect unresolved differences of opinion.

Over its forty-year history, the Coalition has been exercising prophetic obedience by responding to the laments of community residents about housing, education, health, and employment, all basic ingredients of human flourishing, and working alongside residents to discern and enact courses of collective action. Through Coalition campaigns, the community exercises its collective power through prayer, rallies, by holding leaders accountable in government, economic and business institutions, by calling to account tenement owners and school officials, and by finding solutions through negotiations. With an established track record of effectively defending neighbors against destructive economic and social forces at work in the community, the Coalition, in collaboration with the Bronx Cooperative Development Initiative, is now developing an offensive strategy for promoting economic democracy through the development of worker cooperatives, in order to generate shared wealth and ownership of assets among Bronx residents. It is still too soon to know what will become of this effort. But the project's core values, vision, and strategy are shared and have been effective in revitalizing communities in other major cities in the United States and in other places around the world.

Do the *sensus fidei* and the *sensus fidelium* play roles in the prophetic obedience involved in the work of the Coalition? I think they do, but such a claim merits scrutiny and clarification. The clergy caucus and religiously affiliated Coalition members consistently seek to make explicit how their work for justice is rooted in their faith; and this reflects an individual's *sensus fidei* as well as the *sensus fidelium* of the local people of God. The clergy caucus, whenever it meets, seeks to find ways to integrate the work of the Coalition with caucus members' Christian convictions, and Christian leaders have been open to including the participation of faith leaders from other communities, most often Jews and Muslims in the Bronx. The *sensus fidei* and the *sensus fidelium* are reflected in the two schemas of prophetic obedience. On the one hand, the *sensus fidei* and *sensus fidelium* are evident in the community's heeding, receiving, and responding to the voice of the Spirit perceived in aspirations and laments of their neighborhood and the created world around them, and on the other hand, in countless ways the *sensus fidei* and *sensus fidelium* are in evidence in the reception of and witness to, what is recognized as the Word of God in the community, the scriptures, and the ongoing traditions of handing on and interpreting the scriptures. The two schemas of prophetic obedience here intersect.[17]

Many members of the coalition, but certainly not all, acknowledge being inspired by their faith convictions, but they would certainly not express this in terms of the technical categories *sensus fidei* and *sensus fidelium*. People's perceptions and receptions of religious beliefs about the breath or wind or spirit of the creator God present in the goodness and fecundity of creation, for instance, may motivate organizing efforts for laws and policies fostering environmental responsibility, green building construction, and just water policy. Belief in the God-given goodness and dignity of every human animates advocacy for universal health care, healthy food availability, just wages, housing, and antidiscrimination laws and social practices. Many are inspired by the example of Jesus siding with those who are marginalized, or poor and overwhelmed by demonic powers, or poor to join community organizing efforts to work for justice and peace. Many are motivated by faith-based solidarity with all those who suffer through their belief in the body of Christ, the crucified Jesus Christ, and by extension their belief in the sacred dignity of crucified peoples. The clergy seek to make explicit in gatherings of the Coalition this faith dimension in the midst of members from diverse Christian communities, but they are also respectful of Jewish and Muslim neighbors and people from any religious faith tradition. Inevitably, as well, there are a significant number of members with no congregational or faith affiliation. Amid this diversity, coalition leaders, clergy, and the broader membership work to foster bonds of affection, solidarity, and civic friendship among people of varied faith traditions and people with nonreligious worldviews.

Not surprisingly, members holding such diverse beliefs do disagree, deeply, on some publicly contested matters, including gay marriage and civil unions, birth control, and pro-choice and pro-life issues. Disagreements exist over *hot button* social questions between different faith traditions and also within traditions. Like many other broad-based community organizations, the coalition refrains from explicitly addressing such contested issues, even though individual churches, parishes, and congregations may be politically or pastorally engaged with them.[18]

To reformulate a central concern that the *sensus fidei* and *sensus fidelium* are not being sufficiently recognized in broad-based community organizing, sociologist Richard Wood has pointed out that some religiously affiliated parishes and congregations stand on guard vigilantly against the danger that faith and faith communities will be instrumentalized in community organizing, becoming tools to promote secular agendas.[19] Yet in fact, many, if not most, clergy and members of religious congregations are involved in community organizing because of their faith convictions and commitments rather than the other way around. Their prophetic dedication and sense of obedience are grounded in a more or less explicit awareness of, and attempt to be responsive to, the Spirit and the Word at work in the community. Clergy strive to ensure that faith-inspired receptivity to laments and witness to mercy and justice motivates solidarity in the community and work for justice, both for those who are religious and those who are not. Regularly, coalition clergy invite community organizing groups to realize that their work for justice, for many members, is inspired by a deeper summons to respond to and collaborate with God, who is at work in the struggles of their communities.

I have advanced the claim that prophetic obedience is contrary to blind obedience to authorities or a mob mentality. I now wish to highlight this crucial trait by exploring dynamics of power, conflict, and accountability within broad-based community organizing.

Saul Alinsky conceived of civic life as a battlefield between those who abuse economic and political power and those who are regularly exploited by the abusers. The exploited need to join forces in order to gain sufficient power to work for change. Alinsky's 1945 book *Reveille for Radicals* put the matter simply: "the building of a People's Organization is the building of a new power group . . . [, which is] an intrusion and a threat to the existing power arrangements. . . . A People's Organization is dedicated to an eternal war. It is a war against poverty, misery, delinquency, disease, injustice, hopelessness, despair, and unhappiness."[20] In his 1971 book *Rules for Radicals,* Alinsky differentiated life-giving powers and destructive powers.

> Power is the very essence, the *dynamo* of life. It is the power of the heart pumping blood and sustaining life in the body. It is the power of active citizen participation pulsing upward, providing a unified strength for a common purpose. Power is an essential life force always in operation, either changing the world or opposing change. Power, or organized energy, may be a man-killing explosive or a life-saving drug.[21]

People and institutions exerting destructive power can only be effectively challenged when the dispossessed and marginalized join forces to identify the sources of their shared grief and anger, and then exercise their collective power to advance their interests for the common good.

Alinsky's heirs built on their mentor's basic convictions to develop multidimensional approaches to power analysis. Greg Galuzzo of the Chicago-based

Gamaliel community organization, for instance, claims that in the United States many working class and poor people get the message that their involvement in civic life doesn't really matter. This helps explain the shocking fact that among the over one hundred democracies in the world, the United States is the fourth worst in terms of the percentage of citizens who exercise their right to vote.[22] Galuzzo contends that people with power try to discourage those with less power from using that power, or they try to confuse or deter them from exercising their power wisely.[23] Alinsky's convictions are evident in Galuzzo's formulation: there are two groups with power, power elites who exploit others and those who need to get organized to exercise their collective power to challenge elites to bring about meaningful change. In this framework, two views of power come into view. On the one hand, power can be described in terms of power over others through control by one means or another; on the other hand, power is an ability to act, to do something, a capacity to effect a change. Ed Chambers from Industrial Areas Foundation (IAF) goes beyond Galuzzo's formulation by stating, "from one perspective, power is neutral. It may be used for evil or for good. From another, it is ambiguous because any employment of power by finite human beings, no matter how well intended and successful, will lead to unexpected consequences for self and others."[24]

In the 1980s, over a decade after Alinsky died, Ed Chambers and others in the IAF, in conversation with scholars Leo Penta and Michael Cowan, began to draw on the works of Hannah Arendt and Bernard Loomer to differentiate a unilateral approach from relational approaches to power.[25] It stands to reason that political philosopher Hannah Arendt served as a helpful resource for the IAF, since she too worried about the diminishment of people's civic involvement in democratic societies. She chose not to speak of two kinds of power but preferred to contrast violence, force, or strength with a relational view of power, which she described as something that happens between people in the public realm through communication and action in civic engagement. "Power is what keeps the public realm, the potential space of appearance between acting and speaking men, in existence."[26] In an analogous fashion, Loomer, who was trained in process philosophy and theology, describes a linear approach to power as "the capacity to influence, guide, adjust, manipulate, shape, control, or transform the human or natural environment in order to advance one's purposes." By contrast, relational power is "the ability [of groups] to produce and to undergo an effect. It is the capacity both to influence others and to be influenced by others. Relational power involves both a giving and a receiving."[27]

Arendt and Loomer provided the descendants of Alinsky with a conceptual framework and justification for criticizing the use of power by economic and political elites who take advantage of people in society for their own purposes. At the same time, they commended a relational approach to power to motivate people to become organized and to participate collectively in the public realm in civil society.

More recently, Jeffrey Stout has brought greater precision to this discussion in his study of community organizing in New Orleans by the IAF federation called

Jeremiah in the aftermath of the devastating hurricane Katrina in 2005. Based
on the social analysis employed by the Jeremiah organizers, Stout offers a general
definition of power as "the capacity that an individual, group, or institution has to
produce effects the people would have reason to care about. It is because individuals
in isolation have little power that a power analysis focuses mainly on institutions
and on the people who play consequential roles in them."[28] Stout subdivides this
general definition—"the capacity to produce socially significant effects"—into two
specific forms, which follow the usual Alinsky distinction between two groups of
power holders. On the one hand, "how easy it is . . . for major corporations and their
executives to turn governmental institutions to their own purposes—how easy it
is, in other words, to translate economic and political power that can be exercised
over someone else."[29] These business and political elites, corporations, and institutions exercise power in arbitrary and dominating ways for their own purposes. On
the other hand, citizens in general and especially the marginalized rarely mobilize
their power to promote democratic change (in service of the common good), in
order to hold elites accountable and to prevent them from acting in arbitrary and
dominating ways. The capacity of citizens to produce socially significant effects
applies whether this capacity is exercised or not, whether the effects are intentional
or unintentional, whether they are bad or beneficial.

Stout takes note of an important question raised by Michel Foucault: "whether
the agents of power highlighted in IAF power analysis—namely, individuals,
groups, and institutions—are the only sources of socially significant effects worthy
of consideration, or even the most important ones."[30] For Foucault, in the words
of Stout, there are two "anonymous sources of power. . . . The first is the array of
propositions that people living in a given place at a given time are in a position to
entertain, accept, or reject. The second is the array of possible social identities that
people living in a given place at a given time can acquire, adopt, or attribute." These
are not the result of intentional actions, whether personal, social, or institutional,
but "simply . . . unintended by-products of earlier similar configurations of effects,
interacting with historical contingencies without necessarily needing much direct
help from intentional human agency."[31]

Stout argues that Foucault's claims can supplement the thinking and work of
community organizers without contradicting their agency-oriented approach.

> Agents need not be disempowered by learning how they have been shaped
> by the vocabularies and identities lodged in their discursive and formative
> social practices. To the contrary, such knowledge can and should inform
> deliberate choices concerning which social practices to support, how to
> embed them in institutions, and how the norms and identities embodied
> in them should be revised.[32]

For Foucault, there can be no decisive or ultimate social or political liberation.
There is only the ongoing struggle, which, like the art of wrestling honored in Stoic

asceticism, "consists simply in being ready and on guard, in remaining steady, that is to say, not being thrown, not being weaker than all the blows coming either from circumstances or from others."[33]

These traits commended by Foucault and Stout also correspond to the prophetic character of community organizing. Organizers must acknowledge the ongoing role of struggle in the promotion of grassroots democracy. In other words, they must recognize an agonistic dimension in democracy, in ways that incorporate a politics of lamentations without succumbing to the cynical lamentation of politics.[34] This logic underlies the argument being advanced here. To recognize the role of power makes explicit the unavoidable elements of conflict and tension in the public realm. In coalition work, conflict can serve as an impetus for holding accountability sessions where laments are expressed, and people with the power of money or institutions are brought face-to-face with the relational power of people demanding their dignity and their rights; and for some members of broad-based community organizing groups, these demands are inspired by, and in the name of, the all-powerful God of justice and compassion.[35]

Saul Alinsky has been praised and blamed for his concentration on power and on the use of conflict in democratic tactics. Some Alinksy-inspired community organizing groups have continued to emphasize the constructive importance of conflict, agitation, and tension in dealing with those in power, while others give greater attention to relationship-building and negotiation.[36] In this vein, there is evidence that some community organizations in the United States are changing their approach to conflict and expanding their democratic tactics. In the past, common tactics included direct actions like occupying the office of a *shady* employer, apartment owner, or bank; petition drives; public actions; and accountability sessions. There have, more recently, been greater efforts to learn about behind-the-scenes political dynamics on an issue; to build relationships with political or economic actors; and to learn about economic and policy issues involved in order to be able to address them effectively.[37] A radical democratic distrust of political and business elites has been joined by a more representative approach to democracy. Conflict, the hallmark of Alinsky's model of community organizing, still has a strategic role to play in the public realm, but negotiations and partnerships with a range of stakeholders in the community, including business and government elites, do as well.

The Coalition offers a clear example of a mission-driven organization that strives to promote economic and racial justice motivated for many by religious faith traditions, up to this point in its history, predominantly Christian. The distinctive leadership roles played by community organizers and clergy are particularly noteworthy, as are the ongoing efforts by these two groups to identify the next generation of lay leaders who will play a crucial role in future organizing efforts. Ultimately all these groups, organizers, clergy, and lay leaders, are focused on mobilizing both the members of religious communities and the widest circle of neighbors to participate in the mission of the Coalition and in their particular campaigns for housing, health care and environmental wholeness, education, and economic justice. Some people have particular leadership roles, but all are invited and encouraged to be a part of the mission. As is abundantly clear, every facet of the Coalition's work embodies practices of prophetic dialogue, from one-on-one listening campaigns, to discernment sessions to cut an issue and select strategies, to confronting and negotiating with political, civil services, or business elites, and finally, commitment to the never-ending processes of evaluation and accountability sessions.

Parish Pastoral Councils

The characteristics of prophetic obedience that I have delineated above provide a frame for understanding and cultivating the kinds of skills and practices needed in parish pastoral councils to advance prophetic discipleship among all the members in a parish. Parish vitality and a missionary orientation require nothing less. Parish pastoral councils are the most basic and important expression in the local church of the synodality championed at Vatican II. The term synodality comes from an ancient Greek term σύνοδος (*synodos*). The prefix, syn, means with or together, and ódos is the term for way or road, journey or pilgrimage. Synodos can be translated as finding our way together on a journey, apt for a pilgrim people. This Greek term has a Latin-based correlate, conciliarity (*conciliuum*), and both terms denote collaboration and collegiality by means of participatory structures of church governance through collective discernment and decision making about pastoral planning for mission.

Parish pastoral councils operate at their best when they intersect within the web of local modalities of synodality in dioceses that include diocesan pastoral councils, diocesan synods, presbyteral councils, as well as various structures of decision making used by religious congregations and base Christian communities and movements. At another institutional level, episcopal conferences and the synod of bishops exemplify synodality at national, continental, and global levels of the church.[38] Parish pastoral councils foster the development of grassroots synodality and local, contextual, inculturated theologies in dioceses just as community organizing coalitions provide venues for the involvement of parish members in the promotion of grassroots democracy with people of other faith traditions and worldviews.

I wish to illustrate the characteristics of prophetic obedience at work in parish pastoral councils by considering the intensive program of developing parish pastoral councils and pastoral planning over the past decade across the Diocese of Brooklyn.[39] Bishop Nicholas DiMarzio was installed in Brooklyn as bishop in October 2003. With a desire to devote special attention to improving parish vitality and planning, but without any conscious connection or agenda pertaining to parish and diocesan finances and with no motivating concern about parish restructuring, beginning in 2005 DiMarzio initiated a planning process for parish pastoral councils through the Office of Pastoral Planning. Robert Choiniere was hired by

DiMarzio as the director of this office, and Ellen Ratigan was appointed as associate director, to work with the Vicar for Pastoral Planning Monsignor Neil Mahoney and the Vicar for Evangelization and Pastoral Life Monsignor Frank Caggiano, to develop a diocesan-wide process of council development and pastoral planning. It is noteworthy that Choiniere integrated what he learned from a graduate degree in pastoral ministry with his training in faith-based community organizing. In parish settings, Choiniere applied the expertise he had gained in utilizing one-on-one exercises in community organizing to engage and mobilize parishioners, identify lay leaders, and target issues that concerned the parish community. These basic skills were employed in the interest of the community discerning and developing a pastoral plan based on a parish vision and mission.[40] Between 2005 and 2011 the parishes in the Brooklyn Diocese went through two diocesan-wide processes for parish pastoral planning.

Parish Pastoral Planning in the Diocese of Brooklyn: Phase One

In 2005, the Diocese of Brooklyn began a diocesan-wide process for parish pastoral planning. Various steps were involved. Each of the approximately two hundred parishes in the diocese participated in a formation program for parish pastoral councils. This entailed forming new councils in some parishes, and evaluating and revising already existing council practices in others. The parish pastoral council, along with the pastor and the parish staff, developed a pastoral plan through a dialogical process of discernment that lasted about a year and a half.

One of the most important facets of this parish process involved campaigns of listening, the foundational practice for a dialogical church and the central characteristic of prophetic obedience. These listening campaigns entailed parish pastoral council members conducting thirty-minute one-on-one conversations with members of the parish over several months. The conversations had three objectives: (1) to learn about parish members—their life story, background, work, length of time in the parish, and how they have been involved in the parish and neighborhood; (2) to ask about the parishioners' interests in and concerns about the parish and the neighborhood; and (3) to explore what the parish is doing well and what it could do better. "What do you like about being a member of the parish? What do we do well at our parish? What are your most important concerns about our parish? What could our parish do differently or do more of to be an even more meaningful community for you and others? What are the most important concerns you worry about for yourself and your family, your neighborhood? Why do you feel this is a problem? How do you feel the parish could begin to address that concern?"[41]

As their listening campaign was in progress, the parish pastoral council, staff, and pastor worked in collaboration with the pastoral planning office of the diocese to conduct a parish self-study, including a parish survey. This provided demographics and trends in the composition of the parish and the wider community in the forms of tables and charts: population, age, income, race, ethnicity, housing, movements of people in and out of the area, and poverty statistics. In the idiom of prophetic discernment, this information provided certain indicators of the signs of the times in the parish and neighborhood.

The one-on-ones and the parish self-study laid the groundwork for a three-hour parish-wide assembly, where every sector of the parish met to begin to work together toward the formation of a parish mission statement and goals. The Book of Wisdom provided the motto for their undertaking: "Where there is no vision, the people will perish" (29:18). Three topics were discussed in small groups. First, groups were asked the following questions: Imagine what message Jesus might have for the parish to lead us into the future. How can the identity and mission of the community as a Catholic Church be realized? And what is special about our parish?

Second, after the statistical data about the parish and neighborhood was presented, small groups discussed the following: "What do I expect of my parish? How should our parish reach out to the broader community in our neighborhood? What do our demographics and data suggest that we need to do as we move into the future?"

Third, those assembled assessed the parish in terms of seven essential elements in the faith life and mission of the parish, topics previously introduced to the parish through parish bulletins and homilies: worship; faith formation; community; service; leadership, stewardship, and temporalities; and evangelization. Small groups briefly discussed, "which of these essential elements do we need to focus on now and why?"[42]

Based on the findings of this assembly, the parish pastoral council and the pastor prepared a mission statement and goals. The mission statement of the parish was to address four topics: (1) identity: name, location, unique character, and history; (2) purpose: based on core beliefs, values, and the reason for the parish's existence; (3) function: the parish's commitments and what it does and for whom; and (4) future: specific challenges and elements that need strengthening. Once the council and the pastor agreed on the mission statement, they generated a set of goals for a new parish pastoral plan.[43]

In the weeks that followed, the mission and goals of the parish were distributed to the community at Mass. Parishioners were invited to commit themselves to one of the goals of special concern to them, and then to fostering the work of that goal by helping to set forth objectives and to develop a plan for implementation. This stage provided opportunities for parishioners to offer feedback, to further the development of concrete objectives and implementation strategies, and to participate in the process of reception of the preliminary pastoral mission and goals. On a subsequent Sunday, parish members were invited to sign up to work with a group of parishioners on implementing certain goals. The pastor, council members, and parishioners participated in reflection groups to delineate particular goals at a second parish assembly with the same objective. A year after the inception of the process, parishes were ready to publish the parish pastoral plan and to begin implementation. Roughly six months after the implementation process began, an initial evaluation of the plan was conducted, with all those who had been involved invited to participate.

Between January 2005 and March of 2007, all of the approximately two hundred parishes of the Diocese of Brooklyn went through this process, revitalizing existing or initiating new parish pastoral councils, and updating or formulating new pastoral plans. The process aimed to cultivate among parish members greater participation in the life and mission of the parish, and the majority of parishes benefited from taking part. However, some parishes still struggled. One can speculate as to why: sometimes members might not have had the communication and deliberation skills necessary for collective discernment; they might have had limited experience using the powers of their imagination, or insufficient comprehension of how the social imaginary works in groups like parishes, to be able to understand at deeper levels how the essential elements might inform parish life and mission, and how these dimensions could be implemented in the daily life of the parish; the negative dynamics of declining parish numbers and financial problems may have been difficult to overturn.

The efforts of the Office of Pastoral Planning of the Diocese of Brooklyn to revitalize and initiate parish pastoral councils illustrate what I have identified as many of the two frames of prophetic obedience: on the one hand, heeding, receiving, and responding to the voice of the Spirit of God in the aspirations and laments of people and the created world, and the corresponding heeding, receiving, and responding to the Word of God through witness in word and deed. This axis of obedience finds a crucial wellspring in listening campaigns with parish members that employ one-on-one and small group encounters to bring to light individual and communal aspirations and laments, which, through the deliberation of the parish pastoral council, can activate the identity of the parish as a dialogical church.

Certain traits that I have identified with prophetic obedience in the previous chapter were not explicitly addressed in the formation materials prepared by the Office of Pastoral Planning but are germane to the topics addressed. In the Brooklyn process, the most important skills associated with prophetic obedience pertain to collective discernment and how lay leaders and councils collaborate with pastors and staff members to heed and respond to what has been heard, in order to assess current parish practices and fashion a parish vision and pastoral plan that build on positive cooperation, and that lead to effective programs in the parish and address limitations and problems.

For the parish pastoral council to engage in its ministerial function of discernment requires creating a hospitable context for developing collegial, collaborative relationships among members. This context of collaboration creates the conditions, a climate, for building genuine bonds of affection, and partnerships that can foster honest mature collective discernment and deliberation. Such a climate is antithetical to, and works against, paternalistic clericalism and dominating personalities. On the other hand, the council exercises prophetic obedience by resisting the exclusionary power dynamics of cliques, elites, and majority blocs, as well as groupthink or certain mob mentalities, within the council and parish. Prophetic obedience on the council and in the parish ultimately requires that people heed, receive, and respond to the various voices in the parish and the neighborhood, and that they be especially attentive to the aspirations and laments of those on the margins or excluded.

Closely associated with issues of power dynamics in the council and parish is the crucible for every prophetic community: the prophetic character of parish pastoral councils requires learning how to proceed through a discerning process in situations of conflict and struggle that inevitably surface in parish life. These can range from the clash of personalities, to fundamental disagreements about matters of substance, to situations of apparent or real impasse. Prophetic discipleship summons each Christian to cultivate the skills to find one's way in, and through, conflict and struggle—what can be called the agonistic dimensions of synodality—to know when to take a stand, when to stand firm even when the majority disagrees, and when to step back and change one's mind and heart—all the while practicing hospitality, generosity of spirit, and a reconciling heart.[44] Parish pastoral councils are called on to exercise prayerful discernment to reach consensus. This practice is not strictly identified with majority rule and certainly not with political maneuvering. Nor should councils promote consensus at the expense of repressing or sidestepping genuine difficulties, conflict, and struggle. Prophetic obedience requires that there be room for differentiated consensus, where communities find space for open agreement amidst disagreement, for *dissensus* that allows for the agonistic character of councils and synods, and that sets up the conditions for developing honest and evolving consensus over time, and for undergoing fruitful change and growth.

Although the Office of Pastoral Planning did not use the particular formula *discerning the signs of the times* in their written materials or oral presentations, the category aptly names the efforts of parishes to identify historical, social, and cultural factors that bear on the life of the parish. This is particularly evident in cases of gathering information about the racial, ethnic, and economic profiles of parishioners and the surrounding neighborhood, as well as migration patterns. All of this information is relevant for the process of discernment involved in prophetic obedience. Still, the questions can be raised: Are the council and the parish at large exploring all the relevant signs of the times? Are they detecting all the factors of prime significance for the life and mission of the parish? This will receive more attention below.

Not surprisingly, there is also no explicit mention of the formula *sensus fidei* or *sensus fidelium* in the resource materials provided by the Office of Pastoral Planning. Such technical theological categories are rarely utilized in the local church. Yet a strong argument can be made that some or all of the essential elements of the faith life and mission of the church that parishes were asked to reflect on provide a selective or preliminary grid or frame for considering some of ingredients of the *sensus fidei* and *sensus fidelium,* which are decisive for parish discernment and assessment of areas of personal and collective responsibility and accountability. I will return to this issue, too, below.

Finally, one finds in the Brooklyn materials no explicit development of the mission of the parish in terms of prophetic dialogue such as was formulated by the missionary order of the Society of the Divine Word and further developed by members Stephen Bevans and Roger Schroeder (as discussed in Chapter 5). Nonetheless, one can reasonably draw the conclusion that when following the diocesan guidelines, parish pastoral councils were developing pastoral plans and missions that corresponded with basic features of prophetic dialogue as outlined by the Divine Word Missionaries.

Strategic Pastoral Planning in a Crisis Situation: Phase Two

The plot thickened. In the aftermath of the parish renewal process that took place between 2005 and 2007 in the Diocese of Brooklyn, it became increasingly clear that certain signs of the times were impinging on, and working against, the diocese's promotion of parish pastoral life. The constellation of factors involved included demographic shifts in parish membership caused by people changing parishes or leaving the church entirely; the impact of migration patterns on local, regional, and national levels; the decreasing number of priests and religious vocations; and the disparity of the financial health among parishes. One momentous sign of the times was the clergy sex abuse and its aftermath; a second was the financial crisis in the US economy in 2008. In the wake of these, the financial situations of numerous parishes and dioceses across the country deteriorated precipitously due to legal expenses, payments to victims, and compensation for psychological assistance to victims of clergy abuse. In Brooklyn, these losses were compounded by the weakening economy that negatively impacted the salaries of staff, the financial debts of many parishes, and the resources needed for building maintenance and development in each parish and in the diocese as a whole.

In 2010, Bishop DiMarzio introduced a new Diocesan Strategic Planning Process for all the parishes, whose aim was to address diocesan financial and human resources difficulties. The United States and global financial crisis of 2008 contributed to significant losses in the investment portfolio of the diocese and seriously hampered their ability to subsidize financially struggling parishes. By 2010, the Diocese of Brooklyn had been commited to pay out $12 million because of the sex abuse scandal, only half of which was covered by insurance. The diocese was facing an annual deficit of $8 million. Demographic shifts and decreases in parish membership were compounded by a decreasing number of priests. On top of those factors, there were the usual brick-and-mortar issues pertaining to parish building maintenance and structural improvements. On multiple fronts, the bishop and clergy of Brooklyn, as in dioceses across the United States, were challenged to face up to their historical lack of transparency and disclosure, and their parental or paternal code of secrecy around financial and other matters. Among other effects, then, these crises impelled the bishop and clergy to pull back the veil of secrecy and to move toward greater transparency in their financial practices and decision making.

To address severely strained resources, Bishop DiMarzio felt compelled to close and consolidate parishes. Desiring to gather data and to consult widely in order to make the necessary decisions, the bishop launched a new pastoral planning process on March 1, 2010. This parish-based process involved evaluating the signs of vibrancy and the greatest strengths in each parish, as well as deliberating about the greatest challenges or areas of concern at present and in the foreseeable future. The 2010 process revisited topics and parish dynamics addressed in the previous parish evaluation, but this time in light of key demographic and financial factors and with deeper analyses of basic elements in the parish's mission.

In order to determine pertinent signs of the times pertaining to the vitality and viability of all the parishes, key demographic factors were assessed. Each parish prepared a parish data report that included pastoral data providing the numbers of parishioners, annual baptisms, marriages, and funerals; and financial data pertaining to building maintenance, debt, and staff salaries. They compiled data about parish ministries, groups, and activities and the number of active participants in each. Based on the data gathered, a parish engagement ratio was determined by calculating a participation ratio for the parish—the ratio between attending parishioners and parishioners that participate in the life of the parish beyond Mass attendance.[45] There was a further differentiation made between all those who participate and those who participate in multiple ministries. So, for instance, within the total number of Mass attendants (100 percent) there may be 20 percent who are engaged in ministries or activities and 2.5 percent who are highly engaged.

Every parish conducted a parish assembly or a parish leadership meeting between April 13 and 24, 2010, to discuss the parish data reports. During the two weeks following this gathering the parish pastoral council, parish finance committee, and parish trustees convened to complete a planning questionnaire. This completed the parish self-study that was then to be submitted to the planning commission and summarized for the parishes. The commission reviewed the study and communicated with each parish in September 2010.

DiMarzio's next step was to construct a diocesan strategic planning process to make the cuts in parishes necessary to protect the economic viability of the diocese.[46] A forty-two–member planning commission composed of members of the diocesan curia (vicars general, episcopal vicars, and chancellor), parish priests, religious, deacons, and laypeople was established to make recommendations to the bishop. This commission worked with the information provided by the in-depth parish self-studies, in which all parishioners had been encouraged to become involved. As a part of this evaluation process, the planning commission visited each parish to discuss its self-study.

The commission engaged all the parish stakeholders—pastors, parish staff members, lay leaders involved in the parish pastoral council and financial council.

Together they considered data on Mass attendance, patterns in sacramental celebrations, fluctuations in the number of parishioners, building maintenance issues, budget deficits, income, clergy availability, demographics, and geography. The central focus of attention was on the financial health of the parish and its demographic vitality.

Based on the information provided by all parishes, the commission submitted proposed recommendations to Bishop DiMarzio. The bishop made no decision at that point concerning a plan of action. Instead the commission met again with each parish group, and its recommendations were communicated with these leaders, who had a chance to respond. The commission reviewed these responses and prepared a final recommendation for the bishop, which provided the basis for the bishop's decision. Three worship sites were initially closed, and some were told to merge with other parishes. A third option was offered by the bishop to some parishes that were struggling: he requested that some parishes prepare a strategic action plan to identify their challenges and devise a plan to address them in twelve to eighteen months.[47]

Discerning Parish Vitality

Those parishes that were required to develop a strategic action plan were grouped according to the seriousness of the problems they were facing, based on the reports they had submitted and the consultations that had taken place with the forty-two–member panel committee: red, yellow, or green, based on their solvency and vitality.

The diocesan planning office next designed an instrument entitled the Foundations and Indicators of Parish Vibrancy following the seven categories on mission that were used during the earlier 2005–2007 phase: worship, faith formation, community, service, leadership, stewardship, and evangelization. As previously noted, these seven categories suggest a selective grid of constitutive elements of the *sensus fidei* and *sensus fidelium*. This document provided a way for struggling parishes to assess their own parish activities in terms of these categories, broadening and deepening the understanding of the parish mission by drawing on biblical motifs and church teachings. The parish pastoral and finance councils were invited once again to assess the strengths of their parish and those areas that needed attention. These councils were encouraged to consult with resource people in the wider community about how to address practically the issues identified.

The Foundations and Indicators document delineated fundamental convictions based on scripture, church teaching, and pastoral practices about each of the seven basic ingredients of the mission of the local parish, and specified indicators corresponding with each of these foundations that should be evident in the life of the parish. Parishes may have previously identified these foundational ingredients and indicators in the initial parish pastoral planning process, but this document provided those parishes whose pastoral vision statements and concrete strategies were more limited with greater detail and direction for their pastoral planning. Drawing on

Vatican II and other church teachings and policies, the Foundations and Indicators document offered basic criteria or benchmarks pertaining to parish life.

For example, under the first essential element, worship, foundation 1 states, "Eucharistic celebrations are vibrant and encourage the full, conscious, active participation of all." Indicators are delineated pertaining to the presiders, the range of liturgical ministers, music ministry, and the cultural diversity of the parish. The second essential element, faith formation, has for its first foundation: "Life long faith formation programs exist to serve all members of the parish." The third essential element, community, had for its fifth foundation: "Parish leadership consults with all parishioners on a periodic basis considering future planning efforts and programming for the parish." The fourth element, service, is specified in terms of various foundations: the parish "provides opportunities and ministries for parishioners to directly serve those in need" (no. 1); "works in collaboration with Catholic Charities and/or others to provide referrals and assistance to people in need" (no. 2); "participation in special collections to . . . aid organizations . . . to respond to emergency situations" (no. 3); "encourages parishioners to be active in civic life" (no. 4) through elections and by "advocating for" and by participation in "local and global issues of social justice." The fifth essential element, leadership, includes foundational convictions about parish pastoral and finance councils, the ministries of all the baptized, and the formation of lay leadership. Stewardship and temporalities is the sixth essential element that pertains to foundational convictions about the parish exercising financial responsibility, including for parish buildings and assets. The seventh essential element, the evangelizing mission of the parish, is delineated in terms of indicators in each of the previous essential elements. This more detailed tool for evaluation addresses many features of prophetic discipleship.

In summary, I have argued that the practices designed by the Office of Pastoral Planning of the Diocese of Brooklyn and utilized by the parishes throughout the diocese correspond with basic ingredients involved in the exercise of prophetic obedience in a dialogical church. These practices also reflect a concerted effort to implement the teachings of Vatican II about synodality and conciliarity in the local church. Let me conclude this chapter by raising a number of open-ended questions that merit further consideration.

Further Observations and Questions

The first question is this: How does communal discernment, as a distinctive feature of prophetic obedience and discipleship, contribute to genuine synodality in the local church? Stated differently, how does communal discernment operate in participatory structures within parishes and dioceses? There are a variety of ways that communal discernment has developed and been employed, and over the past fifty years members have wrestled with how best to cultivate communal discernment in deliberative processes in the church. During the pontificates of John Paul II and Benedict XVI, special emphasis was given in doctrinal statements and in canonical stipulations to the norm that all synods and conciliar bodies should be consultative only.[48] This emphasis flowed from the conviction that clerical officeholders are the designated legislators and decision makers of the church by virtue of their ordination. The resulting official formulation stipulates that participatory structures of governance in the church are not in the strict sense decision making but are offering information and advice to those in higher levels of authority. The authority to render judgments and decisions in these collective ecclesial bodies resides in the primacy of ordained office, whether it be the pope in the instance of the synod of bishops; the pope and derivatively the curia for episcopal conferences; the bishop in cases of diocesan synods, diocesan pastoral councils, and presbyteral councils; and the pastor in the case of the parish pastoral council. Some bishops and priests have encouraged active roles for the nonordained in decision making by councils and synods in matters of importance. There have also been periodic laments by bishops, priests, and laypeople that their involvement in participatory structures is curtailed and undermined by the consultative-only canonical restriction. Oftentimes questions raised about participatory structures of decision making in the church prompt the rejoinder or reminder that the synodal character of the church does not mean that the church is a democracy. As noted in previous chapters, Cardinal Ratzinger warned that synods and councils should not be reduced to majority rule. Yet, to call into question the consultative-only formulation and policy, or more narrowly the precise conditions under which it is operative or not in collective bodies in the church, is not to deny that the legitimate authority of popes, bishops, and clergy can be manifest and should be respected in certain forms of decision making. The challenge going forward is to assess the consultative-only doctrine and canons in light of the teaching of Vatican II about the prophetic anointing of all the faithful in baptism and their exercise of prophetic obedience and diverse forms of authority especially through synodal forms of discernment and decision making.

A second question can be posed in a variety of ways. How can parish pastoral councils, with the pastor and pastoral staff, cultivate within the parish community at large the prophetic practice of discerning the signs of the times? Parishioners in Brooklyn were asked to raise their awareness of a targeted set of issues concerning the demographics of their parish and neighborhood. These demographics included racial and ethnic composition, migration patterns of people from around the world who arrive in the United States and make their homes in the Diocese of Brooklyn, the many other modes of mobility that shape the local church, and the economic situations and strata among the community being served. Attending to these data provided a preliminary groundwork for exploring deeper signs of the times.

Another way of formulating this question is to ask, can the kinds of issues surfaced by means of community organizing about local signs of the times be relevant for the parish community? For example, are there people in the parish and neighborhood who are struggling to find work, jobs with a living wage, and health care? What are the conditions of the local schools, their curricula, educational environments, buildings, and how are the children of parish members and neighborhood residents served by these schools as well as children in other socio-economic sectors of the larger metropolitan area? How does the racial and ethnic diversity of the parish, and the various social and cultural issues this involves, influence decision making not only in terms of pastoral planning about liturgy, religious education, and the promotion of lay ecclesial ministries, but also in terms of the attention given to struggles in areas of employment, housing, education, health care, policing, prisons, and policies of jurisprudence? Granting the attention given in the parish data gathered to the number of people attending Mass, baptisms, marriages, vocations, and funerals, the vitality of the parishes cannot be adequately assessed if the spiritual needs of members are being addressed without integrating those spiritual issues with people's aspirations and laments pertaining to the basic necessities of life and conditions for human flourishing for parish members and for their surrounding community.

Consideration of the signs of the times in parishes by means of demographics can help introduce people to discussions of larger historical, social, cultural dynamics at work in the parish and neighborhood, the local church and city, which can further be set in relation to larger regional, national, and global patterns. The issue of race provides one example of an intractable problem that is often avoided or overlooked in the parish and diocese. This is also evident in the Bronx and in New York City more generally. Protests of racial profiling in *stop-and-frisk* policing practices in the Bronx and citywide escalated during the final years of Mayor Bloomberg's administration. Unarmed black men have been killed by police officers at a disproportionately high rate in New York. This issue is not just local but national. An inordinately high percentage of people of color are in prisons, again locally and nationally. Schools in neighborhoods with high percentages of populations of people of color have practices that create a policing culture—students enter their schools through metal detectors; police officers are often stationed in the schools; students are sent home for very minor disciplinary problems. All of these contribute to what has been called the cultivation of a school-to-prison pipeline. These local and national phenomena are, in turn, part of longer historical and wider global patterns associated with the slave trade, colonialism, and the migration of people from the Global South to the north, patterns inscribed in the flesh of the many people of color in places like the Bronx and Brooklyn. These complex and neuralgic issues cannot be addressed in meaningful ways unless churches, in collaboration with their neighbors and local civic organizations, begin to raise awareness among their members of how patterns of racism are related to local, national, and international factors that contribute to transgenerational poverty and the ongoing dehumanization of people of color and immigrant populations.

In light of the treatment of the signs of the times in the previous chapter, the second question can once more be reformulated: What would it mean to face reality and bear the weight of reality in parishes? To this end, what kinds of social scientific and theological resources and inquiry would be helpful in parish settings? In some diocesan contexts social scientific analysis of the demographic patterns affecting local churches has been conducted in terms of immigration, refugees, Mass attendance, and church involvement.[49] This has been complemented more recently by greater attention to the variegated lived experiences of people in local communities. In these ways, one could argue, there has been a great deal of attention given to the signs of the times since Vatican II. Yet an adequate social discernment of the signs of the times requires not only gathering data, but expanding one's engagement with larger historical and social realities. It also necessitates building bonds of solidarity by participating in works of mercy and work for justice. Joe Holland and Peter Henriot called for this kind of approach in the 1980s, building on the legacy of Catholic Action from earlier in the twentieth century.[50] Just as parishes and dioceses have developed extensive programs of initiation into adult faith formation, parishes could also promote programs of formation in prophetic discipleship, spirituality, and community-building that elicit a deeper analysis and discernment of the signs of the times.[51] Such formation would, of course, include ongoing study of Catholic social teaching drawn from official writings of popes and episcopal conferences, and interwoven with biblical, theological, and philosophical resources. But official social teaching is not a finished deposit to be handed on and implemented in cookie-cutter fashion. Rather it constitutes a living tradition that needs to be engaged, discussed, and no doubt debated in parish forums and adult formation programs. So many pressing issues in the public arena rarely get discussed in parish settings: matters pertaining to poverty and economic disparity, gender and racial justice, war and peace, and the environment. The challenge is for parishes to continue to widen the circle of parishioners who are cultivating solidarity, works of mercy, and work for justice as a part of their evangelizing mission, spiritual formation, and in the liturgical life and aesthetics of the parish.

A third line of inquiry asks, does the *sensus fidei* and *sensus fidelium* have any bearing on the work of the parish pastoral council for and with the parish, and if so how? I have suggested that the seven essential elements of faith that were used in the Diocese of Brooklyn to assess parish pastoral work offer a rudimentary framework that corresponds with dimensions of the *sensus fidei* and *sensus fidelium*. So, for instance, the elements of worship, faith formation, service, and evangelization provide formal and simple articulations of basic features of Catholic Christian faith, yet in each category there is much of the content of faith that is implied but unarticulated. The perception, recognition, and reception of the professed faith of the church by individuals and groups demand much greater scrutiny and exploration, especially in terms of the daily life and practices of believers.

The creedal core of faith, pertaining to Christians' deepest convictions about the triune God, the human person, salvation, the church and the world, sacraments, and human destiny in history and in eternity, is nowhere explicitly addressed in the Brooklyn process. This is not surprising. And yet the essential elements of the faith life and mission of the parish as articulated by the Brooklyn Office of Pastoral Planning—worship, faith formation, community, service, leadership, stewardship and temporalities, and evangelization—provide cognitive, affective, and moral scaffolding in every parish for all of these doctrinal areas—the triune God, the human person, salvation, and so on. Moreover, parish communities are deeply informed by their participation in the baptismal and Eucharistic faith of the church, the scriptures that are publicly read and commented on in the liturgy, and the creeds they profess in public worship. All of these provide a grammar, narratives, and rhetorical moorings for the living faith of the church. Participating in these mediums of the faith of the church helps create and sustain bonds of shared love and knowledge, motivations for worship, and incentives for works of mercy and work for justice.

At the same time, the parish community and lay and ordained ecclesial ministers should not be naïve in their approach to the mystery of faith as it is perceived, received, and lived out in the everyday lives of people in the parish. Beyond the dynamic core of faith that is shared, there are distinctive forms of personal piety and spirituality, and myriad ways of understanding, interpreting, and engaging the faith of the church as it illuminates the mystery of the triune God, the identity of Jesus Christ and the Spirit, the human person, the church, the world, time and eternity; and these may not be shared by all parishioners whether they be conscientiously devoted, lapsed, or anywhere in between. The faith of the church is accordingly always a matter of contestation and negotiation for individuals, families, and in ever-wider circles of the parish community and the local diocesan church. This is the structure and dynamic of the everyday life of faith. Just as Catholics recognize various levels of authority in the teachings of the church, and a hierarchy of truths that is variously shared with members of other Christian churches and communities, so too in the parish, members can be bound together in affection, commitment, worship, and faith-in-action by many core beliefs and practices, and yet struggle with and question dimensions of these very beliefs and practices. That this is so is a sign of a vital, searching faith, a faith that is anything but moribund.

At any given liturgy, the celebrant and homilist works out of a particular form and style of spirituality, and a particular theological orientation toward the identity and mission of Jesus Christ and the church, that certain members of the parish may not share. The same can be said of the ministers of liturgical music, religious educators, and other lay or ordained ecclesial leaders. Every pastor, council, and parish community at some level of consciousness realizes something it would not hurt to publicly acknowledge: that there are certain beliefs and practices of the church that are a cause of concern, lament, and dissent in the hearts and minds of individual parishioners, and likely among families, age groups, and racial and ethnic populations. Numerous people who attend Mass, however frequently, have serious questions about the faith of the church. But parishes rarely offer opportunities for people to acknowledge and discuss these questions openly.

One of the most widely known examples of a contested matter of the Catholic faith in our day illustrates the matter. How does the faith of the church address the experience of the diversity of sexual orientations? The US bishops have become outspoken public advocates against gay and lesbian civil unions and marriage. There is now a campaign under way to fire teachers in Catholic elementary and middle schools who are in an active gay or lesbian relationships. At times, the church's strong unyielding moral claim may be united with a soft pastoral position toward gays and lesbians. One can find parishes that have an open policy of hospitality toward gay and lesbian members and that welcome their involvement in parish ministries and outreach. Other parishes operate with a don't ask, don't tell policy. And there are still other parishes where priests and lay ecclesial ministers may express rejection or hostility toward gay and lesbian members. This range of positions discloses and foments painful tensions and conflicts for many gay and lesbian members of the church, and their parents, siblings, relatives, and friends. What if one's conscience, based on prayerful inquiry into the belief in God's creation and the destiny of people, cannot abide by the official teachings of the church on this issue? In this and other cases, the *sensus fidei* of individuals and the *sensus fidelium* of a significant percentage of the people of God may not be in agreement with the communicated faith of the church. Many active Catholics, especially among the young, have reached the conclusion that, while they share—and love—the faith of the Catholic church in so many ways, it is hypocritical to remain active in a church that violates some of their most self-consciously considered convictions. The parish should not be naïve about these and other matters of disagreement, and the pastor and the council should promote a culture of sensitivity surrounding them. Under certain conditions, the parish might search for ways to create forums for people to talk about their own experiences and struggles surrounding painfully contested issues. This kind of discussion should also be promoted at the diocesan levels through councils and synods, and at the national level through forums organized by episcopal conferences. Consulting the people of God in matters of faith and doctrine requires cultivating prophetic dialogue in service of prophetic obedience.

A fourth question for further exploration concerns how a parish pastoral council exercises its prophetic obligation in a way that resists blind obedience to the will of another individual or a group, or to unquestioned ecclesial or cultural assumptions and practices. This question is important because prophetic obedience is, as I have claimed in agreement with others, the antithesis of blind obedience. Parish pastoral councils, like other expressions of the synodal character of the church, are arenas where this claim is tested. When parish pastoral councils deliberate about the parish mission, strategic pastoral plan, and courses of action, there is an exercise of power. Whenever decision making is involved, there are power dynamics inevitably at work. Parish leaders' efforts to make decisions that advance the gospel and the good of the community are inevitably intertwined with the convictions, interpretations of the gospel and the good of the community, and interests of individuals and subgroups involved. As a result council meetings are a space where conflicts of convictions, interpretations, and interests inevitably arise. When they do, they should be faced; acknowledged and placed on the table; and, when appropriate, discussed, rather than left to operate covertly, unconsciously, or under the table. Too often religious people, perhaps more often Catholics, including clergy and people involved in parish pastoral councils, are conflict averse. People *go along*, taking the lead of the pastor or dominant personalities rather than talking through potentially challenging issues that impinge on the vitality of the parish. People sometimes simply lower their expectations about addressing concerns that people feel passionately about, or they just walk away, rather than experiment with generous and honest ways to face conflict and to face the difficulties involved in addressing them.

Prophetic obedience in councils requires cultivating practices that favor talking through difficult matters when they arise with patience, generosity of spirit, tact, and honesty. To enact these skills requires avoiding polarizing postures. At times it may necessitate taking a stand against authoritarian or paternalistic personalities, lay or clergy, without denying the need for strong individual leadership and different kinds of personalities in councils. It may demand vigilant resistance to mob mentalities or groupthink bred by cliques with special interests or elites with special knowledge, without denying the quest for collective wisdom oriented toward honest consensus among the council as a whole, and respectful of the special and legitimate charisms and passions of subgroups that have important contributions to make in the parish. Pastors, council members, and the parish staff must develop a culture of care for one another and culture of honesty as the basis for developing processes of mutual accountability in the parish. This usually means that the parish's ministries, vision, pastoral objectives, and courses of action should be reviewed every few years. Like community organizing groups, parish councils should also evaluate significant events, particular ministries, and the quality of prayer, preaching, and hospitality. Only when the council along with the pastor and pastoral team can together affirm the gifts and resources of the parish community, while also communicating with one another about ways the parish is falling short of its missionary mandate, will parish vitality and growth be fostered.

Mention of mutual accountability within the parish context fostered by the parish pastoral council surfaces larger questions about whether the church at large fosters open processes of accountability, where the use of secrecy and the avoidance of certain controversial topics can be resisted and overcome. The clergy sex abuse scandal was a watershed event in terms of exposing the lack of structures and practices of accountability for priests and bishops, and the widespread clerical culture of secrecy in the Catholic Church. A different example is provided by the moratorium, that is, the imposed silence placed by John Paul II and Cardinal Joseph Ratzinger on open discussions of the theological possibility for ordaining women. The church has failed to create safe spaces and cultures that foster open conversation about a variety of issues concerning racism, the role of women in the church and society, and sexual diversity.

Parish pastoral councils are by design mission oriented. The foundational work of the council is to exercise imagination, to evoke and design an ecclesial social imaginary that can ground a pastoral strategy for promoting the mission of the parish. This endeavor depends on collegiality, collaboration, and partnership among the pastor, the lay ecclesial ministers, the parish staff, and the parish pastoral council. Together these leaders should be on the lookout for the next generation or next wave of lay leaders for ministry and for the parish pastoral council, and actively invite such persons to discern whether they have a call to leadership. But their most important collective aim is to help advance the mission of all the faithful of the parish: in their everyday lives, among their families, in their jobs, in civic life, in works of mercy and work for justice, in the mystical and political dimensions of prophetic identity. The transformation of a parish into a mission-driven community ultimately depends on the cultivation of an approach to mission that is, by design, focused on prophetic dialogue and prophetic obedience.

This chapter has sought to demonstrate ways that the various traits involved in prophetic obedience are operative in the communal processes employed by parish pastoral councils in the Diocese of Brooklyn and by the Northwest Bronx Community and Clergy Coalition. Broad-based community organizing and parish pastoral councils offer two of the clearest examples of prophetic obedience in a dialogical church. In fact, the processes used to advance grassroots democracy through community organizing and local synodality through parish pastoral councils are not only structurally similar. They are also analogous in their processes of discernment of the Spirit at work in the community in aspirations and laments; and they share some of the deepest orienting convictions of the *sensus fidei* and *sensus fidelium* in terms of a Word received and witness given. These connections provide the basis for a powerful synergism or dynamic field of interaction between parishes promoting local forms of synodality and coalitions promoting grassroots democracy.

I have emphasized throughout my treatment that prophetic obedience in a dialogical church must be based on and nourished by practices of heeding, receiving, and responding to the voice of the Spirit, discerned in aspirations and laments that express the joys and hopes, and frustrations and failures, of the precarious life of the people of God, just as they are based on and nourished by the Word of God received, witnessed to, and proclaimed in word and deed. Prophetic obedience demands that individuals and communities regularly return to their frustrations and failures not only in the neighborhood and the parish community, but also in broad-based community organizations and parish pastoral councils. Periodic listening campaigns and accountability sessions provide the necessary opportunities to surface the power of these deepest unfulfilled aspirations, and to lift up the unresolved disappointments and disturbances at the work of individuals and the community. The ongoing vitality of the community depends on the ability to draw on the energy found in such aspirations and laments. This capacity provides the wellspring for the summoned self and the commissioned church.

Chapter 7

INDIVIDUATION AND COMMUNION:
SUMMONED SELF AND
COMMISSIONED CHURCH

To say that the vision of the church as the people of God has been eclipsed by the official ecclesiology of communion over the past three decades does not mean that inspiration offered by this theology did not remain influential in various places or that official teachings during the pontificates of John Paul II and Benedict XVI avoided the category of people of God altogether. And to speak of the ascendance and heyday of an official ecclesiology of communion between 1978 and 2013, one associated with centralization, clericalism, and paternalism, is not to claim that every ecclesiology of communion is so defined. The theological and pastoral challenge at present, one that has been boldly advanced by Pope Francis, is to develop the prophetic character of the people of God in keeping with practices of synodality and conciliarity in ways that complement and remain in mutually accountable relationship with the church understood as communion. This important, unfinished task of the council must be worked out at multiple levels: in teaching and practice, canon law, and church structures. In closing, I want to signal one deeper conceptual issue that must be addressed if the relationship between the prophetic character of the people of God and the church understood as communion is to be successfully clarified.

The issue can be posed in the form of a question: how can the prophetic summons of individuals and the prophetic commission of local churches and small mission-driven communities be affirmed and actuated as a basic dimension of the church understood as communion? The difficulty is that cultivating a person's individual identity and vocation, and a community's distinctive identity and mission, processes I shall speak of here using the technical term *individuation*, are viewed by some theologians and church leaders as contrary and antithetical to communion. Individuation and communion are frequently cast as comparable to the polarity of individualism and communitarianism—that is, as mutually exclusive. This false and misleading characterization and comparison often informs theological assessments and contributes to widespread difficulty in conceiving prophetic obedience in relation to ecclesial communion. Let me identify three laments in the church that illustrate the problem.

Lamenting Three Signs of the Times

First, an alarming number of young people in the United States born since the 1960s (Generation X, born 1962 to 1980, and the Millennial generation, born 1981 to 1995) choose not to pursue their personal life aspirations or to struggle with their life difficulties in church communities.[1] They have, researchers tell us, "a weaker and more tentative affiliation with the institutional church than previous generations."[2] This is especially troubling because these same young people often acknowledge spiritual hungers, seek to give a meaningful account of themselves, and are searching for a sense of purpose and destiny in their personal lives. Yet churches in the United States, recent studies have documented, "provide almost nothing for the developmental tasks that are accomplished when people are in their twenties and thirties. [As a result,] younger adults are having to invent their own ways of making decisions and seeking support for those decisions."[3] These changing patterns of church affiliation among younger people are taking place in the aftermath of "a seismic shift [that] has occurred in the church—a shift from the compliance-based approach of the 1940s and '50s to the conscience-based approach of more recent decades. As a result, young Catholics still think of themselves as Catholic, and they are more religious than many older people realize, but, compared to their pre–Vatican II grandparents, they are more likely to be Catholic on their own terms."[4]

Second, many US women today, whether or not they self-identify as feminists, seek to pursue and realize their identities freely as equals with men, even as they continue to struggle against restrictive female roles in the family, society, and in churches.[5] Studies continue to confirm that women consistently "exhibit a greater commitment to, involvement with and belief in religion."[6] But women, both young and old, including many Catholics, are often frustrated and angered by much in their churches. For many Catholic women, these frustrations include teachings on gender complementarity and feminine genius; dismissive responses to arguments of Catholic feminists; and the attitudes and actions of clergy who do not recognize their struggles for greater freedom, who fail to give full voice to the testimonies of women from the scriptures and the history of Christianity, and who restrict them in exercising church leadership in the everyday life of the church. In the face of this, a significant percentage of Catholic women have chosen to leave their parishes in search of church communities more attuned to their quest for full participation, whether by ordination or simply by allowing the full exercise of women's leadership in the church's varied ministries.[7] Other Catholic women disagree with their church's policies and practices on women's roles but remain dedicated to their faith traditions and continue to participate in their church communities. Some of these women vocalize their laments, taking a stance of loyal opposition; others suffer in silence with anger repressed or displaced.[8] It should come as no surprise that younger Catholic women are increasingly less devout; less orthodox; and they practice their religion less, if at all.[9]

A third lament arises from the widely divergent experiences of local churches in Africa, Asia, and Latin America during the postcolonial period and of their descendants in immigrant communities in US cities like New York. In the course of the twentieth century, members of local churches in the Southern Hemisphere began increasingly to wrestle with the legacy of a Eurocentric Christianity that had been transplanted on their soil generations ago, usually by well-intentioned missionaries. In the United States, a long-practiced integrationist approach to Catholic parish identity has frequently met with resistance among the range of immigrants who are transforming the face of US Catholicism, with large numbers from Latin America and the Caribbean, as well as smaller but significant numbers of immigrants from Catholic populations in African countries and from Asia, most notably the Philippines and Vietnam.[10] The last thirty years have seen a variety of attempts by immigrants in local churches to acknowledge and respect communal memories and cultural practices, and to draw on aspects of local indigenous culture and sometimes diverse religious traditions to inculturate the Christian faith.[11] Yet these efforts have at times been discredited or met with resistance by religious authorities, resulting in frustration and anger among immigrant or indigenous populations. During this same period of time, we have also witnessed growing membership in Pentecostal churches in the Global South and among their descendants in US cities, churches that offer their own, oftentimes strongly appealing approaches to incorporating these local cultural and religious traditions.[12]

What can be learned from these laments? I will explore this question by considering two potential responses.

How Is One to Respond to These Three Signs of the Times?

Option One: Resist Individualization by Promoting Ecclesial Communion

One option is to criticize these three phenomena as manifestations of the ascendance of individualism and its debilitating effects on persons and communities during the modern period. Seen from this perspective, individualization may be differentiated into three cumulative phases or dimensions that track with the unfolding of modern liberal ideology: secularization; liberation movements; and epistemological, moral, cultural, and religious relativism. In Catholic theology, we see this argument exemplified by the theology of Joseph Ratzinger over the course of his career, including in his official statements as Pope Benedict XVI. This approach is also associated with the positions and policies of Pope John Paul II.[13]

As a counterforce to the destructive processes of individualization identified with individualism, official Catholic teaching has advanced an ecclesiology of communion that emphasizes the centrality of church community, beliefs, and practices for shaping people's identities and way of life. Developed during the pontificates of John Paul II and Benedict XVI, and drawing on classical scriptural and theological categories and important passages from the documents of Vatican II, this official Catholic ecclesiology of communion was embodied in the new code of canon law, the universal catechism, and in various curial policies and decrees.[14]

Instead of speaking of personal individuation, key proponents of communion ecclesiology, such as Joseph Ratzinger and Eastern Orthodox theologian and Metropolitan of Pergamon John Zizioulas, have espoused Christian personalism. Christian personalism, as they describe it, acknowledges the importance of interpersonal and social relationships in the formation of the human person according to sacramental, canonical, creedal, and catechetical standards. But this approach can place restrictions on the freedom of critical or creative thought and action by individuals or communities when they call into question official teachings and practices.[15] As we have seen, communion ecclesiology as developed in Catholic theology since the mid-1980s has been intended by its architects to be a corrective to certain post–Vatican II receptions of an ecclesiology of the people of God deemed to have resonances with secularization, misguided liberation movements, and suspect programs of inculturation. This official Catholic approach to communion ecclesiology, with its particular vision of personalism, seeks to address the longings of youth to purify the allegedly liberal impulses operative in feminism (and in other liberation theologies), and to protect both against the encroachment of indigenous traditions and Pentecostal and evangelical sects into Catholic communities, and against the threat of hybrid and multiple forms of religious belonging associated with cultural and religious pluralism. On this view, to overcome the problems associated with modern liberal individualism, or its postmodern variations, one needs to communicate effectively—in preaching, religious education, and faith formation—a clearly demarcated ecclesial identity and mission handed on in faith-specific traditions of belief and practice, through the exercise of strong episcopal and clerical leadership. The outstanding question raised by this option is whether it sufficiently addresses the striving for individuation by individual persons and local communities.

Option Two: Advocate Prophetic Individuation-in-Communion

A second option, which I will describe and defend here, advances the promotion of personal and collective individualization by way of a conception of individuation in community, or to state it theologically, prophetic individuation-in-communion.[16] Seen from this second vantage point, efforts by representatives of the Catholic Church to repudiate the aspirations of young adults, women, and postcolonial local churches in the Global South, and immigrant populations in the United States, by reducing them to manifestions of modern individualism—and thus as signs of moral and spiritual deficiency and decay—are defective, destructive, and counterproductive. Contemporary theology, and ecclesiology in particular, need a far more complex analysis and assessment of modern and postmodern processes of individualization. The argumentative flaw emerges whenever all forms of *individuation* are judged to be *individualistic,* and it is assumed that any form of individuation repudiates a constructive role for religious and civic communities in forming identity and influencing life goals. I argue, on the contrary, that some forms of individuation, personal and collective, do grant the importance and necessity of communities and, for theology, an ecclesiology of communion, but without subscribing to a reductively harmonious understanding of relationships. My approach affirms individuation, with its correlative roles for freedom, conscience, criticism, and creativity, as the indispensable source of vitality, evolution, and maturation for persons and communities. To affirm the call and mission of individuation, moreover, one inevitably must acknowledge the constructively agonistic or conflictive character of negotiating diversity and plurality in communities. Theologies and policies of communion may seek to circumvent or squelch the agonistic dimension of individuation, but they do so at the expense of the vitality of the church.

I have chosen to employ the term *individuation* rather than the more traditional and commonly used term *personalism.* In recent theology, personalism is sometimes deployed in ways that leave insufficient room for the critical and creative ways individuals and groups exercise freedom in identity formation and life orientation. Moreover, Catholic versions of personalism often assume a universalist, centralized, and classicist understanding of the church that fails to take adequate account of the historical and contextual character of local communities, especially on the periphery, and the efforts of these communities to promote the creation of more polycentric sources of creative energy in the church.

The individuation of persons and of local communities is necessary in order to enable churches to effectively cultivate both inclusive policies of belonging of diverse peoples, and a shared mission orientation that acknowledges and honors cultural and religious pluralism as necessary for, rather than obstacles to, an adequate theology of communion. Individuation so understood is not individualistic in the sense of being egoistic or selfish, nor is it based on an atomistic and libertarian sense of the self that engenders isolation, consumerism, and materialism. Individuation, in fact, describes the life-long processes of personal and communal identity formation and missionary orientation and activity. I contend that there is no genuine ecclesial communion without genuinely individuated persons and local communities, and there is no Christian individuation without effective, dialogical communication associated with vibrant communities of faith.

Conceptual Clarification

Individuation names the life-long endeavor by individuals and groups to discover, construct, negotiate, and actualize a sense of identity, through which they pursue animating desires and address challenging concerns. My assumption is that individuating processes have been operative in every generation, even in periods in history and in societies where collective forms of consciousness have predominated. However, various social dynamics associated with modernization have led in our times to growing awareness of personal and collective individuation. In Catholic ecclesiology, attending to modes of individuation provides a complement and a needed corrective to classical views of the human person and community informed by a stable, if not static, social and cosmic worldview, on the basis of which integration and communion were established by means of traditional beliefs, practices, and exercises of hierarchical authority.

No less important, individuation as I seek to formulate it here also offers a stark alternative to modern and postmodern understandings of personal individuality that are egoistic, atomistic, and self-centered—in other words, individualistic. Such egoistic views of individuality strongly inform dimensions of liberal theory, consumer culture, pop psychology, and lifestyle enclaves. Equating individuality with the pursuit of personal satisfactions, self-improvement, consumption, and leisure, egoistic individualisms fail to give sufficient credit to the role of communities, traditions, and practices in the formation of the self, and are unable to articulate and defend larger collective goals and goods.

In short, *individuation* needs to be differentiated from *individualism*. Too often they are conflated. Personal and collective modes of individuation can involve discovery and actualization through communal relations and modes of communication that operate with a comprehensive, interpersonal, and social view of the self and community. The practices and discourses of individuation may at times contribute to, but are ultimately not reducible to, personal and collective forms of individualism.

What is distinctive about individualism, and why does it (rightly) draw criticism from a Christian theological perspective? Sociologist Steven Lukes has shown that the term has taken on distinctive traits in France, Germany, (North) America, and England. Significantly, the term was initially used in derision. Its French form, "*individualisme*,' grew out of the negative reaction to the French Revolution and to its alleged source, the thought of the Enlightenment."[17] Edmund Burke, Joseph de Maistre, Louis de Bonald, and Claude Henri de Saint-Simon and their heirs were joined in "their critique of the Enlightenment's glorification of the individual, their horror of social atomization and anarchy, as well as their desire for an organic, stable, hierarchically organized, harmonious social order."[18] These French authors identified diverse historical frameworks for the emergence of individualism, "variously traced to the Reformation, the Renaissance, the Enlightenment, the Revolution, to the decline of the aristocracy or the Church or traditional religion, to the Industrial Revolution, to the growth of capitalism or democracy, . . . [and yet] there is a wide agreement in seeing it as an evil and a threat to social cohesion."[19]

Charles Taylor and Michael Sandel have argued that the defenses of liberalism by both John Rawls and Ronald Dworkin are excessively individualistic and fail to fully account for the importance of communities in the formation of the self and in promoting the moral good of society.[20] Charles Taylor maintains that Dworkin's and Rawls' liberalism offers a universal standpoint based on reason from which a person creates oneself and continues to change course over one's life span. Taylor finds this understanding of the self atomistic and untenable.[21] In fact, he argues, people come to realize a sense of self through their participation in communities, traditions, institutions, and practices. These inform their sense of the self and of the goods of society.

Others take aim at liberal individualism as it is embodied in modern economic theory, for instance, in the thought of Ludwig von Mises and Friedrich von Hayek, the architects of the Austrian school of economics.[22] In the United States, extreme forms of economic liberalism have most recently become associated with Ayn Rand, libertarianism, and the proponents of the Tea Party.[23] The Austrian school of economics has been criticized by Steven Lukes and Angus Sibley for excessive and exaggerated individualism that undermine any conception of the common good, solidarity, and social justice in the civic arena, and thereby promote antigovernment animus and corporate greed.[24]

It is worth noting that the tradition of German romanticism developed its own, positive, doctrine of *Individualität* and *Eigentümlichkeit*, which surfaced initially in the writings of Wilhelm von Humboldt, Novalis, Friedrich Schlegel, and Friedrich Schleiermacher, which was subsequently widely received. This tradition offered an alternative to the Enlightenment version of the self based on reason and freedom, and sought to articulate the individuality of persons and communities as emerging from interpersonal bonds of affection, and communal forms of life and belief. Charles Taylor speaks of the embodiment of this tradition in terms of the "expressive individualism" of intellectual and artistic elites who "searched for the authentic way of living or expressing themselves throughout the nineteenth century." In the twentieth century, "this kind of self-orientation seems to have become a mass phenomenon. Its most obvious manifestation has perhaps been the consumer revolution."[25] The more communal orientation of this tradition, especially in its nineteenth-century beginnings, lends support to my case for understanding individuation as distinct from individualism.[26]

Collective individuation can pertain to any group identified by a shared past, common convictions, aspirations, and practices. When considering Christian groups, and particularly Catholic ones, individuated groups can be any community that has fashioned and affirmed a particular set of traditions of belief and practice, cultures and institutions, memories and hopes through forms of collective discernment and decision making. We will explore some examples of collective individuation in the final part of this chapter, using new ecclesial movement to illustrate. However, my larger argument is that cultivating collective individuation is necessary for the vitality of the church across the whole spectrum of ecclesial life: in practices of synodality and conciliarity within local parishes and dioceses; in conciliar modes of decision making in men's and women's religious communities; in analogous forms of communal discernment and decision making in small mission-driven communities, and so on.

Is it possible to offer examples of collective forms of individualism? These can perhaps be found among persons who seek out what Robert Bellah has called life-style enclaves, wherein individuals with similar tastes pursue an egoistic vision of the good life based on the coincidence of self-interests rather than seeking a substantive community that is oriented around a multivocal, diversely embodied, but thick vision of human flourishing and the common good.[27] In this regard, Bellah also speaks of self-interest politics, in which individuals join groups to advance their personal interests but are unable to articulate and advance collective shared goods.[28]

If one were seeking to identify instances of collective individualism in Catholic ecclesiology, one might explore the criticisms of the eighteenth-century views identified as Gallicanism in France, Febronianism in Germany, and Josephinism in Austria, and the wider charge against conciliarism. As in the case with so many accusations of heresies, the question would be whether the targets named are guilty of the charges leveled against them. Parochialism, as well, is by its definition a form of collective individualism that calls into question and threatens wider networks of relationships and collective action.

Theologically Justifying Individuation

There are several theological arguments that provide warrants for the personal and collective individuation I am advocating here. One concentrates on the implications of the doctrine of creation, a second on the identity and mission of Jesus of Nazareth and the correlative demands of Christian discipleship, and a third based on the charisms of the Holy Spirit. In fact, theologians over the years have given much attention to charism and vocation as important avenues for reflecting on the distinctive features of individuals and individuality in the Christian tradition.[29] Let me identify several influential theological trajectories.

Medieval theologian and philosopher John Duns Scotus (1266–1308) is widely recognized for drawing attention to what makes persons and things distinctive.[30] He wrote of this in terms of their individual uniqueness, which he called *haecceitas*. Often translated as *thisness*, *haecceitas* refers to the distinctive qualities, properties, or characteristics that identify the particularity of a person or object in contrast to the *whatness* or *quiddity* of a person or object, which refers to universal qualities shared by all examples of its kind. Scotus's notion of *haecceity* had a significant impact on the poetry of nineteenth-century Jesuit Gerard Manley Hopkins, whose doctrine of *inscape* celebrates the glory of God at work in the individuation process in all of creation, including humans.[31] In the twentieth century, Scotus's views were likewise important for Thomas Merton's differentiation of the true and the false self.[32]

Early nineteenth-century German Catholic theologian Franz Anton Staudenmaier, a foremost Catholic contemporary critic of the influential philosophy of Georg Friedrich Hegel, gave considerable attention to individuality in a book devoted to the *pragmatism of spiritual gifts*. Staudenmaier described the human journey from slavery into the freedom of individuality, which is manifested in the individuality of persons, families, and peoples.[33] It is interesting to note that a century later, Hans Urs von Balthasar, who was indebted to Staudenmaier's critique of Hegel, likewise devoted special attention to the role of the individual mission of Jesus Christ and of the Christian disciple.[34]

Staudenmaier's and Balthasar's lines of argument overlap with one I have advanced in Chapter 4: Jesus realizes his individual vocation and mission not only by being obedient to the Father, but also by his obedience to the Spirit. This is depicted in the gospels in the episode of the anointing of the Spirit in the baptism of the Lord (Mk 1:9–11; Mt 3:13–17; Lk 3:21–22; cf. Jn 1:32–34). Here Jesus's identity as messianic son of God is made manifest, and immediately thereafter the Spirit compels him into a wilderness, a desert, a wasteland where he is tempted by evil spirits that call into question the precise nature of his identity and mission (Mk 1:12–13; Mt 4:1–11; Lk 4:1–13). What is at stake in this conflict is precisely the individuation of Jesus. Jesus's public mission begins after this struggle, and Luke's gospel capitulates this scene by having Jesus proclaim a reading from Isaiah that speaks about obedience to voice of the Spirit in the cries of the poor, the captives, the blind, and the oppressed (Lk 4:18–19). Jesus's heeding, receiving, and responding to the call of the Father and of the Spirit are the basis for his unfolding identity and mission. In keeping with Staudenmaier's work on a theology of individuation and Hans Urs von Balthasar's theology, which draws on Staudenmaier, this can contribute to a Christian understanding of the triune God, in which the individuating identities and missions of the Spirit and the Son are realized in communion with the Father or divine source. Such a theology of the triune God can provide inspiration not only for an emphasis on Trinitarian theology as a justification for ecclesial communion, but precisely for an ecclesiology of individuation in communion.

Three philosophical motifs are pertinent for the theologian's reflection on individuation. First, the classic Kantian Enlightenment theme of coming of age, maturity, and adulthood represents the individual's call to break free from authoritarianism in order to have the courage to think for oneself. This coming-of-age motif is associated with the reform-minded desire to break free from clericalism and paternalism in the church and other forms of authoritarianism in society, and it is a theme articulated theologically in the contemporary writings of Paul Lakeland and Johann Baptist Metz.[35] Charles Taylor has developed a complex philosophical analysis and defense of the modern and postmodern quest for individual authenticity in an age often criticized for its individualism, secularism, relativism, and nihilism.[36] And philosopher Judith Butler has given special attention to individuation in her analysis of the human person in terms of gender performance, the precariousness of life, and the summons to give an account of oneself, a treatment that is receiving increasing attention in theology.[37]

Without denying the benefits of these theological and philosophical resources and rationales for individuation, I am specifically arguing that individuation also be considered as a distinguishing feature of prophetic identity. The recovery of the prophetic character of all the baptized in the writings of the Second Vatican Council provides a particularly fruitful theological framework for understanding and justifying an ecclesiology of personal and collective individuation in communion. Prophetic individuation identifies a distinctively Christian understanding of personal and collective Christian identity, one that provides a necessary complement to the sacramental ecclesiology of communion. One of the greatest achievements of the Second Vatican Council was to reclaim the biblical motif of the people of God, which includes the affirmation of the prophetic character of all believers as a lens for interpreting the historical pilgrim character of the church. Through the anointing of the Spirit in baptism, the council taught that all believers share in the priestly, kingly, and prophetic identity and mission of Jesus Christ; all are called to participate as equal members in the mission of the church. Associated with the prophetic character of the baptized is the *sensus fidei*, the instinct of faith that enables individuals and communities to perceive the faith of the church, to discern its meaning for life and action, to witness to the truth of the faith in word and deed, and to be attentive and responsive to the signs of the times. In short, the prophetic anointing initiates a call to be attentive to the signs of the times, and to be honest in facing reality, in discernment, and in action. To do this requires receptivity to the Word of God and a willingness to communicate it. But no less important, it requires heeding the voice of the Spirit of God in the aspirations and laments of people and of the entire created world. The prophetic witness of individuals and communities finds its source of inspiration and motivation in the aspirations of those who search for fullness of life, and in the lamentations of those who struggle with the conditions of precarious life. Prophetic individuation provides the necessary complement to the church understood as communion.

The Quest for Individuation-in-Communion in the Church

Having clarified the basic terms in the argument, let us return to the original problem. Why are so many young adults pursuing their quest for meaning, identity, and life projects unaccompanied by a church community? Why are women leaving the church out of frustration or anger and joining other churches, or giving up on Christianity or religion altogether? Why are many people in the Southern Hemisphere, including Africans, Latin Americans, and Asians, or immigrant populations in the United States, leaving Catholic parishes and dioceses to join Pentecostal churches or churches that preach the gospel of prosperity, or communities that practice indigenous religious traditions disassociated from Christianity?

We can expand the field of inquiry. Why is it that an increasing number of people are becoming unaffiliated from their religious communities? And why is it that some people choose to remain in their parishes but with chronic disappointment and chronically low expectations for their communal life?

The Pursuit of Engaging Ecclesial Social Imaginaries

What are these people seeking and not finding? Here I find helpful a category developed by Charles Taylor. People are looking for what Taylor calls social imaginaries, ways of envisioning the world that capture their attention, engage their life passions, and address their laments; these people seek social imaginaries that help them face honestly the precariousness of life, and that help them gather together in communities and communicate with each other about what is most pressing and what is most cherished. In the words of Taylor, these social imaginaries identify "the ways in which [people] imagine their social existence, how they fit together with others, how things go on between them and their fellows, the expectations which are normally met, and the deeper notions and images which underlie these expectations."[38] Social imaginaries are first of all "the way ordinary people 'imagine' their social surroundings . . . often not in theoretical terms, [but] in images, stories, legends;" secondly they provide a collective vision that is persuasive for groups of people; and thirdly, they provide a "common understanding which makes possible common practices, and a widely shared sense of legitimacy."[39]

In various writings, Taylor explores the quest for and realization of social imaginaries at the macrolevel of history, tracing various groups, societies, and practices in diverse periods in history. I wish to suggest, however, that social imaginary can also name a particular ecclesial odyssey and reality found in grassroots, local faith communities and in intermediate-level institutions. The social imaginary of the church is not reducible to an ecclesiology of communion that emphasizes the sacramental communion of local churches and the universal church, but should also thrive on the collective individuation of the local church, imagined and narrated as a prophetic people of God on pilgrimage in particular historical and social settings. A diocese, a parish, a small Christian community, an ecclesial movement can develop its own distinctive ecclesial social imaginary, which then serves to individuate that community's identity and mission, and to sustain the life of individuals and the group.

Vibrant Christian communities large and small invite their members into distinctive ecclesial social imaginaries. Through symbols and stories, communities provide an imaginative construal of Christianity that helps individuals understand themselves within a network of social relations both within the community and in relation to the larger society. Moreover, ecclesial communities establish and mobilize participation in common practices that identify the community and its mission. The way a community embodies and passes on these symbols, stories, and practices provides the basis for the community's legitimacy and its vitality for members and newcomers. There are, however, churches that seem to have legitimacy but not vitality. A crisis of vitality may, in fact, mask—or be a symptom of—a crisis of legitimacy. And such crises frequently signal an inability or failure on the part of the group and its leaders to foster personal and collective individuation.

Ecclesial social imaginaries are vital when communities are creative, imaginative, experimental, and practical in drawing on their symbols, stories, and practices to engage people's passions, to address openly the challenges of everyday life, and to bear in life-giving ways the weight of realities associated with the signs of the times. This is not to deny the importance of traditional practices associated with ecclesial existence. But it is the ways in which traditional texts and practices are invoked and embodied that account for their vitality. Creativity and willingness to experiment are particularly important because collective individuation is a work of the creative and productive imagination. Collective individuation is also a work of practical reasoning, or *phronesis*, which is the Greek philosophical term for practical wisdom associated with the Latin word for prudence; and it entails practices of rhetoric, the Greek and Latin art of constructing persuasive speech based on sound argument by a person of character, crafted to engage the passionate reason of the audience.

Official Structures of Church Participation: The Often Disappointing Option

In the wake of the Second Vatican Council, members of the Catholic Church have witnessed canonically prescribed efforts to realize a revised and revitalized ecclesial imaginary at every level of the church. Whereas the pre–Vatican II imaginary portrayed parishes and local churches as offering relatively uniform replicas or imitations of the imaginary of the universal church, Vatican II's ecclesial imaginary became self-consciously pluriform, and in the process of reception during the decades after the council, increasingly contested.[40]

Many post–Vatican II local churches cultivated dialogical practices by implementing canonically prescribed structures for discerning identity and mission, which we have explored in Chapters 1 and 2.[41] As we have seen illustrated in New York, this is a story of a difficult transition still under way—from the church associated with a centralized, hierarchical, and clerical ecclesiology to a dialogical ecclesiology; from pyramidal structures to intersecting circles; from a unidirectional approach to communication practices associated with synodality, conciliarity, collegiality, widespread consultation, and collaboration.

To make this kind of paradigm shift requires learning new skills and developing new social practices of dialogical discernment and decision making, all crucial for advancing collective and personal individuation. There are, the evidence suggests, significant numbers of parishes and local churches where these communicative skills are being learned and these social practices developed, with real consequences for how a community prays, forms community, welcomes new members, and serves its members, those in its neighborhood and region, and even through global outreach. The data also shows many failed attempts, setbacks, and frustrations. In my judgment, the failure to realize a dialogical ecclesiology is one of the primary reasons why people do not find parishes and local churches conducive to personal and collective individuation. This failure contributes to the widespread phenomenon of people "believing without belonging" and "belonging without believing;"[42] and it has been an all-too-common tragedy and setback during the post–Vatican II period. One effect of the resurgence of the people of God ecclesiology ushered in by the election of Pope Francis has been the emergence of an agenda to revitalize synods of bishops and episcopal conferences in the universal church. This salutary development needs, however, to be complemented by the implementation of the unfulfilled promise of local practices of synodality and conciliarity in dioceses and parishes introduced at Vatican II.

Catholics' struggles and failures to advance a dialogical ecclesiology that can promote personal and collective individuation in parishes and dioceses have led me to look for other examples outside of the usual structures. Fruitful examples of individuation-in-communion at the parish and diocesan levels do exist, and they should be promoted in every way, but they are not always common, or contagious, but often controversial. As we conclude, I think it valuable to identify places outside of ordinary parish and diocesan structures where young people, women, and local groups are engaged and inspired to individuate personally, to become committed to, and to participate actively in, vibrant communities of faith that are individuating collectively.

Alternatives: From Catholic Action to New Ecclesial Movements

Parish and diocesan church structures can, and do, provide participants with ecclesial social imaginaries, but there exist alternative communities that many believers find more attractive and effective. Among these alternatives are groups identified during the period before and after the council in terms of Catholic Action and, more recently, especially during the Pontificate of John Paul II, as new ecclesial movements.[43]

As we saw in Chapter 1, the people of God theology of the council provided deeper theological moorings for lay involvement in the mission of the church in the world, often under the banner of Catholic Action, described by Pope Pius XI in 1931 as "the participation of the laity in the apostolate of the hierarchy."[44] The roots of Catholic Action go back to the nineteenth century. To recapitulate, a general form that began in Italy fostered a paternalistic approach to the laity's participation in the hierarchy's apostolate of advancing Catholic Christendom, marked by polemical hostility against liberalism and Protestantism, and sometimes with anti-Jewish animus. Other, specialized forms of Catholic Action cultivated associations among social groups (e.g., workers, students, doctors, lawyers, married couples) interested in addressing social issues, and were often associated with antipoverty efforts and the promotion of grassroots democracy locally and nationally. These specialized forms were often contrasted with devotional societies that fostered personal spirituality (e.g., Holy Name Society or the Legion of Mary).[45]

Cardinal Suenens at the World Council of Lay Apostolate in October 1957 argued that the name Catholic Action was being too narrowly identified with social action groups who promoted activist and sometimes confrontational practices, most notably Joseph Cardijn's program of see, judge, act embraced by the Young Christian Workers movement. At the council Suenens repeated this critique and championed efforts to cultivate a multiplicity of forms of Catholic Action that could also include groups more oriented toward spirituality and the spiritual works of mercy.[46]

The council commended Catholic Action explicitly and, in a concession to critics like Suenens, defined it broadly to include associations of all sorts (*Apostolicam Actuositatem*, 20). Importantly for our argument here, by affirming a plurality of forms of Catholic Action associations and movements in the promotion of contextualized missions, the council established an important precedent and principle for inculturation and social outreach. After the council, with the ascendance of new ecclesial movements like the Charismatic Renewal, Cursillo, Focolare, Sant'Egidio, Communione e Liberazione, Opus Dei, and the Neochatechumenal Way, this principle remained of vital importance.[47]

It is also significant that, after the council, Catholic Action, as it had been articulated and disseminated by Joseph Cardijn among the Young Christian Workers and among groups involved in the international Pax Romana movement, became influential around the world. Gustavo Gutiérrez served for a while as a chaplain for Pax Romana in Peru, and Paulo Freire was involved in Catholic Action in Brazil. In the United States, Cardijn's model of see, judge, act influenced the work of the Christian Family Movement associated with Patrick and Patricia Crowley, and it bore certain affinities with Dorothy Day and Peter Maurin's Catholic Worker Movement. In the Bronx, as we have witnessed, Catholic Action convictions were in evidence both before and after the council as lay leaders, priests, and bishops collaborated to promote grassroots democracy by means of broad-based community organizing, joining with people from other Christian traditions, other religions, and those with no explicit faith convictions to respond to neighbors' laments and aspirations.

Today the spirit of specialized forms of Catholic Action is very much alive in the proliferation of various programs—many developed over the last twenty-five years—designed to promote faith in action for Catholic college and university graduates: Jesuit Volunteer Corps, the Vincentian Volunteers, the Lasallian Volunteers, the Augustinian Volunteers, the Franciscan Network for Human Rights, and more.[48] Other groups also flourished during the period of the Second Vatican Council and should be noted. The Holy Name Society, the St. Vincent De Paul Society, the Catholic Youth Association, and the Knights of Columbus all were able to generate interest and energy among groups of Catholics in parish and diocesan settings before and after the council.[49]

After the council, an array of what came to be called new ecclesial movements, some with origins prior to the council, some after, attracted increasing numbers of people. Many of these new groups began in Europe and spread to other parts of the world, but they originated only rarely in the United States where parish- and diocese-based groups were more common. These communities offer members distinctive personal and communal forms of spirituality combined with different missionary orientations. Some are ecumenical like Taizé; others are Catholic with an ecumenical and interfaith orientation like Focolare and Chemin Neuf. There are groups focusing on charitable and social justice activities like the Community of Sant'Egidio and L'Arche. Other movements concentrate on nurturing particular styles of communal prayer and spiritual practice like the Charismatic Renewal and Cursillo.

Groups such as Opus Dei, Communion and Liberation, and the Neocatechumenal Way bear closer resemblance to General Catholic Action movements that earlier flourished in Italy. These movements have developed close ties with the Vatican and have a special loyalty to the pope and papal pastoral priorities.[50] Some are very committed to the curial articulations and agendas of communion ecclesiology. John Paul II and Benedict XVI have been personally supportive of groups like Opus Dei, Communion and Liberation, the Neocatechumenal Way, and the Focolare Movement. Often contrasted with the aforementioned groups, and more frequently originating outside of Europe, are various forms of base Christian communities. These base communities foster small-group faith sharing about everyday Christian existence in the family, the workplace, and in society at large; and some, but by no means all, are integrated into parish or diocesan life.[51] Finally, whereas loyalty to the pope is associated with new ecclesial movements like Opus Dei and Focolare, there are a variety of groups that are vocally critical of certain curial policies, including policies advancing catechetical and juridical ecclesial communion. These groups, We Are Church, Call to Action, Voice of the Faithful, Women Church, Futurechurch, and others, promote reform in the church, drawing on diverse ecclesiological metaphors and models.

The agenda of We Are Church is reflective of the animating concerns of a number of these Catholic reform-minded groups. They call for (1) a church that brings together brothers and sisters in Christ with equal respect for all the people of God, (2) granting women the power to participate fully in the life and ministry of the church, (3) lifting mandatory celibacy for priests, (4) encouraging a more positive understanding of sexuality, and (5) teaching the gospel as a message of joy. The Vatican has not fostered closer relations with these reform-minded groups, and in many instances local bishops have been hostile toward them.

Each of these groups is distinctive. Each has its particular founders, charisms, traits, practices, and missions. The central fact I am drawing attention to here is this: these groups have individuated as communities, and people, including many young people, have been inspired to participate in them as places where they, in turn, find themselves encouraged and empowered to individuate as Christian disciples in community.

Why Are People Attracted to Catholic Action
and New Ecclesial Movements?

Why are new ecclesial movements thriving now in some places, and why are older Catholic Action approaches being reborn into new forms in certain Catholic universities and parish settings? And what can we learn from them? One major reason these groups can be so effective, I am convinced, is the simple fact that they promote personal and local communal Christian processes of individuation. Members receive a sense of belonging by participating in the collective individuation of the group, which, in turn, nurtures their own personal individuation. These groups invite people to individuate in a community committed to personal and communal prayer and a distinctive mission orientation—some serve the poor; some work as peace builders through conflict resolution; others focus on ecumenical and interfaith relations; still others are dedicated to work for social justice through politics, legal work, and by promoting economic reform; a significant number, as well, are devoted to promoting official teachings such as right-to-life issues. By creating shared communal milieus in which each member is invited to make a radical commitment to pursue one's spiritual aspirations, to discover and to form one's own identity and mission, these groups foster both a strong sense of personhood and a strong sense of belonging.

My further argument is that these new ecclesial movements, like the myriad forms of Catholic Action, offer social imaginaries that hold appeal precisely because they effectively initiate people into vibrant Christian communities particularly adept at communicative practices. In order to substantiate this claim we would need to gather much more information about the modes and styles of communication in relation to the particular themes they address and the basic content and contours of their basic convictions. Real, significant differences obtain among these movements, their convictions, and their communicative practices, and these differences must not be discounted. Yet all of these communities invite people to offer radical witness to the gospel in the postmodern world in word and deed. They cultivate personal individuation and collective individuation in identity and mission by means of communicative interaction.

Young people, women, people in the Global South, and immigrant populations in the United States will continue to drift away from the church, or be driven away, if the church proves unable to promote personal and collective individuation as it fosters communion. It is crucial that these dimensions of the prophetic charism, bestowed on all believers, be allowed to flourish, so that the faithful may become full and active participants in the life and mission of a church that is attuned to the sense of the faithful and responsive to the signs of the times. Above all, cultivating the prophethood of all believers requires communities that foster the adult exercise of reason and freedom, the priority of conscience, of memory and hope conditioned by an ascetic alertness to the precariousness of life, and attentiveness to, and solidarity with, the aspirations and laments of all of God's children and the earth.

Are the many forms of Catholic Action and the new ecclesial movements signs of the agency of the Spirit at work in the church and the world in the wake of Vatican II? Do they all have lessons to teach? I have proposed that all of them teach us about the need for personal and collective individuation. Yet just as every parish and diocese should be assessed and held accountable by lay leaders and clergy in reference to the church at large, so each group needs to be scrutinized and discerningly assessed by their members and within its wider ecclesial setting.

Massimo Faggioli and others have observed that the various modes of Catholic Action and their offshoots that have flourished, and I would add are being reborn in parish and diocesan settings, respect local episcopal and clerical processes of discernment and decision making, specifically synodal and conciliar, whereas many new ecclesial movements have regularly sought to circumnavigate grassroots forms of synodal collaboration with local churches and communities, while pledging allegiance and confessing devotion to the papacy and centralized policies and priorities.[52] This is a matter of no small concern. At the heart of genuine ecclesial individuation and communion are practices that cultivate lay leadership and collaboration with priests and bishops, and that repudiate clericalist, patriarchal, or hypercentralized visions of the church. A crucial feature of prophetic individuation is the cultivation of grassroots synodality in the local church—especially at the periphery—and grassroots democracy and civic engagement in work for justice in local communities. The Spirit blows where it will, but when we witness the people of God in local churches struggling to advance grassroots forms of synodality and democracy it is a confirmation that the Spirit has not been extinguished and a new outpouring of the Spirit heralded at Vatican II is possible in our own day.

Pastoral synods and councils and faith-based community organizing only thrive when they are engaging the aspirations and laments of people living under the concrete conditions of precarious life. Prophetic obedience in a dialogical church communion, a church that is a sacramental sign of the breaking in of the coming kingdom of God, requires no less. The Archdiocese of New York has been the focus of this reflection on constructing a local theology and mission for the church today, but this story is being told and retold in countless ways and variations, in different contexts with different driving aspirations and urgent needs. These diverse, dynamic matrices, scattered across the globe, set the stage for the next phase of the reception of Vatican II, and for the church as a prophetic people of God in communion.

Notes

Introduction

¹ Bradford E. Hinze, *Practices of Dialogue in the Roman Catholic Church: Aims and Obstacles, Lessons and Laments* (New York: Continuum, 2006).

² Johann Baptist Metz, *Unterbrechungen* (Gütersloh: Gütersloher Verlagshaus, 1981); on negative contrast experience, see Schillebeeckx, "Church, Sacrament of Dialogue," in *God the Future of Man*, trans. by N.D. Smith (New York: Sheed and Ward, 1968), 136; Edward Schillebeeckx, *The Understanding of Faith* (New York: Seabury, 1974), 91–101; Pierre Bourdieu, *Outline of a Theory of Practice*, trans. Richard Nice (Cambridge: Cambridge University Press, 1977), 80–83, Pierre Bourdieu, *The Logic of Practice*, trans. Richard Nice (Stanford: Stanford University Press, 1990), 86; Judith Butler, *Precarious Life: The Powers of Mourning and Violence* (New York: Verso, 2004); Judith Butler, *Frames of War: When Is Life Grievable?* (New York: Verso, 2010).

³ For examples of ethnographic studies that raise important theological questions for ecclesiology, see Jerome P. Baggett, *Sense of the Faithful: How American Catholics Live Their Faith* (Oxford: Oxford University Press, 2009); John C. Seitz, *No Closure: Catholic Practice and Boston's Parish Shutdowns* (Cambridge, MA: Harvard University Press, 2011); Mary McClintock Fulkerson, *Places of Redemption: Theology for a Worldly Church* (New York: Oxford University Press, 2007); Pete Ward, ed., *Perspectives on Ecclesiology and Ethnography* (Grand Rapids: William B. Eerdmans, 2012); Christian B. Scharen, *Explorations in Ecclesiology and Ethnography* (Grand Rapids: William B. Eerdmans, 2012); a comparable approach is pursued by Agbonkhianmeghe E. Orobator, S.J., *From Crisis to Kairos: The Mission of the Church in the Time of HIV/AIDS, Refugees and Poverty* (Nairobi, Kenya: Paulines, 2005).

⁴ Richard Gaillardetz, "The 'Francis Moment': A New Kairos for Catholic Ecclesiology," *CTSA Proceedings* 69 (2014): 63–80, http://ejournals.bc.edu.

⁵ Pope Francis interviewed by Antonio Spadaro, S.J., "A Big Heart Open to God," *America*, September 30, 2013, http://americamagazine.org/pope-interview.

⁶ See the analysis of the people of God theology by Maria Clara Lucchetti Bingemer, in "The *Sensus Fidei* in the Recent History of the Latin American Church," *Proceedings of the Catholic Theological Society of America* 70 (2015): 48–59; and the numerous references to "God's holy faithful people" by Austin Ivereigh, in *The Great Reformer: Francis and the Making of a Radical Pope* (New York: Henry Holt, 2014), esp. 110–17.

⁷ In his initial interview with Spadaro, Francis emphasizes that "religious men and women are prophets. . . . Being prophets may sometimes imply making waves. . . . Prophecy makes noise, uproar, some say 'a mess.' But in reality, the charism of religious people is like yeast: prophecy announces the Spirit of the Gospel" ("A Big Heart Open to God," http://americamagazine.org/pope-interview, p. 6). Pope Francis also affirms the prophetic character of all the people of God when he states "This witness (to the social teaching of the church) belongs to the entire People of God, who are a People of prophets," in "Address of

Pope Francis to Members of the International Theological Commission," December 6, 2013; http://w2.vatican.va.

⁸ Papal and curial statements on participatory structures of governance during the pontificates of Paul VI, John Paul II, and Benedict XVI are assessed in Bradford E. Hinze, "Synodality in the Catholic Church," *Theologische Quartalschrift* 192 (2012): 121–30.

⁹ Pope Francis, "Address to the Leadership of the Episcopal Conferences of Latin America during the General Coordination Meeting," July 28, 2013, http://w2.vatican.va.

¹⁰ "A Big Heart Open to God."

¹¹ Ibid.

¹² This sentence follows from the previous quotation from ibid.

¹³ *Evangelii Gaudium*, no. 31 [hereafter cited as EG].

¹⁴ Ibid.

¹⁵ EG, no. 28. Besides promoting parish life, Francis acknowledges that "other Church institutions, base communities and small communities, movements, and forms of association" that are "a source of enrichment for the Church, raised up by the Spirit for evangelizing different areas and sectors." In a finely balanced formulation that has direct relevance for my argument in my final chapter he states, "Frequently [these communities, movements, and associations] bring a new evangelizing fervor and a new capability for dialogue with the world whereby the Church is renewed. But it will prove beneficial for them not to lose contact with the rich reality of the local parish and to participate readily in the overall pastoral activity of the particular Church" (EG, no. 29).

¹⁶ CELAM has been credited with employing dialogical processes with the people of God at their General Conferences of Medellín, Colombia (1968), Puebla, Mexico (1979), Santa Domingo, Dominican Republic (1992), and Aparecida, Brazil (2007) where Bergoglio was actively involved in preparing the final report.

¹⁷ On October 18, 2013, Archbishop Lorenzo Baldisseri, secretary general of the synod of bishops, requested that bishops' conferences distribute a series of questions "immediately as widely as possible to deaneries and parishes so that input from local sources can be received." See "Pastoral Challenges to the Family in the Context of Evangelization," http://www.vatican.va.

¹⁸ EG, no. 257. Citing proposition 55 (of 58 propositions) from the XIIIth Ordinary General Assembly of the Synod of Bishops, which convened October 7–28, 2012, to discuss the theme of The New Evangelization for the Transmission of the Christian Faith.

¹⁹ EG, no. 27.

²⁰ EG, nos. 119–20. In his address to the CELAM leadership on July 28, 2013, Francis underscored the important role at Aparecida of "see, judge and act," the method associated with the Cardijn method of Catholic action, which was associated with the postconciliar practices of CELAM. He spoke of the discernment of the *sensus fidei* as part of the church's identity as a prophetic people of God in his address to the members of the International Theological Commission on December 6, 2013.

²¹ EG nos. 226–27.

²² Pope Francis, "Greeting of Pope Francis to the Synod Fathers During the First General Congregation of the Third Extraordinary General Assembly of the Synod of Bishops" (October 6, 2014), http://w2.vatican.va/content/francesco/en/speeches/2014/october/documents/papa-francesco_20141006_padri-sinodali.html.

²³ John Henry Newman, *On Consulting the Faithful in Matters of Doctrine*, intro. by John Coulson (New York: Sheed and Ward, 1961).

[24] Theologians share an analogous duty as they interpret, explain, and defend the apostolic faith of the church, which likewise demands that they continue to engage and wrestle with the sense of the faithful as it witnesses to and bears on the creative and practical embodiment of the living tradition of the church.

[25] Johann Baptist Metz, *Faith in History and Society: Toward a Practical Fundamental Theology*, trans. J. Matthew Ashley (New York: Continuum, 2007).

[26] Matthias Scharer and Bernd Jochen Hilberath, *The Practice of Communicative Theology: An Introduction to a New Theological Culture* (New York: Crossroad, 2008); Forschungskreis Kommunikative Theologie/Communicative Theology Research Group, *Kommunikative Theologie Selbstvergewisserung unserer Kultur des Theologietreibens/Communicative Theology: Reflections on the Culture of Our Practice of Theology* (Vienna: LIT Verlag, 2006); Dennis M. Doyle, "Interruptive Connections: The Promise of Communicative Theology," *Ecclesiology* 10 (2014): 251–58.

[27] Richard L. Wood, *Faith in Action: Religion, Race, and Democratic Organizing in America* (Chicago: University of Chicago Press, 2002); Mary McClintock Fulkerson, *Places of Redemption: Theology for a Worldly Church* (New York: Oxford University Press, 2007); Luke Bertherton, *Resurrecting Democracy: Faith, Citizenship, and the Politics of a Common Life* (New York: Cambridge University Press, 2015).

[28] See earlier works by Don S. Browning, *A Fundamental Practical Theology: Descriptive and Strategic Proposals* (Minneapolis: Augsburg Fortress, 1991), Richard R. Osmer, *Practical Theology: An Introduction* (Grand Rapids: William B. Eerdemans, 2006), *The Wiley-Blackwell Companion to Practical Theology*, ed. Bonnie J. Miller-McLemore (Malden, MA: Wiley-Blackwell, 2012), *Invitation to Practical Theology: Catholic Voices and Visions*, ed. Claire E. Wolfteich (New York: Paulist Press, 2014), *Opening the Field of Practical Theology: An Introduction*, ed. Kathleen A. Cahalan and Gordon S. Mikoski (Lanham, MD: Rowman & Littlefield, 2014).

Chapter 1

[1] John XXIII closed his December 25, 1961, apostolic constitution, *Humanae Salutis*, which convoked the council with the prayer, "Renew your wonders in our time, as though by a new Pentecost." See Thomas Hughson, "Interpreting Vatican II: 'A New Pentecost,'" *Theological Studies* 69 (2008): 3–37.

[2] Charles Taylor, *A Secular Age* (Cambridge, MA: Belknap Press of Harvard University Press, 2007), 171–72.

[3] Patrick Granfield, "The Church as *Societas Perfecta* in the Schemata of Vatican I," *Church History* 48 (1979): 431–66.

[4] Jan Grootaers, "The Drama Continues between the Acts: 'The Second Preparation' and Its Opponents," in *The History of Vatican II*, 5 vols., ed. Giuseppe Alberigo and Joseph A. Komonchack (Maryknoll, NY: Orbis Books, 1995–2006), 2:399–404.

[5] John O'Malley, *What Happened at Vatican II* (Cambridge, MA: Belknap Press of Harvard University Press, 2008), 47.

[6] On the original schema and topics, see Gérard Philips, "Dogmatic Constitution of the Church: History of the Constitution, in *Commentary on the Documents of Vatican II*, ed. Herbert Vorgrimler (London: Burns and Oates, 1967), 1:105–10; Joseph A. Komonchak, "The Struggle for the Council During the Preparation of Vatican II," in *History of Vatican II*, 1:285–298; Richard R. Gaillardetz, *The Church in the Making: Lumen Gentium, Christus Dominus, Orientalium Ecclesiarum* (Mahwah, NJ: Paulist Press, 2006), 8–27.

⁷ On people of God ecclesiology in *Lumen Gentium*, see Yves M.-J. Congar, "The Church: The People of God," in *The Church and Mankind: Dogma, Concilium*, ed. Edward Schillebeeckx (Glen Rock, NJ: Paulist Press, 1965), 1:11–37; Congar, "The People of God," in *Vatican II: An Interfaith Appraisal*, ed. John H. Miller (Notre Dame, IN: University of Notre Dame Press, 1966), 197–207.

⁸ Alberto Melloni, "The Beginning of the Second Period: The Great Debate on the Church," *History of Vatican II*, 3:80.

⁹ Richard R. Gaillardetz develops with great effectiveness the dynamic of the people of God called and sent on mission in his *Ecclesiology for a Global Church: A People Called and Sent* (Maryknoll, NY: Orbis Books, 2008).

¹⁰ Karl Rahner, "Membership of the Church According to the Teaching of Pius XII's Encyclical '*Mysti Corporis Christi*,'" in *Theological Investigations*, vol. 2 (Baltimore: Helicon Press, 1963), 82–83; Congar, "The People of God," 204–5.

¹¹ Cardinal Léon-Joseph Suenens on December 4, 1962 delivered a speech at the council that proposed a framework for envisioning the entire work of the council in terms of the church's nature (*ad intra*) and mission (*ad extra*). He described a dialogical church—a dialogue within the church between the bishops and the faithful; a dialogue with other Christians and members of other religions; and a dialogue with the modern world; see *History of Vatican II*, 2:343–44.

¹² A minority of bishops at the council feared that chapter two undermined and eviscerated Vatican I, and they complained relentlessly to Paul VI. This influenced two major interventions by Paul VI.

The first and most disruptive was the introduction of a prefatory explanatory note (*nota explicativa praevia*) for chapter three on the hierarchy. Although it was repeatedly acknowledged in the approved document that collegial authority operates with and with due subordination to the pope, the minority believed that the supreme jurisdictional authority over the universal church that had been affirmed at Vatican I was being jettisoned or placed at risk. The *nota praevia* clarified limitations imposed on the college: (1) bishops are not equal in a juridical sense with the pope; (2) although bishops become a member of the college by ordination, this ability to act as such must be exercised and canonically established by means of being in hierarchical communion with the head of the college and its members; (3) while the supreme authority of the college over the whole church cannot operate without the head, it is possible that the head can act on his own for the good of the whole church; and (4) in the strict sense a collegial action is not always operative, but can only occasionally be exercised "with the consent of the head." This interpretation of *Lumen Gentium* established conditions for reaffirming centralized authority in the church after the council. On the so-called Black Week, see *History of Vatican II*, 4:388–452, esp. 417–28.

A second action taken by Paul VI was the formation of a synod of bishops as a vehicle for exercising its collegial role. With the bishops poised to establish the synod of bishops as an instrument of collegiality with its own integrity, Paul VI on his own initiative (*motu proprio*) issued a decree *Apostolicam Sollicitudo* instituting this body, not with its own integrity and decision-making authority, but as an instrument of the pope, with his agenda, and with only consultative status in relation to the pope, and by extension, the papal curia's own authority. The curia and the synod of bishops, mediated by the curia, are thus conceived as both instruments of the pope. See John W. O'Malley, *What Happened at Vatican II* (Cambridge, MA: Belknap Press of Harvard University Press, 2008), 238–46, 252–53.

¹³ For an overview of the concerns about the synods of bishops, see Bradford Hinze, "Collegiality and Restraint: The Synod of Bishops," in *Practices of Dialogue in the Roman Catholic Church* (New York: Continuum, 2006), 157–78; for Joseph Ratzinger's rejoinder to the complaints, see "The Structure and Tasks of the Synods of Bishops" (1985), in *Church, Ecumenism and Politics: New Essays in Ecclesiology* (New York: Crossroad, 1988), 46–62.

¹⁴ *Quadragesimo Anno* nos. 96, 138; Pius XI began to clarify the meaning of Catholic Action in 1922 in his first encyclical, *Ubi Arcano Dei Consilio*, nos. 54, 58; and in 1928 he formulated what has become the classic definition: "Catholic Action has no other purpose than the participation of the laity in the apostolate of the hierarchy" (Pius XI letter to Cardinal Bertram, November 13, 1928, in Odile M. Liebard, ed., *Clergy and Laity: Official Catholic Teachings* (Wilmington, NC: McGrath, 1978), 30–34, at 31, cited in Patrick J. Hayes "Catholic Action in the Archdiocese of New York," in *Empowering the People of God: Catholic Action before and after Vatican II*, ed. Jeremy Bonner et al. (New York: Fordham University Press, 2013), 22.

¹⁵ For general and specialized forms of Catholic Action, see Étienne Fouilloux, "The Antepreparatory Phase: The Slow Emergence from Intertia (January, 1959–October, 1962), in *History of Vatican II*, 1:78; on Suenens, see Jan Grootaers, "The Drama Continues between the Acts. The 'Second Preparation' and Its Opponents," in *History of Vatican II*, 2:443–45. Some bishops from the United States and the United Kingdom complained that the name Catholic Action risked being ecumenically insensitive.

¹⁶ Pope John XXIII used the expression the church of the poor a month before Vatican II started while addressing the problem of underdeveloped countries. This inspired a group of about fifty bishops to meet to promote these concerns at the council. They developed two short documents that were introduced through back channels to be incorporated into the council documents, but with no effect. For more on the church of the poor, see the collection of essays in Norbert Greinacher and Alois Müller, eds., *The Poor and the Church* (New York: Seabury Press, 1977), 11–16, 56–61, 97–105, 109–11; Also see Alberto Melloni, "Poverty of the Church—Poverty of Culture: A Contribution of Giuseppe Dossetti to Vatican II," *Theological Studies* 75 (2014): 485–501.

¹⁷ On Catholic Action, see Bradford E. Hinze, "Vatican II and U.S. Catholic Communities Promoting Grassroots Democracy" in *The Legacy of Vatican II*, ed. Massimo Faggioli and Andrea Vicini (New York: Paulist Press, 2015), 152–81, and Massimo Faggioli, *Sorting Out Catholicism: A Brief History of the New Ecclesial Movements* (Collegeville, MN: Liturgical Press, 2014), 152–81; Kevin Ahern, *Structures of Grace: Catholic Organizations Serving the Global Common Good* (Maryknoll, New York: Orbis Books, 2015).

¹⁸ Paul VI, Motu Proprio, *Ecclesiae Sanctae 1a*, nos. 15–17, pertaining to Vatican II decrees, *Christus Dominus*, no. 27; *Presbyterorum Ordinis*, no. 7.

¹⁹ The influential New York priest sociologist, Philip J. Murnion, prepared a report issued in March 1968, entitled *The Archdiocese of New York: Prospects and Recommendations for the Future*, which was commissioned by a group of priests of the archdiocese and which issues a closing set of recommendations that overlap with the memorandum but also raises larger concerns about emerging social patterns: urban/suburban, declining vocations, social groups (ethnicity, race, and class, but no mention of gender issues and generational shifts).

²⁰ See Regina Bechtle, "The Impact of Women Religious on the Church of New York," *Review for Religious* 68 (2009): 230–49, at 232.

²¹ Elizabeth Ann Seton founded the Sisters of Charity guided by the missionary vision and spirituality of Vincent de Paul and Louise de Marillac (originally established in Emmitsburg, Maryland in 1809). Three sisters from this community traveled to New York in 1817 to open an orphanage. As the group of sisters grew, they extended their mission by starting the Catholic school system in 1833 with a special commitment to the education of girls. In 1846, they established their own congregation, the Sisters of Charity of New York, and within three years they opened St. Vincent's Hospital.

²² From a letter of Mother Loretto Bernard to her congregation, 1962, Archives of the Sisters of Charity, cited in Mary Elizabeth Earley, S.C., *The Sisters of Charity of New York, 1960–1996*, vols. 4 and 5 (Bronx, NY: Sisters of Charity of New York Press, 1997), 4:6.

²³ Ibid., 4:10.

²⁴ Quote taken from Sister Margaret Dowling, in Ana María Díaz-Stevens, *Oxcart Catholicism on Fifth Avenue: The Impact of the Puerto Rican Migration upon the Archdiocese of New York* (Notre Dame, IN: University of Notre Dame Press, 1993), 151; citation taken from Mary Cole, *Summer in the City* (New York: Kenedy & Sons, 1968), 131.

²⁵ Details taken from the Sisters of Charity newsletter, *Community*, quoted in Earley, *The Sisters of Charity of New York*, 4:18; Fox's three principles of Summer in the City were to create a public forum, foster creativity, and promote human relationship, as discussed in *Summer in the City*, 122–44.

²⁶ The US and International Missions of the Sisters of Charity are described by Earley, *The Sisters of Charity of New York*, 5:375–480.

²⁷ Sister Miriam Cleary, O.S.U., addressed the Sisters of Charity in 1973 on the subject of using an approach to discernment based on the spirituality of Ignatius of Loyola in corporate decision making during their official deliberative assemblies. Community members recognized that they already knew this method and employed it in their daily lives and they collectively decided to employ it at their assemblies.

²⁸ Evelyn M. Schneider, who was the superior general of Sisters of Charity of New York in 1971, sent to the members of the community a 63-page report on the Chapter of Affairs conducted in three sessions in August 1969, July 1970, and August 1970, with the title *That We May Have Life. Reflections and Decisions, Chapter of 1969–1970* (Mount Saint Vincent: New York, January 1971).

²⁹ Earley, *The Sisters of Charity of New York*, 4:41.

³⁰ Ibid., 4:67–68.

³¹ The Sisters of Charity convened chapters in 1960, 1963, 1966, 1969–70, which were subsequently called assemblies in 1971–73, 1973–75, 1977–79, 1983–87, 1991, 1995, and special convocations in 1982, 1986; Earley, *The Sisters of Charity*, 4:124.

³² Sisters of Charity of New York Website; http://www.scny.org/about-us/our-mission/

³³ Sisters of Charity of St. Vincent De Paul of New York, *Constitution*, 15–16 (1984). The Sisters of Charity participated in two groups of women religious in the Archdiocese of New York. The Archdiocesan Council of Women Religious was composed of the superiors of each of the congregations of women in the archdiocese. Some women religious took particular note of the formation of the Senate of Clergy, an elected body of representatives, and they wanted their own voices heard and demanded to be collaborators in the decision-making processes in the archdiocese. To this end, they formed, in 1969, with the approval of Cardinal Spellman, the Sisters' Council of the Archdiocese of New York that elected representatives from over fifty congregations and over eight thousand sisters in the archdiocese. This body functioned for more than twenty years before dissolving in 1994.

[34] Terence J. Cooke letter, February 19, 1969, to be read at all Masses on February 23. Archives of the Archdiocese of New York, St. Joseph's Seminary, Dunwoodie, New York (Hereafter Archdiocesan Archives), Parish Councils File.

[35] Resume of Inaugural Meeting of the Committee on Parish Councils held on October 10, 1969. Archdiocesan Archives, Parish Councils File .

[36] Myles Bourke, "Draft of Pastoral Lettter # 1: From the Task Force of the Parish Council Committee, Subject, The Rationale of Parish Councils." Archdiocesan Archives, Parish Councils File.

[37] Msgrs. George A. Kelly and Francis M. Costello were the first co-chairmen of the Commission on Parish Councils beginning shortly after Vatican II. Msgr. William B. O'Brien, in November 1970, signed a memo as director of the Commission of Parish Councils. Fr. Henry Mansell became director in 1972. Parish Councils File.

[38] The career of Philip J. Murnion who died in 2003 merits a study of its own. Ordained in 1963, he was first assigned to a black parish in Harlem at the center of the Civil Rights and Antipoverty Movements. He earned a doctorate in sociology from Columbia in 1971 and then began the Archdiocesan Office of Pastoral Planning where he studied parish life and ministry in New York, which he subsequently did at a national level. In 1978, he was chosen to head the Parish Project of the US bishops until 1982, and in 1981, he became director of the Notre Dame Study of Catholic Parish Life. He founded the National Pastoral Life Center in 1983. His studies of the emerging phenomenon of lay ministry commissioned by the US bishops appeared as *New Parish Ministries* in 1992 and *Parishes and Parish Ministers* in 1999. Murnion was also involved at various times in the work of the priests' senate and presbyteral council. John A. Maguire, the archdiocesan chancellor during Cardinal Spellman's years, recommended that the cardinal enlist the services of two sociologist priests, George A. Kelly and Joseph P. Fitzpatrick, S.J., from Fordham University to study the great postwar migration of Puerto Ricans into New York. This was a precursor to the work of the Office of Pastoral Research and Planning. In 1952, Kelly "estimated that the Puerto Rican population of the archdiocese was already 300,000 and that it would reach 880,000 by 1960" (Thomas J. Shelley, *The Archdiocese of New York: The Bicentennial History 1808–2008* [Strasbourg, France: Éditions du Signe, 2007], 520). This eventually led to rescinding national/ethnic parishes and sending half the class of the seminary upon graduation to receive training in Spanish and Puerto Rico culture at the Catholic University of Puerto Rico in Ponce, during the years when Fr. Ivan Illich began to serve as vice rector in 1956.

[39] Ruth Narita Doyle, "The Social Context of Pastoral Ministry: The Work of the Office of Pastoral Research and Planning of the Archdiocese of New York" (Ph.D. dissertation, Fordham University, 1994).

[40] There were two major research projects on the hopes and experiences of Latinos and the black community in the Archdiocese of New York during the time of Ruth Doyle's work for the archdiocese. Office of Pastoral Research, *Hispanics in New York: Religious, Cultural and Social Experiences/Hispanos en Neuva York: Experiencias Religiosas, Culturales y Sociales*, 2 vols. (New York: Office of Pastoral Research, 1982). Office of Pastoral Research and Office of Black Ministry, *One Faith, One Lord, One Baptism: The Hopes and Experiences of the Black Community in the Archdiocese of New York*, 2 vols. (New York: Archdiocese of New York, 1988). Ruth Narita Doyle served as a consultant and researcher for the Secretariat of Cultural Diversity in the Church of the USCCB and in particular for the *Asian and Pacific Island Affairs Survey 2011*, which included an analysis of the growth of Asian population in the fourteen districts of the USCCB between 2000 and 2010.

⁴¹ Memorandum from the Commission on Parish Councils at the December 10, 1971, meeting. Vicariate councils have played a major role in New York. In 1971, three regional councils (east Bronx, northern Westchester, and Orange County), served as models. Archdiocesan Archives, Parish Councils File.

⁴² Memo from Msgr. William B. O'Brien, November 9, 1971, to Terence Cardinal Cooke. Archdiocesan Archives, Parish Councils File

⁴³ Appendices E and F from the May 21, 1974, Priests' Senate Progress Report, *Considerations for an Archdiocesan Pastoral Council, and Diocesan Pastoral Council*. The proposal as submitted to the priests' senate was defeated at this meeting by a vote of nineteen to twenty-four. The Minutes from the October 1974 meeting reported that a revised proposal on the archdiocesan pastoral council was approved. The Archdiocesan Pastoral Constitution and By-Laws received minor revisions in the composition of the lay membership in 1992 and the original draft of the composition of the membership remained largely intact as found in the memo to Msgr. Henry Mansell from Fr. Stephen Kelly on October 8, 1992, subject, Draft of APC Constitution. Archdiocesan Archives, Presbyteral Council File.

⁴⁴ Appendix E, Priests' Senate Progerss Report. Archdiocesan Archives, Presbyteral Council File.

⁴⁵ Letter from Archbishop Henry J. Mansell, Archbishop of Hartford, Connecticut, to author, March 29, 2010. The archives of the New York Archdiocese are incomplete for the archdiocesan pastoral council.

⁴⁶ Jill Jonnes, *South Bronx Rising: The Rise, Fall, and Resurrection of an American City* (New York: Fordham University Press, 2002), 4, revised edition of Jill Jonnes, *We're Still Here: The Rise, Fall, and Resurrection of the South Bronx* (Boston: Atlantic Monthly Press, 1986). For Catholic and Protestant churches in some areas in the Bronx in the third quarter of the nineteenth century, see Eveyln Gonzalez, *The Bronx* (New York: Columbia University Press, 2004)—Mott Haven, twenty-four; Melrose, twenty-eight; Morrisania-Hunts Point, thirty-seven.

⁴⁷ My analysis is based on Alexander von Hoffman, *House by House, Block by Block: The Rebirth of America's Urban Neighborhoods* (New York: Oxford University Press, 2003), 18–76.

⁴⁸ See Claude J. Mangum, "'Have We Not All One Father?': A Historical Review of Black Catholics in the Archdiocese of New York," in Office of Pastoral Research and Office of Black Ministry, *One Faith, One Lord, One Baptism*, 2:129–203.

⁴⁹ Gonzalez, *The Bronx*, 99, 100, 110, 113. See Catholic Church, *Hispanics in New York: Religious, Cultural and Social Experiences/Hispanos en Nueva York: Experiencias Religiosas, Culturales Y Sociales*, 2 vols. (New York: Office of Pastoral Research, Archdiocese of New York, 1982).

⁵⁰ Von Hoffman, *House by House*, at 21.

⁵¹ Ibid., 22.

⁵² Ibid., 22. Also see Jonnes, *South Bronx Rising*, 233, quote taken from letter of Charles F. Kirby, deputy fire chief, to John T. O'Hagan, the chief of the fire department.

⁵³ Greg Lobo Jost, longtime deputy director of the University Neighborhood Housing Program in the Bronx, offered helpful insight into the combination of factors that influenced the Bronx fires, drawing on the works of Joe Flood, *The Fires: How a Computer Formula, Big Ideas, and the Best of Intentions Burned Down New York City—And Determined the Future of Cities* (New York: Riverhead Books, 2010), and Deborah Wallace and

Rodrick Wallace, *A Plague on Your Houses: How New York Was Burned Down and National Public Health Crumbled* (New York: Verso, 2001).

⁵⁴ Dean Brackley, *Organize! A Manual for Leaders* (New York: Paulist Press, 1990), 1.

⁵⁵ Thomas J. Shelley, *The Bicentennial History of the Archdiocese of New York, 1808–2008*, 584.

⁵⁶ Neil A. Connolly and James F. Cox, "The Challenge of Being a Pastor: Two Views," *Clergy Report* 8 (December 1978): 1.

⁵⁷ Cardinal Cody kicked Egan out of Chicago. Egan was involved with peace activities with Theodore Hesburg, C.S.C., president of the University of Notre Dame. Hesburg invited Egan to come to Notre Dame, along with Roach, to take on full-time positions in promoting social ministry. In 1976, when Egan and Roach took up full-time positions at Notre Dame, Philip Murnion from the Office of Pastoral Research in New York was elected chairperson, and Sister Margaret Cafferty from San Francisco, who had played a key role in organizing the Detroit "Call to Action" Conference initiated by the US bishops as the culmination of a long process reflecting on the legacy of liberty and justice during the nation's bicentennial celebration, was chosen as executive director.

⁵⁸ Tuite, Fagen, and Gorman all knew Chicagoan and former seminarian Edward Chambers, who would take the place of Saul Alinsky as the head of IAF in Chicago. Cardinal Cody severed ties between the Archdiocese of Chicago and the IAF in 1979, and Chambers was instrumental in moving the main office of IAF to New York.

⁵⁹ Dean Brackley, *People Power*, illustrated by Larry Nolte (New York: Paulist, 1989); Dean Brackley, *Group Exercises with "People Power"* (New York: Paulist Press, 1989).

⁶⁰ Brackley, *Organize! A Manual for Leaders*; Dean Brackley and the team of trainers of South Bronx People for Change, *Workshops with "Organize!" A Manual for Trainers* (New York: Paulist Press, 1990).

⁶¹ Cf. Harry Fagan's earlier book, *Empowerment: Skills for Parish Social Action* (Mahwah, NJ: Paulist Press, 1979).

⁶² I make this connection between Latin American liberation theology and community organizing in the tradition of Saul Alinsky because of the involvement of theologian Dean Brackley who was trained in liberation theology, as well Kathy Osberger who had experience in Chile and Peru, and Neil Connolly in Puerto Rico, and their training in community organizing with Harry Fagan. The more Connolly learned about Latin American liberation theology, the more he recognized the work of the South Bronx People for Change in that light. Dean Brackley, *Divine Revolution: Salvation and Liberation in Catholic Thought* (Maryknoll, NY: Orbis Books, 1996). The relation of liberation theology and community organizing is complex, contested, and merits closer scrutiny. Saul Alinsky was a proponent of grassroots democracy on a range of issues pertaining to economic, labor, housing, safety, all of which intersected with matters of racial justice. He recognized the role of conflict in democratic life, but he was not a proponent of class conflict as often associated with Marxism. On this he was in agreement with Jacques Maritian. This must be further examined in the works of those Catholics trained or influenced by Alinsky: Ed Chambers, Ernesto Cortes, Michael Gecan, Tom Gaudette, Greg Galuzzo, John Baumann, Leo Penta, and others, who came to influence the main community organizing networks: IAF, Pacific Institute for Community Organizing (now known simply as PICO), Gamaliel, National People's Action. Pertinent issues are not only about class struggle and conflict, but also about the formation of communities based on preferential relations with poor and marginalized people, the analysis of structures of injustice, and

the mobilization of people through a social imaginary—a theological and ethical vision of promoting human flourishing and the common good. Discussion of liberation theology and Alinsky-influenced community organizing can be found in Mary Beth Rodgers, *Cold Anger: A Story of Faith and Power Politics* (Denton: University of North Texas Press, 1990); Mark R. Warren, *Dry Bones Rattling: Community Building to Revitalize American Democracy* (Princeton, NJ: Princeton University Press, 2001); Dennis A. Jacobsen, *Doing Justice: Congregations and Community Organizing* (Minneapolis: Augsburg Fortress, 2001); Luke Bretherton, *Christianity and Contemporary Politics* (Boston: Wiley-Blackwell, 2010); *Resurrecting Democracy: Faith, Citizenship and the Politics of a Common Life* (New York: Cambridge University Press, 2015). Also see Helene Slessarev-Jamir, *Prophetic Activism: Progressive Religious Justice Movements in Contemporary America* (New York: New York University Press, 2011).

[63] Bob Stern and Neil Graham took on full-time work with the program along with Nora Cunningham and Muriel Long. Peter Gavigan rededicated himself to community development as he was introduced to it at St. Athanasius with Connolly and Gigante.

[64] Quote from interview with Paul Brant in Jonnes, *South Bronx Rising*, 345.

[65] The original priests and parishes are Daniel Peake, St. Margaret of Crotona, Riverdale; John Carlin, St. Gabriel's, Riverdale; Peter McNulty, Visitation, Van Cortlandt Park; Msgr. John T. Doherty and Howard Calkins, St. John's, Kingsbridge; Auxiliary Bishop Patrick Ahern, Our Lady of Angels, Kingsbridge; John Flynn, St. Anne's, Williamsbridge; Msgr. John Costello, St. Brendans, Kingsbridge Heights; Philip Shannon, St. Philip Neri, Kingsbridge Heights; Fr. Jim Flynn, then John Jenick, Our Lady of Refuge, Fordham Heights; Msgr. Francis X. Reilly, St. Martin of Tours, Belmont; Louis G. Martella, Our Lady of Mount Carmel, Belmont; Msgr. Tom McNulty, Our Lady of Mercy, Belmont; William Krupa, O.S.A., St. Nicholas of Tolentine, University Heights; John C. McCarthy, Holy Spirit, University of Morris Heights; Martin Miller, O. Carm., St. Simon Stock.

[66] Jonnes, *South Bronx Rising*, 355.

[67] Ibid., 349, 264.

[68] Ibid., 349.

[69] There were efforts made to reach out to fledgling Jewish groups that were responding to poverty-related issues in the neighborhoods, but the Jewish groups wanted to develop their own organizations and chose to join forces strategically with the coalition rather than as regular members of the coalition.

[70] The Protestant churches in the early period of the coalition included Calvary United Methodist Church on University Avenue, Featherbed Lane Presbyterian Church, Lutheran Church of the Epiphany, Bedford Park Presbyterian, University Heights Presbyterian, African American Church in the University Heights neighborhood.

[71] Alinsky's personal failure in the Chelsea district of New York in the 1950s had convinced him that grassroots community organizing in New York City was just not feasible. The elites were too powerful and the city's welfare establishment (referring to the many agencies funded to solve people's problems for them and in many cases to provide jobs) deterred people from identifying issues and solutions together. The coalition used Alinsky's methods, but proved him wrong about New York. Alinsky's methods evolved among his heirs after he died in 1972. On Alinsky in New York, see Sanford D. Horwitt, *Let Them Call Me Rebel: Saul Alinsky, His Life and Legacy* (New York: Vintage Books, 1992), 279–305. On the evolution of his methods, see Mark R. Warren, *Dry Bones Rattling: Community Organizing to Revitalize American Democracy* (Princeton, NJ: Princeton University Press,

2001), Richard L. Wood, *Faith in Action: Religion, Race, and Democratic Organizing in America* (Chicago: University of Chicago Press, 2002).

[72] To be specific about the coalition lineage of national community organizers, Roger Hayes was trained in community organizing in Chicago by Shel Trapp, former Methodist minister, in the Northwest Community Organization. Trapp was trained by Tom Gaudette who came under the influence of Saul Alinsky and became involved in community organizing in 1957 through his involvement in the Christian Family Movement in his Catholic parish. Gaudette trained many organizers besides Trapp, including Gail Cincotta and Jesuits Greg Galuzzo and John Baumann. Hayes shared an apartment with Greg Galuzzo and John Baumann. Baumann subsequently founded PICO in Oakland, California in 1972. Galuzzo was hired as executive director of the community organizing network called Gamaliel in 1986. None of these were trained through the IAF associated with former Catholic seminarian Ed Chambers.

[73] The original ten neighborhood associations were North Kingsbridge, Kingsbridge/ Marble Hill, Mosholu/Woodlawn, Kingsbridge Heights, Bedford Park, Fordham/Bedford, University Heights, South Fordham, Jerome/Webster, and Belmont/Crotona. These are listed on the Bronx African American Archival Survey of Fordham University. www.fordham.edu/academics/programs_at_fordham_/bronx_african_americ/archival_survey/northwest_bronx_comm_27930.asp.

[74] Early in 1975, clergy representatives of the coalition reached out to the West Bronx Jewish Community Council (formerly identified as the Northwest Bronx Jewish Community Conference) that was committed to addressing issues of poverty and care for the elderly. They talked about ways of cooperating. They agreed not to compete for funding, to find ways to link the organizations that would not be an amalgamation or fusion, but that would retain and honor their separate identities. Coalition board minutes from February 17, 1975 and March 24, 1975. Northwest Bronx Community and Clergy Coalition Archive, Boxes 261, 264 (The Bronx County Historical Society, Bronx, New York).

[75] Phone interview with Anna Marie Reinthaler, May 10, 2010.

[76] Margaret Groarke, "Organizing against Overfinancing: The Northwest Bronx Coalition Campaign against Freddie Mac," *Bronx County Historical Society Journal* 39 (2002): 68–86, at 71; see also Margaret Groarke, "Using Community Power Against Targets Beyond the Neighborhood," *New Political Science*, 26 (2004): 171–88.

[77] Sarah Gay (St. Johns Kingsbridge), Peter Rosenbaum (Our Lady of Angels), Anna-Marie Rheinthaler (Our Lady of Refuge), Christine Reeves, James P. Shea (attorney), James Stenerson (St. Brendan), and Mr. Joseph Zimzi (Our Lady of Mount St. Carmel).

[78] Based on the author's interview with Mary Dailey who was organizer at the coalition from 1986 to 2005, and executive director beginning in 1994; Julissa Reynoso, "Putting out Fires before They Start: Community Organizing and Collaborative Governance in the Bronx USA," *Law and Inequality* 24 (2006): 213–267, at 239.

[79] Reynoso, "Putting out Fires before They Start," 213.

[80] Jonnes, *South Bronx Rising*, 354–55.

[81] Chicago organizers Gale Cincotta and Shel Trapp were key figures in the national campaign for HMDA in 1975 and the Community Reinvestment Act (CRA) of 1977. In 1972, they established the National Training and Information Center in 1972 to address issues of housing foreclosures and bank redlining and in the same year started the National People's Action organization, a coalition of roughly three hundred community organizations in the United States. See Michael Westgate, *Gale Force: Gale*

Cincotta: The Battles for Disclosure and Community Reinvestment (Cambridge, MA: Education & Resources Group, 2011).

[82] The National Housing Institute's main instrument was the magazine *Shelterforce*, designed initially to provide a how-to resource for tenant activists. See www.shelterforce. org/about/shelterforce/. The first issue appeared in April 1975.

[83] Jonnes, *South Bronx Rising*, 356.

[84] Eventually the coalition's Neighborhood Reinvestment Committee, which was composed of coalition organizers and leaders Denis Boyle, Bill Frey, Jim Mitchell, Roger Hayes, Joe Muriana, Lois Harr, John Reilly, and Jim Buckley, launched the Fordham Bedford Housing Corporation, which owns and manages 116 buildings. The University Neighborhood Housing Program runs another eighteen buildings. The Fordham Bedford Community Services provides a variety of services for young people, those in financial need, and immigrants.

[85] This history is explored in more detail in Jonnes, *South Bronx Rising*, 354–62.

[86] Jonnes, *South Bronx Rising*, 362–75, at 370.

[87] Northwest Bronx Community and Clergy Coalition 1983 *Year-End Program Report* (Coalition Archives); see also Edward J. Buckley, "A Tree Grows in the Northwest Bronx," *Fordham Magazine*, 1984, http://unhp.org/publications/press/a-tree-grows-in-the-northwest-bronx.

Chapter 2

[1] See the Cologne Declaration signed by 163 German-speaking theologians from West Germany, the Netherlands, Austria, and Switzerland which states: "One of the critical achievements of Vatican II—the opening of the Catholic Church to collegiality between pope and bishops—is being stifled by recent Roman efforts and centralization," *Origins* 18 (March 2, 1989): 633–34. The Catholic Theological Society of America issued a statement: "Do Not Extinguish the Spirit," *Origins* 20 (December 27, 1990): 461, 463–67.

[2] This debate is associated with an exchange between Cardinals Joseph Ratzinger and Walter Kasper between 1999 and 2001 analyzed by Kilian McDonnell in "The Ratzinger/Kasper Debate: The Universal Church and Local Churches," *Theological Studies* 63 (2002): 227–50; For Kasper's comprehensive ecclesiology, see *The Catholic Church: Nature, Reality and Mission* (New York: Bloomsbury, 2015). For further analysis, see Gerard Mannion in *Ecclesiology and Postmodernity: Questions for the Church in Our Time* (Collegeville, MN: Liturgical Press, 2007). For a critical analysis in terms of communion ecclesiology, see Bernd Jochen Hilberath, "Kirche als communio. Beschwörungsformel oder Projektbeschreibung?" *Theologische Quartalschrift* (hereafter ThQ) 174 (1994): 45–65; Bernd Jochen Hilberath, "Communio hierarchica. Historischer Kompromiss oder hölzernes Eisen?" ThQ 177 (1997): 202–219; Bernd Jochen Hilberath, "Vorgaben für die Ausarbeitung der Communio-Ekklesiologie, in *Communio—Ideal oder Zerrbild von Kommunikations?* ed. B. J. Hilberath (Basel, Freiburg, Wien: Herder, 1999), 277–98. Bernd Jochen Hilberath, "Communio—Gift oder gift? Zu Risiken und Nebenwirkungen eines Kirchenkonzepts," ThQ 193 (2013): 321–35; Dennis Doyle, *Communion Ecclesiology: Visions and Versions* (Maryknoll, NY: Orbis Books, 2000); and Brian P. Flanagan, *Communion: Diversity, and Salvation* (London: T&T Clark, 2011); Brian P. Flanagan, "Communion Ecclesiologies as Contextual Theologies," *Horizons* 40 (2013): 53–70;

Scott MacDougall, *More Than Communion: Imagining an Eschatological Ecclesiology* (New York: Bloomsbury/T&T Clark, 2015). While agreeing with the substance of the arguments by Hilberath, Doyle, Flanigan, and MacDougall, I wish to concentrate on what the vision of the church as a prophetic people of God contributes to ecclesiology and ecclesial praxis.

³ Pope John Paul II, Apostolic Constitution *Sacrae disciplinae leges* (1983), in *Code of Canon Law, Latin-English Edition* (Washington, DC: Canon Law Society of America, 1999), xxx.

⁴ See Bradford E. Hinze, "The Reception of Vatican II in Participatory Structures of the Church: Facts and Friction," *Canon Law Society of America Proceedings* 70 (2009): 28–52.

⁵ See the discussion of the *nota explicativa praevia* in section The People of God in the Ecclesiology of *Lumen Gentium*, in Chapter 1; as well as John A. Alesandro, "General Introduction," *Code of Canon Law: Text and Commentary*, ed. James E. Coriden, Thomas J. Green, Donald E. Heintschel (New York: Paulist, 1985), 1–22, at 9–10.

⁶ James H. Provost, " 'The People of God': Law or Politics?" *Annual Convention of the Canon Law Society of America Proceedings* 42 (1980): 44–59, at 57. He references Robert T. Kennedy, "Shared Responsibility in Ecclesial Decision-Making," *Studia Canonica* 14 (1980): 5–23; James H. Provost, "The Working Together of Consultative Bodies—Great Expectations?" *Jurist* 40 (1980): 257–81.

⁷ This problem surfaced in 2004 by the National Review Board report on the sexual abuse crisis, mentioned by Thomas J. Green, "Selected Issues in Developing Structures of Diocesan Communion," *Jurist* 69 (2009): 418–41, at 423; but also take special note of Green's valuable comments on discernment, consultative-only, and greater levels of collaborative decision making: 425n29, 428–29, 431–34, 439–41.

⁸ Joseph A. Komonchak, "A New Law for the People of God: A Theological Evaluation," *Canon Law Society of American Proceedings* (1981): 14–43, at 25–27; Komonchak further comments on the suspicions and restrictions introduced by the code in relation to the exercise of episcopal authority at 37–39, 41–42.

⁹ James A. Coriden, "The Holy Spirit and Church Governance," *Jurist* 66 (2006): 339–73; also see James Coriden, "The Holy Spirit and Canon Law: An Exploration," *Canon Law Society of America Proceedings* (1996): 134–47.

¹⁰ Coriden, "The Holy Spirit and Church Governance," 355–56.

¹¹ Ibid., 370–71. Coriden obliquely references the prophetic office of all the faithful in his proposal on the teaching function (ibid., 368). His argument is entirely in keeping with the argument I am advancing here, but my treatment in Chapter 5 of the Spirit's work in heeding laments and in prophetic obedience offers additional claims beyond Coriden's word-centered approach to prophecy.

¹² Komonchak, "A New Law for the People of God," 42, quote from Hubert Miller, "Ius condendum de personis in genere," *Periodica* 68 (1979): 136–37.

¹³ See Thomas J. Green, "Subsidiarity during the Code Revision Process: Some Initial Reflections," *Jurist* 48 (1988): 771–99; Thomas J. Green, "The Latin and Eastern Code: Guiding Principles," *Jurist* 62 (2002): 235–79; Joseph Komonchak, "Subsidiarity in the Church: The State of the Question," in *The Nature and Future of Episcopal Conferences*, ed. Hervé Legrand, Julio Manzanares, and Antonio Garcia y Garcia (Washington, DC: Catholic University of America, 1988), 298–349; John J. Burghard, "The Interpretation and Application of Subsidiarity in Ecclesiology: An Overview of the Theological Literature

and Canonical Literature," *Jurist* 58 (1998): 279–342; Ad Leys, *Ecclesiological Impacts of the Principle of Subsidiarity* (Kampen, the Netherlands: Uitgeverij, 1995).

[14] The members of the commission are cited by Thomas J. Green, "The 1982 Papal Consultation Concluding the 1917 Code Revision Process," *Jurist* 67 (2007): 364–431, at 364nn3and4.

[15] Extraordinary Synod II, "Final Report of *Origins*15 (December 19, 1985): 441, 443–53, at 448.

[16] Joseph A. Komonchak quotes Danneels' Initial Report in his valuable analysis, "The Synod of 1985 and the Notion of the Church," in *Chicago Studies* 26 (1987): 330–45.

[17] Concerns were raised about episcopal conferences and subsidiarity in the document, even though they were also widely appreciated during the deliberations of the bishops.

[18] Joseph Ratzinger's writings on the people of God ecclesiology and the body of Christ ecclesiology spans the course of his career, including *Volk und Haus Gottes in Augustins Lehre von der Kirche* (München: Karl Zink Verlag, 1954); *Theological Highlights of Vatican II* (New York: Missionary Society of St. Paul the Apostle, [German 1966], 1966); *Das neue Volk Gottes: Entwürfe zur Ekklesiologie* (Düsseldorf: Patmos Verlag, 1969); Joseph Ratzinger and Hans Maier, *Demokratie in der Kirche: Möglichkeiten und Grenzen* (Limberg, Austria, 2000); Ratzinger's interview with Vittorio Mesori, *The Ratzinger Report: An Exclusive Interview on the State of the Church* (San Francisco: Ignatius Press, 1985); "The Ecclesiology of the Second Vatican Council" with "Appendix: Modern Variations of the Concept of the People of God," in *Church, Ecumenism and Politics: New Essays in Ecclesiology* (New York: Crossroad, [German 1987], 1988); *The Call to Communion: Understanding the Church Today* (San Francisco: Ignatius, [German 1991], 1996); *Politik und Erlösung: Zum Verhältnis von Glaube, Rationalität und Irrationalem in der sogenannten Theologie der Befreiung* (Opladen, Germany: Westdeutscher Verlag, 1986); "On the Ecclesiology of Vatican II," *L'Osservatore Romano* (English Edition), January 23, 2002, 5–7.

[19] Hermann Pottmeyer, "The Church as Mysterium and as Institution," *Synod 1985—An Evaluation*, eds. Giuseppe Alberigo and James Provost (Edinburgh: T and T Clark, 1986), 99–109, at 100.

[20] Joseph Komonchak, "The Theological Debate," in *Synod 1985—An Evaluation*, 53–63, at 56, with note referring to chapter 3 of *The Ratzinger Report*.

[21] Ibid., 54.

[22] See the work of the International Theological Commission, *L'unique Eglise du Christ* (Paris: Le Centurion, 1985); "Select Themes of Ecclesiology on the Occasion of the Twentieth Anniversary of the Closing of the Second Vatican Council" (1985), in *International Theological Commission: Texts and Documents, 1969–1985*, ed. Michael Sharkey (San Francisco: Ignatius, 1989), 269–304, esp. 271–82, 286–88, 300–1.

[23] Komonchak's introduction to *Synode extraordinaire. Célébration de Vatican II* (Paris: Cerf, 1986), 9–31, at 20, cited by José Comblin, *People of God* (Maryknoll, NY: Orbis Books, 2004), 212n4. This passage is repeated in the quote but not accurately cited.

[24] Komonchak, "The Theological Debate," 55–56, with footnote to *The Ratzinger Report* and his essay "The Ecclesiology of Vatican II," both from 1985 and the survey essay by Giuseppe Colombo, "Il 'popolo di Dio' e il 'mistero' della Chiesa nell-ecclesiologia postconciliare," *Teologia* 10 (1985): 97–169.

[25] Komonchack, "The Synod of 1985 and the Notion of the Church," 333.

[26] Comblin, *The People of God*, 55–58.

²⁷ See Elmar Klinger, "Das Volk Gottes auf dem Zweiten Vatikanum. Die Revolution in der Kirche, Volk Gottes, Gemeinde und Gesellschaft," in *Jahrbuch für Biblische Theologie*, vol. 7 (Neukirchen-Vluyn [Germany]: Neukirchener Verlag, 1992), 305–20. See the Festschrift for Klinger, *Das Volk Gottes: Ein Ort der Befreiung* (Würzburg: Echter, 1998), especially Herbert Vorgrimler, "Volk Gottes oder Communio?" 41–53.

²⁸ It is also noteworthy that during this same period of time among Orthodox, Anglican, and Protestant churches, communion ecclesiology became increasingly influential and provided a widely shared ecclesiological vision that has served as a point of ecumenical convergence and fruitful contestation.

²⁹ Congregation for the Doctrine of the Faith, "Letter to the Bishops of the Catholic Church on Some Aspects of the Church Understood as Communion," (1992), http://www.vatican.va/roman_curia/congregations/cfaith/documents/rc_con_cfaith_doc_28051992_communionis-notio_en.html, nos. 8 and 9. See also Ratzinger, *Church, Ecumenism, and Politics*, 75; Ratzinger, *Call to Communion*, 44.

³⁰ Walter Kasper, "Zur Theologie und Praxis des bischöflichen Amtes," in *Auf neue Art Kirche Sein: Wirklichkeit—Herausforderungen—Wandlungen* (Munich: Berdward bei Don Bosco, 1999), 32–48.

³¹ The curial resistance to the exercise of the magisterial authority of US episcopal conferences is treated by Bradford E. Hinze, *Practices of Dialogue in the Roman Catholic Church* (New York: Continuum, 2006), 90–111, at 99–104.

³² See "Theological and Juridical Status of Episcopal Conferences," *Origins* 17 (April 7, 1988): 731–37. For background and commentary, see *Episcopal Conferences: Historical, Canonical and Theological Studies*, ed. Thomas J. Reese (Washington, DC: Georgetown University Press, 1989); and Joseph Ratzinger's statement to the US Bishops, "The Bishop as Teacher of the Faith," *Origins* 18 (March 23, 1989): 681–82.

³³ The distinction of effective and affective collegiality in the work of episcopal conferences can be detected in John Paul II's *motu proprio Apostolos suos* (1998, no. 12), his Apostolic Exhortation *Pastores Gregis* on Bishops (2003, no. 8), and the Directory for the Pastoral Ministry of Bishops, *Apostolorum Successores*, issued by the Congregation for Bishops in 2004 (no. 28). Further questions were raised about voting requirements and the need for a *recognitio* by curial offices before a document is approved for dissemination. See Joseph Komonchak, "Episcopal Conferences," *Chicago Studies* 27 (1988): 311–28; Joseph A. Komonchak, "The Roman Working Paper on Episcopal Conferences," *Episcopal Conferences: Historical, Canonical, and Theological Studies* (Washington, DC: Georgetown University Press, 1989), 177–204.

³⁴ Another manifestation of the repressive curial policy during the John Paul II and Benedict XVI pontificates is in evidence in the efforts made to investigate and discipline theologians in a manner that rivals if not exceeds the practices during the Modernist controversy. See Bradford E. Hinze, "A Decade of Disciplining Theologians," in *When the Magisterium Intervenes: The Magisterium and Theologians in the Church Today*, ed. Richard R. Gaillardetz (Collegeville, MN: Liturgical Press, 2012), 3–39.

³⁵ Congregations of the Bishops and the Evangelization of Peoples, "Instruction on Diocesan Synods," *Origins* 27 (October 23, 1997): 324–32, at 328, citing *Christus Dominus* 8 and Canon 381 on the authority of the bishops.

³⁶ John Paul II, "Address on the Participation of the Laity in the Priestly Ministry," *L'Osservatore Romano*, English Edition, May 11, 1994; cf. *Lumen Gentium*, no. 31 and John Paul II, Post-Synodal Apostolic Exhortation, *Christifideles Laici*, no. 15. The various facets

of the debate that surfaced in response to The Declaration "Dominus Iesus: On the Unicity and Salvific Universality of Jesus Christ and the Church" issued by the Congregation for the Doctrine of the Faith in 2000 intersect with the issues being raised in this chapter about the understanding of the church as communion and the exercise of hierarchical authority. For the document see http://www.vatican.va/roman_curia/congregations/cfaith/documents/rc_con_cfaith_doc_20000806_dominus-iesus_en.html.

[37] Congregation for the Clergy and 7 other Roman Dicasteries, "On Certain Questions Regards the Collaboration of the Non-Ordained Faithful in the Sacred Ministry of the Priest," http://www.vatican.va/roman_curia/congregations/cclergy/documents/rc_con_interdic_doc_15081997_en.html.

[38] The authority of the pastor in pastoral councils at the diocesan and parish level was reasserted in a 2002 instruction devoted to "The Priest, Pastor, and Leader of the Parish Community" issued by the Congregation for the Clergy, http://www.vatican.va/roman_curia/congregations/cclergy/documents/rc_con_cclergy_doc_20020804_istruzione-presbitero_en.html; and in 2004 the Directory for the Pastoral Ministry of the Bishops (*Apostolorum successores*) released by the Congregation of Bishops, http://www.vatican.va/roman_curia/congregations/cbishops/documents/rc_con_cbishops_doc_20040222_apostolorum-successores_en.html.

[39] If I were to consider the ongoing reception of the people of God ecclesiology in the Archdiocese of New York during the era of Cardinal Timothy Dolan, I would need to review and assess all of the local churches' structures identified in Chapter 1 and this chapter. This would include a consideration of the continued lack of an Office for Parish Pastoral Councils, Dolan's reestablishment of the archdiocesan pastoral council, and an assessment of his more active engagement with the presbyteral council. Special consideration would need to be given to the widely negative assessment given to the advisory processes used in closing elementary schools and high schools and in closing and consolidating parishes between 2012 and 2015. In principle, the issue is not that difficult decisions have to be made, but how those shareholders in the community are engaged in the process of discerning and decision making.

[40] Pat F. Rossi, *The Eighteenth Synod of the Archdiocese of New York: Perspectives on the Theology of the Local Church and Its History* (Cambridgeshire, UK: Melrose Books, 2009), 81.

[41] Ibid., 95.

[42] For a different episcopal style in conducting a diocesan synod, see my analysis of Cardinal John Deardon's leadership in the Archdiocese of Detroit in 1969 and Archbishop Rembert Weakland's approach in the Archdiocese of Milwaukee in 1987, in Hinze, *Practices of Dialogue in the Roman Catholic Church*, 38–63.

[43] Rossi, *The Eighteenth Synod*, 136n39, from "Plans for Implementing the Proposals of the Eighteenth Synod," *Metropolitan Tribunal*, December 22, 1988, 1–4.

[44] Rossi, *The Eighteenth Synod*, "Appendix C: Pre-Synodal Meeting Outlines for Subjects of Concerns," 161.

[45] Ibid., 157.

[46] Auxiliary Bishop Austin B. Vaughn, who was widely known for being outspoken on pro-life issues, rose near the end of the synod, after deliberations and voting had taken place, and urged that a pro-life and antiabortion stance be advanced in every phase of implementing the synod. This final proposal was approved by acclamation, not by vote.

[47] These quotations are taken from the "Recommendations of the Senate of Clergy Concerning the Formation of the Presbyteral Council," October 13, 1983, and found in

the record of minutes from the senate in the Archives of the Archdiocese of New York, St. Joseph's Seminary, Dunwoodie, New York (hereafter Archdiocesan Archives).

[48] Archdiocese of New York, *Senate Progress Report*, March 1984, Archdiocesan Archives, Presbyteral Council File.

[49] Archdiocese of New York, "Four Priority Recommendations to Archbishop Egan from the Priests' Council," May 18, 2000, Archdiocesan Archives, Presbyteral Council File.

[50] David M. Herszenhorn, "Archdiocese Cuts 23 Jobs in New York," *New York Times,* May 12, 2001.

[51] Manny Fernandez, "Letter to Priests Is Critical of Archbishop's Leadership," *New York Times* (October 15, 2006).

[52] Assembly 2003, Enactment 2. Sisters of Charity Archives, Bronx, New York, Assembly 2003 Box.

[53] Quote taken from Sister Regina Bechtle, "Journey Home or Journey into Exile?" *The Occasional Papers of the Leadership Conference of Women Religious,* Winter 1996, 12; in Mary Elizabeth Earley, *The Sisters of Charity of New York 1960–1996*, Vol. V, 482.

[54] *Parish and Parish Councils* (hereinafter cited as *Handbook*), available online at http://sjtemahopac.org/documents/2014/10/parishcouncilhandbook.pdf.

[55] This approach was widely adopted following the work of Mary Benet McKinney, OSB., *Sharing Wisdom: A Process of Group Decision Making* (Allen, TX: Tabor, 1987, repr., Chicago: Thomas More Press, 1998); William J. Rademacher and Marliss Rogers, *The New Practical Guide for Parish Councils* (Mystic, CT: Twenty-Third Publications, 1988), and Mark F. *Fischer, Pastoral Councils in Today's Catholic Church* (Mystic, CT: Twenty-Third Publications, 2001); Mark F. Fischer, *Making Parish Councils Pastoral* (Mahwah, NJ: Paulist Press, 2010).

[56] *Handbook*, 7.

[57] Ibid.

[58] "Origin of a Parish Council," undated document released with the closing of the Office for Parish Councils. Archdiocesan Archives, Parish Council File.

[59] Cardinal O'Connor and Neil Connolly disagreed and clashed about a number of issues pertaining to pastoral matters in the South Bronx during the first years of O'Connor's years in New York. This animosity probably contributed to Connolly's reassignment. Connolly took initial steps in making this transition by meeting with the staff at St. Mary's Parish, which was mourning the loss of their beloved pastor. Shortly thereafter, O'Connor asked for a meeting and apologized to Connolly and said that he could stay in the South Bronx if he wished. Connolly said he had already started the transition and rejected the offer. Their differences in ecclesiology and political ideology must be balanced by O'Connor's ability to apologize and open the door for Connolly to stay in the Bronx. The details of this period are described in Neil Connolly's memoirs, which I had access to thanks to Angel Garcia, his longtime assistant.

[60] Jim Rooney, *Organizing the South Bronx* (Albany: State University of New York Press, 1995), 112.

[61] Ibid., 110.

[62] Ibid., 111.

[63] This corresponds with the judgment of Kathy Osberger stated in an e-mail exchange, August 28, 2010.

[64] Dean Brackley e-mail to author, May 24, 2010.

[65] Julissa Reynoso describes the coalition's "evolution of an adversarial methodology," in her article "Putting out Fires before They Start: Community Organizing and Collabora-

tive Governance in the Bronx, USA," *Law and Inequality* 24 (2006): 213–267, at 215, and 218–19. This line of argument corresponds to Richard L. Wood, Brad Fulton, and Kathryn Partridge, *Building Bridges, Building Power: Developments in Institution-Based Community Organizing* (Syosset, NY: Interfaith Funders, 2013), 20; and Richard L. Wood, *Faith in Action: Religion, Race, and Democratic Organizing in America* (Chicago: University of Chicago Press, 2002), 178.

[66] Julissa Reynoso, drawing on the work of Margaret Groarke, differentiates direct action which "consisted of dozens of busloads of people appearing at an elected official's or a bureaucrat's office with a bullhorn and a demand for the target to meet with the organization," and a hit, which is "a surprise visit to a target, usually one who has ignored the organization's requests for a meeting, or failed to keep commitments." "Putting out Fires before They Start," 230n105, citing Margaret Groarke, "Organizing against Overfinancing: The Northwest Bronx Coalition Campaign Against Freddie Mac," *Bronx County Historical Society Journal* 39 (2002): 68–86, at 80.

[67] This central argument of Reynoso's argument is summarized in "Putting out Fires before They Start," 242–43, 259–60, 262. Former executive director of the coalition, Mary Dailey, states the abiding challenge: "An organization wins and has a host of relationships in play, it has a lot to lose. Every time that the organization complains or critiques its former targets (now allies or partners) it puts a relationship at risk. The heart of success is getting this balance right, ensuring that risks are taken on clear matters of principle and that the organization never puts too many relationships at risk simultaneously" (cited in ibid., 260n333).

[68] When James Mumm became the new executive director in June 2005, he initiated a shift to an institutional-based model for the coalition composed of churches, tenant associations, and school associations, based on the model espoused by the Gamaliel training center in Chicago, which he combined with the long-standing connection with the National People's Action. In keeping with the institutional model of organizing Mumm initiated the payment of membership dues for all affiliated churches, tenant associations, and school groups.

[69] Reynoso, "Putting out Fires before They Start," 241.

[70] Ibid., 241–42.

[71] On the problems associated with religious personalism, see Wood, *Faith in Action*, 264–67.

[72] On the role of religion to promote passionate engagement, while cultivating the need for accepting ambiguity in the midst of contestation and negotiating compromise, see ibid., 250–57. On the prophetic role of religious groups, see ibid., 17, 278.

[73] The risk of the instrumentalization of religion by community organizing results when there is not a proper balance maintained between the instrumental role of religion and the ethical and religious considerations of religious beliefs and practices. Wood, ibid., 161–94, especially 185–94, and 292.

[74] On the problems of moralism and therapeutic culture in religious culture, see ibid., 219–58.

[75] Ibid., 219–57, 276–79; Faith in Public Life, *Be Not Afraid? Guilt by Association, Catholic McCarthyism and Growing Threats to the U.S. Bishops' Anti-Poverty Mission* (2013), http://www.faithinpubliclife.org/wp-content/uploads/2013/06/FPL-CCHD-report.pdf.

[76] Groarke, "Organizing against Overfinancing," 71. Also see Margaret Groarke, "Using Community Power Against Targets Beyond the Neighborhood, *New Political Scientist* 26 (2004): 171–88.

⁷⁷ Three housing campaigns took place over the 1980s. As Reynoso explains, following the work of Groarke and conversations with Mary Dailey, Project Reclaim "aimed at rehabilitation of vacant buildings and keeping rents affordable"; ONTOP was a "city-wide campaign to increase non-profit ownership, repairs, and rehabilitation at affordable rents"; and another "city-wide campaign against Major Capital Improvement rent increases" ("Putting out Fires before They Start," 233–34).

⁷⁸ Groarke, "Organizing against Overfinancing," 72.

Chapter 3

¹ Emmanuel Katongole with Jonathan Wilson-Hartgrove, *Mirror to the Church: Resurrection Faith after Genocide in Rwanda* (Grand Rapids: Zondervan, 2009), 163.

² Peter Steinfels mourns the increasing number of people, especially young people, leaving the church, in "Further Adrift: The American Church's Crisis of Attrition," in *Commonweal*, October 18, 2010; Marian Ronan grieves the treatment of women and homosexuals in *Tracing the Sign of the Cross: Sexuality, Mourning, and the Future of American Catholicism* (New York: Columbia University Press, 2009); and Bryan N. Massingale mourns the failure of the church to address the problem of racism in *Racial Justice and the Catholic Church* (Maryknoll, NY: Orbis Books, 2010); Gerald A. Arbuckle explores the importance of hearing laments in church and processing them honestly to promote healing and growth in *The Francis Factor and the People of God: New Life for the Church* (Maryknoll, NY: Orbis Books, 2015).

³ Antonio Rosmini, *Of the Five Wounds of the Church*, trans. H. P. Lidden (New York: E.P. Dutton, 1883 [1848]).

⁴ Ibid., 16.

⁵ For my investigation of selected instances of implementing synodal practices in the post–Vatican II church, see Bradford E. Hinze, *Practices of Dialogue in the Roman Catholic Church: Aims and Obstacles, Lessons and Laments* (New York: Continuum, 2006); for an overview, see Bradford E. Hinze, "The Reception of Vatican II in Participatory Structures of the Church: Facts and Friction," *Proceedings of the Canon Law Society of America* 70 (2008): 28–52.

⁶ Theologians who draw special attention to laments or comparable genres, experiences, or memories invariably employ critical *background theories* (using Francis Schüssler Fiorenza's formulation) and *explanatory methods* (as described by Paul Ricoeur) in their investigations to augment and offset commonplace phenomenological and hermeneutical assumptions. So, for example, Edward Schillebeeckx's *negative contrast experiences* and Johann Baptist Metz's *anamnestic solidarity* and *Leiden an Gott* reflect the influence of the critical theories of Max Horkheimer, Theodor Adorno, Walter Benjamin, and Ernst Bloch.

⁷ Recent attention to the category of impasse in theology has been inspired by Constance Fitzgerald, O.C.D., "Impasse and Dark Night," in *Women's Spirituality: Resources for Christian Development*, ed. Joann Wolski Conn (Mahwah, NJ: Paulist Press, 1986), 287–311. Bryan N. Massingale selected "Impasse . . . and Beyond" as the theme for the 2009 annual convention of the Catholic Theological Society of America. See the Catholic Theological Society of America Proceedings, 2009, at http://ejournals.bc.edu/ojs/index.php/ctsa/issue/view/572.

⁸ On dialectic in theology, see Bernard Lonergan, *Method in Theology* (New York: Herder and Herder, 1972), 235–266; Robert M. Doran, *Theology and the Dialectics of History* (Toronto: University of Toronto Press, 1989).

⁹ Congregation for the Doctrine of the Faith, "Letter to the Bishops of the Catholic Church on Some Aspects of the Church Understood as Communion," *Origins* 22 (June 25, 1992): 108–12, no. 9.

¹⁰ Walter Kasper, "Zur Theologie und Praxis des bischöflichen Amtes," *Auf neue Art Kirche Sein. Kirklicheiten—Herausforderungen—Wandlungen* (Munich: Bernward bei Don Bosco, 1999) 32–48, at 44.

¹¹ For documentations and analysis, see Kilian McDonnell, "The Ratzinger/Kasper Debate: The Universal Church and Local Churches," *Theological Studies* 63 (2002): 227–50 and Medard Kehl, "Der Disput der Kardinäle: Zum Verhältnis von Universalkirche und Ortskirchen," *Stimmen der Zeit* 128 (2003): 219–32.

¹² The emergence of this paradigm among curial officials is associated with the central role of Cardinal Joseph Ratzinger as the head of the CDF during the papacy of John Paul II. Ratzinger credits the importance of Henri de Lubac's work on the body of Christ and its relation to Eucharistic ecclesiology, which "thus opened . . . up to the actual questions of the Church's legal order and the relationships between the local and the universal church" (*Church, Ecumenism, and Politics: New Essays in Ecclesiology* [New York: Crossroad, 1988] 14). Ratzinger comments on the central contribution of Hans Urs von Balthasar to the work of Communio theology in "Communio: A Program," *Communio* 19 (1992): 436–49.

¹³ See, for example, Peter De Mey, "Is 'Affective' Collegiality Sufficient? A Plea for a More 'Effective' Collegiality of Bishops in the Roman Catholic Church and Its Ecumenical Implications," in *Friendship as an Ecumenical Value*, ed. Antoine Arjakovsky and Marie-Audie Tardivo (Lviv, Ukrane: Catholic University Press, 2006), 132–53.

¹⁴ For representative texts, see The World Council of Churches, *The Nature and Mission of the Church: A Stage on the Way to a Common Statement*, Faith and Order Statement 198 (Geneva: World Council of Churches, 2005); The North American Orthodox-Catholic Theological Commission, "Steps towards a Reunited Church: A Sketch of an Orthodox-Catholic Vision for the Future" (2010), http://assemblyofbishops.org/news/scoba/towards-a-unified-church; U.S. Lutheran-Roman Catholic in Dialogue X, *The Church as Koinonia of Salvation: Its Structures and Ministries*, ed. Randall Lee and Jeffrey Gros (Washington, DC: United States Catholic Conference of Bishops, 2005); Anglican-Roman Catholic International Commission (ARCIC), "The Gift of Authority (Authority in the Church III)" (1998), http://www.prounione.urbe.it/dia-int/arcic/doc/e_arcicII_05.html.

¹⁵ See the commentaries on chapter two by Yves M.-J. Congar, "The Church: The People of God," in *The Church and Mankind*, Concilium Theology in the Age of Renewal, Dogma, ed. Edward Schillebeeckx (Glen Rock, N.J.: Paulist Press, 1964), 11–37; Yves M.-J. Congar, "The People of God," in *Vatican II: An Interfaith Appraisal*, ed. John H. Miller (1966), 197–207.

¹⁶ See Giuseppe Alberigo and James Provost, eds., *Synod 1985—An Evaluation*, Concilium: Religion in the Eighties, ed. Giuseppe Alberigo and James Provost, Edinburgh: T and T Clark, 1986), 188; The assessment of Joseph Komonchak is quoted in Chapter 2 from "The Synod of 1985 and the Notion of the Church," in *Chicago Studies* 26 (1987): 330–45, at 333.

¹⁷ Walter Brueggemann, *The Message of the Psalms: A Theological Commentary* (Minneapolis: Augsburg, 1984), 51–58, at 54; also see Walter Brueggermann, *Theology of the Old Testament: Testimony, Dispute, Advocacy* (Minneapolis: Fortress, 1997), 317–406, esp. 373–99.

¹⁸ Claus Westermann, "The Structure and History of the Lament," in *Praise and Lament in the Psalms*, trans. K. R. Crim and R. N. Soulen (Atlanta: John Knox Press, 1981[1954]), 165–213.

¹⁹ Westermann argues that the lament is only complete when it has three dimensions pertaining to God, the one who laments, and the enemy (ibid., 169). Westermann speaks of the structure in terms of an address (or introductory petition), lament, turning toward God (or confession of trust), petition, vow of praise (170). For a similar delineation, see John Kselmann and Michael Barré, "Psalms," in *New Jerome Biblical Commentary*, ed. Raymond E. Brown, Joseph A. Fitzmyer, and Roland E. Murphy (Upper Saddle River, NJ: Prentice-Hall, 1990), 34:9.

²⁰ For Brueggemann, the ultimate theological significance of the lament is a speech pattern that "shifts the calculus and redresses the redistribution of power between the two parties" of the petitioner and God. The petitioner stands up to God and as a result "is taken seriously and legitimately granted power" so that through this discourse of lament "the petitioner is heard, valued, and transmitted as serious speech." In the context of cult (or prayer), one infers that God "hears" and takes the lament seriously. The larger implication is that "such a speech pattern and social usage keep all power relations under review and capable of redefinition;" see "The Costly Loss of Lament," in *The Poetical Books: A Sheffield Reader* (Sheffield, UK: Sheffield Academic Press, 1997), 84–97, at 87–88; originally in *Journal for the Study of the Old Testament* 36 (1986): 57–71.

²¹ One of the interesting features of laments is that they provide a space to accuse the other of being perverse, sacrilegious, and godless, while at the same time recognizing that the enemy acts friendly toward the lamenter (Ps 55:21), greets (Ps 144:8), and spends time (Ps 41:5–6) with the lamenter. See Westermann, "Structure and History of the Lament," 180–81, 188–94.

²² The solace offered to the lamenter by the larger narrative promise of the covenant, the prophet's consoling hope, the sage's confidence, and the psalmist's prayers of trust and gratitude were occasionally called into question and judged as less than fully credible as, for example, during the repression at the hands of the forces of the Hellenistic empire. In this period, complaints became severed from petitions, professions of trust, rededication, and gratitude borne of new orientation. Kathleen O'Connor and Diane Bergant argue that when stripped to its barest literary form, the lament is difficult medicine with no prognosis in sight. Diane Bergant, *Lamentations* (Nashville: Abingdon Press, 2003); Kathleen M. O'Connor, *Lamentations & The Tears of the World* (Maryknoll, NY: Orbis Books, 2002); a wider range of issues are explored in the collection *Lamentations in Ancient and Contemporary Cultural Contexts*, ed. Nancy C. Lee and Carleen Mandolfo (Atlanta: Society for Biblical Literature, 2008).

²³ Markus Öhler, "To Mourn, Weep, Lament and Groan: On the Heterogeneity of the New Testament Statements on Lament," in *Evoking Lament: A Theological Discussion*, ed. Eva Harasta and Brian Brock (New York: T&T Clark, 2009), 150–65, at 150.

²⁴ Stephen P. Ahearne-Kroll, *The Psalms of Lament in Mark's Passion* (Cambridge: Cambridge University Press, 2007).

²⁵ The contention that the expression of human laments and the groaning of creation comes from the Spirit is based on Paul's claims in Romans 8:22–26 and 1 Corinthians 2:10. See Joseph A. Fitzmyer, *Romans, Anchor Bible Commentary* (New York: Doubleday, 1992), 504–21; Robert Jewett, *Romans: A Commentary*, Hermeneia Series (Minneapolis: Fortress, 2007), 504–24. Jewett traces the motif of creation groaning to Job 31:38–40 with allusion to Genesis 3:17–18; and Fitzmyer recognizes not only the threat of divine judgment, but also

the promise of new life through the travail of creation, a motif found in Hebrew scriptures and in Greco-Roman literature (Jewett, *Romans*, 517; Fitzmyer, *Romans, Anchor Bible Commentary*, 509). I would further hypothesize that lament is one form found in speaking in tongues (*Glossolalia*) relevant to Paul's understanding of the discourse of the Spirit. These scriptural insights invite us to expand our understanding of the Spirit as the mouth of God, as developed by Symeon the New Theologian, *On the Mystical Life, Vol. 1: The Church and the Last Things*, trans. Alexander Golitzen (Crestwood, NY: St. Valdimir's Press, 1995), 118–22.

   [26] See Krister Stendahl, "The Apostle Paul and the Introspective Conscience of the West," in *Paul among Jews and Gentiles* (Minneapolis: Augsburg Fortress, 1976), 78–96.

   [27] Benjamin H. Dunning, *Aliens and Sojourners: Self as Other in Early Christianity* (Philadelphia: University of Pennsylvania Press, 2009).

   [28] Hans Urs von Balthasar, in *The Glory of the Lord: A Theological Aesthetic*, vol. 1, *Seeing the Form* (Crossroad/Ignatius, 1982), discusses how Paul weeps "over the deformations of the Church wrought by sinners" (Phil 2:21, 3:18), "the Gospel's wicked servants," while offering himself as a model of Christ. Peter, on the other hand, "weeps for himself." Balthasar draws the conclusion, typologically rich, but logically strained, that "both weep over the same thing, namely, the failure of the institutional Church. They weep over the gap which yawns in the Church between person and office, whereas Christ wanted to impress upon the Church his own identity" (Balthasar, *Glory of the Lord*, 566).

   [29] The logic of lament that leads to conversion and rededication, gratitude and praise is expressed in the literary structure of individual lament psalms and in the dynamic of the entire psalter, characterized by Brueggemann in terms of psalms of orientation, disorientation, and new orientation, and in the larger canonical polyphony where laments are imbedded in redemptive and consoling narratives and prophecies, sage wisdom or apocalyptic visions. See Brueggemann, *Theology of the Old Testament: Testimony, Dispute, Advocacy*.

   [30] Augustine, *Enarrationes in Psalmos Corpus Christianorum: Series Latina*, vols. 38–40 (Turnhout, Belgium: Brepols Publishers, 1956); Augustine, *Expositions of the Psalms*, Works of Saint Augustine: A Translation for the 21st Century, III/15–III/20, intro. Michael Fiedrowicz, trans. Maria Boulding, ed. John E. Rotelle, O.S.A. (Hyde Park, NY: New City Press,), 21. In his "General Introduction" to vol. 1 of Boulding's translation, III/13–66, Fiedrowicz summarizes his landmark study, *Psalmus Vox Totius Christi: Studien zu Augustins "Enarrationes in Psalmos"* (Freiburg im Breisgau, Germany: Herder, 1997). Michael C. McCarthy explores the psalms of lament and ecclesiology in "The Revelatory Psalm: A Fundamental Theology of Augustine's 'Enarrationes in Psalmos'" (Ph.D. dissertation, University of Notre Dame, 2003), 243–339; see also Jason Byassee, *Praise Seeking Understanding: Reading the Psalms with Augustine* (Grand Rapids: Eerdmans, 2007).

   [31] Augustine, "Exposition 2 of Psalm 34," *Expositions of the Psalms*, III/16, 64–65.

   [32] Brian Brock, "Augustine's Incitement to Lament, from the *Enarrationes in Psalmos*," in *Evoking Lament*, 182–203, at 186.

   [33] Augustine, "Exposition 1 of Psalm 101," *Expositions of the Psalms*, III/19, 51.

   [34] See McCarthy, "Revelatory Psalm," 243–339, esp. 284–301; and Michael C. McCarthy, "An Ecclesiology of Groaning: Augustine, The Psalms, and the Making of the Church," *Theological Studies* 66 (2005): 23–48.

   [35] This translation of Augustine's comments, *Enarrationes in Pslamos* 30 (2) s. 3.1, vol. 38, 213, is by McCarthy in "An Ecclesiology of Groaning," 26; cf. *Expositions of the Psalms*, III/15, 347.

   [36] "An Ecclesiology of Groaning," 45.

[37] *Expositions of the Psalms*, III/16, 37:13–14, 156–57; cf. "An Ecclesiology of Groaning," 26.

[38] "An Ecclesiology of Groaning," 27.

[39] Ibid., 29; also see Fiedrowicz, "General Introduction," 50–57.

[40] "An Ecclesiology of Groaning," 34.

[41] Augustine, "Exposition 2 of Psalm 26," *Expositions of the Psalms*, III:15, 274.

[42] McCarthy ("Revelatory Psalm," 194–214, 252–300) elucidates how Augustine finds reading the psalms a therapy of the affections and catalyst for social dynamics, especially in performance.

[43] On the testimony of apostles, martyrs, and ascetics, see ibid., 301–35.

[44] Fitzgerald, "Impasse and Dark Night"; Constance Fitzgerald, " From Impasse to Prophetic Hope: Crisis of Memory," *Catholic Theological Society of America Proceedings* 64 (2009): 21–42.

[45] Fitzgerald, "Impasse and Dark Night," 287–88.

[46] Ibid., 288.

[47] Ibid., 291.

[48] Fitzgerald, "From Impasse to Prophetic Hope," 22. Here Fitzgerald's approach is informed by John of the Cross, *Ascent of Mount Carmel*, in *The Collected Works of St. John of the Cross*, trans. Kieran Kavanaugh and Otilio Rodriguez (Washington, DC: Institute of Carmelite Studies Publications, 1991), bk. 3, chaps. 1–15; and John of the Cross, *Dark Night of the Soul*, bk. 2 in *Collected Works*.

[49] Fitzgerald "From Impasse to Prophetic Hope," 23; the quotation is taken from Hein Blommestijn, Jos Huls, and Kees Waaijman, *Footprints of Love: John of the Cross as a Guide in the Wilderness* (Leuven, Belgium: Peeters, 2000), 74.

[50] Fitzgerald, "From Impasse to Prophetic Hope," 24.

[51] John of the Cross, *The Dark Night of the Soul* 2.21.11, in *Collected Works*, 448–49.

[52] Fitzgerald, "Impasse and Dark Night," 289.

[53] Ibid., 290.

[54] Michael J. Buckley, S.J., "Atheism and Contemplation," *Theological Studies* 40 (1979): 680–99, at 696; see also Buckley's treatment of ideology and purity of heart in *Papal Primacy and the Episcopate: Towards a Relational Understanding* (New York: Crossroad, 1998), 22–31.

[55] Ignatius of Loyola, *Spiritual Exercises and Selected Writings*, ed. George E. Ganns (New York: Paulist Press, 1991), no. 317, 202; translations occasionally revised in light of Timothy M. Gallagher's translation and observations in his *Discernment of Spirits: An Ignatian Guide for Everyday Life* (New York: Crossroad, 2005), 62–66. Belgian Bert Daelemans, S.J., by private communication, offered helpful insight into Ignatius' *Spiritual Exercises*.

[56] *Spiritual Exercises*, no. 322, 203.

[57] *Spiritual Exercises*, no. 331, 206.

[58] On the rules of discernment for the second week of the exercises, see Timothy M. Gallagher, *Spiritual Consolation: An Ignatian Guide to the Greater Discernment of Spirits* (New York: Crossroad, 2007), 11–14, 59–60.

[59] *Spiritual Exercises*, no. 333, 206.

[60] J. Peter Schineller, S.J., "The Pilgrim Journey of Ignatius: From Soldier to Laborer in the Lord's Vineyard and Its Implications for Apostolic Lay Spirituality," *Studies in the Spirituality of Jesuits* 31/4 (September 1999), 1–14.

[61] The *Constitutions of the Society of Jesus and Their Complementary Norms* (St. Louis: Institute of Jesuit Sources, 1996), pt. VII, nos. 622–26, 284–91.

[62] Schineller, "The Pilgrim Journey of Ignatius," 23.

[63] Three superior generals have promoted practices of common apostolic discernment. Pedro Arrupe in his letter of December 25, 1971, *Acta Romana Societas Iesu*, vol. 15 (Rome: Typis Polyglottis Vaticanis, 1972), 767–73; Peter Hans Kovenbach, in his annual letter of 1986, *Acta Romana Societas Iesu*, vol. 19 (1987), 720–40; Adolfo Nicolás, "Common Apostolic Discernment," *Review of Ignatian Spirituality* 40 (2009): 9–20. To what extent practices of communal discernment have been developed by Jesuit or Ignatian-based communities like Christian Life Communities merits further investigation. It is clear, however, that Ignacio Ellacuría was keenly aware of the work of communal discernment in his emphasis on the *historicization* of the *Spiritual Exercises* (inspired by the philosophy of Xavier Zubiri), and on the collective use of the creative imagination in the discernment of a *proyecto social* (social project) in communities and universities dedicated to apostolic mission.

Chapter 4

[1] On the shift to a dialogical ecclesiology, see Bradford E. Hinze, *Practices of Dialogue in the Roman Catholic Church* (New York: Continuum, 2006); Bradford E. Hinze, "Ecclesial Repentance and the Demand for Dialogue," *Theological Studies* 61 (2000): 213–14; Bradford E. Hinze, "On Fostering Ecclesial Dialogue: Engaging Contrasting Ecclesiologies," *Ecclesiology* 4 (2008): 166–82. On the transitions from Christocentric to more pneumatological and Trinitarian ecclesiologies, see Bradford E. Hinze, "Releasing the Power of the Spirit in a Trinitarian Ecclesiology," in *Advents of the Spirit: An Introduction to the Current Study of Pneumatology*, ed. Bradford E. Hinze and D. Lyle Dabney (Milwaukee, WI: Marquette University Press, 2001), 345–79.

[2] This argument uses the term *reception*, but the claims being advanced merit further development in terms of the philosophy and theology of recognition as found in the work of many, including Paul Ricoeur, *The Course of Recognition*, trans. David Pellauer (Cambridge, MA: Harvard University Press, 2005), and Judith Butler, *Frames of War: When Is Life Grievable?* (London: Versa, 2010). On recognition and theology, see Kathryn Reinhard, "Recognizing the Spirit: An Ecclesial Pneumatology" (Ph.D. dissertation, Fordham University, 2015); Kevin W. Hector, *Theology without Metaphysics: God, Language, and the Spirit of Recognition* (Cambridge, MA: Cambridge University Press, 2011).

[3] See Brian Leary, S.J., "Christian and Religious Obedience," *Review for Religious* 44 (1985): 513–20. Religious obedience is described as a particular expression of Christian obedience, both of which are rooted in Philippians 2:7; A. Paul Dominic, S.J., "The Threefold Call," *Review for Religious* 40 (1981): 283–96, examines scriptural roots for obedience, in all four gospels.

[4] I am not considering in this chapter the distinctive place of the vow of obedience taken in religious life in relationship to the obedience that is required of all Christians. For a treatment of the latter that has influenced my position, see Judith K. Schaefer, *The Evolution of a Vow: Obedience as Decision Making in Communion*, Communicative Theology Series, vol. 11 (Zürich: LIT Verlag, 2008).

[5] See my comments on the selective use of the principles devised for revising the code in light of the teachings of Vatican II in Bradford E. Hinze, "The Reception of Vatican II in Participatory Structures of the Church: Facts and Friction," *Proceedings of the Canon Law Society of America Annual Convention* 70 (2009): 28–52.

⁶ Paternalism is defined by Paul Misner as "the practice of making decisions for persons who are of age and otherwise de jure capable of speaking for themselves, decision, that is, that could well be left to the groups or individuals directly concerned, or at least to negotiations with them," *The New Dictionary of Catholic Social Thought* (Collegeville, MN: 1994), 712, cited in Peter J. Bernardi, *Maurice Blondel, Social Catholicism, & Action Française* (Washington, DC: Catholic University of America Press, 2009), 11–16, at 13n22,

⁷ Latin quotation cited in Archbishop John Quinn, "A Permanent Synod? Reflections on Collegiality," *Origins* 31 (April 18, 2002): 730–36, 734 and 736n41, and examined by Yves Congar, "*Quod omnes tangit, ab omnibus tractari et approbari debet*," *Revue historique du droit français et etranger* 36 (1958): 210–59.

⁸ This angle of approach into a certain sphere of dialogue draws on the work of a wide variety of theologians, but I want to acknowledge, in particular, the attention to repression utilizing Jacques Lacan in the work of Joerg Rieger, *Remember the Poor: The Challenge to Theology in the Twenty-first Century* (Harrisburg, PA: Trinity, 1998), and Joerg Rieger, *God and the Excluded: Visions and Blindspots in Contemporary Theology* (Minneapolis: Fortress Press, 2001).

⁹ See John P. Boyle, *Church Teaching Authority: Historical and Theological Studies* (Notre Dame, IN: University of Notre Dame Press, 1985); Ladislas Örsy, *The Church: Learning and Teaching* (Collegeville, MN: Michael Glazer/Liturgical Press, 1987).

¹⁰ Meghan Clark, "Subsidiarity as a Two-Sided Coin" (March 8, 2012), http://catholicmoraltheology.com/subsidiarity-is-a-two-sided-coin/, describes the principle in terms of making decisions "at the lowest level possible and the highest level necessary" in light of analysis of papal social teaching on the subject from Pius XI, *Quadregesimo Anno* (1931) to Pope Benedixt XVI in *Caritas in Veritate* (2009). See John Burkhard, "The Interpretation and Application of Subsidiarity in Ecclesiology: An Overview of the Theological and Canonical Literature," *Jurist* 58 (1998): 279–342; Joseph Komonchak, "Subsidiarity in the Church: The State of the Question," *Jurist* 48 (1988): 298–349; and Ad Leys, *Ecclesiological Impacts of the Principle of Subsidiarity* (Kampen, the Netherlands: Kok, 1995).

¹¹ Joseph Ratzinger, *Introduction to Christianity*, trans. J. R. Foster (New York: Crossroad/Seabury, 1969), 57.

¹² Joseph Ratzinger, *Behold the Pierced One*, trans. Graham Harrison (San Francisco: Igantius, 1986), 61–69, at 65; and Ratzinger's dissertation, *Volk und Haus Gottes in Augustins Lehre von der Kirche* (K Zink, 1954, reissued St. Ottilien: EOS-Verlag, 1992).

¹³ Josef Ratzinger, "Free Expression and Obedience in the Church," in *The Church: Readings in Theology* (New York: P. J. Kenedy & Sons, 1963), 194–217, at 202. This essay goes on to discuss the church's prophetic witness in contrast to the church as a whore (*casta meretrix*) based on the sinfulness of the church's members, citing Hans Urs von Balthasar's work on this subject. The church assumes the mantle of the prophets (ibid., 210), now as witness who suffers martyrdom for the truth, which likewise places limits on critical protest. "Obedience as obedience takes on a new aspect: the obligation of 'bearing witness,' the duty to strive for the integrity of the Church, to battle against the 'Babylon' within her that raises its head not only among the laity, not only among individual Christians, but even higher up within the very core of the Church's structure" (ibid., 211–12). He draws the conclusion that "what the Church needs today, as always, are not adulators to extol the status quo, but men whose humility and obedience are no less than their passion for truth; men who brave every misunderstanding and attack as they bear witness;

men who, in a word, love the Church more than ease and the unruffled course of their personal destiny" (ibid., 212).

[14] Ratzinger, *Introduction to Christianity*, 130; he develops a dialogical eschatology on pages 270–78.

[15] Ratzinger, *Behold the Pierced One*, 15. The church is described as the object of the dialogue between Jesus and the Father, which provides the Trinitarian basis for the church in Joseph Ratzinger, *The God of Jesus Christ*, trans. Robert J. Cunningham (Chicago: Franciscan Herald Press, 1979), 73.

[16] Ratzinger, *Behold the Pierced One*, 41.

[17] Joseph Ratzinger/Pope Benedict XVI, *Jesus of Nazareth: Part One, from the Baptism in the Jordan to the Transfiguration* (San Francisco: Ignatius Press, 2007), 7.

[18] Joseph Ratzinger/Pope Benedict XVI, *Jesus of Nazareth: Part Two, Holy Week from the Entrance into Jerusalem to the Resurrection* (San Francisco: Ignatius Press, 2011), 161, quoting Christoph Schönborn, *God's Human Face: The Christ-Icon*, trans. Lothar Krauth (San Fracisco: Ignatius Press, 1994), 102–33, at 126–27.

[19] Ratzinger/Benedict, *Jesus of Nazareth, Part Two*, 161.

[20] Hans Urs von Balthasar, *The Cosmic Liturgy: The Universe According to Maximus the Confessor*, trans. Brian E. Daley (San Francisco: Ignatius Press, 2004 [1941]); see the central role of Maximus in Hans Urs von Balthasar, *Theo-Drama: Theological Dramatic Theory*, trans. Graham Harrison (San Francisco: Ignatius Press; New York: Crossroad, 1988), 2:189–334, at 201–3 (hereafter *Theo-Drama*).

[21] Hans Urs von Balthasar, *The Glory of the Lord: A Theological Aesthetics*, vol. 1, trans. E. Leiva-Merikakis (San Francisco: Ignatius Press; New York: Crossroad, 1982), 478.

[22] *Theo-Drama*, 1:34–37, at 34.

[23] *Theo-Drama*, 1:646; also see the Dialogue Principle, ibid., 626–43.

[24] *Theo-Drama*, 3:174–75; M. Nédoncelle, *La Réciprocité des consciences* (Paris: Aubier, 1942).

[25] On the mission of the Son and Trinitarian Inversion, see *Theo-Drama*, 3:149–259, esp. 183–91 at 187.

[26] *Theo-Drama*, 3:188. In the words of Kathryn Tanner, "the general tenor of [the father and son's] relationship as interpreted by Hans Urs von Balthasar and Joseph Ratzinger, one could summarize ... [in] this way: sent to his death by the Father, under relentless pressure from the Spirit, the Son exhibits in his human life the blind obedience of an inferior before the heartless command of an implacable superior, demanding from him nothing less than self-sacrifice and extreme acts of self-evacuation and self-renunciation." Kathryn Tanner, *Christ the Key* (Cambridge: University Press, 2010), 212.

[27] *Theo-Drama*, 3:174–75.

[28] Hans Urs von Balthasar, *Theo-Logic. Theological Logical Theory* (San Francisco: Ignatius Press, 2004), 2:147–48.

[29] Walter Kasper, *The God of Jesus Christ*, trans. Matthew J. O'Connell (New York: Crossroad, 1984), 290; *Der Gott Jesu Christ* (Mainz, Germany: Matthias-Grünewald, 1982), 353. Walter Kasper, *Jesus the Christ*, trans. V. Green (London Burns and Oates; New York: Paulist Press, 1976), discusses the obedience of Jesus and the role of the Holy Spirit in relation to the hypostatic union on pages 249–52. "The Spirit as the personal bond of the freedom of the love between the Father and Son is the medium into which the Father freely and out of pure grace sends the Son, and in which he finds in Jesus the human partner in whom and through whom the Son obediently answers the Father's mission in an historical

way, , , , The freedom of love in the Holy Spirit has its own plausibility, power to convince, radiance, light and beauty, and by this it impresses man without coercing him" (ibid., 251–52). The latter insight Kasper attributes to volume one of Balthasar, *The Glory of the Lord*. See Balthasar's discussion of Kasper's position in *Theo-Drama*, 3:185–86. Whether Balthasar's doctrine of Trinitarian inversion and his formulation of the role of the Spirit in the obedience of the Son would ultimately violate Kasper's later formulation is open to discussion, but on the fundamental character of the Son's obedience to the Father and the Spirit's role in the relation of the Father and the Son, the differences are not decisive.

    30 Kasper, *The God of Jesus Christ*, 277–79; also see Matthias Joseph Scheeben, *The Mysteries of Christianity*, trans. Cyril Vollert (St. Louis, MO: Herder, 1946); Joseph Pohle, *The Divine Trinity: A Dogmatic Treatise,* trans. Arthur Preuss (St. Louis, MO: Herder, 1925); Ludwig Ott, *Fundamentals of Catholic Dogma*, trans Patrick Lynch (St. Louis, MO: B. Herder, 1960). I owe a debt of gratitude to Ralph Del Colle for discussions about these and related matters during his lifetime.

    31 On the monarchy of the Father, see Wolfhart Pannenberg, *Systematic Theology*, vol. 1. Trans. Geoffrey W. Bromiley (Grand Rapids: Eerdmans, 1991), 274–80, 324–27; John Zizioulas seeks to defend the Father as cause *arche* or *monarchia* without denying the equiprimordial character of Trinitarian identity as a communion of persons, "The Father as Cause: Personhood Generating Otherness," in *Communion and Otherness*, ed. Paul McPartlan (T & T Clark, 2006), 113–54. "The Fatherhood of God . . . has nothing in common with human fatherhood; no analogy between the two is possible. Human father-hood presupposes a division in human nature, that is, individuality before relationality, since the entity of the human father is already established prior to that of his son. It would therefore appear impossible in such a context to speak of the idea of divine Fatherhood as 'oppressive' or 'paternalistic' or 'sexist', and so on. All fears that by maintaining the biblical language of God the Father we encourage sexism in religion and society are dissolved in such a relational ontology" (ibid., 122–23).

    32 This paternalistic and hierarchical approach has recently been modified by Ormond Rush utilizing two analogies. The first is based on giving and receiving: "Within the imma-nent Trinity, the Father is Giver and Receiver, the Son is Receiver and Giver, the Spirit is the dynamic of mutual reception. Within the economy of salvation, the Spirit is the dynamic of receiving and giving between God and humanity, so as to constitute the principle of humani-ty's reception of divine revelation." The second analogy is based on conversation or dialogue: "The Father speaks forth the Word and receives a Word in reply; the Son is Listener and Speaker; the Spirit is the Dialogue between the Speaking and Listening of Father and Son. The word that goes forth from the Father is received (listened to) so totally by the Son that he becomes the Word; the (perfectly echoed) word of response by the Son is received (fully accepted) by the Father as the validated Word of God. The Son is, at once, the Word Spoken and the Word Received. In the process of divine self-communication within God, the Spirit is the Dialogue between the Father and the Son. In the process of divine self-communication between the Triune God and humanity, the Spirit is the Dialogue who enables response to God's Word of Address to humanity." Ormond Rush, *The Eyes of Faith: The Sense of the Faithful and the Church's Reception of Revelation* (Washington, DC: Catholic University of America Press, 2009), 32–33.

    33 Walter Kasper emphasizes the inward and outward dialogical character of the church in his latest and most thorough life work on ecclesiology, *The Catholic Church: Nature, Reality and Mission* (New York/London: Bloomsbury/T&T Clark, 2015[German,

2011]), see esp. 269–73, 277–81, 289–347, esp. 344–47. But he makes no explicit connection with the dialogical character of God's identity and mission other than when he states, "We only know that this dialogue [here he is speaking about ecumenical dialogue] and this way are the vocation of Jesus and a work of the Holy Spirit" (ibid., 346). While privileging communion ecclesiology, notice his particular attention to the discernment of the people of God in addressing "existential problems, the joys and hopes, the fears and sorrows of the people" (invoking *Gaudium et Spes* 1) in his section on the parish (ibid., 278–79).

[34] My criticism of the classical approach to the Spirit that focuses on passivity and restricts the divine communication is stated forcefully by Denis Edwards, *Breath of Life: A Theology of the Creator Spirit* (Maryknoll, NY: Orbis Books, 2004), 154–55.

[35] See Tanner, *Christ the Key*. Tanner shares my interest in exploring the relationships among the three persons of the Trinity as narrated in the gospel stories (ibid., 159). Like Ratzinger and Balthasar, and following the scriptural and traditional spotlight, Tanner focuses on Jesus's obedience to the Father (ibid., 35, 82), sustained by the Spirit to "do the Father's will completely" (ibid., 165, 181–87, 218–19). Tanner speaks about dialogical approaches to the Trinity, ones that advance the perfectly reciprocal relations among the perichoretic communion of Trinitarian persons to support progressive politics, but she argues that the Trinity is more than dialogical and that this approach fails to account for the "non-mutual relation of subordination to the Father" in prayer and in the Son's unity with the will of the Father (ibid., 230–31, cf. 182).

[36] Elizabeth Johnson, *Women, Earth, and Creator Spirit* (New York: Paulist Press, 1993); Elizabeth Johnson, *Ask the Beasts: Darwin and the God of Love* (New York: Bloomsbury Academic, 2014); Denis Edwards, *Breath of Life*; Denis Edwards, *Partaking of God: Trinity, Evolution, and Ecology* (Collegeville, MN: Liturgical Press [Michael Glazier], 2014).

[37] Some claim, "the Holy Spirit is not said to be at work in creation in this passage" of Paul, but it is the individuals in community that are beckoned to renewal. Kirsteen Kim recounts these critical remarks in relation to the Canberra Assembly of the World Council of Churches in 1991, in *The Holy Spirit in the World: A Global Conversation* (Maryknoll, NY: Orbis Books, 2007), 148, referencing Eduard Schweizer, "On Distinguishing Between Spirits," *Ecumenical Review* 41 (1989): 406–15, at 408, and Hans Hübner, "The Holy Spirit in Holy Scripture," *Ecumenical Review* 41 (1989): 324–38, at 324, 332–33, 336.

[38] See John J. Collins, *Introduction to the Hebrew Bible* (Minneapolis: Fortress Press, 2004), 47–137.

[39] I agree with Elizabeth Johnson on the need to retrieve a diversity of names of God, male and female terms, in scripture and tradition; see Elizabeth Johnson, *She Who Is: The Mystery of God in Feminist Theological Discourse* (New York: Crossroad, 1992), 76–103.

[40] See the helpful analysis by Mary Rose D'Angelo, "*Abba* and 'Father': Imperial Theology and the Traditions about Jesus," *Journal of Biblical Literature* 111 (1992): 611–30; Mary Rose D'Angelo, "Theology in Mark and Q: *Abba* and 'Father' in Context," *Harvard Theological Review* 85 (1992): 149–74; for a defense of the Fatherhood of God, see John D. Zizioulas, "The Father as Cause," in *Communion and Otherness*, 133–54.

[41] Similar formulations can be found in Psalms 31:2, 34:5–6, 17–18, 40:1, 77:1, 78:1, 80:1, 81:5b–13, 83:1, 86:1, 6, 7, 88:2. There are many other examples of this obedience of the Father to the suffering of humanity (mediated by the Spirit): Abraham bargains with God (Gn 18:16–33). Tobit 3:1–16; Genesis: 21:17, 29:33; 1 Kings 8:44–45; 2 Kings 19:16: "Incline your ear, O Lord, and hear"; Isaiah 59:1: "See, the Lord's hand is not too short to save, nor his ear too dull to hear." Walter Brueggemann overlooks hearing when he identi-

fies various verbal forms in his *Theology of the Old Testament: Testimony, Dispute, Advocacy* (Minneapolis: Fortress Press, 1997), 145–212.

[42] Abraham Heschel, *The Prophets*, 2 vols. (Peabody, MA: Hendrickson, 2009 [1962]), 1:57.

[43] Heschel, *The Prophets*, 1:151.

[44] Ibid., 2:1–6.

[45] Ibid., 2:4.

[46] Adela Yarbro Collins, *Mark: A Commentary*, Hermeneia Series (Minneapolis: Fortress Press, 2007), 673–83, at 676–77; John R. Donahue and Daniel J. Harrington, *The Gospel of Mark*, Sacra Pagina Series (Collegeville, MN: Liturgical Press, 2002).

[47] José Comblin, *Cry of the Oppressed, Cry of Jesus: Meditation on Scripture and Contemporary Struggle* (Maryknoll, NY: Orbis Books, 1984), is very clear that the cries (or laments) of suffering men and women, even in the Exodus, reflect the work of the Spirit crying out, but surprisingly he fails to make the connection to the cry of Jesus on the cross as the voice of the Spirit crying out; ibid., 53–58, cf. 23–25; in José Comblin, *The Holy Spirit and Liberation* (Maryknoll, NY: Orbis Books, 1989), Comblin expands on his reflection on the role of the Spirit in bringing forth speech in the cries of the poor, (ibid., 61–75, esp. 66–67). He speaks of prophets giving voice to the cry of the poor, but he does not describe it in terms of the prophetic ministry as being an obedient response to the lamentations of those suffering. Leonardo Boff in *Cry of the Earth, Cry of the Poor* (Maryknoll, NY: Orbis Books, 1997) offers no connection between the Spirit and the cries of the poor, nor with the cry of the earth.

[48] On learning (obedience) through suffering, see Harold W. Attridge, *The Epistle to the Hebrews: A Commentary on the Epistle to the Hebrews*, Hermeneia Series (Philadelphia: Fortress Press, 1989); Charles H. Talbert, *Learning Through Suffering. The Educational Value of Suffering in the New Testament and Its Milieu* (Collegeville, MN: Liturgical Press, 1991); N. Clayton Croy, *Endurance in Suffering: Hebrews 12:1–13 in Its Rhetorical, Religious, and Philosophical Context* (Cambridge: Cambridge University Press, 1998).

[49] Attridge, *Epistle to the Hebrews*, 147–54.

[50] This latter move, concerning obedience to the true apostle, has justified a hierarchical order and an office carrying on the apostolic ministry. I do not want to call into question the connections to obedience to the apostolic ministry (and all that subsequently surfaced about the exercise of episcopal ministry), but I do want to consider whether the apostolic ministry in this larger framework requires rethinking the hierarchical assumption that has required some form of subordination, superior to inferior. A similar line of interrogation would be needed when treating the Ephesians text that posits an analogy between the obedience of a wife to a husband, and of the church to Christ, as the head of the body of Christ (Eph 5:21–33).

[51] Thomas Aquinas treats the seven gifts of the Spirit in Isaiah 11:2 in his treatment of understanding (ST II–II, Q. 8, A. 1), knowledge (Q. 9, A. 1), fear (Q. 19, A. 9), and wisdom (Q. 45, A.1). On one occasion he correlates the gift of knowledge with the beatitude blessed are those who mourn (Q. 9, 4) and ponders Augustine's claim "Knowledge befits the mourner, who has discovered that he has been mastered by the evil which he coveted as though it were good" (*De Serm. Dom, in monte* iv). Thomas concludes, "it is by forming a right judgment of creatures that man becomes aware of the loss (of which they may be the occasion), which judgment he exercises through the gift of knowledge." The knower rejoices in the knowledge, but mourns the thing that the knower has wrongly conceived, used, and loved.

[52] Elizabeth Teresa Groppe, *Yves Congar's Theology of the Holy Spirit*, AAR Series (New York: Oxford University Press, 2004).

[53] John R. Levison, *Filled with the Spirit* (Grand Rapids: William B. Eerdmans, 2009), 12. While I am receptive to the benefits of Levison's interpretations advanced in the interest of purging anachronisms in interpretations of the Hebrew Bible and the Christian scriptures and am not averse to accepting them on a case-by-case basis, a theologian cannot use this rationale as an excuse to avoid constructive imaginative theological interpretations of earlier materials informed by later passages.

[54] Levison, *Filled with the Spirit*, 15, 19.

[55] Levison, *Filled with the Spirit*, 43–47, 66.

[56] Levison, *Filled with the Spirit*, 80.

[57] The obedience of the triune God is not simply about the economic Trinity, but it also reveals the attention and receptivity that is a part of the loving interaction in the mutual relations in the immanent Trinity. Whether it is David Coffey's return model that offers a variation or completion of a very Augustinian logic, Thomas Weinandy's Thomistic approach, or some sort of interpersonal or social model of the Trinity, there is a need for attention to the mutual attentiveness and receptivity not only in the economic Trinity, but also within the inner Trinitarian relations. See David Coffey, *Deus Trinitas: The Doctrine of the Triune God* (New York: Oxford University Press, 1999); and Thomas Weinandy, *The Father's Spirit of Sonship: Reconceiving the Trinity* (Edinburgh: T & T Clark, 1995). And as a result the doctrines of the obedience of faith and the reception of doctrine must be situated within a larger Trinitarian frame of reference than is often offered that is scriptural, spiritual, and ecclesiological.

[58] As W. Norris Clark and David Coffey speak of receptivity as a positive perfection, which corresponds to self-communication. W. Norris Clark, *Person and Being: The Aquinas Lecture* (Milwaukee: Marquette University Press, 1993), 20–24; 82–93; David Coffey, *Deus Trinitas*, 101, 153.

[59] On safeguarding the monarchy of the Father, see ibid., 31. "Within the inner-trinitarian life, the Holy Spirit is the Dialogue between the Father and Son; in God's outreach to humanity, it is the Spirit of Dialogue who facilitates the reception of the Word of God in human history. To foster a culture of dialogue is to foster the work of the Holy Spirit for the sake of a more faithful reception of God's Word" (ibid., 276). Rush's proposal seeks to capture the dialogical character of the triune God that we saw portrayed by Joseph Ratzinger, Hans Urs von Balthasar, and above all Walter Kasper delineated in section two of this chapter. By featuring the Spirit as the dialogue between the father and the son and the Spirit who facilitates reception of the Word of God in history, I wish to suggest that Rush has failed to accentuate fully the active role of the Spirit in being sent by the Source to be the mouthpiece for groaning creation and grieving humanity. The further repercussion, to be explored in the next chapter, is that the prophetic character of faith is primarily formulated for him in terms of reception of the Word of God, whereas I wish to argue that it is just as important that we recognize the agency of the Spirit in the work of intercession.

[60] The quotation is from Karen Kilby, "Perichoresis and Projection: Problems with Social Doctrines of the Trinity," *New Blackfriars* 31 (2000): 432–45, at 443, who refers to Kathryn Tanner's treatment of how an emphasis on the transcendence of God can function differently in the political realm in *The Politics of God* (Minneapolis: Fortress Press, 1992); Tanner returns to the issues of the Trinity and politics in *Christ the Key*, 140–246; for Orthodox reflections, see John Behr, "The Trinitarian Being of the Church," St. Vladi-

mir's Theological Quarterly 48 (2003): 67–88, and Radu Bordeianu, *Dumitru Staniloae: An Ecumenical Ecclesiology* (New York: Bloomsbury/T&T Clark, 2011).

[61] Kilby, "Perichoresis and Projection," 442. Kilby has as her target the ascending theological opinion, or as she prefers to put it "the new orthodoxy," of the social Trinitarians espoused by Moltmann, Gunton, and others. She does not deny the legitimacy of a social analogy relative to a psychological analogy, or other analogies. Rather she is critical of how they use the concept *perichoresis*. "First . . . to name what is not understood, [in this case] what whatever it is that makes the three Persons one. Secondly, the concept is filled out suggestively with notions borrowed from our own experience of relationships and relatedness. And then, finally, it is presented as an exciting resource Christian theology has to offer the wider world in its reflections upon relationships and relatedness" (ibid.).

[62] See Bernhard Nitsche, "*Die Analogie zwischen dem trinitarischen Gottesbild und der communialen Struktur von Kirche. Desiderat eines Forschungsprogrammes zur Communio-Ekklesiologie,*" in *Communio—Ideal oder Zerrbild von Kommunikation?* ed. Bernd Jochen Hilberath, Quaestiones Disputatae 176 (New York: Herder, 1999), 81–114, at 87.

[63] Michael Buckley, *Papal Primacy and the Episcopate* (New York: Crossroad, 1998), 27–31.

[64] Ian A. McFarland, *Listening to the Least: Doing Theology from the Outside* (Cleveland: Pilgrim Press, 1998).

Chapter 5

[1] For a discussion of the prophetic office (*munus propheticum*) and its identification with the office of teaching (*munus docendi*) in *Lumen Gentium* 25–27 and *Christus Dominus* 11–21, see Ormond Rush, *The Eyes of Faith: The Sense of the Faithful and the Church's Reception of Revelation* (Washington, DC: Catholic University of America Press, 2009), 56–62, 246; and Peter De Mey "The Bishop's Participation in the Threefold *Munera*: Comparing the Appeal to the Patterns of the *Tria Munera* at Vatican II and in the Ecumenical Dialogues," *Jurist* 69 (2009): 31–58. Classic sources include John Henry Newman "Lectures on the Prophetical Office of the Church," in *The Via Media of the Anglican Church*, ed. intro. notes by H. D. Weidner (Oxford: Clarendon Press, 1990); Yves Congar wrote before Vatican II that "In the threefold division of the Church's powers that correspond to the same division of Christ's messianic offices, prophecy is equivalent to magisterium or the teaching function," in Yves Congar, *Lay People in the Church*, trans. Donald Attwater (Westminster, MD: Newman Press, 1967), 271.

[2] Joseph Blenkinsopp, *A History of Prophecy in Israel. Revised and Enlarged* (Louisville, KY: Westminster John Knox Press, 1996), 223–24; John J. Collins, *Introduction to the Hebrew Bible* (Minneapolis: Fortress Press, 2004), 420–22.

[3] Thomas Hughson, "Interpreting Vatican II: 'A New Pentecost,'" *Theological Studies* 69 (2008): 3–37.

[4] *Lumen Gentium* 25 uses the term *colluctatione*, which is translated as "wrestling," and the text goes on to cite Ephesians 6:12, which corresponds to the term Παλη, translated as "struggle" in this NRSV translation.

[5] There is a long history of resistance to apocalyptic and prophetic figures and movements in Christianity. See, for example, Bonaventure's critique of the visions of Joachim of Fiore in *Collationes in Hexaemeron*, which is the subject of Joseph Ratzinger, *The Theology of History of St. Bonavanture*, trans. Zachery Hayes (Chicago: Franciscan

Herald Press, 1971). Also see Niels Christian Hvidt, *Christian Prophecy: The Post-Biblical Tradition* (New York: Oxford University Press, 2007), and "Das Problem der christlichen Prophetie: Niels Christian Hvidt im Gespräch mit Joseph Kardinal Ratzinger," *Communio* 2 (1999): 177–88.

6 Johannes Weiss, *Jesus' Proclamation of the Kingdom of God*, trans. Richard Hyde Hiers and David Larrimore Holland (Philadelphia: Fortress Press, 1971).

7 E. P. Sanders, *The Historical Figure of Jesus* (New York: Penguin, 1995); Dale C. Anderson, *Constructing Jesus: Memory, Imagination, and History* (Grand Rapids: Baker Academic, 2010); N. T. Wright, *Jesus and the Victory of God* (Philadelphia: Fortress, 1997).

8 This emphasis on the eschatological character of Jesus's identity stands in opposition to a noneschatological interpretation of Jesus's life and ministry associated with the work of John Dominic Crossan, *The Historical Jesus: The Life of a Jewish Mediterranean Peasant* (San Francisco: Harper, 1991); and Marcus Borg, *Jesus: A New Vision: Spirit, Culture, and the Life of Discipleship* (San Francisco: Harper, 1987).

9 John Meier, *A Marginal Jew: Rethinking the Historical Jesus,* 4 vols. (New York: Doubleday, 1991-2009); Ben F. Meyer, *The Aims of Jesus* (London: SCM Press, 1979); Adela Yarbo Collins, *Is Mark's Gospel a Life of Jesus? The Question of Genre* (Milwaukee, WI: Marquette University Press, 1990); Elisabeth Schüssler Fiorenza, *Jesus: Miriam's Child, Sophia's Prophet: Critical Issues in Feminist Christology* (New York: Bloomsbury, 1994); and Luke Timothy Johnson, *Prophetic Jesus, Prophetic Church: The Challenge of Luke-Acts to Contemporary Christians* (Grand Rapids: Wm. B. Eerdmans Publishing Co., 1911).

10 Edward Schillebeeckx, *Jesus: An Experiment in Christology*, trans. Hubert Hoskins (New York: Seabury, 1979); Edward Schillebeeckx, *Christ: The Experience of Jesus as Lord*, trans. John Bowden (New York: Seabury, 1980).

11 Karl Rahner identifies Jesus as "the great prophet, the absolute, eschatological bringer of salvation" in "Prophetism," in *Encyclopedia of Theology: The Concise Sacramentum Mundi*, ed. Karl Rahner (New York: Seabury, 1975), 1286–89, at 1288; Rahner, *Sacramentum Mundi*, 5:110–13, at 112, for an early study of Rahner's theology by Kinshasa-based theologian René de Haes, S.J., *Pour une Théologie du Prophétique. Lecture Thématique de la Théologie de Karl Rahner* (Louvain, Belgium: Éditions Nauwelaerts/Paris: Béatrice-Nauwelaerts, 1972); Yves Congar, *Jesus Christ* (New York: Herder and Herder, 1966), 16; see also Victor Dunne, *Prophecy in the Church: The Vision of Yves Congar* (Frankfurt am Main: Peter Lang, 2000), 28–32.

12 See Hans Urs von Balthasar's rejection of the prophetic identity of Jesus Christ. "The evangelists do not characterize Jesus as a prophet (they express only the opinion of the crowd about the words and deeds of Jesus), nor does Jesus characterize himself as a prophet, but rather places himself with his particular fate in the succession of the martyred prophets" (*The Glory of the Lord: A Theological Aesthetics: VII: Theology: The New Covenant* (San Francisco: Ignatian Press, 1989 [German, 1969]), 78, also see 80. His Christology is Chalcedonian and deeply indebted to Augustine and Maximus the Confessor, with a soteriology focused on the representative character (*Stellvertretung*) character of Jesus's death. Balthasar later concedes that we must consider Jesus's calling in terms of the call of the prophets in the Old Testament, but this remains of secondary significance (Hans Urs von Balthasar, *Theo-Drama: Theological Dramatic Theory*, trans. Graham Harrison (San Francisco: Ignatius Press; New York: Crossroad, 1988), 3:156 [hereafter *Theo-Drama*]). For Balthasar a prophetic identity and mission is superseded within his rendering of the Trinitarian drama of Jesus Christ in which divine and human natures and freedom are hypostatically united.

Consequently, the significance and implications of prophetic identity and mission for Jesus Christ and his disciples can be overlooked. His appreciation of the dynamic of individuation in the mission and person of Jesus Christ is aptly sounded in his Trinitarian reflections. Yet the prophetic quality of the process of individuation is lacking. See *Theo-Drama*, 3:149–259.

[13] Ratzinger's approach to Christology and the church is in many ways similar to Balthasar's, but his most recent statements about the prophetic identity of Jesus are more complex and nuanced. Throughout his academic career, and as prefect of the Congregation for the Doctrine of the Faith, he did not address the prophetic character of Jesus's identity. He was critical of liberation and political theologies for subscribing to the new eschatological awareness that he associates with the root of prophetism in Marxism by focusing more on social issues rather than the traditional topics of eschatology. Nevertheless, he concedes, "Jesus himself belongs to the tradition of prophetic expectation." Joseph Ratzinger, *Dogmatic Theology: 9 Eschatology: Death and Eternal Life*, trans. Michael Waldstein, ed. Aidan Nichols (Washington, DC: Catholic University of America Press, 1988 [1977]), 28, cf. 59. In the first of his three-volume meditation on Jesus of Nazareth he gave greater attention to the prophetic character of Jesus Christ. He begins with the institution of prophecy associated with Moses by quoting Deuteronomy: "And there has not arisen a prophet since in Israel like Moses . . . whom the Lord knew face to face (34:10)." Joseph Ratzinger/Pope Benedict XVI, *Jesus of Nazareth: From the Baptism in the Jordan to the Transfiguration* (New York: Doubleday, 2007), 3. Jesus is portrayed in John's gospel as the fulfillment of the prophet who sees God face to face and in the Sermon on the Mount; "Jesus stands before us neither as a rebel nor as a liberal, but as the prophetic interpreter of the Torah" (ibid., 126). He does not abolish the Torah, but fulfills it; "and he does so precisely by assigning reason its sphere of responsibility for acting within history. Consequently, Christianity has to reshape and reformulate social structures and 'Christian social teaching" (ibid., 126–27). Of all the aspects treated in the synoptic episode recounting Peter's confession, "the common element . . . is that Jesus is classified in the category 'prophet,' an interpretative key drawn from the tradition of Israel" (ibid., 291–92). But ultimately the New Testament presents Jesus as more than and different from the prophets. "He is the Prophet who, like Moses, speaks face-to-face with God as with a friend; he is the Messiah, but in a different sense from that of a mere bearer of some commission from God" (ibid., 304). In the volume of *Jesus of Nazareth* devoted to Holy Week (San Francisco: Ignatius Press, 2011), Ratzinger claims that there is a "relativization of the cosmic" with a "personalist focus, this transformation of the apocalyptic visions . . . is the original element in Jesus' teaching about the end of the world: this is what it is all about" (ibid., 51). This argument brings us close to Balthasar's position. Any prophetic identification between the prophets and Jesus and his followers is superseded. The dynamics of prophetic identity and mission are thereby diminished for understanding the identity and mission of Jesus and the church.

[14] John Paul II, *Redemptor Hominis*, 1979, 19. Cf. *Christifideles Laici*, 1988, 9, 14.

[15] Key documents and policy decisions associated with the emergence of the official Roman Catholic theology of Communion during the Pontificates of John Paul II and Benedict XVI are treated in Chapter 2.

[16] Paul Tillich, *The Dynamics of Faith* (New York: Perennial Classics, 2001 [1957]), 33; Paul Tillich, *Systematic Theology* (Chicago: University of Chicago Press, 1957–1963), 1:37, 227, 3:245.

[17] John Paul II, *Veritatis Splendor*, 1993; *Fides et Ratio: On the Relationship between Faith and Reason*, 1998; on John Paul II's encyclical, see Lieven Boeve, "The Swan or the Dove? Two

Keys for Reading *Fides et Ratio*;" Jeannine Hill Fletcher, "Reason, Holiness and Diversity: *Fides et Ratio* Through the Lens of Religious Pluralism;" John E. Thiel, "Faith, Reason, and the Specter of the Enlightenment: A Nonfoundationalist Reading of John Paul II's *Fides et Ratio*," and Anthony Godzieba, "The Meanings of *Fides et Ratio*: Patterns, Strategies, and a Prediction," in *Philosophy and Theology* 12 (2000): 3–52; Philip Rossi, "After *Fides et Ratio*: New Models for a New Millennium", *Philosophy and Theology* 12 (2000): 419–29; Richard J. Bernstein, "Faith and Reason," 1999, http://www.booksandculture.com/articles/1999/julaug/9b4030.html; William L. Portier, "Thomist Resurgence," *Communio* 35 (2008): 494–504.

[18] Joseph Ratzinger, *Turning Point for Europe* (San Francisco: Ignatius [German 1991], 1994); Joseph Ratzinger, "Relativism: The Central Problem of Faith Today," *Origins* 26, no. 20 (October 31, 1996): 309, 311–17; and on "the dictatorship of relativism" homily addressed to conclave on April 18, 2005, http://www.vatican.va/gpII/documents/homily-pro-eligendo-pontifice_20050418_en.html; Joseph Ratzinger, *Values in a Time of Upheaval* (San Francisco: Ignatius; New York: Crossroad, 2006).

[19] See, e.g., Portier, "Thomist Resurgence."

[20] This multifaceted approach to reality will be developed in the section on the signs of the times in terms of the contributions of Edward Schillebeeckx, Ignacio Ellacuría, and Hans Joachim Sander.

[21] See LG, 10–12, 25–27, 34–36; on the bishop (*Christus Dominus*, 11–21), priests (PO, nos. 2–4), and on the laity (AA, no. 2). I do not question the historical significance and systematic advantages of speaking about the priestly and kingly offices in conjunction with the prophetic office, which draws on venerable traditions about the baptism of the Lord. If there was more space, we could explore the debate about the validity of this teaching by people like Wolfhart Pannenberg and the relative importance and interrelatedness of these three motifs.

[22] This is based on Kenan B. Osborne, *Ministry: Lay Ministry in the Roman Catholic Church: Its History and Theology* (Mahwah, NJ: Paulist Press, 1993), 546–47, cited in Peter De Mey, "The Bishop's Participation in the Threefold *Munera*: Comparing the Appeal to the Pattern of the *Tria Munera* at Vatican II and in the Ecumenical Dialogues," *Jurist* 69 (2009): 31–58, at 35–36.

[23] I agree with the common opinion that what *Lumen Gentium* and *Apostolicam Actuositatem* say about the participation of all the faithful in the kingly office through governing appears truncated and underdeveloped (see LG, 12, 36; AA, 2); and certain issues pertinent to the kingly office are interrelated with the prophetic character of all the faithful.

[24] This translation is *Vatican Council II: The Basic Sixteen Documents, Constitutions, Decrees, Declarations*, completely revised translation in inclusive language, general editor, Austin Flannery (Northport, NY: Costello/Dublin, Ireland: Dominican Publications, 1996). The English translation by Walter M. Abbott and Joseph Gallagher, *The Documents of Vatican II* (New York: American Press/Association Press, 1966), changes the order of the sentences and instead of "guided by the sacred magisterium which it faithfully obeys," closes the paragraph with "All of this it does under the lead of a sacred teaching authority to which it loyally defers."

[25] Blenkinsopp, *A History of Prophecy in Israel*; also see David E. Aune, *Prophecy in Early Christianity and the Ancient Mediterranean World* (Grand Rapids: William B. Eerdmans, 1983).

[26] John J. Collins, *Introduction to the Hebrew Bible* (Minneapolis: Fortress Press, 2004), 283; he continues "In the Hebrew Bible, the most frequent term for such interme-

diaries is *nābi*'. The etymology of this word is disputed, but it most probably means 'the one who is called'. . . . Other figures, who are called 'seers (*rō'eh, ḥōzeh*) or 'men of God,' are also subsumed under the category prophecy. In general, prophecy is distinguished from divination, which attempts to discern the will of the deity by various means, such as the examination of the liver of a sacrificial victim or observing the flight of birds. (In principle, the distinction is between spontaneous inspiration, presumably by a deity, and ritual consultation, which requires human initiative. In practice, the line between prophecy and divination is not always clear.").

²⁷ Walter Brueggemann, *Theology of the Old Testament. Testimony, Dispute, Advocacy* (Minneapolis: Fortress Press, 1997), 622. His formulation continues, "Prophecy culminates as this cadre of individual persons and their remembered, transmitted words (and actions) are stylized into a fixed body of literature and achieve canonical status. Stated in brief, prophecy as mediation refers both to *individual persons* and to a *literary corpus*."

²⁸ This word-oriented framework for understanding prophecy is common among theologians. In twentieth-century Catholic theology, it can be found in the work of Karl Rahner, Yves Congar, and Hans Urs von Balthasar. See Rahner's Word-centered approach to prophecy in his description in "Prophetism", but also in his interpretation of Thomas Aquinas's position on the obediential potency, a receptivity to God's Word and grace. Marie-Dominique Chenu operated with a Word-centered approach to prophecy, but gave special attention to the social dimension of obediential potency, vis-à-vis the *praeparatio evangelica* in certain signs of the times. M.-D. Chenu, "The Signs of the Times," in *The Church Today: Commentaries on the Pastoral Constitution on the Church in the Modern World*, ed. Group 2000 (Westminster, MD: Newman Press, 1967), 43–59, at 57.

²⁹ See Karl Rahner, "Prophetism," *The Encyclopedia of Theology*, 1286–89, and his earlier treatment of mystical visions and prophecies, which includes a typology of prophecies, in *Visions and Prophecies* (New York: Herder and Herder, 1963). Joseph Ratzinger's treatment of prophecy begins with his *Habilitationsschrift* on *The Theology of History in St. Bonaventure*, trans. Zachary Hayes (Chicago: Franciscan Herald Press, 1971). Yves Congar, *True and False Reform in the Church*, trans. Paul Philibert (Collegeville, MN: Liturgical Press, 2011). Hans Urs von Balthasar, *The Glory of the Lord: A Theological Aesthetics, VI. Theology: The Old Covenant* (San Francisco: Ignatius, 1991), 215–300. For more recent Catholic theologians, see Richard Gaillardetz and Catherine Clifford, "Reimagining the Ecclesial/Prophetic Vocation of the Theologian," *Proceedings of the Catholic Theological Society of America* 65 (2010): 43–62; and Niels Christian Hvidt, *Christian Prophecy: The Post-Biblical Tradition* (New York: Oxford University Press, 2007), 52–58, 167–84.

³⁰ My attention to lamentations in prophetic discourse provides a necessary means to attend to a variety of aspects of reality and power dynamics from various theoretical vantage points. Besides biblical and theological resources, I have been influenced by the contributions of Saul Alinsky and his heirs in the work of community organizing, and the theoretical discussions associated with Michel Foucault's analysis of power and discourse in society and Judith Butler on precarity and grief, and by Bonnie Honig on the politics of lamentations and agonistic theories of democracy. See Saul D. Alinsky, *Reveille for Radicals* (New York: Vintage Books, 1989), Saul D. Alinsky, *Rules for Radicals: A Pragmatic Primer for Realistic Radicals* (New York: Vintage Books, 1989); Michel Foucault, *Discipline and Punish: The Birth of the Prisons* (New York: Vintage Books, 1995); Michel Foucault, *Power / Knowledge* (New York: Vintage Books, 1980); Judith Butler, *Precarious Life: The Powers of Mourning and Violence* (London / New York: Verso, 2004); Judith Butler, *Frames of War: When Is*

Life Grievable? (London / New York: Verso, 2010); Bonnie Honig, *Antigone, Interrupted* (Cambridge, MA: Cambridge University Press, 2013).

[31] Blenkinsopp, *A History of Prophecy in Israel*, 53, 63, 73.

[32] Ibid., 36, 49, 66, 73.

[33] See, for example, the emphasis given to the forms and functions of prophetic discourse in David E. Aune, *Prophecy in Early Christianity and the Ancient Mediterranean World* (Grand Rapids: Eerdmanns, 1983), 18–19, 49–80, 88–100, 114–20, 163–70, 247–338.

[34] Martin Buber, *The Prophetic Faith* (New York: Harper & Row, 1949), 3.

[35] Abraham Joshua Heschel, *The Prophets*, 2 vols. (Peabody, MA: Hendrickson, 2009), 1:151.

[36] Walter Brueggemann, *The Prophetic Imagination* (Minneapolis: Fortress Press, 2001), 11.

[37] Brueggemann, *Theology of the Old Testament*, 624–25.

[38] Sandra Schneiders, *Buying the Field: Catholic Religious Life in Mission to the World* (Mahwah, NJ: Paulist Press, 2013), 3:469–70, 474.

[39] On the complex and disputed manifestations of Montanism, see the work of William Tabbernee, *Montanist Inscriptions and Testimonia: Epigraphic Sources Illustrating the History of Montanism* (Washington, DC: Catholic University of America Press, 1996); William Tabbernee, *False Prophecy and Polluted Sacraments: Ecclesiastical and Imperial Reactions to Montanism* (Boston: Brill, 2007); and Vera-Elisabeth Hirschmann, *Horrenda Secta: Untersuchungen zum frühchristlichen Montanismus und seinen Verbindungen zur paganen Religion Phrygiens* (Stuttgart, Germany: Steiner, 2005). Congar articulates the antithesis between the legitimate exercise of the prophetic Spirit in reform and problematic pneumatic movements by his axiom: "The only valid prophecy in the church is in the service of the church's apostolicity" (*True and False Reform in the Church*, 189).

[40] It was not until Pope Pius XII in his encyclical *Mystici Corporis Christi* that the threefold messianic offices of Jesus Christ as priest, prophet, and king became associated with those in the body of Christ who possess sacred powers through ordination. See Peter de Mey, "The Bishop's Participation in the Threefold *Munera*: Comparing the Appeal to the Pattern to the *Tria Munera* at Vatican II and in the Ecumenical Dialogues," *Jurist* 69 (2009): 31–58, at 34.

[41] See John J. Ign. Von Döllinger, *Prophecies and the Prophetic Spirit in the Christian Era: An Historical Essay*, trans. Alfred Plummer (London: Rivingstons, 1873); Hvidt, *Christian Prophecy: The Post-Biblical Tradition*.

[42] Yves Congar, identifies various classic theologians on the prophetic charism being given to the entire church: Ireneneus, *Adversus Heresies*, V, 6; Eusebius, *Ecclesiastical History*, V,7,6; II, 32, 4; III, 11,9; Justin Martyr, *Dialogue with Trypho*, 82; Thomas Aquinas, *Summa Theologiae*, IIa-IIae, QQ. 171–712. Congar, *True and False Reform in the Church*, 176–87.

[43] See John Henry Newman, *On Consulting the Faithful in Matters of Doctrine*, intro by John Coulson (New York: Sheed and Ward, 1961), 76. See also the 1871 edition of John Henry Newman, *The Arians of the Fourth Century* (Westminster, MD: Christian Classics, 1968). Newman states: "The Catholic people, in the length and breadth of Christendom, were the obstinate champions of Christian truth, and the bishops were not. . . . This is a remarkable fact; but there is a moral in it. Perhaps it was permitted in order to impress upon the Church . . . the great evangelical lesson that, not the wise and powerful, but the obscure, the unlearned and the weak constitute her real strength. It was mainly by the faithful people

that paganism was overthrown; it was by the faithful people, under the lead of Athanasius and the Egyptian bishops, and in some places supported by their bishops and priests, that the worst of heresies was withstood." Quoted by Coulson, in Newman, *On Consulting the Faithful*, 109–10; on Khomiakov, see Timothy Ware [Bishop Kallistos Ware], *The Orthodox Church* (New York: Penguin, 1963), 255. In 1848, the Orthodox Patriarchs stated in a letter to Pope Pius IX, "Among us, neither Patriarchs nor Councils could ever introduce new teaching, for the guardian of religion is the very body of the Church, that is, the people (*laos*) itself." Khomiakov in correspondence with William Palmer on this letter by the Patriarchs wrote, "The Pope is greatly mistaken in supposing that we consider the ecclesiastical hierarchy to be the guardian of dogma. The case is quite different. The unvarying constancy and the unerring truth of Christian dogma does not depend upon any hierarchical order; it is guaranteed by the totality, by the whole people of the Church, which is the Body of Christ." Khomiakov text is from correspondence in W. J. Birkbeck, *Russia and the English Church During The Last Fifty Years* (London: Rivington, Percival, 1895), 94, cited in Ware, *The Orthdox Church*, 255.

⁴⁴ Ormond Rush, *The Eyes of Faith: The Sense of the Faithful and the Church's Reception of Revelation* (Washington, DC: Catholic University Press of America, 2009), 175–214.

⁴⁵ This formulation is indebted to my collaboration with Bernd Jochen Hilberath, Matthias Scharer, Mary Ann Hinsdale, and the Communicative Theology Research Group influenced by the I-We-It-Globe formulation of Theme Centered Interaction developed by Ruth C. Cohn. For an introduction, see Matthias Scharer and Bernd Jochen Hilberath, *The Practice of Communicative Theology: An Introduction to a New Theological Culture* (New York: Herder and Herder, 2008).

⁴⁶ Schneiders, *Buying the Field*, 3:426–30.

⁴⁷ For a valuable description of the shift that took place before and after Vatican II and a constructive theological and psychological proposal, see Judith K. Schaefer, *The Evolution of a Vow: Obedience as Decision Making in Communion*, Communicative Theology—Interdisciplinary Studies (Vienna: LIT Verlag, 2008).

⁴⁸ Paul Lakeland, *The Liberation of the Laity: In Search of an Accountable Church* (New York: Crossroad, 2003); *Catholicism at the Crossroads: How the Laity Can Save the Church* (New York: Continuum, 2007); Paul Lakeland, *Church: Engaging Theology: Catholic Perspectives* (Collegeville, MN: Liturgical Press, 2009). Lakeland does not advance his argument in terms of the prophetic character of the faithful. However, many of the traits that he associates with this liberated laity are precisely the ones I am emphasizing that have their historical source and theological justification in a theology of the prophetic office and prophetic discipleship of all the faithful.

⁴⁹ Sandra Schneiders, *Prophets in Their Own Country: Women Religious Bearing Witness to the Gospel in a Troubled Church* (Maryknoll, NY: Orbis Books, 2011), 81; a similar argument is made in terms of Prophetic obedience in ministry, in *Buying the Field*, 3:465–71.

⁵⁰ In two volumes of her trilogy, *Religious Life in a New Millennium*, Sandra Schneiders develops her argument about the prophetic character of the religious life form. Sandra M. Schneiders, *Finding the Treasure: Locating Catholic Religious Life in a New Ecclesial and Cultural Context*, (Mahwah, NJ: Paulist Press, 2000), 1:313–58); and *Buying the Field*, 3:355–595.

⁵¹ Pope Francis has emphasized that "religious men and women are prophets. ... Being prophets may sometimes imply making waves. ... Prophecy makes noise, uproar, some say

'a mess.' But in reality, the charism of religious people is like yeast: prophecy announces the Spirit of the Gospel" ("A Big Heart Open to God," *America*, September 30, 2013, http:// Americamagazine.org/pope-interview). Victor Dunne identifies a number of theologians who have written about the prophetic character of the religious life form besides and before Sandra Schneiders began advancing this argument. Yves Congar's theology of prophecy suggested that monastic communities of religious life serve a prophetic function in the church. More recently, Dunne argues, the prophetic character of religious life has been more thoroughly explored in terms of a critical countercultural witness to the gospel, discernment of the signs of the times, and new imaginative ways of being church. See Victor Dunne, *Prophecy in the Church: The Vision of Yves Congar* (Frankfurt am Main: Peter Lang, 2000), 164–67.

[52] Schneiders, *Buying the Field*, 3:124–25; Pope Francis stated, "This witness (to the social teaching of the church) belongs to the entire People of God, who are a People of prophets," in "Address of Pope Francis to Members of the International Theological Commission," December 6, 2013, http://w2.vatican.va/content/francesco/en/speeches.

[53] Blenkinsopp, *A History of Prophecy in Israel*, 54; also see ibid., 24, 62, 136–37, 228.

[54] Moberly discusses the debates about how the latter criterion has been assessed as "partisan hindsight" based on some kind of "objective" deuteronomistic tradition, or unable to negotiate the ideological struggle involved in the canon formation process that includes this passage. R. W. L. Moberly, *Prophecy and Discernment* (Cambridge: Cambridge University Press, 2006), 70–99.

[55] Ibid., 125–27.

[56] Ibid., 232–33.

[57] Ibid., 221–54.

[58] Ibid., 254. "If my argument is at all along the right lines, then intrinsically it will not be possible to acquire some (as it were, divine) perspective from which one can look down upon the human fray and profound upon its rights and wrongs. Rather it is only possible for those who engage in the fray, and who seek to discern responsibly within the fray, who may be able rightly to recognize those who speak and act for God. But there is no guarantee either that their discernment will be clear and whole, rather than mixed and partial, or that their discernment, even if entirely faithful, will be heeded by those who should heed. . . . In other words, the struggles of life continue. The exercise of discernment offers the hope, however, that the life-transforming and wonder-bestowing reality of God may genuinely be appropriated and make the struggles supremely worthwhile."

[59] Joseph T. Lienhard, "On 'Discernment of Spirits' in the Early Church," *Theological Studies* 41 (1980): 505–29.

[60] Ibid., 529.

[61] Antony D. Rich, *Discernment in the Desert Fathers: Diákrisis in the Life and Thought of Early Egyptian Monasticism* (Blethchley, UK: Paternoster, 2007).

[62] Ibid., 230–31.

[63] See Evagrius of Pontus, *Talking Back* Antirrhêtikos: *A Monastic Handbook for Combating Demons*, trans. and intro. David Brakke (Trappist, KY: Cistercian Publications/ Collegeville, MN: Liturgical Press, 2009).

[64] John Cassian, *The Conferences*, Ancient Christian Writers, trans. Boniface Ramsey (Mahwah, NJ: Paulist Press, 1997), 59–80.

[65] Ignatius also addressed the question of religious obedience in his autobiography on obedience to the pope, Ignatius of Loyola, *Spiritual Exercises and Selected Works*, ed. George E. Ganss (Mahwah, NJ: Paulist, 1991), nos. 46–47; for other sources including his

key letters in which Ignatius addressed the topic of obedience in July 1547, January 1548, March 1548, and esp. March 26, 1553, and March 26, 1553, in Ignatius of Loyola, *Letters of St. Ignatius*, trans. W. J. Young (Chicago: Loyola University Press: 1959), 287–95, see primary and secondary sources in notes by Ganss in Ignatius of Loyola, *The Constitutions of the Society of Jesus*, trans. and commentary George E. Ganss (St. Louis, MO: Institute of Jesuit Sources, 1970), nos. 547–52.

[66] Ignatius of Loyola, *The Constitutions of the Society of Jesus*, no. 547; and *The Constitutions of the Society of Jesus and Their Complementary Norms* (St. Louis, MO: The Institute of Jesuit Sources, 1996), Norms, pt. VI, nos. 149–56.

[67] It is widely recognized that Ignatius subscribed to a resolutely feudal and thus hierarchical understanding of the exercise of authority in the church, which he incorporated into his understanding of the exercise of leadership in the Society of Jesus. As a result, the *Exercises* can promote deep institutional loyalty and profound levels of obedience to religious superiors and hierarchical authorities in the church. See Ignatius of Loyola, "Rules for Thinking, Judging, and Feeling with the Church," in *Spiritual Exercises and Selected Works*, nos. 352–70, 211–24. Yet, at other times, Ignatius's *Exercises* have been known to foster versions of obedience that have instigated conflict with institutional leaders and those who hold office in the church and in civil society. How these two impulses in the *Exercises* are to be adjudicated must remain an open question worthy of further consideration.

[68] Three superior generals have drawn attention to the need to develop practices of common apostolic discernment. Pedro Arrupe in his letter of December 25, 1971, *Acta Romana Societas Iesu*, vol. 15 (Rome, 1972), 767–73; Peter Hans Kolvenbach, in his annual letter of 1986, *Acta Romana Societas Iesu*, vol. 19 (Rome, 1987), 720–40; Adolfo Nicolás, "Common Apostolic Discernment," *Review of Ignatian Spirituality* 40, no. 122 (2009): 9–20; on the experience of the Adrian Dominicans, see Bradford E. Hinze, *Practices of Dialogue in the Roman Catholic Church*, 130–56.

[69] George Ganss's editor's forward to Ladislas Orsy, "Toward a Theological Evaluation of Communal Discernment," *Studies in the Spirituality of Jesuits* 5 (1973): 139–88. Orsy urges caution in assessing the meanings and applicability of the term discernment to communal modes of deliberation: "Communal discernment is no substitute for critical intelligence" (ibid., 171); "Consolations and desolations are not necessary criteria of truth" (173); "The discerners are not infallible. Hence the outcome of every discernment process is fallible" (ibid., 175); and "If consensus can be reached, praise be to God; if not, let us recall that to disagree is Catholic" (ibid., 178).

[70] Dean Brackley, *The Call to Discernment in Troubled Times* (New York: Crossroad, 2004).

[71] Ibid., 152.

[72] Ibid., 205.

[73] The axiom was formulated by Ruth Cohn and developed by Matthias Scharer and Bernd Jochen Hilberath, *The Practices of Communicative Theology*, 126–27; Forschungskreis Kommunikative Theologie/Communicative Theology Research Group, *Kommunikative Theologie: Selbtsvergewisserung unserer Kultur des Theologietreibens/Communicative Theology: Reflections on the Culture of Our Practice of Theology* (Vienna: LIT Verlag, 2006), 126–29.

[74] Schneiders, *Prophets in Their Own Country*, 96.

[75] Ibid., 97; also see Schneiders, *Buying the Field*, 3:364.

[76] Rich, *Discernment in the Desert Fathers*, 114.

[77] Ibid., 116; see John Cassian, *The Institutes*, trans. Boniface Ramsey (New York: Newman Press, 2000), bk. 4, esp. nos. 7–10; and Cassian, *Conferences*, conference 2, no. 10.

78   Rich, *Discernment in the Desert Fathers*, 191.

79   *The Constitution of the Society of Jesus*, notes by George Ganss, 248n7.

80   Evagrius of Pontus wrote in the fourth century a handbook to help monks "talk back" to demons that lead individuals and communities astray; see *Talking Back*. See Bradford E. Hinze, "Talking Back, Acting Up: Wrestling with Spirits in Social Bodies," in *Interdisciplinary and Religio-Cultural Discourses on a Spirit-Filled World: Loosing the Spirits*, ed. Kirsteen Kim, Veli-Matti Kärkkäinen, and Amos Yong (New York: Palgrave Macmillan, 2013), 155–70.

81   For examples of the diverse roles played by prophets, see Congar, *True and False Reform in the Church*, 172–76.

82   This is reminiscent of Joseph Ratzinger's impatience with synodal forms of delibera-tion and some of their outcomes expressed in his critical remarks about majority rule as he experienced them in the German synods and conciliar assemblies, reflected in his formula— "I don't believe in committees, but in prophetic existence." This implies an antithesis of prophetic existence and the deliberations of committees, which may or may not have been intended. Joseph Ratzinger offered his response to a question posed to 200 individuals by the editor Otto Mauer of the periodical *Wort und Wahrheit* requesting an evaluation of the state of the Catholic Church. See Joseph Ratzinger, *Wort und Wahrheit* 27 (1972): 197–98, cited in *Encounters with Karl Rahner: Remembrances of Rahner by Those Who Knew Him*, ed. and trans. Adreas R. Batlogg, Melvin E. Michalski with the assistance of Barbara G. Turner (Milwaukee, WI: Marquette University Press, 2009), 127–28n17. "What are most needed are spiritual initiatives—people who without inhibition, authentically and in an exemplary way live what is the very heart of the gospel. I do not believe in committees but in prophetic existence. That cannot be imposed, (therein lies our helplessness): one can only encourage one to live in this way. The spiritual renewal of Christianity in the individual, the attempt at a possible decisive following of Christ, could be a way of preparing for a new awakening."

83   Against the rule of the mob, Joseph Ratzinger in the 1970s and 1980s repudiated the principle of majority rule in the church in his treatment of the democratic character of the church; and John Burkhard has also emphasized the need to heed not only the voices of those who are observant and practicing believers among the people of God, but that we must heed the marginal voices that fall outside of the acceptable consensus in the church; prophet obedience cannot be reduced to poll or vote results. Prophetic obedience is to the voice of the Spirit amidst the people of God. This obedience is constituted by attentiveness, reception, and a discerning response to the aspirations and laments of the people of God.

84   My effort to link prophetic approaches to politics and an agnostic approach to democracy is indebted to the following scholars: Judith Butler, *Precarious Life: The Powers of Mourning and Violence*; Judith Butler, *Frames of War: When Is Life Grievable?*; Bonnie Honig, *Political Theory and the Displacement of Politics* (Ithaca, NY: Cornell University Press, 1993); Bonnie Honig, *Antigone Interrupted*; William E. Connolly, *Identity/Differ-ence: Democractic Negotations of Political Paradox* (Ithaca, NY: Cornell University Press, 1991); Ernesto Laclau and Chantal Mouffe, *Hegemony and Socialist Strategy: Towards a Radical Democratic Politics* (London: Verso 2001); Chantal Mouffe, *The Democratic Paradox* (London: Verso, 2005); Chantal Mouffe, *Agonistics: Thinking the World Politically* (London: Verso, 2013). For a critical assessment of this theory of agonistic democracy, see Francis Schüssler Fiorenza, "Prospects for Political Theology in the Face of Contemporary Chal-lenges," in *Political Theology: Contemporary Challenges and Future Directions*, ed. Michael

Welker, Francis Schüssler Fiorenza, and Klaus Tanner (Louisville, KY: Westminster John Knox Press, 2013), 37–59; Francis Schüssler Fiorenza, "Faith and Political Engagement: Political Theology in a Pluralistic World" (Presidential Address to the American Theological Society, March 28, 2014).

[85] Ormond Rush, *The Eyes of Faith: The Sense of the Faithful and the Church's Reception of Revelation*; John Burkhard, "Sensus fidei: Meaning, Role and Future of a Teaching of Vatican II, *Louvain Studies* 17 (1992): 18–34; John Burkhard, "Sensus Fidei: Theological Reflections Since Vatican II: I. 1965–1984," *Heythrop Journal* 34 (1993): 41–59; John Burkhard, "Sensus Fidei: Theological Reflections Since Vatican II: II. 1985–1989," *Heythrop Journal* 34 (1993): 123–36; John Burkhard, "Sensus Fidei: Recent Theological Reflection (1990–2001), Part I," *Heythrop Journal* 46 (2005): 450–75; John Burkhard, "Sensus Fidei: Recent Theological Reflection (1990–2001), Part II," *Heythrop Journal* 47 (2006): 38–54; also see Daniel Finucane, *Sensus Fidelium: The Use of a Concept in the Post-Vatican II Era* (San Francisco: International Scholars Publication, 1996).

[86] Ibid.

[87] The valuable sociological study of Jerome Baggett, *Sense of the Faithful: How American Catholics Live Their Faith* (New York: Oxford University Press, 2009), needs to be evaluated in light of his use of the category sense of the faithful in light of how theologians use this term.

[88] For an Ignatian and Jesuit approach to discernment and its relevance for ecclesial processes of discernment, see Amanda C. Osheim, *A Ministry of Discernment: The Bishop and the Sense of the Faithful* (Collegeville, MN: Liturgical Press, forthcoming).

[89] Rush here attends to the comments made by Burkhard, *The Eyes of Faith*, 246–51, at 248, and in note 11 which refers to Burkhard, "Sensus Fidei: Recent Theological Reflection (1990–2001). Part I," 463–64; and Burkhard, "Sensus Fidei: Recent Theological Reflection (1990–2001). Part II," 46–48.

[90] On differentiated consensus, see the work of Harding Meyer, *Grundkonsens-Grunddifferenz: Studie des Straßburger Instituts für Ökumenische Forschung Ergebnisse und Documente*, ed. André Birmelé and Harding Meyer (Frankfurt am Main: Verlag Otto Lembeck, 1992), 126; cf. ibid., 43, 38.

[91] Rush, *The Eyes of Faith*, 81.

[92] See, for example, Karl Rahner, "Yesterday's History of Dogma and Theology for Tomorrow," in *Theological Investigations*, vol. 18, trans. Edward Quinn (New York: Crossroad, 1983), 3–35.

[93] GS, no. 4 [cf. GS, nos. 11, 44], PO, no. 9, AA, no. 14; Unitatis Redintegratio, no. 4.

[94] See Henri de Lubac, *The Motherhood of the Church* (San Francisco: Ignatius Press, 1982 [1971]), Joseph Cardinal Ratzinger, "Appendix: Modern Variations of the concept of the People of God," (1986), in *Church, Ecumenism, and Politics* (New York: Crossroad, 1988), 31–29; Joseph Ratzinger, "On the Relation of the Universal Church and the Local Church in Vatican II," *Frankfurter Allgemeine Zeitung*, December 22, 2000.

[95] Giuseppe Ruggieri, "Zeichen der Zeit: Herkunft und Bedeutung einer christlich-hermeneutischen Chiffre der Geschichte," in *Das Zweite Vatikanische Konzil und die Zeichen der Zeit Heute*, ed. Peter Hünermann (Freiburg: Herder, 2006), 61–70.

[96] See M.-D. Chenu's comments on "faith and history" in *Une école de théologie: Le Saulchoir.*" For Congar the expression "signs of the time" acknowledges the historicity of the world and the church, and that the historicity of the world must have an echo or response in the church; see Ruggieri, "Zeichen der Zeit," 63.

⁹⁷ Norman Tanner, "The Church in the World (Ecclesia ad extra)," in *History of Vatican II*, vol. 4, ed. Giuseppe Alberigo and Joseph A. Komonchak (Maryknoll, NY: Orbis Books/Leuven, Belgium: Peeters, 2002), 270–79, 288–94; Gilles Routhier, "Finishing the Work Begun: The Trying Experience of the Fourth Period," *History of Vatican II*, vol. 5, ed. Giuseppe Alberigo and Joseph A. Komonchak (Maryknoll, NY: Orbis Books/Leuven, Belgium: Peeters, 2006), 122–76, at 143–47; Peter Hünermann, "The Final Weeks of the Council," in ibid., 363, 585, at 386–90.

⁹⁸ Marie-Dominique Chenu, "The Signs of the Times," in *The Church Today*, 43–59, at 51, 52, 53, 54.

⁹⁹ On the refractoriness of reality, see Edward Schillebeeckx, *Christ: The Experience of Jesus as Lord*, 30–64, esp. 34–35; on negative contrast experience, see Edward Schillebeeckx, "Church, Sacrament of Dialogue," in *God the Future of Man*, trans. by N. D. Smith (New York: Sheed and Ward, 1968), 136; Edward Schillebeeckx, *The Understanding of Faith* (New York: Seabury, 1974), 91–101; Schillebeeckx, *Christ*, 5–6, 29–79, 817–21; *Church: The Human Story of God* (New York: Crossroad, 1990), 16, 20–21.

¹⁰⁰ This trilogy, "*El hacerse cargo de la realidad, El cargar con la realidad, El encargarse de la realidad*," was first formulated in Ellacuría's essay "Hacia una fundamentacíon filosófica del método teológico Latinamericano," *Estudios Centroamericanos* 323–324 (1975): 409–25; the critical edition is found in Ignacio Ellacuría, *Escritos teológicos*, vol. 1 (San Salvador: UCA [Universidad Centroamericana] Editores, 2000), 187–218, passage from pages 206–8; I am following the translation of David Ignatius Gandolfo, "Human Essence, History and Liberation: Karl Marx and Ignacio Ellacuría on Being Human" (Ph.D. dissertation, Loyola University Chicago, 2003), 223n4; cf. Kevin Burke, who translates this passage as "realizing the weight of reality, shouldering the weight of reality, and taking charge of the weight of reality," in *The Ground Beneath the Cross: The Theology of Ignacio Ellacuría* (Washington, DC: Georgetown University Press, 2000), 100–8; see also Michael E. Lee, *Bearing the Weight of Salvation: The Soteriology of Ignacio Ellacuría* (New York: Crossroad, 2009), 42–50, at 48–49.

¹⁰¹ For the weightiness of reality in Ellacuría's formulation, see Lee, *Bearing the Weight of Salvation*, 48–49, 124, 129; Mark Lewis Taylor offers further valuable resources for considering the weightiness of reality in his engagement with the theories of Jean Luc Nancy and Pierre Bourdieu on the weight of the world, *The Theological and the Political: On the Weight of the World* (Minneapolis: Fortress Press, 2011), 25, 38, 40–41,

¹⁰² Ignacio Ellacuría, "Utopia and Propheticism from Latin America: A Concrete Essay in Historical Solidarity," in *A Grammar of Justice: The Legacy of Ignacio Ellacuría*, ed. J. Matthew Ashley, Kevin Burke, and Rodolfo Cardenal (Maryknoll, NY: Orbis Books, 2014), 7–55; cf. Ignacio Ellacuría, "Utopía y profetismo desde América Latina: Un ensayo concreto de soteriología histórica," originally published in *Revista Latinoamericana de Teología* 17 (1989): 141–84; reissued in the critical edition, *Escritos teológicos*, vol. 2, pp. 233–93.

¹⁰³ J. Matthew Ashley, Kevin Burke, and Rodolfo Cardenal, *A Grammar of Justice*, 8.

¹⁰⁴ Lee, *Bearing the Weight of Salvation*, 97.

¹⁰⁵ Hans-Joachim Sander, *Gaudium et Spes,* in *Herders Theologische Kommentar zum Zweiten Vatikanischen Konzil* (Freiburg im Breisgau: Herder Verlag, 2005), 4:581–869; Hans-Joachim Sander, "Von der Exclusion zur Wahrnehmung der pluralen modernen Welt" and "Einführung der kontextlosen Kirche im Singular zur pastoralen Weltkirche im Plural—ein Ortswechsel durch Nicht-Ausschließung prekärer Fragen", and "Ein Ortswechsel des Evangeliums—die heterotopien der Zeichen der Zeit", in *Herders Theologischer Kommentar zum*

Zweiten Vatikanischen Konzil (Feiburg in Breisgau: Herder Verlag, 2006), 5:381–83, 383–94, 434–39. See Michel Foucault, "Of Other Spaces: Utopias and Heterotopias," in *Architecture/ Mouvement/Continuité*, October 1984, originally "Des Espace Autres," March 1967.

[106] Hans-Joachim Sander, "Pushed to a Precarious Flexibility: Where to Go If Tradition Has No Answer and Apocalypse Is No Alternative," in *Edward Schillebeeckx and Contemporary Theology*, ed. Lieven Boeve, Frederiek Depoortere, and Stephan van Erp (London: T&T Clark, 2010), 163–82, at 177, 178. Sander's claim that Johann Baptist Metz offers a flawed utopian theology (174–75) merits further scrutiny. His description of heterotopia in term of liquidity is based on the work of Zygmunt Bauman, *Liquid Modernity* (Cambridge: Policy Press, 2000); Also see Sander, *Gaudium et Spes*, 4:864–69.

[107] Brueggemann, *Theology of the Old Testament*, 495–502, at 496.

[108] Divine Word Missionaries, Mission in Dialogue, General Chapter 2000, "Listening to the Spirit: Our Missionary Response Today," July 14, 2000, http://www.svdcuria.org/ public/mission/docs/gc15stat/gc15en.htm. Subsequent references to this document will be cited in the text.

[109] Stephen B. Bevans and Roger P. Schroeder, *Constants in Context: A Theology of Mission for Today* (Maryknoll, NY: Orbis Books, 2004), 284. Their position is reformulated in a textbook for missiologists, ecclesiologists, missionaries, and practical theologians in Stephen B. Bevans and Roger P. Schroeder, *Prophetic Dialogue: Reflections on Christian Mission Today* (Maryknoll, NY: Orbis Books, 2011). Stephen Bevans offers further elaborations in "Prophetic Dialogue and Intercultural Mission," in *Intercultural Mission*, ed. Lazar T. Stanislaus and Martin Ueffing (New Delhi: ISPCK, 2015), 2:201–14; and Stephen B. Bevans, "Mission as Prophetic Dialogue: A Roman Catholic Approach," in *Understanding the Mission of the Church*," ed. Craig Ott (Grand Rapids: Baker Academic, forthcoming).

[110] Bevans and Schroeder, *Constants in Context*, 284.

[111] Ibid., 398.

Chapter 6

[1] See my various publications on parish pastoral councils and community organizing beginning with Bradford E. Hinze, *Practices of Dialogue in the Roman Catholic Church: Lessons and Laments* (New York: Continuum, 2006).

[2] Others have commented on the connection between community organizing and prophetic discourse and action. For Richard Wood community organizing offers a "prophetic challenge to public policy regarding poverty and inequality" and that such a "prophetic tradition remains salient enough to undergird and make sense of the conflict inherent in civic engagement." See Richard L. Wood, *Faith in Action: Action, Race, and Democratic Organizing in America* (Chicago: University of Chicago Press, 2002), 74, 278. Helene Slessarev-Jamir identifies a variety of qualities of prophetic political activism, including an inclusive concern for the marginalized and the commitment to creating a vision of an alternative future "in which human relationships to one another and the natural world are repaired." See Helene Slessarev-Jamar, *Prophetic Activism: Progressive Religious Justice Movements in Contemporary America* (New York: New York University Press, 2011), 4; see also ibid., 35–66, 73, 84–86. I acknowledge these features, but I focus on the traits developed in the last chapter to illuminate and evaluate community organizing.

[3] My description of the steps involved in community organizing follows the lead of Wood, *Faith in Action*. Other resources include Mark R. Warren, *Dry Bones Rattling:*

Community Building to Revitalize Democracy (Princeton, NJ: Princeton University Press, 2001); Heidi J. Swarts, *Organizing Urban America: Secular and Faith-Based Progressive Movements* (Minneapolis: University of Minnesota Press, 2008); Jeffrey Stout, *Blessed Are the Organized: Grassroots Democracy in America* (Princeton, NJ: Princeton University Press, 2010); Luke Bretherton, *Christianity and Contemporary Politics: The Conditions and Possibilities of Faithful Witness* (Malden, MA: Wiley-Blackwell, 2010); and Luke Bretherton, *Resurrecting Democracy: Faith, Citizenship and the Politics of a Common Life* (Cambridge: Cambridge University Press, 2015). Also see Mark R. Warren and Richard L. Wood, *Faith-Based Community Organizing: The State of the Field* (Jericho, NY: Interfaith Funders, 2001); Mary Ann Ford Flaherty and Richard L. Wood, *Faith and Public Life: Faith-Based Community Organizing and the Development of Congregations* (Syosett, NY: Interfaith Funders, 2004), and Richard L. Wood, Brad Fulton, and Kathryn Partridge, *Building Bridges, Building Power: Developments in Institution-Based Community Organizing* (Syosett, NY: Interfaith Funders, 2013).

[4] Bretherton speaks eloquently about the importance of listening campaigns and draws out theological implications in *Christianity and Contemporary Politics*, 99–104, 213–17.

[5] Interview with Saul Alinsky, *Playboy Magazine*, 1972, posted at *The Progressive Report: Empower People, Not Elites*, http://www.bahaistudies.net/neurelitism/library/alinsky_interview_1967.pdf, seventh of twelve parts, Success Versus Co-optation.

[6] I would support using Catholic teaching about the common good to analyze and evaluate the move from self-interests to shared interests and shared goods in relation to the doctrine of the common good, but I doubt that this often takes place in community organizing. Luke Bretherton is ambivalent about speaking about the common good. He has preferred to speak about common goods in the field of political action and not the common good, which "seems only an ever-deferred horizon of possibility rather than a plausible political reality under conditions of a fallen and finite political life, although, arguably, its deferred status does not render conceptualizing the common good irrelevant as it may still be operative as a regulative ideal or guiding point of reference. In this latter sense it is quite proper to talk about 'the' common good of a particular society. However, a second issue is that it is not clear at what level the common good is to be pursued—local, regional, national, or global." Bretherton, *Christianity and Contemporary Politics*, 28–29n69.

[7] Besides fostering a public culture of accountability for people with power and authority, community organizing also fosters an internal institutional culture of mutual accountability and responsibility by regularly holding evaluation sessions. Wood, *Faith in Action*, 46.

[8] Wood, *Faith in Action*.

[9] Stout, *Blessed Are the Organized*.

[10] Bretherton, *Christianity and Contemporary Politics*; Bretherton, *Resurrecting Democracy*.

[11] This information on the CBA reached between KARA and KNIC is taken from http://northwestbronx.org/what-we-do/k-a-r-a/. For a news analysis and assessment, see Laura Flanders, "After 20-Year Fight, Bronx Community Wins Big on Development Project Committed to Living Wages and Local Economy," *Yes! Magazine*, January 3, 2014. http://www.yesmagazine.org/commonomics/kingsbridge-armory-community-benefits-agreement.

[12] http://web.mit.edu/colab/work-project-bronx.html.

[13] On the history and four branches of the Mondragon Corporation—finance, industry, retail, and knowledge—see http://www.mondragon-corporation.com/eng/.

[14] On the Evergreen Cooperative Initiatives, see http://evergreencooperatives.com; and for more information on the Cooperative Home Care Associates, see http://www.chcany.org.

[15] Economic Democracy Vision statement (materials from coalition meeting in 2013 on file with author).

[16] See Mary Beth Rogers, *Cold Anger: A Story of Faith and Power Politics* (Denton: University of North Texas Press, 1990). There is a quote that is attributed, but never with citation, to Augustine, "Hope has two beautiful daughters. Their names are anger and courage; anger at the way things are, and courage to see that they do not remain the way they are." On aggression and fortitude, see Thomas Aquinas, *Summa Theologiae* II-II, Q. A. 10, Ad. 3: Fortitude has two acts, namely, endurance and aggression. Aristotle, *Ethics* iii.4: "Of all the cases in which fortitude arises from a passion, the most natural is when a man is brave through anger, making his choice and acting for a purpose, i.e., for a due end; this is true fortitude." See Michael P. Jaycox, "Righteous Anger and Virtue Ethics: A Contemporary Reconstruction of Anger in Service to Justice" (Ph.D. dissertation, Boston College, 2014).

[17] For treatment of religious practices and theological reflections involved in community organizing; see Richard Wood on prayer and faith traditions, the role of religious communities in confessing credentials, the problem of instrumentalizing religious traditions, and the limitations and pitfalls of moralistic faith traditions and therapeutic ones; see Wood, *Faith in Action*, 23–52, esp. 37–40, 68–76, 164–74, 219–257; Luke Bretherton agrees with Wood but offers a wider analysis of theological and ethical issues involved, in particular, the Augustinian instincts or leitmotifs in community organizing in contrast to assumptions taken from Rawlsian liberalism, Thomistic contruals of natural law and the common good, and liberation theology; see *Christianity and Contemporary Politics* and *Resurrecting Democracy*. Mark Warren describes the shifting theology of community organizing from the time of Alinsky to more recent approaches of the Industrial Area Foundation associated with the views of Ed Chambers and Ernesto Cortes; Warren, *Dry Bones Rattling*, 40–72. Further information on the shift from Alinsky to Cortes and Chambers is in Rogers, *Cold Anger*, 11–40, 127–43.

[18] Many broad-based community organizations have had a long-standing commitment to identify areas pertaining to economic and racial justice, and have explicitly not engaged in lesbian, gay, bisexual, and transgender issues and legislation that affect contraception and abortion. This has been a source of contention. Certain high-profile religious organizations have accused community-organizing groups of engaging in proabortion, procontraception, and progay marriage, in an effort to tarnish their reputations before established religious funding sources. John Gehring, *"Be Not Afraid:" Guilt by Association, Catholic McCarthyism and the Growing Threats to the U.S. Bishops Anti-Poverty Mission*,Report of the Faith in Public Life, June 2013, http://www.faithinpubliclife.org/wp-content/uploads/2013/06/FPL-CCHD-report.pdf.

[19] Wood, *Faith in Action*, 72; also see the statement by John Baumann, ibid., 297.

[20] Saul Alinsky, *Reveille for Radicals* (New York: Vintage Books, 1969), 132–33.

[21] Saul Alinsky, *Rules for Radicals: A Practical Primer for Realistic Radicals* (New York, Vintage Books, 1989), 51.

[22] Economist Intelligence Unit, *Democracy Index 2010: Democracy in Decline* http://graphics.eiu.com/PDF/Democracy_Index_2010_web.pdf.

[23] Greg Galuzzo, Leadership Workshop on Community Organizing, October 16, 2010, St. Nicholas of Tolentine Church, Bronx, New York (Notes on file with author.)

[24] Edward T. Chambers with Michael A. Cowan, *Roots for Radicals: Organizing for Power, Action, and Justice* (New York: Continuum, 2003), 28.

[25] Leo J. Penta, "Power, Relationship, and Social Change," *Social Philosophy Today* 10 (1995): 267–80; Leo J. Penta, "Hannah Arendt: On Power," *Journal of Speculative Philosophy* 10 (1996): 210–29.

[26] Hannah Arendt, *The Human Condition* (Chicago: University of Chicago Press, 1998), 200.

[27] Bernard Loomer, "Two Conceptions of Power," originally appeared in *Process Studies* 6 (Spring 1976): 5–32. For analysis of dominative and transformative power in modern religious and social thinkers, including Arendt, Loomer, Foucault and others, see Christine Firer Hinze, *Comprehending Power in Christian Social Ethics* (Atlanta, GA: Scholars Press, 1995).

[28] Stout, *Blessed Are the Organized*, 55. This ethnographic study of post-Katrina New Orleans illustrates theoretical arguments advanced in Jeffrey Stout, *Democracy and Tradition* (Princeton, NJ: Princeton University Press, 2004).

[29] Stout, *Blessed Are the Organized*, 57.

[30] Ibid., 302n33.

[31] Ibid.

[32] Stout believes that Foucault is wrongly inclined to reduce domination to any form of power over people, rather than "the defining trait of relationships in which one person or group is in a position to exercise power arbitrarily over others. . . . Exercising power over someone is not necessarily a bad thing, but domination is" (ibid.). While this might be true, Stout concedes he has not explored the later works of Foucault that may mitigate or nuance Foucault's earlier position.

[33] Foucault maintains that this Stoic asceticism was distinct from Christian asceticism, but I wish to suggest that Faith-Based Community Organizing cultivates a Stoic-like approach to social struggle as a spiritual mode of asceticism. Michel Foucault, *The Hermeneutics of the Subject: Lectures at the Collège de France 1981–1982*, trans. Graham Burchell (New York: Picador, 2005), 322.

[34] I introduced this topic in the last chapter, on a politics of lamentation and the lamentations of politics; see Bonnie Honig, *Antigone Interrupted*.

[35] See Wood, *Faith in Action*, on the use of power in community organizing.

[36] On the use of conflict, discomfort with it, and disagreement about using it, see Wood, *Faith in Action*, 46–49, 242–50, 274–75; Swarts, *Organizing Urban America*, 15–16; Stout, *Blessed Are the Organized*, 114–24.

[37] Wood, Fulton, and Partridge, *Building Bridges, Building Power*, 20. Richard Wood noticed in 2002 a new trend among faith-based community organizing was emerging that was indebted to the heritage of representative democracy. "This cultural shift both reflects and allows the organizations' practice of partnership and negotiation vis-à-vis institutional leaders in the political and economic arenas. . . . Radical democratic distrust of elites would make partnership and negotiation with political elites morally and politically suspect." But certain networks (like PICO) have taken a step beyond Alinsky's legacy by "partial[ly] embrac[ing] . . . a more representative understanding of democracy [that] makes such partnership imaginable and desirable" (Wood, *Faith in Action*, 178).

[38] On parish and diocesan pastoral councils, episcopal conferences, and the synod of bishops, see Hinze, *Practices of Dialogue*; and Bradford E. Hinze, "The Reception of Vatican II in Participatory Structures of the Church: Facts and Friction," *Proceedings of the Canon Law Society of America Annual Convention* 70 (2009): 28–52; on the Brooklyn Priests'

Senate, see Alden Brown, *A Hierarchical Communion: The Priests' Senate of the Diocese of Brooklyn, 1966–1983* (Lulu.com, 2013).

[39] As we learned in the first two chapters the Archdiocese of New York actively promoted the development of parish pastoral councils in the decade after the council and again during the time when John O'Connor was cardinal archbishop. The proactive approach to parish pastoral councils in the Archdiocese of New York began to wane during the time when Edward Egan was cardinal archbishop; the office was closed in 2001 and has not been reactivated since Timothy Dolan has become the episcopal ordinary of the archdiocese.

[40] The model of pastoral councils developed in Brooklyn was influenced by Mary Ann Gubish and Susan Jenny, *Revisioning the Parish Pastoral Council: A Workbook* (Mahwah, NJ: Paulist Press, 2001); also see Mark F. Fischer, *Pastoral Councils in Today's Catholic Parish* (Mystic, CT: Twenty-Third Publications, 2001); Mark F. Fishcer, *Making Parish Councils Pastoral* (Mahwah, NJ: Paulist Press, 2010). For the background to these developments, see Hinze, *Practices of Dialogue*, chap. 1.

[41] Pastoral Planning Office, "One to One Listening Conversations," in *Vibrant Catholic Life: Enriching Faith, Responding to Challenges: An Introduction to Pastoral Planning Diocese of Brooklyn 2005*, 10–12. The Planning Committee responsible for the preparation of this document was composed of Rev. Msgr. Frank Caggiano, Rev. Msgr. Neil Mahoney, Robert Choiniere, Rev. Peter Mahoney, Rev. Joseph Lynch, S.M., Rudy Vargas, IV, and Francios Pierre-Louis. This document was produced and copied by the Office of Pastoral Planning, coordinated by Jeanne Nick.

[42] Pastoral Planning Office, "The Parish Assembly," in *Vibrant Catholic Life*, 17–20.

[43] Pastoral Planning Office, "Writing a Parish Mission Statement," in *Vibrant Catholic Life*, 21.

[44] Karl Rahner discusses the inevitable and constructive role of conflict in the church in "Toleration in the Church," in *Meditations on Freedom and the Spirit* (New York: Crossroad [Seabury Press], 1978), 75–115; and Karl Rahner, "Yesterday's History of Dogma and Theology for Tomorrow," *Theological Investigations*, vol. 18 (New York: Crossroad, 1983), 3–34.

[45] Robert Choiniere, "Engaging Metric: Seeking a Measurement for Parish Vibrancy" (Office of Stewardship and Pastoral Planning, Diocese of Brooklyn, November 1, 1999). Document on file with the author.

[46] Bishop DiMarzio described this process in an opinion essay for the *NY Daily News* on November 21, 2010.

[47] As Choiniere explained, "If those parishes are able to address those goals then they are on the right track and the correction has been successfully made. If, though, they [were] unable to alter their course, and many times this is for reasons far beyond the control and ability of the local community, then the planning commission . . . move[d] to other means to address the persistent challenges either through merger or closure of a worship site." (Personal communication, October 28, 2013).

[48] This issue is treated in Hinze, *Practices of Dialogue*, 250; Bradford E. Hinze, "The Reception of Vatican II in Participatory Structures of the Church: Facts and Friction," *Proceedings of the Canon Law Society of America Annual Convention* 70 (2009): 28–52; and Bradford E. Hinze, "Are Councils and Synods Decision Making? A Roman Catholic Conundrum in Ecumenical Perspective," in *Receiving "The Nature and Mission of the Church": Reality and Ecumenical Horizons for the Twenty-First Century*, Ecclesiological

Investigation Series, vol. 1, Series ed. Gerard Mannion, vol. eds. Paul M. Collins and Michael A. Fahey (New York: T & T Clark [Continuum], 2008), 69–84.

[49] On the contributions of Philip J. Murnion, an ordained priest of the Archdiocese of New York and sociologist by training, see Chapter 1, note 37; and Ruth Narita Doyle, *The Social Context of Pastoral Ministry: The Work of the Office of Pastoral Research and Planning of the Archdiocese of New York* (Ph.D. dissertation, Fordham University, 1994); see Chapter 1, notes 38–39.

[50] Joe Holland and Peter Henriot developed the pastoral circle in *Social Analysis: Linking Faith and Justice* (Washington, DC: Center of Concern, 1983). This approach has been expanded, revised, and reconsidered in light of critical questions in Frans Wijsen, Peter Henriot, and Rodrigo Mejía, eds., *The Pastoral Circle Revisited: A Critical Quest for Truth and Transformation* (Maryknoll, NY: Orbis Books, 2005).

[51] The program JustFaith was originally designed by Jack Jezreel in 1989 in Louisville, Kentucky, based on the model of the Rite of Christian Initiation of Adults. This program has become nationwide with the support of partners, Catholic Relief Services, Catholic Campaign for Human Development, Bread for the World, Maryknoll, and with financial support from Catholic Charities, USA; see http://JustFaith.org.

[52] Pope Francis, "Greeting of Pope Francis to the Synod Fathers During the First General Congregation of the Third Extraordinary General Assembly of the Synod of Bishops (October 6, 2014), http://w2.vatican.va/content/francesco/en/speeches/2014/october/documents/papa-francesco_20141006_padri-sinodali.html.

[53] Pope Francis, *The Joy of the Gospel: Evangelii Gaudium* (Washington, DC: United States Catholic Conference of Bishops, 2013), nos. 227–28.

Chapter 7

[1] In 2012 the Pew Forum on Religion & Public Life published a report on the dramatic increase of people in the United States with no religious affiliation: one-fifth of the entire population and one-third of those under thirty: "'Nones' on the Rise: One-in-Five Adults Have No Religious Affiliation," http://www.pewforum.org/unaffiliated/nones-on-the-rise. aspx. See the insightful and entertaining book by Kaya Oakes, *The Nones Are Alright: A New Generation of Believers, Seekers, and Those in Between* (Maryknoll, NY: Orbis Books, 2015).

[2] Dean R. Hoge, William D. Dinges, Mary Johnson, and Juan L. Gonzales, *Young Adult Catholics. Religion in the Culture of Choice* (Notre Dame, IN: University of Notre Dame Press, 2001), 219. Also see Christian Smith and Melinda Linquist Denton, *Soul Searching. The Religious and Spiritual Lives of American Teenagers* (New York: Oxford University Press, 2005); Christian Smith with Patricia Snell, *Souls in Transition. The Religious Lives of Emerging Adults* (New York: Oxford University Press, 2009); Christian Smith, Kyle Longest, Jonathan Hill, and Kari Christoffersen, *Young Catholic America: Emerging Adults In, Out of, and Gone from the Church* (New York: Oxford University Press, 2014).

[3] Robert Wuthnow, *After the Baby Boomers: How Twenty- and Thirty-Somethings Are Shaping the Future of American Religion* (Princeton, NJ: Princeton University Press, 2007), 12.

[4] This judgment is advanced by William D'Antonio, James Davidson, Mary Gautier, and Katherine Meyer in their assessment of the book by Smith et al., *Young Catholic America*, in comparison with their work, *American Catholics in Transition* (Lanham, MD: Rowman and Littlefield Publishers, 2013); "Assumptions in Study on Young Catholics Lead to Unnec-

essarily Grim Outlook," in *National Catholic Reporter,* December 6, 2014, http://ncronline.
org/news/people/assumptions-study-young-catholics-lead-unnecessarily-grim-outlook .

⁵ See Christine Firer Hinze, *Glass Ceilings and Dirt Floors: Women, Work, and the
Global Economy* (Mahwah, NJ: Paulist Press, 2015).

⁶ Robert Putnam, and David E. Cambell, *American Grace: How Religion Divides and
Unites Us* (New York: Simon and Schuster, 2010), cited in Patricia Wittberg, "A Lost Generation? Fewer Young Women Are Practicing Their Faith: How the Church Can Woo Them
Back," *America Magazine,* February 20, 2012, http://americamagazine.org/issue/5129/
article/lost-generation.

⁷ D'Antonio et al., *American Catholics in Transition,* reaches this alarming conclusion: "Our findings suggest that Catholic women, and especially younger cohorts, are less
willing than in the past to live with the tension posed by loyalty to the Church while
simultaneously being excluded from full participation in its practices. This is a major
development. . . . [t]he ramifications of an ongoing decline—if the patterns we observe
were to continue over the next 25 years—do not portend well for the future vitality of the
Church" (ibid., 156).

⁸ Miriam Therese Winter, Adair T. Lummis, and Allison Stokes, *Defecting in Place.
Women Claiming Responsibility for Their Own Spiritual Lives* (New York: Crossroad, 1994);
Kate Dugan, Jennifer Owens, eds., *From the Pews in Back: Young Women and Catholicism*
(Collegeville, MN: Liturgical Press, 2009).

⁹ Wittberg, "A Lost Generation?"

¹⁰ See D'Antonio et al., *American Catholics in Transition,* 32; the resistance to an
integrationist or assimilationist paradigm is increasingly found, for example, in Timothy
Matovina, *Latino Catholicism: Transformation in America's Largest Church* (Princeton, NJ:
Princeton University Press, 2011), and the research project of Hosffman Ospino, *Hispanic
Ministry in Catholic Parishes: A Summary Report of Findings from the National Study of
Catholic Parishes with Hispanic Ministry* (Huntington, IN: Our Sunday Visitor, 2015).

¹¹ Laurenti Magesa, *Anatomy of Inculturation: Transforming the Church in Africa*
(Maryknoll, NY: Orbis Books, 2004); Laurenti Magesa, *What Is Not Sacred? African Spirituality* (Maryknoll, NY: Orbis Books, 2013); Felix Wilfred, *The Sling of Utopia: Struggles
for a Different Society* (Delhi, India: ISPCK, 2005); Diego Irarrazaval, *Inculturation: New
Dawn of the Church in Latin America* (Maryknoll, NY: Orbis Books, 2000).

¹² Philip Jenkins, *The Next Christendom: The Coming of Global Christianity* (New
York: Oxford University Press, 2011); Frans Wijsen and Robert Schreiter, eds., *Global Christianity: Contested Claims* (Amsterdam: Rodopi, 2007); Allan Anderson, Michael Bergunder,
Andre F. Droogers, and Cornelis van der Lann, eds., *Studying Global Pentecostalism: Theories
and Methods* (Berkeley: University of California Press, 2010).

¹³ Joseph Ratzinger's critique of modern currents of thought can be traced back to his
Introduction to Christianity (London: Burns and Oates, 1968), and found in his critique of
liberation theologies and theologies of religious pluralism. For comments on secularism, see
Joseph Ratzinger, *The Ratzinger Report: An Exclusive Interview on the State of the Church*
(San Francisco: Ignatius Press, 1986), and for other illustrations, see Lieven Boeve and
Gerard Mannion, eds., *The Ratzinger Reader: Mapping a Theological Journey* (London: T
& T Clark, 2010).

¹⁴ Promulgated by Pope John Paul II, *Code of Canon Law* (Washington, DC: Canon
Law Society of America, 1999), the revised code was drafted by a preparatory commission,
and can be found at http://www.vatican.va/archive/ENG1104/_INDEX.HTM; *Catechism*

of the Roman Catholic Church (Washington, DC: United States Catholic Conference, 1997), the preparation of Catechism was under the leadership of twelve cardinals, with Cardinal Joseph Ratzinger as chair, in consultation with bishops conferences from around the world; the document can be found at http://www.vatican.va/archive/ENG0015/_ INDEX.HTM. Congregation for the Doctrine of the Faith, "*Redemptionis Sacramentum*: On Certain Matters to Be Observed or to Be Avoided Regarding the Most Holy Eucharist," 2004; Congregation for the Doctrine of the Faith, "On Some Aspects of the Church Understood as Communion," 1992; Congregation for the Doctrine of the Faith, "*Dominus Iesus*: On the Unicity and Universality of Jesus Christ and the Church," 2000.

[15] In Catholic circles, Christian personalism is associated with a variety of philosophers and theologians, from Jacques Maritain, Martin Buber, and Emmanuel Mounier, to Karol Józef Wojtyla and many others. Orthodox theologian John Zizioulas has consistently argued against considering the person as an individual, while acknowledging the person's uniqueness. On this contrast of person and individual, Zizioulas cites works by Jacques Maritain and Nikolai Berdyaev in *Eucharist, Bishop, Church: The Unity of the Church in the Divine Eucharist and the Bishop during the First Three Centuries* (Brookline, MA: Holy Cross Orthodox Press, 2001 [dissertation originally published in 1965]); also see John Zizioulas, *Being as Communion* (Crestwood, NY: St. Vladimir's Seminary Press, 1985), 27–65, esp. 164–65n85.

[16] The ecclesiology I am advancing here bears some resemblance to the anthropology advanced by Alistair I. McFadyen, *The Call to Personhood: A Christian Theory of the Individual in Social Relationships* (Cambridge: Cambridge University Press, 1990), but my argument draws predominantly on Catholic authors and later philosophical debates, in contrast to McFadyen's focus on Protestant theologians.

[17] Steven Lukes, *Individualism* (Colchester, UK: European Consortium for Political Research Press, 2006), 21.

[18] Ibid., 22.

[19] Ibid., 26–27.

[20] Daniel Bell, "Communitarianism," in Edward N. Zalta, ed., *The Stanford Encyclopedia of Philosophy* (2012), http://plato.stanford.edu/archives/spr2012/entries/communitarianism/. See Charles Taylor, "Atomism," in *Philosophy and the Human Sciences: Philosophical Papers 2* (Cambridge: Cambridge University Press, 1985), 188–210; Charles Taylor, *Sources of the Self: The Making of the Modern Identity* (Cambridge: Cambridge University Press, 1989), 53–90; Charles Taylor, *The Ethics of Authenticity* (Cambridge, MA: Harvard University Press, 1991), originally published as *The Malaise of Modernity*. Also see the formulation by the former student of Taylor, Michael J. Sandel, *Liberalism and the Limits of Justice* (Cambridge: Cambridge University Press,1998).

[21] One might agree with Taylor's critique of social atomism and his defense of the role of communities and traditions in the formation of the self and in society. But many are not convinced that John Rawls's position, which is one of Taylor's targets, is susceptible to these charges. Taylor may have a legitimate concern but the precise target needs to be clarified. Taylor refers to the "thin theory of the good" offered by John Rawls, *A Theory of Justice* (Oxford: Oxford University Press, 1972), 88–89.

[22] Taylor's own critique of atomism was, in fact, aimed at the views of the libertarian thinker Robert Nozick. See Robert Nozick, *Anarchy, State, and Utopia* (New York: Basic Books, 1977), which offers a libertarian critique of Rawls's *Theory of Justice*.

[23] Lukes discusses this position in *Individualism*. A critique of Ayn Rand and the reception of her work among libertarians is leveled by a group of Catholic scholars in "On

All of Our Shoulders: A Catholic Call to Protect the Endangered Common Good," http://
www.onourshoulders.org; also see Vincent Miller, "Saving Subsidiarity," *America Magazine*
July 30, 2012, http://americamagazine.org/issue/5147/article/saving-subsidiarity.

[24] Angus Sibley, *The "Poisoned Spring" of Economic Libertarianism: "Menger, Mises,
Hayek, Rothbard: A Critique from Catholic Social Teaching of the "Austrian School" of
Economics* (Washington, DC: CreateSpace Independent Publishing Platform, 2011); for a
critique of Hayek and the libertarian approach to individualism, see Lukes, *Individualism*.

[25] Charles Taylor, *Varieties of Religion Today: William James Revisited* (Cambridge,
MA: Harvard University Press, 2002), 80.

[26] Jeannine Hill Fletcher's study of an interfaith group of women demonstrates ways
that individuals within a given religious tradition can have complex assessments of individual
beliefs, what I would speak of in terms of a differentiated reception of beliefs and practices
internally among members of particular religious traditions. See Jeannine Hill Fletcher,
Motherhood as Metaphor: Engendering Interreligious Dialogue (New York: Fordham University Press, 2013).

[27] Taylor, *Sources of the Self*, 507–8; see Robert Bellah et al., *Habits of the Heart. Individualism and Commitment in American Public Life* (Berkeley: University of California
Press, 1985). On distinction between associations based on self-interest and associations for
the common good, see James Luther Adams, *Voluntary Associations: Socio-Cultural Analyses
and Theological Interpretation,* ed. J. Ronald Engel (Chicago: Exploration Press, 1986).

[28] There has been criticism of the politics of identity that reflects the mobilization of
groups based on race, ethnicity, nationality, or gender. See the works of critical social and
political theorists like Iris Marion Young, *Justice and the Politics of Difference* (Princeton,
NJ: Princeton University Press, 1990), Iris Marion Young, *Responsibility for Justice* (New
York: Oxford University Press, 2011); Charles Taylor et al., *Multiculturalism: Examining
the Politics of Recognition*, ed. Amy Gutmann (Princeton, NJ: Princeton University Press,
1994). Catholic ecclesiologists need to give further consideration to the roles that such self-
identified groups can play in advancing the shared political and social goals of the group
within larger pluralistic circles of cohabitation, wherein the need for critical and agonistic
modes of discourse is acknowledged such as previously associated with the work of Judith
Butler and Bonnie Honig. See M. Shawn Copeland, *Enfleshing Freedom: Body, Race, and
Being* (Minneapolis: Fortress Press, 2010).

[29] See Edward P. Hahnenberg, *Awakening Vocation. A Theology of Christian Call*
(Collegeville, MN: Liturgical Press, 2010).

[30] For a recent defense of John Duns Scotus, see Dan Horan, "Beyond Essentialism and
Complementarity: Toward a Theological Anthropology Rooted in Haecceitas," *Theological
Studies* 75 (2014): 94–117; Dan Horan, *Postmodernity and Univocity: A Critical Account of
Radical Orthodoxy and John Duns Scotus* (Minneapolis: Fortress Press, 2014).

[31] Catherine Phillips in her introduction to *Gerard Manley Hopkins, The Major Works*,
Oxford World's Classics (New York: Oxford University Press, 2002), describes the influence
of John Duns Scotus's treatment of *haecceitas*, often translated as thisness and suggesting a principle of individuation, which informs Hopkins' treatment of inscape. For Phillips on haecceitas
and inscape, see xxiii; for Hopkins on John Duns Scotus and inscape, see 204–05, 211.

[32] Thomas Merton, "Things in Their Identity," and "Integrity," in *New Seeds of Contemplation* (New York: New Directions Books, 1961), 29–37, 98–103.

[33] Franz Anton Staudenmaier, *Der Pragmatismus der Geistesgaben oder das Wirken des
göttlichen Geistes im Menschen und in der Menchheit* (Frankfurt am Main: Minerva, 1975);

Franz Anton Staudenmaier, "Der Pragmatismus der Geistesgaben: Ein Versuch," in *Theologische Quartalschrift* (1828) 389–432, 608–40. On this subject, see Bradford E. Hinze, "Tracing Trinity in Tradition: The Achievement of Franz Anton Staudenmaier," *Zeitschrift für Neuere Theologiegeschichte/Journal for the History of Modern Theology* 8 (2001): 34–57; and Bradford E. Hinze, "Roman Catholic Theology: Tübingen" (on Johann Sebastian Drey, Johann Adam Möhler, Franz Anton Staudenmaier, and Johann Baptist Hirscher), in *The Blackwell Companion to Nineteenth Century Theology*, ed. David Fergusson (Hoboken, NJ: Wiley-Blackwell Publishers, 2010), 187–213.

[34] Hans Urs von Balthasar, *Theo-Drama: Theological Dramatic Theory*, trans. Graham Harrison (San Francisco: Ignatius Press; New York: Crossroad, 1988), 3:149–282, 447–64.

[35] Paul Lakeland, *The Liberation of the Laity: In Search of an Accountable Church* (New York: Continuum, 2003); Johann Baptist Metz, *Faith in History and Society: Toward a Practical Fundamental Theology*, trans. J. Matthew Ashley (New York: Crossroad, 2007).

[36] Taylor, *Ethics of Authenticity*.

[37] Judith Butler, *Gender Trouble* (New York: Routledge, 2006); Judith Butler, *Giving an Account of Oneself* (New York: Fordham University Press, 2005).

[38] Charles Taylor, *A Secular Age* (Cambridge, MA: Belknap Press of Harvard University Press, 2007), 171. Benedict Anderson, *Imagined Communities: Reflections on the Origin and Spread of Nationalism* (London: Verso, 1983, 1991), 1–19.

[39] Taylor, *A Secular Age*, 172.

[40] In fact, the cookie-cutter ecclesiology was never really fully realized on the ground. There was always more pluralism in practice. While the pre–Vatican II church and theology provided a plurality of spiritualities, vocations, and group missions, post–Vatican II church and theology of the people of God acknowledged and promoted pluralism within the parish and within the diocese. This official recognition of individuation and pluralism in parishes and dioceses fosters the enrichment offered by diversity and even hybridity, without being doctrinally, liturgically, or practically boundless or spineless.

[41] For an investigation of ecumenical and interfaith dialogues, see Bradford E. Hinze, *Practices of Dialogue in the Roman Catholic Church* (New York: Crossroad, 2006), 179–238.

[42] World Council of Churches, *The Nature and Mission of the Church*, Faith and Order Paper 198 (Geneva: WCC, 2005), no. 51; this formula relies on the work of Grace Davie beginning with *Religion in Britain since 1945: Believing without Belonging* (Cambridge, MA: Blackwell, 1994).

[43] Pope John Paul II actively promoted good relations with many of these new ecclesial groups as he prepared for the new millennium. Many groups were invited to Rome to celebrate Pentecost in May 1998 with the pope, who saw them as signs of the work of the Spirit in the church, and again in June 2006 with Benedict XVI. Reform-oriented groups, such as We Are the Church, have not been invited to participate in these gatherings.

[44] Pius XI, *Quadregesimo Anno*, nos. 96, 138.

[45] For historical background on Catholic Action and various examples, see Massimo Faggioli, *Sorting out Catholicism: A Brief History of the New Ecclesial Movements*, trans. Demetrio S. Yocum (Collegeville, MN: Liturgical Press, 2014; Italian edition, 2008); and *Empowering the People of God: Catholic Action before and after Vatican II*, ed. Jeremy Bonner, Mary Beth Fraser Connolly, and Christopher Denny (New York: Fordham University Press, 2013).

[46] Giuseppe Alberigo and Joseph A. Komonchak, eds., *History of Vatican II, vol. 1: Announcing and Preparing Vatican II* (Maryknoll, NY: Orbis Books/Leuven, Belgium:

Peeters, 1995). Before and during the council, there was "sometimes quite [a] lively debate between what was called 'general' Catholic Action, Italian in origin, which took no account of special conditions of life in its parish-based mass-movements (men, women, young people, girls), and what was called 'specialized' Catholic Action, which was broken down into groups (workers, farmers, students, sailors . . .) and was national in structure" (ibid., 78); on Suenens, see Giuseppe Alberigo and Joseph A. Komonchak, eds., *History of Vatican II, vol. 2: The Formation of the Council's Identity* (Maryknoll, NY: Orbis Books/Leuven, Belgium: Peeters, 1997), 443–45. Some bishops from the United States and the United Kingdom complained that the name Catholic Action risked being ecumenically insensitive.

[47] Faggioli, *Sorting out Catholicism*; Massimo Faggioli, "Between Documents and Spirit: The Case of the 'New Ecclesial Movements,'" in *After Vatican II: Trajectories and Hermeneutics*, ed. James L. Heft and John O'Malley (Grand Rapids: Eerdmans, 2012), 1–22; Massimo Faggioli, "Inclusion and Exclusion in the Ecclesiology of the New Catholic Movements," in *Ecclesiology and Exclusion: Boundaries of Being and Belonging in Postmodern Times*, ed. Dennis M. Doyle, Timothy F. Furry, and Pascal D. Bazzell (Maryknoll, NY: Orbis Books, 2012), 199–214; Massimo Faggioli, "The Neocatechumenate and Communion in the Church," *Japan Mission Journal* 65 (2011): 31–38; Brendan Leahy offers a sympathetic analysis in *Ecclesial Movements and Communities: Origins, Significance, and Issue* (Hyde Park, NY: New City Press, 2011).

[48] For more on the activities associated with Catholic colleges and universities, see Bradford E. Hinze, 2012 presidential address to the College Theology Society, "The Tasks of Theology in the *Proyecto Social* of the University's Mission," *Horizons* 39 (2012): 282–309.

[49] James M. O'Toole recounts these examples of Catholic Action in his book *The Faithful: A History of Catholics in America* (Cambridge, MA: Harvard University Press, 2010), 145–266.

[50] There were concerns raised by the curia and specifically Pope Benedict XVI about the innovative character of the monthly liturgies celebrated by Neocatechumenal Way pertaining to the readings, who preaches the homily, "echo"—dialogue homilies—about the exchange of peace, about the manner of receiving communion at a cloth-covered table situated in the middle of the church. They were required to adhere to the approved liturgical books neither adding nor subtracting from the prescribed texts and rites.

[51] Bernard Lee and William D'Antonio et al., *The Catholic Experience of Small Christian Communities* (Mahwah, NJ: Paulist Press, 2000); Bernard Lee and Michael A. Cowan, *Gathered and Sent: The Mission of the Small Church Community* (Mahwah, NJ: Paulist Press, 2003).

[52] Faggioli, "Between Documents and Spirit" and "The Neocatechumenate and Communion in the Church."

Index